Old South, New South

OLD SOUTH, NEW SOUTH

Revolutions in the Southern Economy Since the Civil War

GAVIN WRIGHT

Basic Books, Inc., Publishers   New York

Library of Congress Cataloging-in-Publication Data

Wright, Gavin.
  Old South, New South.

  Bibliographic references. p. 275.
  Includes index.
  1. Southern states—Economic conditions. 2. Southern
states—Industries—History. I. Title.
HC107.A13W67 1986   330.975'04   85–43106
ISBN 0–465–05193–6

CONTENTS

PREFACE

_____

THIS BOOK is the outcome of nearly twenty years of work and thought on the economics and history of the American South. Writers of books on the South are obliged by tradition to declare at the outset whether they are or are not native to the region. In my case, though I have gone South whenever possible during these two decades, I am no Southerner. Those who are Southerners are often skeptical about the capacity of outsiders to comprehend their regional culture. Even the distinguished southern economist William H. Nicholls wrote in 1960:

> I feel that only a Southerner born and bred can fully appreciate the intensity of feeling with which most Southerners hunger for possessing the soil, love outdoor life, and appreciate leisure.[1]

In this he may be right. There is no claim here that this book captures the essence of the southern mind or resolves the enigmas of southern culture and identity. But I have come to the conclusion that in economic history it helps to be an outsider, because outsiders can see more easily how the southern experience has fit into national and international economic currents over the past two centuries. That is the contribution that this book attempts.

One of the things I have come to understand, for example, is that the passionate southern attachment to the soil was a

post–Civil War phenomenon. Slaveholding farmers and planters moved from place to place so often they seldom had time
to sink roots. When slavery ended, like players in a game of
musical chairs they seized whatever land they occupied at the
time and held it tenaciously, reorienting an entire economy
in the process. The focus on this sort of economic effect—
changing relationships between location and economic activity—is the unifying theme of the chapters that follow. It is
carried through from the opening chapters on slavery to the
conclusion, which reports that the entity formerly known as
the Southern economy no longer exists.

This view of southern economic history should be seen as
part of a lifelong effort by an American to persuade his fellow
Americans to look at their nation's economy in the context of
global history. The first lectures in economic history I ever
heard, by William N. Parker at Yale University, taught me that
nations are not necessarily economies and vice versa; subsequent years have only deepened my appreciation for that mes-
sage. But my appreciation has also deepened for the distinctive
place of American economic history in that global story.
Though there is nothing eternal about any nation as an economic entity, the United States seemed for almost two centuries to be an economy unto itself, with its own markets, its
own laws, its own technology, and its own business culture.
What is important to see about this phase of our national history
is not so much that, in reality, international forces were at
work at all times (as they certainly were), but that the era of
the seemingly isolated American economy was indeed a phase
of history, and that it is now past. Just as outsiders can see
some things about the South that escape Southerners, southern
economic history is a useful vehicle for seeing aspects of our
national history more clearly, because for generations the
South was the largest and most cohesive region standing inside
the country but outside the country's economic mainstream.
The South was a "colonial economy" because at every point
Southerners had to deal with the large and often oblivious
economic colossus to the North. It was said of South Carolina
at the time of its secession from the Union that it was "too
small for a republic but too large for a lunatic asylum." The

South may not have been too small or too large, but it was too Southern to be part of the American mainstream, yet too American to have its own economy. Today the South is prospering, but it is also losing its identity. The experience of absorption into larger economic spheres is one that all Americans should ponder because it resembles a phenomenon that our communities and our country as a whole will increasingly have to confront in the future.

This book also attempts to refute the well-known definition of an economist as "a man who states the obvious in terms of the incomprehensible." Though the subject matter includes some of the basic building blocks of economics, the object has been to write as nontechnically as possible for a general audience. There are plenty of numbers, but no equations, regressions, or formal statistical procedures. On the theory that for some readers a picture is worth a thousand words, there are a handful of analytical diagrams; but even these are largely set apart so as not to disrupt the flow of the text. Despite all this effort at communication, it remains fundamentally an economics book whose contribution is to interpret southern economic history in a unified fashion. It does not try to cover or explain all related aspects of southern history. Specialized economic readers should still find that the arguments of the book are addressed to them as well as to others, but more technical formulations and debates are left for the academic journals.

Some readers may wonder how the book relates to my previous volume, The Political Economy of the Cotton South.[2] For the most part, it is a sequel; Political Economy deals with slavery, while Old South, New South covers the economy since the Civil War. Where material overlaps, I have dealt relatively briefly here with topics discussed at length earlier. Concerning the transition to the postbellum agricultural regime, however, there are two definite changes. In Political Economy, I treated the entire South in a single framework; here, in response to the persuasive arguments of economic historians Jay Mandle, Peter Temin, and David Weiman, I separate the plantation from the nonplantation areas. More important, in Political Economy I tended to adopt the small farmer's view of things, in which

the loss of self-sufficiency and the postwar move to commercialization were somewhat fortuitous, the result of a conjunction of circumstances whose effects proved irreversible. This
still seems to me a good characterization of the "slippery slope"
on which small farmers often found themselves, but I now
argue that from the standpoint of the region as a whole the
postemancipation pressures toward commercialization were
deep and powerful. Indeed, these effects go to the heart of the
economics of slavery and emancipation. Chapter 2 is a fairly
thorough revision and restatement of my views on the economic effects of slavery.

My debts to others are innumerable, and only a few can be
acknowledged here. One of the pleasures of teaching is learning
from one's students, and in the field of southern economic
history this pleasure has been mine many times over. A year's
visit at Stanford in 1978 was especially enlightening, as I came
away a member of three thesis committees; all three of the
research projects were on the South, and all have influenced
my thinking in basic ways. Cathy McHugh studied the family
labor system in textiles; David Weiman the experience of small
up-country farmers; and Warren Whatley mechanization. In
the case of Warren Whatley, I have drawn on not only his
research on the mechanization of cotton, but also on material
from an ongoing study of black labor history on which we are
collaborating. Back at Michigan, I continued learning from
Martha Shiells, who was a world-class research assistant for
several years and with whom I coauthored an article on night
work that figures prominently in chapter 7.

Colleagues at Michigan and at Stanford have been generous
with encouragement and criticism during the development of
the book, especially Gregory Clark, Paul David, Carl Degler,
Alex Field, Nate Rosenberg, Gary Saxonhouse, Steven Webb,
and Warren Whatley. Among the many others who have of-
fered advice or assistance, I would like especially to thank
Leonard Carlson, David Carlton, Stanley Engerman, Elizabeth
Fox-Genovese, Eugene Genovese, Claudia Goldin, Robert
Higgs, Robert Margo, Dale Newman, Roger Ransom, Don
Schaefer, Rebecca Scott, Richard Sutch, Peter Temin, and Tom

Terrill. Gilbert Fite kindly sent an advance copy of his book, *Cotton Fields No More*, and Gary Kulik shared his unpublished paper on the Birmingham pig iron industry. No one should make the mistake of holding any of these individuals accountable for the views set forth in this volume, however.

In my effort to write something readable, I have had the aid and friendly-but-persistent criticism of Steven Fraser, my editor at Basic Books. As an active labor historian himself, he has a good ear for the devices economists use to preserve their incomprehensibility, and he refused to let me use them. The final product is still undoubtedly imperfect, but any expository virtues it may have owe a lot to Steven Fraser.

I am grateful too for the love and understanding of my wife Cathe and our sons Anders and Nicholas, for whom the book has mainly been a time-consuming distraction from the rest of life. Some day I will write a book with Cathe's title (which continues to be "Soil, Toil, and Moil"), but that book will not be about history, economics, or the South.

Old South, New South

Where did this New South come from, and what became of the Old? This book is an attempt to answer these questions.

1

OLD SOUTH, NEW SOUTH

———————

ECONOMIC HISTORY teaches that events of the distant past continue to shape our lives in the present, but the American South today appears to be a region that has thrown off its history. Long the most backward and impoverished section of the United States, the South since 1940 has persistently outpaced the rest of the nation in the growth of incomes, industry, jobs, commerce, construction, and education. Headlines in the business press display the revolutionary change in the country's view of the South and its economy: "Business Loves the Sunbelt (and Vice Versa)"; "Southern States: Markets on the Move"; "New Rich South: Frontier for Growth"; "How Times Have Changed in the South."[1] As recently as the 1960s, southern race relations and poverty were national embarrassments, but today the South is "guiltless, optimistic, on display," as one observer put it:

> The South has risen again, all right, just as we all said it would, but nobody quite imagined the manner of its rising. . . . Certainly the South today looks better—more successful and prosperous, less defensive—than it has looked for more than a century.[2]

The suddenness of change and the completeness of the transformation seem to defy not only the historian's presumption of continuity in human relationships but the economist's venerable belief that "nature does not take great leaps."[3]

Where did this New South come from, and what became of the Old? This book is an attempt to answer these questions, but in a roundabout way, through a new interpretation of southern economic history since the Civil War. In the process of trying to understand the contemporary South, we have to confront the very different concerns of past generations, which historians still ponder. What was the source of southern economic "backwardness"? Did slavery stunt the economic development of the South, or was it "wartime destruction and social upheaval which prevented rapid recovery from the impact of the Civil War"?[4] Did industrial development lag because the South was a "colonial economy," held back by outside ownership of mines, mills, forests and means of transport?[5] Or did southern poverty arise from "its labor-repressive system of agricultural production, which posed a major obstacle not only to economic development, but also to democracy"?[6] If we could answer these questions and grasp the historical Southern economy, the explanation for the modern renaissance of the South would fall into place like the last piece of a jigsaw puzzle. The chapters that follow find elements of truth in all of these interpretations, but there is a larger truth to be found by examining their common premise: that there *is* a "Southern economy" and that it does have a history of its own.

Searching for the Historical Southern Economy

Much economic thinking about the South, and indeed much economic thinking generally, employs what William N. Parker calls the "international horse race" approach, based on the conception that economies are countries, or countries economies, and that the heart of the subject is the comparative growth performance of these entities.[7] The urban specialist Jane Jacobs, in a lively recent polemic called *Cities and the Wealth of Nations,* indicts the economics profession for persisting in "the idea that national economies are useful and salient entities for understanding how economic life works and what its structure may be."[8] By this she does not mean simply that large regions like the South need separate treatment, for she is equally critical of the famous "New South" advocate Henry Grady for thinking in terms of "large, amorphous regional economies" rather than the bustling, innovative urban centers that in Jacobs's view are fundamental. There is nothing self-evident about the idea that a region is an economy or an economic entity.

Perhaps a region develops an economic identity as a result of its geography, its climate, land, and resources. Consider this 1964 statement by the great historian of the Southwest, Walter Prescott Webb:

> The South is the only region in the United States that fronts the sea on two sides. . . . It has one-third of the good farm land in the nation. . . . It has two-thirds of all the land with forty inches of rainfall or more. . . . It has enormous deposits of coal and iron which have hardly been touched. It is the region richest in natural resources.
>
> Now I asked myself this question, I would like to ask it of every Southerner: Would you consider the purchase of a piece of real estate that had all these natural advantages, all of this real and potential wealth? In short, would you buy the South as an investment?[9]

That is one possibility—the South as a bundle of resources, a space on the map, a piece of real estate.

Even to consider this conception, however, is to reject it as a basis for a "Southern economy." The southerly parts of the country today have precious little geographic unity. There are vacation spots on the coasts, oil and natural gas reservoirs in the Gulf states, mountains and minerals in Appalachia and the Ozarks, flat rural prairies over broad stretches of the interior. Why would we want to group these areas together, merely because they occupy one contiguous corner of our national map? In truth, the South never had much homogeneity on a purely geographic basis, even in the days when agriculture predominated. Some recent writers, lacking Webb's enthusiasm, have seized on the idea that poor soil and limited resources are the key to southern economic history.[10] The contrasting views serve to underscore the point that resources and soil have "quality" and acquire value only in a social context. To an economist, whether soil is fertile or mediocre and

5

whether resources are abundant or sparse will be determined not by intrinsic physical properties of the land, but by the level of demand, the state of knowledge, and the organization of property rights and markets. In the eighteenth century, few people doubted that the soil and climate of the tobacco-, rice-, and indigo-growing colonies were more productive than those of the North. Today the pundits are saying the same. If southern soil and resources became mediocre in the intervening two centuries, we would still have to address the question of why so many people chose to live there and suffer during this long hiatus. Plainly, North Carolina sociologist Rupert Vance had it right when he wrote: "History, not geography, made the solid South."[11]

A more promising starting point is the people, the Southerners. Shared historical experience has produced a more-or-less distinctive southern people, with a set of attitudes, traits, practices, and traditions that persist into our own day.[12] No doubt, interest in the southern backwardness of the past and the "rise of the New South" in the present reflects a genuine concern for the economic welfare of this group of people who, over the decades, have endured more than their share of economic hardships. But if we are honest with ourselves, we will have to admit that no one ever follows the fortunes of this group in any consistent way. When we read that "the South made substantial gains in income between 1929 and 1948,"[13] do we take this to include the incomes of the four million native-born Southerners who left the region during these years? And when we read: "It is well known that since World War II, and especially since the early 1960s, the South has enjoyed more economic growth than the United States as a whole," are we to assume that the enjoyments of the Harvard Ph.D.'s at the Raleigh–Durham Research Triangle—or the transplanted New Yorkers who report that "It's hard to meet anybody in Atlanta who's from the South"—have all been carefully deducted from the totals?[14] Shared subcultures do not make an economy.

There is a more telling problem. When white Americans refer to "Southerners," they almost invariably mean southern

whites.[15] Throughout most of American history, the economic
fortunes of most black Americans were intimately bound up
with the economic life of the South, yet they were not full
citizens and surely had their own views about white culture.
The spokesmen of the past who carried on about the exploited,
colonial South and the need for regional progress typically gave
little thought to the black stake in that regional interest. And
while no modern economist would admit to sharing that view,
accounts of the southern ascendancy often pass over the fact
that the first three decades of that resurgence coincided with
massive black out-migration from the region. Isn't this part of
the story too? If southern economic history means merely the
record of economic events that happened to occur in a particular geographic space on the map, it is not worth writing. Is
there, or has there ever been, a Southern economy after all?

The way out of this quandary is to abandon the notion of a
Southern economy as a timeless entity engaged in a horse race
with other economies, in favor of the view that the historical
Southern economy was a particular configuration that derived
its identity through its interaction with national and international economies in particular epochs. Contrary to Jane Jacobs's
view, there *was* a southern regional economy, though today it
has virtually disappeared. This book maintains that the defining feature of this economy in the post–Civil War era was that
the South constituted a separate regional labor market, outside
the scope of national and international labor markets that were
active and effective during the same era. Since the concept of
a "labor market" is an abstraction, this is less an explanation
for the economic course of the southern states than a way of
organizing the subject. Explaining and defining this view is
the task of the following chapters.

Many readers may find the emphasis on labor markets puz-
zling and discomfiting; perhaps they share the view of one
American official of the 1890s:

No sophistry is more demonstrable than that contained in the
phrase "the labor market," a phrase which grates upon the ear
and offends the moral sense—for it seems to classify men with

7

machinery, and fails to take into account human impulses and feeling, the heart and brain in their effect upon the energy and excellence of human industry.[16]

But as much as we may not like to acknowledge labor markets, they do exist and they do affect our lives. Subsequent chapters will show that this was true even in the postslavery South, where, according to many experts, a market for labor neither existed nor functioned. Properly understood, the concept of a labor market does not deny "human impulses and feeling"; instead, the regional character of the labor market is the economic counterpart of the observation that Southerners have been a distinct people with a distinct culture. The entire intellectual subdiscipline of international economics has grown up around the plausible assumption that factors of production (labor and capital) are highly mobile within countries but not between countries. Labor in particular is attached to countries for a host of reasons: distance, information, language, family, familiarity, loyalty. Every one of these played a role in maintaining the separateness of the southern labor market.

Alone among American regions, the South made a serious attempt to become an independent country, and it continued to be a quasi country until recent times. But regional patriotism is not the most important factor; modern surveys indicate that "regional consciousness" is, in fact, higher among highly educated Southerners who have traveled or lived outside the region than it is among the poorly educated who have never left the South.[17] The regionalism that people are conscious of is less potent than the regionalism they take for granted, and this is what southern blacks had in common with southern whites. They may not have shared the same culture, but they did share the same labor market. The South has been distinctive in many ways besides its wage rates: in its farming methods, in its racial segregation, in its entrepreneurship, in its political economy. But this book argues that all of these differences have their roots in the separateness of the southern labor market.

The regional labor market was not the conscious creation of human agents. From early in the nineteenth century, agricultural migration tended to occur along east-west lines, for reasons of familiarity with crops, soil, and climate. The institution of slavery, however, was crucial in shaping these "natural" migratory tendencies into two distinct cultural and economic channels. Labor market channels that originated in agriculture carried over into mining, manufacturing, and other types of employment, and long after the demise of slavery, north-south regionalism persisted in the labor market. It did not persist because of heavy-handed legal barriers or debt peonage or the convict labor system, but because people moved to places they knew about, where the environment and the people were familiar, and where they had family or friends who could help them get settled and find work. This was as true for blacks as for whites, perhaps even more so. The South was not a prison, and there was no smoking gun to keep blacks and poor whites in the region. But employers were well aware of these ties of family and race and made use of them in labor recruitment and job-design policies, which therefore served to reinforce and maintain the initial regionalism. From a modern perspective, one might suppose that north-south differences would inevitably decline over time. But as relative southern wages fell in the late nineteenth century—while European immigrants filled the unskilled industrial jobs of the North—both the economic and cultural gaps actually widened and in many respects were greater in the 1920s and 1930s than they had been since the Civil War itself.

Now when economists hear an expression like "separate regional labor market," one often hears in response an obscure-sounding but important question: "What about the factor-price equalization theorem?" They are referring to the proposition in international trade theory that holds that if factors of production such as labor cannot move between countries, commodity trade can still accomplish what factor migration cannot. Labor-abundant countries will export labor-intensive goods, while labor-scarce countries export land- or capital-intensive goods. In equilibrium, wages will be equalized as fully as if labor itself had actually moved. But there are two specific reasons why this theory did not apply to the pre–World War I South. To be effective, factor-price equalization requires that countries or regions be "not too different" in their endowments; in equilibrium, each country has to produce some amount of each major commodity. But the North and South at the turn of the twentieth century were "very different," specifically in that the South grew exotic commodities (above all, cotton) that could not be produced in the North. This fact is closely related to the second reason, which is that the southern resource allocation was primarily determined in relationship to the international economy. There is no more reason to think that interregional trade should have pulled southern wages up to U.S. national norms than to expect that international trade should have pulled these wages down to levels prevailing in countries like Egypt and India.

The principle of factor-price equalization became increasingly important, however, in the twentieth century. On the one hand, the new threat of out-migration in the wake of World War I led southern employers to be, if anything, even more defensive and suspicious of outside influences than they had been before. On the other hand, as the international demand for cotton stagnated in the 1920s and 1930s and the Southern economy, with its eye on national markets, turned toward industry, the threat of internal low-wage competition loomed ever larger in national politics. The response was a set of policies that undermined the foundations of the separate southern labor market between 1930 and 1950 and produced a revolution that ultimately opened today's South to its modern transformation.

Revolutions in Southern Economic History

There is no doubt that the southern labor market originated during the slave era, and, indeed, the bulk of this book may be viewed as an extended essay on the economic consequences of slavery. Of course, the institution of slavery has its own story, its own origins and history, and if we trace these back to the seventeenth and eighteenth centuries in America, the lines intermingle with elements of climate, geography, and the international political economy of tobacco, sugar, rice, and indigo. But in the nineteenth century, slavery prevailed in the South because it was accepted and legally enforced there; slavery disappeared in the North because it was rejected and legally abolished there. In contrast to sugar, which virtually required large-scale investment and coerced labor for successful cultivation, cotton could easily have spread as a small farm crop. Because of slavery, however, the North and the South developed as separate economies, each with its own dynamic logic. The economic structure generated under slavery took many years to overcome. The most basic and lasting legacy of this era, however, was the simple fact of separateness itself.

Property rights in human beings shaped the investment strategies, the economic geography, and the political economy of the South. As compared to the American North, the incentives of slave property tended to disperse population across the land, reduce investments in transportation and in cities, and limit the exploration of southern natural resources. Above all, slave owners had no incentives to open up labor market links with outside areas, and the resulting inelasticity of the labor supply squeezed out labor-intensive manufacturing activity, such as the pre-war textile industry which grew during the 1840s but stagnated during the cotton boom of the 1850s. We can see these effects not just by contrast with the North, but by the marked changes in direction of economic activity after the war. The new incentives associated with simple land ownership led to a reallocation of land from corn to cotton, new enthusiasm for railroads and local development, and the rise of new manufacturing and mining sectors. Whether or not they had been slaveholders, the postwar landlords were a "new class" in a significant economic sense. The material foundation for their economic interest was no longer movable, and for this reason their enterprise and their politics were linked more closely to localities and less to global confrontations. Before the war, they favored high-priced labor (because they owned it); after the war, they pressed for cheap labor. In many ways the direction of economic change moved closer to the American mainstream. Chapter 2 describes these changes.

But there was one significant departure from the mainstream: southern labor markets were largely isolated from national and international labor markets, and as the situation emerged in the 1870s, the South was a low-wage region in a high-wage country. Many of the symptoms of southern backwardness may be traced to this economic structure. The major trends and fluctuations in the Southern economy between the Civil War and World War II primarily reflected the changing pace of world cotton demand. Given high rates of population growth, fluctuating demand for cotton, a limited range of profitable alternative crops, and an isolated regional labor market, no feasible program of agricultural improvement could have generated significant convergence toward national norms. Chapter 3 shows that rates of southern industrial progress were rapid by historical standards, but nested as they were in a large agricultural economy with high fertility rates and isolated from national migration flows, southern industries could not penetrate deeply enough to raise the basic agricultural wage. The persistence of backward technologies in agriculture and manufacturing is primarily traceable to the low southern wage. Similarly, though racial segregation and racial discrimination were pervasive in the South, the low incomes of American blacks had much more to do with their place in the low-wage Southern economy than with overt forms of oppression and coercion. There was indeed a labor market in the South between 1870 and 1930, and it operated to reduce wage differentials and some forms of wage discrimination; but it was a *southern* labor market, and it was not effective in closing *regional* differentials between North and South.

Even the institutions of plantation agriculture emerged from market processes. Chapter 4 shows that, contrary to assertions repeated for a century, sharecropping was a high-turnover system, and indebtedness did not prevent blacks or whites from frequently changing landlords. Despite the presence of racism and segregation, market pressures were strong enough to very nearly equalize the wages of black and white unskilled labor. Nor were blacks confined to agriculture. Thousands were employed in sawmills, coal mines, iron works, and tobacco factories. Even when they were excluded, as they were from the textile industry, the base wage for white labor was still closely linked to the wage scale in agriculture—even here, to put it in the contemporary vernacular, mill owners were able to get white labor at a black wage (see chapters 5 and 6). The existence of a regional labor market is the grain of truth in the accusation that southern employers used the issue of race to depress the wages of their white workers.

The southern example thus provides some support for the analysis, dear to many economists, that the free market in labor is the enemy of racial distinctions—that "what no amount of coercion could accomplish" can be achieved "by the silent working of economic forces."[18] But it serves to illustrate even more clearly the limitations of this view. Racial wage distinctions were quickly eliminated in the "spot markets" for raw homogenized common labor, where transactions were short-term and work assignments uniform; but wherever distinctions had to be made, discrimination was the rule, and blacks had little prospect for advancement above the unskilled level. The operation of market forces did little to improve this situation. On the contrary, the spread of labor markets over wider areas operated to preserve and perpetuate racial segregation (see chapter 6). By the 1920s, the work experience and educational histories of the two races had become so different that explicit or implicit racial wage differentials began to appear. Thus blacks were not literally confined to agriculture, but only in agriculture was there much realistic hope for *economic* as opposed to *geographic* mobility. Even here, blacks who prospered often had to pay a steep price in deferential behavior and "knowing their place." If the Old South was something of a separate nation-within-a-nation, it was a white man's country.

If the South was a quasi nation, was there any truth in the charge that its industrial progress was held back by its status as a "colonial economy"? It is true enough that the South produced raw materials and simple unprocessed goods and often had to borrow northern money, but the conspiratorial version of the theory does not hold up. Despite New England's jaundiced attitude, the textile industry grew rapidly, with mostly southern money and some northern help. Ironically, the perception of a colonial relationship reflects the limited flow of outside capital and the marginal importance of the region to most northern business. Inflow of outside capital did not distinguish the South from other regions; but in other cases, capital flows were quickly followed by flows of people, so that the capital soon lost its "outside" identity. This was the time-honored American way of colonization, to capture a territory like California and absorb it so thoroughly into the nation that its colonial origins are forgotten. So long as the South remained isolated, however, its business leaders continued to feel southern and colonized.

There was, however, an important grain of truth in the colonial economy concept. The South was something like a country, but it was a country that lacked a strong indigenous technological community with the capacity to adapt techniques to the region's distinctive labor, resources, and markets. The emergence of the "American system" of technology in the nineteenth century was the decisive step in the U.S. surge to world economic prominence, but there was no real southern counterpart. As recounted in chapter 6, the growth of the Alabama iron and steel industry was repeatedly held back by the need to rely on technology developed elsewhere. U.S. Steel did not suppress the growth of Birmingham, but neither did it put Birmingham at the center of its corporate attention. In part, this is the problem faced by any small country in the shadow of a giant. Scale economies in technological development imply that every country cannot have its own indigenous "appropriate technology." But the South faced a further problem. Because advanced education greatly increased the probability of out-migration, the region was reluctant to invest heavily in schooling and higher education. However desirable it may have been to upgrade the educational system, southern employers had reason to doubt that they or the region could actually capture these benefits. Hence their position in the national economy led them to be more concerned with preserving the isolation of their regional labor supply, to be suspicious rather than welcoming to outsiders and outside ideas. The colonial economy status was thus as much the responsibility of the South as of the North.

Old South, New South

The underpinnings of the old Southern economy may be seen most clearly in the process of its demise (this is recounted in the concluding chapters, 7 and 8). Again and again in the last half-century, patterns and phenomena that were thought to be so deeply rooted in the southern tradition that they could only evolve over the generations were, in fact, dismantled or transformed with astonishing speed. The idea that mechanization would "create a revolution in cotton production, or create any serious labor and social disturbances," was ridiculed as "newspaper bunk" in the 1930s, and as late as 1950 it was said that there was "little likelihood that mechanization will shortly sweep the entire cotton belt."[19] But when the bases of plantation tenancy were undermined by the federal farm programs of the 1930s, the long-delayed mechanization accelerated and was all but complete by the end of the 1950s. Similarly, in industrial areas of the upper South, wage increases during the interwar years (most dramatically under the National Industrial Recovery Act and the Fair Labor Standards Act) destroyed the logic of the family labor system, and the "passing of the mill village" followed soon after.[20] The immediate effect of federal policies on southern blacks was decidedly adverse; economic disparities were widened, and the racial basis for a coalition of white planters and white workers was actually clarified and strengthened. The long-run result was quite different, however. The dislocation, unemployment, and underemployment created by the federal assault on the low-wage Southern economy was the basis for the massive out-migration of unskilled labor during and after World War II. These flows triggered a further chain of responses that in the end produced the final disappearance of the plantation regime and irreversibly altered the regional political economy. Having little of the old low-wage economy to protect, southern property owners opened their doors wholeheartedly to outside flows of capital, government funding, and highly paid labor.

The prime example of a southern tradition thought to be unchangeable was racial segregation. Southern writer Holland Thompson wrote in 1910:

As regards certain phases of the Negro question, opinion, conviction—call it what you will—is fixed, and an absolute making over all Southern society would be required before any considerable change would appear.[21]

This was echoed and re-echoed with equal certainty into the 1960s. Even the eminent historian C. Vann Woodward wrote in 1961:

> The modern South rests on those very foundations and is continuous in its economic, political and racial institutions and doctrines with the order established in 1877. . . . In racial policy, political institutions and industrial philosophy, there has been no break with the founding fathers of the New South.[22]

Yet segregation collapsed in the 1960s, not because of labor market pressures or the rationalism of an industrial society, but because it got in the way of the new southern program to change the region's image and, in effect, persuade the rest of the nation to follow Walter Prescott Webb's advice and "buy the South as an investment." Thompson's premise was thus absolutely correct.

There are many component forces to the recent economic rise of the South: energy, vacation and retirement centers, the space program, a "good business climate," and more. The New South has gone off in many different directions, and it is questionable whether "the Southern economy" any longer has meaning or existence. What these various forces have in common, however, is that they were all unleashed by the effective destruction of the isolated low-wage southern labor market. The southern case is often seen as an economic success story to be held out as an example to the poor countries of the world, a region that managed to "break the vicious circles that thwart development."[23] Perhaps it is more accurate to say that a new economy has moved into the geographic space formerly occupied by the old one.

2

FROM LABORLORDS
TO LANDLORDS:
THE "LIBERATION" OF
THE SOUTHERN ECONOMY

———————

WHAT SORT of an economic class did the slaveholders comprise, and what sort of an economy did they bequeath to the postbellum South? The key to both of these questions is a basic difference between investment in slaves on the one hand, and investment in land and most forms of industrial capital on the other: slaves were movable, the other forms of investment were not. Even for a slave and slave owner who spent a lifetime in one locality, *potential* movability determined value, because a buyer could carry the slave anywhere that slavery was legal. This is the economic essence of the distinction between real and personal property, slaves almost always having been classified as the latter. This simple distinction had a pervasive influence on economic life, affecting population growth, private investment patterns, farming practices, mineral exploration, and political coalitions. Slavery generated a weaker and looser connection between property holders and the land they occupied.

For years historians have debated the question: Were the

slaveholders a traditional prebourgeois class like the great landed classes of Europe, or were they acquisitive, capitalist farmers, pursuing their economic interests like other Americans? The debate continues because, as this chapter shows, the question is badly posed. The issue is not whether slave owners were calculating and accumulating, but whether an economic interest centered in slave property as an object of accumulation led them to behave in the same ways and support the same programs as farmers and industrialists in the free states. Clearly not. The value of investments in slaves was independent of local development, and planters had little to gain from improvements in roads and marketing facilities in a particular area. They had little stake in community life generally, no particular desire to attract settlers by building schools and villages and factories. Since immovable land was a small part of their wealth, they had no great interest in spending time and money looking for precious metals or coal and iron deposits. In these and a multitude of other ways, slave owners were not "bourgeois"; but not because they resembled the landholding classes of Europe, whose agricultural property interest was fixed in geographic space. The concepts of class that derive from that context cannot do justice to a case in which agricultural producers have as their main asset a factor of production that is geographically rootless. They were not landlords but "laborlords."

This is why emancipation was an economic revolution. A popular metaphor among regional spokesmen during the 1870s and 1880s was the notion that slavery had enslaved whites as well as blacks by stifling economic energies in various ways. In an influential article entitled "The Emancipation of the Southern Whites," John W. Johnston of Virginia wrote that the white man of the Old South "was a slave"

> [whose] chains . . . were as inexorable as those that bound the colored race. . . . The negro was a slave to him, and he was a slave to the situation. . . . What did it matter to him if the earth beneath his feet was loaded with all the minerals which contribute to the wealth, convenience or enjoyment of mankind, or that the stream running by his door had waterpower enough to turn a thousand

wheels? He could not utilize them; he was bound hand and foot. . . .[1]

Most recent historians have given short shrift to this conception as economics, dismissing it as so much "mythmaking" by publicists who grossly exaggerated the pace of industrialization in the postwar South.[2] It would seem that a consensus might be formed around the interpretation advanced in 1949 by Robert S. Cotterill:

> The South in the 1880s did not become suddenly *industrial*; it only became suddenly *articulate*. The beginning was not in *manufacturing*, but in *publicity*.[3]

This chapter argues that the New South ideologists had their rhetorical finger on something real, a basic change in the principles and directions of entrepreneurial energies. When slavery was abolished, investment strategies, entrepreneurial designs, and political schemes whose end purpose was to increase the productivity and value of *land* came to the fore. Ironically, in dismissing these writers as "publicists" obsessed with claims of "abounding resources," historians have overlooked the clues to the real economic change that these favorite phrases provide.

Legacies of Accumulation Under Slavery

According to economic historians Roger Ransom and Richard Sutch, the value of slaves in 1860 comprised nearly 60 percent of all agricultural wealth in the five cotton states of Alabama, Georgia, Louisiana, Mississippi, and South Carolina.[4] The value of farmlands and buildings accounted for less than one-third. These figures are conservative. The average slave owner held nearly two-thirds of his wealth in the form of slaves, and in many places the proportion was higher. In Harrison County, Texas, the typical slaveholding household had more than $10,000 in slave property, more than three times the value of its real property. In the antebellum South, wealth and wealth accumulation meant slaves, and land was distinctly secondary. This was not just the perspective of a few giant planters. The owner of as few as three slaves had a larger investment in human beings than the average nonslaveholder had in all other forms of wealth put together. If slave owners were capitalists, they were human capitalists.

It is not difficult to establish theoretically the proposition that the capitalization of labor will, *ceteris paribus,* reduce the flow of savings in an economy. Many writers have overlooked this effect, perhaps because (illustrating the "little bit of learning" adage) it is even easier to spot the fallacy in the crude version of the "capital absorption hypothesis": if a Southerner invests in land and slaves by buying them from another Southerner, the aggregate effect is merely a transfer from one owner to the other, which absorbs no resources. A more subtle model builds on the well-known fact that the level of savings is a function of wealth as well as of income. By analogy to the burden of the national debt, capitalizing labor satisfies the desire to accumulate wealth over the life cycle, and hence reduces the savings available for investment in physical capital.[5] This model could well explain the evidence recently presented by economists Fred Bateman and Thomas Weiss that rates of return in antebellum southern manufacturing were generally high, yet failed to attract investment on a large scale.[6] In this form, however, it is difficult, in the absence of precise knowledge of interregional and international capital flows, to estimate effects on the aggregate regional economy.

The concept of "savings," in any case, is an abstraction, much more slippery in historical context than in modern economies. The endeavor to accumulate wealth took numerous forms in nineteenth-century America, many of which were not savings or investment in conventional terms—for example, land clearing, exploration for minerals, promoting towns and cities, or even raising large families so as to increase the scale of farming operations. Some of these activities were socially productive, others were uncertain or distinctly dubious. But in the free-labor economy, there was a common denominator to many of the items on such a list: they were efforts to accumulate wealth by increasing the value of land, the residual

TABLE 2.1

Canal Mileage by Decade, 1830–50

	1830	*1840*	*1850*
North			
New York	546	640	803
New Jersey	20	142	142
Pennsylvania	230	954	954
Ohio	245	744	792
Indiana	0	150	214
Illinois	0	0	100
South			
Virginia	0	216	216
North Carolina	0	13	13
Georgia	16	28	28
South Carolina	52	52	52
Alabama	0	52	52
Mississippi	0	0	0

SOURCE: Eugene Alvarez, *Travel on Southern Antebellum Railroads, 1828–1860* (University: University of Alabama Press, 1974), 171.

claimant on economic returns. These were the activities that were missing or diminished in an economy whose wealth was dominated by labor. Since it is in the nature of the case that these effects are region-specific (even if there are interregional capital flows), the aggregate implications are that the *spatial* patterns of economic activity, the composition of production, and the growth rates of population and land settlement were altogether different North and South.

TRANSPORTATION AND TOWN BUILDING

Consider table 2.1 which compares canal mileage by decade in various northern and southern states. The cotton boom of the 1830s was at least as vigorous as the national boom, yet canal building was more than five times greater in the North. In the cotton states virtually no canals were built during one of the greatest surges of demand for cotton in history. The differential cannot be explained by saying that canals were "not needed" in the South because natural water routes were abundant, or that canals were unsuited to the porous southern soil. On the one hand, many, and perhaps most, of the northern canals were also "not needed," or not suited to physical con-

TABLE 2.2

Railroad Mileage by Decade, 1840–60

	1840	1850	1860	1860 Mileage Per 1,000 Sq. Mi.
North				
Massachusetts	270	1,042	1,264	157
New York	453	1,409	2,682	56
Pennsylvania	576	900	2,598	58
New Jersey	192	332	560	75
Ohio	39	590	2,946	72
Indiana	20	226	2,163	60
Illinois	26	118	2,799	50
7 States	1,576	4,617	15,012	62
South				
Virginia	341	341	1,731	35
North Carolina	247	249	937	19
Georgia	212	666	1,420	24
South Carolina	136	270	973	32
Alabama	51	112	743	14
Mississippi	50	60	862	19
Louisiana	62	89	335	7
7 States	1,099	1,787	7,001	22

SOURCE: Eugene Alvarez, *Travel on Southern Antebellum Railroads, 1828–1860* (University: University of Alabama Press, 1974), 172.

ditions, the number of outright fiascos far outnumbering the success stories.[7] On the other hand, many areas of the South were largely isolated from market contact, at least in part because of inadequate transportation facilities; in what sense did they not "need" better transportation?[8]

Canal investment might, of course, merely reflect regional attitudes about public involvement in the economy. Railroads, however, were primarily private enterprise in the antebellum period, and here too the South was far behind in relation to its area (table 2.2). Perhaps even more telling than mileage figures are the facts that the level of investment per mile in southern railroads was far below the national average, and that these lines were "generally inferior in construction, rail, motive power and rolling stock."[9] They also featured much longer distances between stopping points. As slavery historians Eugene Genovese and Elizabeth Fox-Genovese observe: "The southern leaders themselves built their transportation system colonial-style: it bound the staple-producing plantation districts to the ports and largely bypassed the upcountry."[10] The phrase "colonial-style" is just right—almost as though they had been built by absentee landlords. That was indeed the missing element: pressure from landowning classes looking for capital gains. That sort of pressure was missing both from private entrepreneurial efforts and from government-supported projects. Indeed, the line between these two categories was often fuzzy, and it may be surprising that contrary to what one might predict on an ideological basis, a higher percentage of southern than northern railroad mileage was state-sponsored. But this is exactly what we should expect on the basis of the movability of investments in slaves. Since slave values were determined in broad regional rather than local markets, only the higher-level governmental units could have the scope and perspective to internalize railroad benefits.

Even at the state level, the effects on slave values may not have been large enough to generate support. The state of Georgia, for example, had no general program of internal improvements, but persistently tried to run its own railroad as a substitute for tax revenue. In Alabama, representatives from Mobile had little success, after years of effort, in interesting the state legislature in internal improvements.[11] In Texas, there were numerous proposals to improve the navigability of the rivers, but the river counties "had no money for the work." There were enthusiastic speeches about railroads, but "few of the many companies formed were able to obtain the necessary capital." The "state plan" for railroad construction emerged only after failed proposals became so numerous that people became tired of the subject. An editorialist observed in 1854: "What now, for instance, is staler and more threadbare than a railroad speech in Texas." And three years later the governor acknowledged that he had lost faith in the effectiveness of land grants as an inducement to construction.[12]

The whole situation was in marked contrast to that in the North, where railroads were pulled in by farmers engaged in "anticipatory settlement," by land speculators, by small-town merchants and by town builders.[13] *Town building*, is a convenient summary term for a cluster of entrepreneurial pur-

23

suits—establishing stores, schools, and roads, arranging real estate sales, attracting services, and above all, publicizing the venture—which centered around the desire to raise the value of local land. The antebellum South had few large cities, but the sparsity of *small towns* was an even more striking feature. In 1853 Alabama had only 30 towns with a population of more than 200, and Mississippi had 29, whereas Indiana had 77 towns of this size in 1833 (when its population was less than half of Alabama's 1853 level). Even Illinois in 1833 had more towns (34) than Alabama did in 1853, though its population was less than one-fifth of Alabama's 1853 level. By 1847, Indiana had 156 towns, though the state had still not reached Alabama's 1853 population.[14]

THE LAND AND THE PEOPLE

The southern railroad figures (and many other comparisons) would not look so deviant if examined on a per capita basis. But doing so would obscure a basic effect of slavery: the slowing of the rate of southern population growth as a result of the South's insulation from outside labor flows (table 2.3). Rates of natural population growth were not markedly different between North and South, but foreign migration was overwhelmingly to the North. We can best think of this as the aggregated effect of the multitudinous microlevel efforts to recruit and entice migrants to particular localities. A thousand small sucking actions combined to turn the North into a giant demographic vacuum cleaner, carrying the Easterners across the prairies and onto the plains, and replacing them with foreigners in northeastern cities. State and national government policy, in turn, reflected this property owner's class interest in keeping migration up. Just how much faster the South would have grown if it had gone this route we will never know, because this sort of activity was not happening there. The one specific proposal to open the South to outside labor flows—the campaign to reopen the African slave trade—was persistently blocked by slaveholder interests in all parts of the South.[15]

The closed character of the southern population, in combination with high geographic mobility on the part of slave own-

TABLE 2.3

Population Per Square Mile

	1850	1860
North		
Massachusetts	123.7	153.1
New Hampshire	35.2	36.1
New York	65.0	81.4
Pennsylvania	51.6	64.8
Ohio	48.6	57.4
Indiana	27.5	37.6
Illinois	15.2	30.6
Iowa	3.5	12.1
South		
Alabama	15.0	18.8
Arkansas	4.0	8.3
Georgia	15.4	18.0
Louisiana	11.4	15.6
Mississippi	13.1	17.1
North Carolina	17.8	20.4
South Carolina	21.9	23.1
Tennessee	24.1	26.6
Virginia	27.8	30.3

SOURCE: U.S. Bureau of the Census, *Historical Statistics of the United States*, Series A-196 (Washington, D.C.: Government Printing Office, 1975), Part 1.

ers and slaves, generated many isolated or declining "backwater" small farm areas in the Southeast. This is surely what Ulrich Phillips had in mind when he argued that the interstate slave trade "drained capital out of the districts where it had been earned."[16] Slave owners had little attachment or loyalty to local areas. Historian James Oakes has stressed the extremely low rates of geographic persistence (that is, high rates of geographic turnover) among wealthy planters: "In Jasper County, Georgia, at the heart of that state's cotton belt and long past its frontier days, nearly sixty percent of the 1850 slaveholders were gone ten years later." Another historian of planter society, Jonathan Wiener, reports similar figures for the wealthiest planters in five Alabama counties. A new study by economist Donald Schaefer, which actually manages to trace observations from one census to another between 1850 and 1860, finds that mobility rates for small slaveholders were even higher, and

25

that slaveholders typically moved much longer distances than nonslaveholders.[17]

As Oakes points out, the rates of mobility for the wealthiest slaveholders were comparable to those of the poorest class of unskilled laborers in the North. But Oakes takes this to mean that the planters were merely acquisitive commercial farmers like those of the North. Wealthy property holders in the North, however, did not behave this way at all. Even home ownership significantly reduced the likelihood of moving, while most of the very rich had stable long-term connections with an urban or regional business community.[18] It was not a question of being calculating or acquisitive, but of what geographic space was encompassed in their calculations, of how they weighed local connections and investments against distant opportunities. James Henry Hammond of South Carolina remarked on the departure "to the West of nearly every one of the young men with whom I was brought up." He considered the idea seriously himself:

> I have been trying to get over my desire for a western plantation, but every time I see a man who has been there it puts me in a fever. . . . I must go West and plant.[19]

He did not yield to the fever in the end, but he made detailed calculations of costs and benefits. In his case, very likely the decision to stay in the East had more to do with political aspirations and personal affairs than with the results of his cost calculations. Most slave owners were more footloose. In one respect this was highly efficient, resulting in a rapid migration of slaves to the areas of highest fertility. But the implication for the regional economy was a sparse population spread thinly and broadly across the countryside. As measured by the yardsticks a Northerner would use, the growth of population and especially of land values, the North outstripped the South decisively.

TABLE 2.4

Value-Added^a in Manufacturing
Per Capita, 1850–60

	1850	1860
Alabama	$ 2.98	$ 5.29
Arkansas	1.53	3.68
Georgia	4.05	6.56
Louisiana	8.34	12.50
Mississippi	2.70	4.35
North Carolina	5.19	6.52
South Carolina	6.36	4.85
Tennessee	4.55	7.72
Texas	3.63	5.31
Virginia	8.09	12.41
10 Southern States	5.27	7.52
Midwest^b	12.14	15.76
Northeast^c	36.02	50.66
United States	20.17	27.42

SOURCES: Donald B. Dodd and Wynelle S. Dodd, *Historical Statistics of the South* (University: University of Alabama Press, 1973); Dodd and Dodd, *Historical Statistics of the United States, 1790–1970*, vol. 2, *The Midwest* (University: University of Alabama Press, 1976); U.S. Bureau of the Census, *Manufactures*, 8th Census (1860) (Washington, D.C.: Government Printing Office, 1865), 677–730.
^{a} "Value-added" is the value of manufacturing output, less the cost of raw materials.
^{b} Includes Illinois, Indiana, Iowa, Kansas, Michigan, Minnesota, Missouri, Nebraska, North Dakota, Ohio, South Dakota, and Wisconsin.
^{c} Includes Maine, New Hampshire, Vermont, Massachusetts, Rhode Island, Connecticut, New York, New Jersey, Pennsylvania, Delaware, Maryland, and Washington, D.C.

MANUFACTURING AND MINING

The closed character of the southern population was directly related to the limited development of manufacturing in the slave economy (table 2.4). The difficulty of supervising slave labor in factories and the "degradation of work" by white laborers have been much exaggerated. The problem was not in production but in the price of labor. The effective regionwide market in slaves raised the eastern price of labor in harmony with southwestern demand. The possibilities of substitution between white and black labor conveyed these effects to white labor as well. Most important, during times of upward labor market pressure in the 1830s and 1850s, the impulse to expand the scope of these markets into lower-wage areas outside the region was missing or deeply submerged in the South. The result was that many manufacturing and urban activities that blossomed during the agriculturally slow years of the 1840s subsequently stagnated under the pressure of labor and capital shortages in the 1850s. Thus, the nature of slave labor markets and the incentives implied by slave property ownership acted to discourage the "cheap labor" manufacturing of the northeastern states.[20]

There was another dimension to nineteenth-century American manufacturing that was not encouraged by slavery: the technology of the era was heavily resource-using, and the American adaptations of European innovations served to accentuate this tendency. The location of cotton textiles might be determined by labor costs, but many industries had to be close to key resources, especially coal and iron ore. The discovery of anthracite coal fields in eastern Pennsylvania in the 1830s gave an early fillip to many kinds of factory activities.[21]

But under slavery, the incentives to search for valuable mineral resources were much diminished. Some discoveries are matters of random luck, but sustained exploration is an economic activity, involving costs and hoped-for returns. In states where land is in private hands, exploration is, in essence, a way of investing in land in hopes of a capital gain. For the same reasons that town-building was more widespread in the free states, there was much less mineral exploration in the slave states. If the slaveholder's "primary interest was in appreciation," it was not land values that he had in mind.[22]

Michael Wayne begins his recent study of the Natchez slaveholding elite with an apocryphal story about a planter who could not trouble himself to investigate a report that gold had been discovered on his land.[23] If it didn't happen, it could have. Gold really was discovered in the Piedmont as early as 1799, and the response of the planters was at least as lethargic as in Wayne's tale. It was not until the 1820s that significant mining activity began, and even then it was seen primarily as a "dull season" supplementary activity for the slaves— "whenever the corn is hoed, the cotton weeded, and the agricultural business which engages them will permit." Outside engineers were "quite critical of the lack of progressive thinking by the proprietors of the land, who invariably seemed to prefer backward methods to more capital-intensive and long-term development." The brief Piedmont gold boom of 1830–36 was largely the work of outsiders, who were not given a warm welcome.[24] The fundamental reason for this response was that the owners had a much larger investment in slave property that would in no way be enhanced by discoveries of gold.

It is sometimes said that the slow industrial development of the slave South is attributable to the fact the main mineral deposits of the region had not yet been discovered. But this lack of discovery was no accident. It was said of the West Indian planters that "if the finest geologist of Europe were to . . . state that indications of coal were evident in the formations of the neighboring mountains . . . no effort would be made to obtain it."[25] The same might be said of the Southerners. The phosphate deposits in South Carolina were known to scientists before the Civil War, but no significant effort was made to search them out precisely and realize their commercial value.[26] Wiener reports that the North-South rail line given state funds in 1850 was "not located, except incidentally, to develop the coal trade."[27] In a striking illustration of the contrast between a land-oriented and a labor-oriented mind-set, union soldiers who camped near Chattanooga during the war were amazed at the abundant but undeveloped coal and iron ore resources, and some of the early postwar growth stemmed from the initiative of these men.[28]

AGRICULTURAL PRACTICES

The use of gold mining as a way of filling in the slave work year illustrates the fixed-cost character of slave labor, the tendency to treat the slaves as the basic investment and to spread their labor across as many acres and tasks as possible.[29] The microlevel counterpart to sparse population was the "extensive system of farming," largely indifferent to yields per acre but seeking every chance to get more labor from slave households and more cash-generating or cost-saving output per slave. This strategy supported a high degree of self-sufficiency on plantations as well as farms. This argument assumes, of course, that plantation slaves could not easily be rented out during the slack seasons.

Slave rental markets did exist, and where slaves were used in manufacturing, construction, mining, and so on, the majority were rented. But over most of the agricultural South, rental markets were not well developed, and the reasons are not difficult to find. One factor was the absence of towns and concentrations of population. A further deterrent lay in the consideration that slaves were valuable property and were being held as part of a long-term accumulation strategy that raised the "transactions costs" associated with any rental arrangement. Rentals could occur, but the rental rate had to reflect the risks of death, mistreatment, or escape, to say nothing of the costs of negotiating responsibilities and settling disputes. These were unavoidable consequences of the fact that slave labor was capitalized and owned by someone at all times. Thus, the highly developed state of long-distance markets in slave *purchase* worked against the spread of localized market relationships in labor as well as commodities.

What most galled the agricultural reformers, however, was the absence of respect for the soil, the practice of "buying land as they might buy a wagon—with the expectation of wearing it out." In his classic *Political Economy of Slavery*, Eugene Genovese presented evidence that use of fertilizer was quite limited, despite well-publicized reform campaigns. He attributed the problem, however, to (among other factors) the "poor quality of the implements that planters could entrust to the slaves" and the "carelessness of slaves [which] made all attempts at soil reclamation or improved tillage of doubtful outcome."[30] This is a supply-side view, in the long tradition of associating slave labor with poor morale, semi-intentional carelessness, and technological backwardness. There is little direct evidence for this view, and it is difficult to reconcile with the fact that a fertilizer revolution began in the Southeast almost immediately after emancipation, when freed slaves were actively withdrawing labor and labor relations were chaotic. More likely, the agricultural practices simply reflected the low priority that planters placed on land investment and maintenance. Soil exhaustion and erosion have received short shrift from historical economists in recent years, but a study by a geographer finds that the antebellum years witnessed the worst soil erosion in southern history, and erosive land use was highly correlated with slavery. The author concludes: "Planters earned well their reputations as 'land killers.' "[31]

Perspectives on the North-South Debate

Northern observers in the late antebellum years had little doubt that the slave South was backward and stagnant. This view was not just based on remoteness and poor information, because eyewitness visits produced some of the most negative impressions. New York politician William H. Seward went South in 1835, 1846, and 1857, for example, and reported each time on the "exhausted soil, old and decaying towns, wretchedly-neglected roads, and in every respect, an absence of enterprise and improvement." He wrote that on every trip he wished that "at least one northern man from every town could be with me to see the practical workings of slavery."[32] Such comments were reiterated and accepted many times over. But what exactly was it that the Northerners were observing? They were certainly not looking at modern statistical aggregates like per capita income, nor at the net worth of typical slaveholders, which would have excited more envy than ruth. They were looking for what they took to be the overt signs of progress—canals, towns, schools, factories, machines in the fields.

Recent articles by Howard Temperley develop the theme of "anti-slavery as cultural imperialism," which is striking but helpful in understanding these perceptions.[33] Northerners tended to attribute their economic success to their own system, and specifically to their own hard work, which their system had encouraged. We can go further: Northerners not only *associated* their economic success with their free institutions, but they came to *define* economic success in a way that only made sense in a free-labor society. For a society of landlords, population growth and land values are natural yardsticks of success. By these criteria, they were right to associate northern progress with "free land and free labor," since unrestricted fee simple property rights in land were as basic to the northern dynamic as slave values were to the South.

In these circumstances, it is not surprising that slave owners were attracted to anti-bourgeois ideologies and that they were able to see through the hypocrisies and injustices of northern society more clearly than most Northerners. But these attitudes had roots in their property interest and reflected the kind of economy that their property interest had created. Since they were above local interests and squabbles, and since their interests were defined most clearly at national and global levels, there is on this reckoning broad appropriateness to Eugene Genovese's view of the Old South as a slave-owners' country unique in world history.

But if the analysis offered here helps to give a new form of support to some older observations about the economics of slavery, it also tends to discredit the venerable contention that slavery was aggressively expansionist in territorial terms. Slave owners were certainly aggressive in politics and in the righteous defense of their institutions, but they were far less expansionist geographically than the Northerners, who filled up the continent at twice the speed. While southern settlers were inching into east Texas, still unable to agree on railroads which would link them to the Pacific, John C. Fremont (explorer and later Republican presidential candidate) had already seized California for the free-soil forces. If the movability of slaves was their decisive feature, why were the owners so slow? The issue is more political economy than economics. Individually, slave owners moved often and quickly; but collectively their interest in rapid territorial expansion was debatable. One consideration was that rapid expansion might depress the price of cotton. But the major reason that southern expansion was slower was that southern population growth was slower, and this reflected a collective interest in high prices that all slave owners shared.

No misconception is more persistent and more inaccurate than the belief that slave owners were divided on the slave-trade issue, the idea that there was a basic cleavage between the "breeders" of the Southeast and the "planters on the make" in the Southwest. The average slave owner of Harrison County, Texas, had $10,000 of slave property that was in no way dependent on developments in that county—or in all of Texas, for that matter. What did they care about filling up Texas? They certainly cared, however, about keeping the African slave trade closed. Sam Houston was elected governor in large part because of a rumor that his opponent was soft on the slave-trade issue.

Here is the grain of truth in the perception that the South was falling behind economically because of slavery, and that this lag was related to a deterioration of their political strength in the Union. By no conventional measure of performance was the South stagnant or declining, nor was slavery unviable economically. But by slowing the growth of the regional population, slavery retarded territorial expansion and political weight. Since this political weight was a factor in secession, and since sheer manpower was a factor in the South's military defeat, in these ways we may say that the economics of slavery contributed to its own demise.

New Channels for Old Energies

The economy that the slave South bequeathed to its successor was dispersed, agricultural, isolated from the outside world; it had a poor transportation system, few cities and towns, and undeveloped markets. The best proof that the antebellum economic structure was shaped by slavery is what happened after the war. Historians may debate "continuity" versus "discontinuity" interminably, because some things changed and some did not. But to an economic historian concerned with the *direction* of structural change, the break was dramatic. The new incentives associated with the change in property rights provide the thread that unifies a wide range of otherwise disparate economic pursuits. Formerly labor was wealth and wealth was chiefly labor; the location and investment decisions of slave owners served to augment the value of particular slaves, and the slave-owner politics served to keep the value of slave labor high in general. After emancipation, the "masters without slaves" were *landlords*, whose concern was to raise the value of output per acre, treating labor as a variable cost. Since land is fixed in place, what occurred was a pronounced *localization* of economic life. Farmers now reoriented their investments and their politics toward raising land yields and land values in particular localities. Local coalitions of landowners began to push for markets, towns, railroads, and eventually factories. "Abounding resources" appeared on all sides, and publicists everywhere.

LAND, LABOR, AND CROPS

The phrase "King Cotton" dates from pre–Civil War political rhetoric, but, in fact, the South moved much more heavily into cotton growing *after* the war than before. The major symptom was the disappearance of self-sufficiency in basic foodstuffs, which had been characteristic of smaller farms as well as of slave plantations, and the initiation of large-scale imports of grains and meats from the Midwest. Table 2.5 shows the decline in southern corn and hog production, to little more than half of their 1860 levels.

The swing toward cotton is a familiar theme in southern history, but its nature is not so well known. There were many pressures and incentives toward specialization in cotton, but behind them all lies the fact that cotton was far more valuable *per acre* than were alternative uses of land. Table 2.6 uses U.S. agriculture department estimates of yields and farm-gate prices (that is, prices received by farmers) for cotton and corn to give some idea how large the differential could be. When extra expenses for fertilizer, implements, and marketing are deducted,

TABLE 2.5

Corn and Hogs Per Capita, Rural Population,
1860–80

| | Corn (bu.) | | Hogs | |
	1860	1880	1860	1880
Alabama	36.3	21.3	1.91	1.05
Arkansas	41.3	31.4	2.71	2.03
Florida	21.0	13.1	2.02	1.18
Georgia	31.3	16.6	2.07	1.05
Louisiana	32.2	14.1	1.21	0.90
Mississippi	37.7	19.5	1.99	1.05
North Carolina	31.1	20.8	1.95	1.08
South Carolina	23.0	12.8	1.47	0.68
Tennessee	49.0	44.0	2.21	1.51
Texas	28.6	20.1	2.37	1.35
Virginia	26.2	22.0	1.10	0.72
11 States	33.1	23.4	1.92	1.14
5 Deep South States	29.0	17.3	1.80	0.97

SOURCES: Donald B. Dodd and Wynelle S. Dodd, *Historical Statistics of the South* (University: University of Alabama Press, 1973); U.S. Census Office, *Compendium of the Tenth Census* (1880) (Washington, D.C.: Government Printing Office, 1883), 681.

the margin in favor of cotton is of course reduced. But my point here is not the net *profitability* of cotton, but the fact that cotton represents an *intensification of land use.* In other words, the higher levels of other inputs per acre is equally part of the process.

Another development that was part of the process was the *eastward* shift of the center of gravity of cotton production. Comparison of geographical patterns in 1859 and 1899 (figures 2.1a and 2.1b) shows that the shift was not at all a continuation of prewar trends. Indeed, the phenomenon has no parallel in American agricultural history. Parts of the Piedmont that were among the oldest cotton-growing areas and had long been considered "exhausted," enjoyed a new revival in cotton growing. And formerly isolated, up-country areas that had been largely bypassed by the slave economy now found themselves pulled into cotton and its associated commercial relationships. There is no more vivid illustration of the impact of slavery on spatial patterns of economic activity. The highlight in the Southeast was the application of fertilizers, while in the plantation areas,

TABLE 2.6

Value of Output Per Acre of Cotton and Corn,
1866–1900

| | Yields × Price Per Acre | | Cotton Yield × Price + Seed − Nonlabor Costs |
	Cotton	Corn	
Alabama	$14.39	$ 7.99	$ 8.58
Arkansas	22.00	9.80	18.95
Georgia	15.24	6.71	8.88
Louisiana	21.68	9.67	16.20
Mississippi	17.98	8.82	12.52
North Carolina	18.60	6.89	11.16
South Carolina	17.37	6.88	10.39
Tennessee	18.49	8.94	15.07
Texas	21.32	11.01	18.82
Unweighted Average	18.52	8.52	13.40
Weighted Average	18.25	7.68	11.70

SOURCES: U.S. Department of Agriculture, Division of Statistics, "The Cost of Cotton Production," Misc. Series, Bulletin no. 16 (Washington, D.C.: Government Printing Office, 1899); U.S. Department of Agriculture, Agricultural Marketing Service, *Cotton and Cotton Seed,* Statistical Bulletin no. 164 (Washington, D.C.: GPO, 1955); U.S. Department of Agriculture, Bureau of Agricultural Economics, "Revised Estimates of Corn Acreage, Yield and Production 1866–1929" (mimeo, 1934); U.S. Department of Agriculture, *Prices of Farm Products Received by Producers,* Statistical Bulletin no. 16 (Washington, D.C.: GPO, 1927).

it was the application of labor; the unifying element was the effort of landlords to raise the value of their land's product.

A major recent book by Roger L. Ransom and Richard Sutch, *One Kind of Freedom,* on the economic consequences of emancipation, emphasizes the withdrawal of black labor from field work, particularly the labor of females and children.[34] This development was undoubtedly real and significant, but the Ransom-Sutch account conveys an impression that the increased scarcity of labor caused a rise in the ratio of land to labor. In reality the change was the opposite. In the plantation areas, per capita allotments of land to black families *declined* by more than 50 percent between 1860 and 1880, much more, in other words, than the estimated fall in labor force participation. This perspective, in turn, raises the question whether the observed labor force withdrawal was entirely voluntary. As economic historians Robert E. Gallman and Ralph V. Anderson suggest, "changes in the work proclivities of freed men

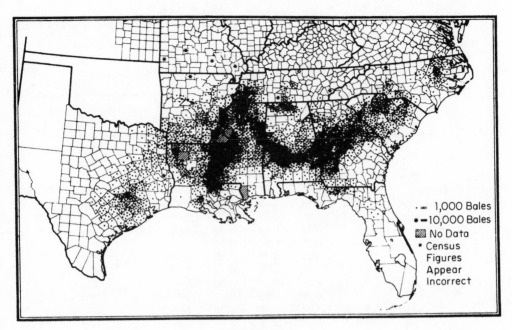

FIGURE 2.1a

Cotton Production, 1859

NOTE: U.S. Department of Agriculture, *Atlas of American Agriculture*, part 5, sec. A (Washington, D.C.: Government Printing Office, 1918), 17.

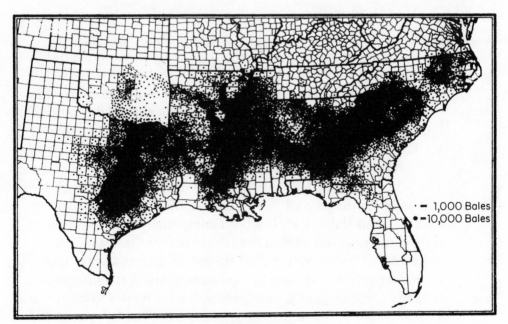

FIGURE 2.1b

Cotton Production, 1899

NOTE: U.S. Department of Agriculture, *Atlas of American Agriculture*, part 5, sec. A (Washington, D.C.: Government Printing Office, 1918), 17.

TABLE 2.7

Improved Acres/Rural Population

	1850	1860	1870	1880	Percentage of Change, 1860–80
Alabama	6.02	6.98	5.42	5.34	−23.5
Arkansas	3.72	4.59	3.94	4.67	1.7
Florida	3.99	4.86	4.27	3.91	−19.5
Georgia	7.35	8.21	6.30	5.87	−28.5
Louisiana	4.14	5.18	3.90	3.91	−24.5
Mississippi	5.78	6.57	5.30	4.76	−27.5
North Carolina	6.43	6.73	5.08	4.82	−28.4
South Carolina	6.57	6.98	4.67	4.49	−35.7
Tennessee	5.28	6.39	5.88	5.96	−6.7
Texas	3.14	4.59	3.88	8.75	90.6
Virginia	8.26[a]	8.31[a]	7.56	6.43	−22.6
11 States	6.22	6.72	5.61	5.68	−15.5
5 Deep South States	6.22	6.97	5.76	5.02	−28.0
10 States[b]	6.32	6.88	5.78	5.25	−23.7

SOURCE: Donald B. Dodd and Wynelle S. Dodd, *Historical Statistics of the South 1790–1970* (University: University of Alabama Press, 1973).
[a] Excludes West Virginia.
[b] Excludes Texas.

may not have been altogether a product of their choice . . . [because] labor no longer had the character of fixed capital to the planter."[35]

Because cotton requires more labor per acre than corn, the shift in crop is closely connected with the rise in the ratio of labor to land. They may be thought of as alternative ways of viewing the same phenomenon: in part, the move to cotton was a *reflection* of greater land intensity, in part it was a *cause*. The Civil War marked a fundamental break in the relative trends of farmland and farm labor in all the southern states except Texas (table 2.7). It would complete the picture neatly if we could now record that the break reflected massive inflows of immigrant labor. Emancipation did, in fact, instantly transform the planters' attitude toward immigration; the former opponents became avid proponents and organizers.[36] But these efforts were not generally successful over the long run, for reasons explored in the following chapter, and the bulk of the postwar population growth was natural increase. Black fertility was high both before and after emancipation, but only after the war did the South emerge as the nation's high-fertility region for the white population.

THE RISE OF INTERIOR TOWNS AND RAILROADS

Economists commonly explain the move into cash crops as a response to improvements in transportation and marketing facilities, and from the standpoint of the individual farmer, whose ability to influence his own market is small, this is perfectly correct. But from the perspective of the regional economy, this amounts to explaining (as the economists would put it) one endogenous variable in terms of another endogenous variable. Both may be attributed more compactly and economically to the change in property rights and the new interest in land values. Despite all the problems of the cotton economy, the immediate postwar years saw a rush of entrepreneurship and new investment in interior towns and the transportation network.

In contrast to the antebellum experience, the South shared fully in the national railroad building boom of 1865–75. Railroad historian John Stover wrote: "By 1866 Southern rail recovery was so complete that nearly every state had new railroad projects in mind and in some cases, work had actually begun."[37] Of more importance than total mileage were the new locational patterns, the penetration of previously isolated counties and towns, and the creation of new trade centers at rail crossings (figures 2.2a and 2.2b). The use of a term like "penetration" should not, however, be taken to mean that these railroads were alien intrusions by large outside interests. In their origins, the new lines were local and regional. A survey of ten major lines and their presidents during the period 1865–80 shows that virtually every one had strong local ties and investments in local enterprises.[38] Railroad stock tended to be widely distributed among local holders, which often included the municipalities themselves.

The local railroads may be thought of as an early phase of the town-building activity that accelerated after the war (figure 2.3). The older cotton factorage system was unable to reestab-

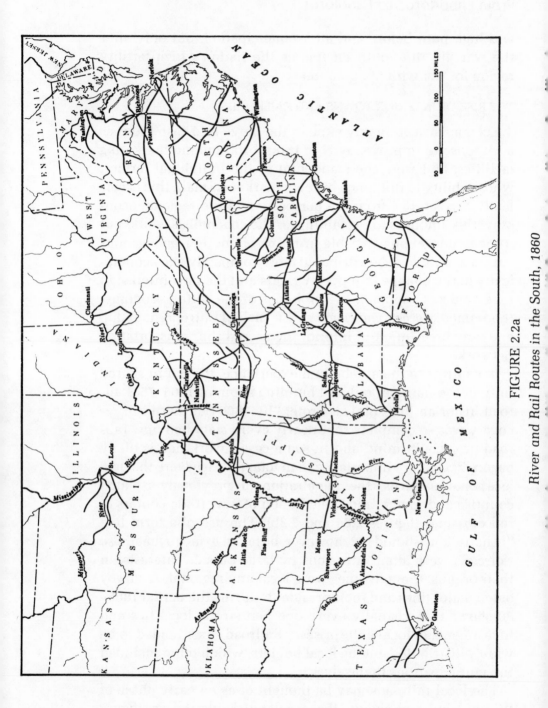

FIGURE 2.2a

River and Rail Routes in the South, 1860

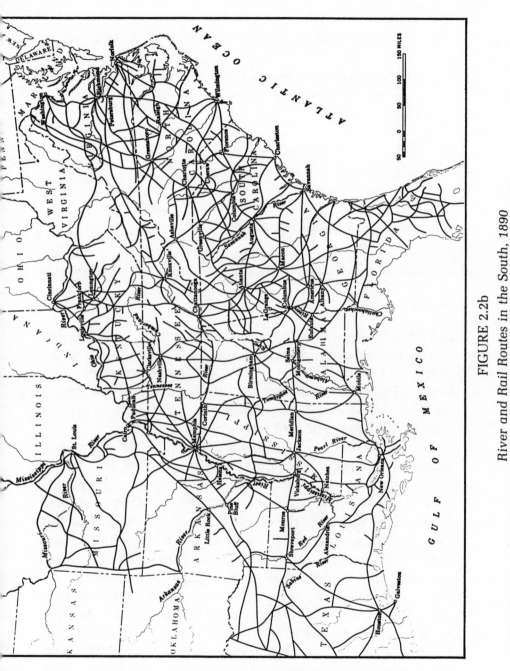

FIGURE 2.2b

River and Rail Routes in the South, 1890

NOTE: Reprinted, by permission of the publisher, from Harold Woodman, King Cotton and His Retainers (Lexington: University Press of Kentucky, 1968), inside back cover. Copyright © 1968 by the University Press of Kentucky.

FIGURE 2.3

Number of Urban Centers in the South, 1790–1950

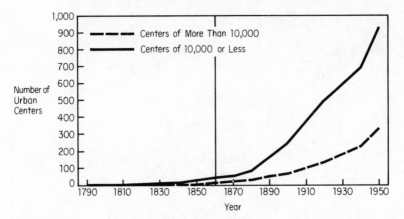

NOTE: Reprinted, by permission of the publisher, from Gavin Wright, "The Strange Career of the New Southern Economic History," *Reviews in American History* 10 (1982):169.
Data from Kenneth Weiher, "The Cotton Industry and Southern Urbanization," *Explorations in Economic History* 14 (1977): 123.

lish itself because of the new competition from scores of rural merchants and country stores offering to advance credit, supply goods, and market cotton, at new and more accessible locations.[39] The speed and discontinuity of this local blossoming suggests that it was in response to an equally discontinuous change, the new system of property rights.

The rise of small interior towns also refutes the notion that southern economic geography simply recorded the limited processing requirements of the staple crops.[40] It may have looked that way before the war, but afterward many of these towns began to service the cotton crop as their main economic function. Increasingly after 1880, cotton pressing and cotton-seed-oil milling came to be central activities for dozens of fast-growing small cities in the cotton regions.[41] There is no technological reason why services such as these could not have been dispersed much earlier. Their emergence after the war reflects on the one hand the channeling of entrepreneurship into location-specific activities and pursuits; on the other hand, it may be seen as a response to the new demands of local landowners for facilities that enhanced the value of their particular land holdings. Recent studies indicate that these developments had the support of landowning planters and farmers.[42]

On this score the New South was doing no more than moving in the direction of the American mainstream. As the economist and social critic Thorstein Veblen put it:

> Habitually and with singular uniformity, the American farmers have aimed to acquire real estate at the same time that they have worked at their trade as husbandmen. . . . They have been cultivators of the main chance as well as the fertile soil.
>
> The location of any given town has commonly been determined by collusion between "interested parties" with a view to speculation in real estate, and it continues through its life-history . . . to be managed as a real estate "proposition." Its municipal affairs, its civic pride, its community interest, converge upon its real estate values.[43]

Crucial to the success of any such enterprise is publicity. Every small chamber of commerce flooded the mails with pamphlets and brochures boosting the local cotton market or promoting wares or real estate. The "booster" spirit of the newspapers was a reflection of the basic economic impulses behind town building itself, the tendency of townspeople to treat their communities as a common enterprise.[44] To dismiss these editors as mere "publicists" is to miss the fundamental redirection of economic energy that followed emancipation.

MANUFACTURING AND RESOURCE DEVELOPMENT

Many readers will have followed the argument thus far in its application to spatial patterns in agriculture and trade, and yet still wonder how the abolition of property rights in labor could directly stimulate mining and manufacturing, as the New South publicists claimed. Since slave labor was employed successfully in mining and even in factories, what basis could there be for the warning in the *Southern Recorder* that Northerners "will yet find out to their sorrow that the destruction of our negro property has laid the foundation for an independence that will strike fatal blows at their prosperity."[45] The "fatal blows" were at least a half-century off, but it is a fact that the 1860s saw the largest percentage increase in southern manufacturing establishments of any decade in the nineteenth century, and after 1880 this growth accelerated (figure 2.4).

FIGURE 2.4

Number of Manufacturing Establishments in All Southern States,
1850 to 1900

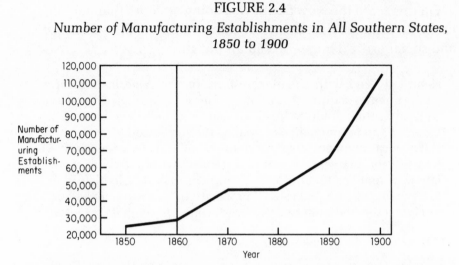

NOTE: Reprinted, by permission of the publisher, from Gavin Wright, "The Strange Career of the New Southern Economic History," *Reviews in American History* 10 (1982): 170.
Data from Donald B. Dodd and Wynelle S. Dodd, *Historical Statistics of the South, 1790–1970* (University: University of Alabama Press, 1973).

There were direct links between these trends and the new localization of economic life, in at least three cases: cotton manufacturing, the fertilizer industry, and the emergence of the coal and iron region in Alabama and Tennessee.

Broadus Mitchell's 1921 classic, *The Rise of the Cotton Mills in the South,* portrayed the spread of cotton mills after 1880 as a public-spirited crusade in which philanthropic and altruistic motives predominated. Since C. Vann Woodward, no analyst (and certainly none of the many economists who have studied the rise of southern textiles) has had any good word to say for this interpretation: surely economic motives must have been foremost, and surely economic conditions must have been ripe.[46] What these critics missed is that the early mill-building movement was an outgrowth of town building.[47] The mills clustered around towns and transportation facilities. Their local supporters were merchants and landowners in the town and surrounding areas. Their rhetoric was boosterism, the town as a collective enterprise. And while the claimed moral/social benefits and philanthropic purposes were undoubtedly exaggerated, there was a sense in which the beneficiaries really

could be seen as "the community": namely, the property holders who all stood to gain, either explicitly in the form of higher
land values, or implicitly through the volume of commerce or
improved local markets for cotton and farm produce.

What was most misleading about the cotton mill rhetoric
was the implication that non-property-owning laborers and
concern for their welfare played a major role. The enthusiasts
certainly did not see *themselves* as potential mill workers, and
the residents of the new mill villages quickly became objects
of revulsion and fear on the part of town residents. It is also
true that an industry needs more than local enthusiasm to
become competitive in a national market, and the supply of
cheap labor was the key to the continued growth of southern
textiles over the subsequent half-century (see the detailed
analysis in chapter 5). Though Mitchell may be rightly criticized for taking the rhetoric of boosterism literally, the point
here is that this rhetoric was intimately linked to one of the
genuine economic impulses behind the industry, and that this
sprang from the abolition of slavery. This indirect connection
is the element of truth in Mitchell's statement that the slave
owners "shut out the average man from economic participation; but with the rise of the cotton mills, the poor whites were
welcomed back into the service of the South."[48]

The location of textile manufacturing has been historically
sensitive to the cost of labor, but many other nineteenth-century industries required close access to fuel and raw materials.
An example is the manufacture of commercial fertilizers,
which began in South Carolina in the 1870s in the wake of the
development of large-scale phosphate mining in the lowland
areas of that state beginning in 1867.[49] The phosphate deposits
which had previously been items of scientific curiosity now
became objects of intense interest and mobilization (table 2.8).
Rice planters began to engage in active prospecting and to consider offers from mining companies. One should not necessarily
think of this search as a response to the new interest in fertilizers among southern farmers generally, because an active international trade in fertilizer had existed for decades prior to
the war, with European markets in phosphate fertilizers from

TABLE 2.8

Shipments and Consumption of South Carolina Phosphate,
1867 to 1892 (in Tons of 2,240 pounds)

Year	Shipped to Foreign Markets	Shipped to Domestic Markets	Manufactured at Home	Total Shipments
1867	0	6	0	6
1868	208	11,654	0	11,862
1869	3,760	24,511	0	28,271
1870	15,632	40,763	0	56,395
1871	42,524	21,907	12,000	76,431
1872	33,168	29,135	10,000	72,303
1873	27,035	32,168	15,000	74,203
1874	52,545	42,430	16,000	110,975
1875	70,546	32,560	19,680	122,786
1876	76,265	38,231	18,850	133,346
1877	102,767	47,053	15,000	164,820
1878	121,742	68,946	17,635	208,323
1879	119,566	60,899	18,900	199,365
1880	61,375	107,358	22,040	190,773
1881	71,168	157,824	38,142	267,134
1882	112,486	168,959	42,900	324,345
1883	123,040	186,720	42,000	351,760
1884	153,609	222,411	56,900	432,920
1885	123,490	193,700	67,000	260,700
1886	160,209	201,600	69,000	430,809
1887	199,700	197,905	83,000	480,605
1888	189,650	237,834	87,000	514,484
1889	143,002	308,643	90,000	541,645
1890	219,822	250,936	116,000	586,758
1891	126,798	295,151	151,000	573,940
1892	124,343	242,942	181,000	548,396

SOURCE: Carroll D. Wright, The Phosphate Industry of the United States, Sixth Special Report of the Commissioner of Labor (Washington, D.C.: Government Printing Office, 1893), 97.

at least 1845. The new deposits were, however, rich enough to affect world and domestic fertilizer prices, so that a real economic symbiosis prevailed between the efforts of two sets of southern landowners to gain more revenue from their holdings.[50] Though the South Carolina phosphate-fertilizer industry dwindled in the twentieth century, the fact that this occurred only confirms the mechanism at work, since it succumbed to the discovery of still richer deposits in Tennessee and Florida; both were the results of active searches.

An industrial development that combined mineral exploration and town building was the coal and iron complex in Alabama and Tennessee, which emerged as the Birmingham steel industry by the end of the century. Birmingham itself began as a real estate venture undertaken by a group of land speculators in association with officials of the Louisville and Nashville Railroad who were interested in freight. But Birmingham was only the most successful of the town-promotion schemes that dotted the northern Alabama countryside with blast furnaces, beginning almost immediately with the post-bellum period.[51] Virtually every industrial beginning may be traced to someone's attempt to make a capital gain on property in land. To be sure, much of this activity was unproductive: towns were promoted on "the merest hint of ore and coal deposits," and many of the blast furnaces were unprofitable.[52] But the net result was that the hills were scoured for coal and iron, settlers and outside investors flowed in, and a major industrial complex emerged (table 2.9). It was a far cry from the economic geography of slavery, but essentially similar to the process by which the northern economy had operated all along.

Property Rights and Political Economy: Did the Planter Class Survive the War?

From the time of C. Vann Woodward's classic *Origins of the New South* (1951), historians have debated whether the old planter class was destroyed by the war, or whether they survived to continue their regional domination. Woodward's answer was that the planter class had not survived, but had given way to a new middle class of merchants, lawyers, and industrialists, and that those who did survive largely accepted the values of these new groups. The many critics of this position have made two main points: first, that the majority of large planters from before the war were able to retain their lands, and hence their positions of economic power, after the war; and second, that the conservative Redeemer governments that

TABLE 2.9

Coal, Iron Ore, and Pig Iron Production in Alabama,
1860–1900 (in Thousands of Tons)

Year	Coal	Iron Ore	Pig Iron	Year	Coal	Iron Ore	Pig Iron
1860	10	4	2	1885	2,492	505	203
1870	13	11		1886	1,800	650	253
1871	20			1887	1,950	675	261
1872	30	22	11	1888	2,900	1,000	401
1873	45	39	20	1889	3,573	1,570	707
1874	50	58	29	1890	4,090	1,898	817
1875	67	44	22	1891	4,760	1,987	796
1876	112	44	22	1892	5,529	2,312	915
1877	196	70	37	1893	5,137	1,742	727
1878	224	75	37	1894	4,397	1,493	592
1879	280	90	45	1895	5,694	2,199	855
1880	380	171	69	1896	5,746	2,042	922
1881	420	220	88	1897	5,894	2,050	948
1882	896	250	101	1898	6,509	2,202	1,026
1883	1,568	385	154	1899	7,485	2,627	1,084
1884	2,240	420	169	1900	8,504	3,095	1,156

SOURCES: U.S. Bureau of the Census, Manufactures, 8th Census (1860) (Washington, D.C.: Government Printing Office, 1865), clxxiii–clxxx; Thomas Mcadory Owen, History of Alabama, vol. 1 (1921; reprint, Spartanburg, S.C.: Spartanburg Reprint Company, 1978), 284, 796–97.

came to power in the 1870s were not wholeheartedly favorable to internal improvement, banks, corporations, and industrial development.[53]

But what is the essence of the "planter class"? In the classical economic tradition handed down from Smith, Ricardo, and Marx, the concept of class is rooted in a factor of production, and class interest represents the interest of that factor. The term *planter class* applied to both slave owners and landlords obfuscates the economics of the matter; according to that standard they were all a "new class," because the interests associated with their property had changed. Whether the same individuals and families happen to be involved may be interesting sociologically, but it is really not an essential question from an economic standpoint. When writers argue that because the "old agrarian class . . . encouraged the New South" in North and South Carolina, "there was no real break in the character of the social support for the Old and New Souths," they are mixing incompatible concepts of class, much the way the New South spokesmen blended conflicting ideologies in their rhetoric.[54] If after the Revolution, the members of a class vigorously pursue goals they staunchly opposed before, in what economic sense has that class survived? Most planters may have held onto their land, but after the war, they had to deal with a non-slave labor market that was a completely new experience and that involved an "ideological capitulation" that took several years to complete.[55] Before they were laborlords, now they were only landlords.

There is also no doubt that the political priorities of planters in economic matters changed direction after the war. A good example is the campaign to close the open range to grazing and other forms of trespassing. For generations the southern range had been open, and property rights in land given lower priority than the rights of small herdsmen and farmers to hunting, fishing, and foraging. After the war, landowners in state after state led campaigns for fence laws, stock laws, strict trespass laws, and enforcement. Often there were bitter protracted struggles between big landowners and small farmers or tenants, who regarded such measures as "calculated seriously to injure their rights and privileges."[56] At the conclusion of one recent study, the author observes:

> The question remains as to why Alabama's range was in no way restricted until after the Civil War. There is a common belief that one of the results of America's bloodiest war was to break the grip of the great landowning class and democratize the South. It then seems odd that the planter class did not get what it had been seeking until *after* the war."[57]

The puzzlement is resolved by the analysis of this chapter: the planters were a "great landowning class" only after the war; previously, they were laborlords more than landlords.

None of this discussion is meant to deny the force of the view, capably expressed by historian Carl Degler, that there were many threads of continuity in southern history over the whole century.[58] The structural legacy of slavery took a long time to undo. For another three-quarters of a century, the state of world cotton demand remained the main determinant of prosperity or depression for the South. The color line remained firm long after slavery. The major continuity, however, was simply the fact of separateness. Even though the South moved toward the American mainstream in its economic behavior, it emerged in the 1870s as a low-wage region in a high-wage country, a consideration that shaped its economic future for another century.

3

THE LONG VIEW OF

SOUTHERN LAND AND LABOR

POLITICAL FACTORS are basic to economic history, but the terms of political discourse in a given era are often well removed from the most important economic trends of that same era. Northerners worried about the expanding slavocracy at a time when the North was more expansionist than the South. The South counted on the political power of King Cotton at just the moment when English cotton demand had passed its peak. A generation later, what appeared to be the historic political confrontation between farmers and capital occurred in 1896, after the organizational roots of the farmers' movement had been destroyed; yet the farmers' defeat came on the eve of a major upswing in their economic fortunes that lasted more than two decades. In the twentieth-century South, concern for "colonial economy" exploitation was high when capital inflows were low, and vice versa. Northern agitation over low wages in textile mill villages arose in the midst of significant increases in these wage levels. And so on. Political actors are not objective, and even if they try to be, it is not easy for a generation to understand its own position in historical terms.

This being the case, it seems wise to try to identify basic contours and components in the economic history of the South from a somewhat rarefied elevation, before embarking on more detailed study of industries and institutions. This chapter advances three propositions:

1. that regional agricultural progress was dictated primarily by the pace of cotton demand, not by productivity;
2. that rates of industrialization and industrial productivity growth in the South were quite respectable by historical standards;
3. that wage and migration indicators show the South as a region with a functioning labor market and a mobile labor force.

If these points are correct, in what sense was the South backward or its economic performance unsatisfactory? The answer to this question is implicit in the third proposition, that the labor market was a *regional* market, largely isolated from national labor markets. Poor quality soil, climate, high fertility rates—none of these would have caused regional poverty if there had been a national labor market. So long as southern population growth remained high and the southern labor market remained isolated, the basic southern wage was bound to remain below national norms, even in the midst of economic growth as conventionally defined. Many of the characteristics of backwardness, such as low-wage, low-skill industry, underinvestment in education, even capital scarcity, were rooted in the regional character of the labor market.

Land, Labor, and Cotton Demand

Whereas before the Civil War, the southern countryside filled up much more slowly than the rural areas of the North and West, thereafter the opposite was true. Table 3.1 displays the vivid contrast between North and South in basic trends over the fifty-year period from 1880 to 1930. In every southern state but Texas, farm acreage per member of the rural population declined steadily and apparently inexorably. (The Texas figures reflect the rise of the cattle kingdom in western Texas, really a distinct phenomenon.) But in every northern state, acreage per person was *rising*, markedly so in the states west of the Mississippi. As a result of the trends, rural population density

TABLE 3.1

Acres in Farms/Rural Population, 1880–1930

	1880	1890	1900	1910	1920	1930
Alabama	16	15	13	12	11	9
Arkansas	16	14	14	13	12	11
Florida	14	12	11	10	10	7
Georgia	19	16	14	13	13	11
Louisiana	12	11	11	9	9	7
Mississippi	15	14	13	12	12	10
North Carolina	17	15	13	12	10	8
South Carolina	15	13	12	11	9	8
Tennessee	15	13	12	12	11	11
Texas	25	27	50	38	36	36
Virginia	15	14	13	12	11	10
11 States	17	16	19	16	16	13
5 Deep South	16	14	13	11	11	9
10 States[a]	14	14	13	12	11	9
Illinois	15	15	15	15	15	15
Iowa	18	20	21	22	22	23
Kansas	24	26	37	36	39	41
Nebraska	25	28	37	44	47	50
Midwest[b]	16	17	20	21	23	23

SOURCES: Donald B. Dodd and Wynelle S. Dodd, *Historical Statistics of the South* (University: University of Alabama Press, 1973); *Historical Statistics of the United States, 1790–1970*, vol. 2, *The Midwest* (University: University of Alabama Press, 1976).

[a] Excludes Texas.

[b] Includes Illinois, Indiana, Iowa, Kansas, Michigan, Minnesota, Montana, Nebraska, North Dakota, Ohio, South Dakota, and Wisconsin.

(the reciprocal of the ratios in table 3.1), which was roughly equal in the two regions as of 1880, was twice as great in the South as in the North by 1930. The comparable figures on acres per farm have to be regarded as somewhat suspect because of the irregular treatment of plantations in the South. Yet the aggregate data in table 3.2 show precisely the same pattern: a steady upward trend in farm size in the North, a steady downward trend in the South.

Several things are noteworthy about these figures. Modern observers often suggest that long-run tendencies toward national economic convergence are very strong, and hence that there was a kind of inevitability about the southern "catch-up" to the rest of the country. Yet here we have evidence, not just of slow convergence but of positive divergence at a basic level over a long historical period. A second observation often

TABLE 3.2

Acres Per Farm, 1880–1930

	1880	1890	1900	1910	1920	1930
Alabama	139	126	93	79	76	68
Arkansas	128	119	93	81	75	66
Florida	141	107	107	105	112	85
Georgia	188	147	118	93	82	86
Louisiana	171	138	95	87	74	58
Mississippi	156	122	83	66	67	55
North Carolina	142	128	101	88	74	65
South Carolina	143	115	90	77	65	66
Tennessee	125	116	91	82	77	73
Texas	209	225	257	269	262	252
Virginia	167	150	119	106	100	98
11 States	157	143	141	115	110	104
5 Deep South	159	130	96	80	73	67
10 States*a*	149	128	98	84	77	70
Illinois	124	127	124	129	135	143
Iowa	134	151	151	156	157	158
Kansas	155	181	241	244	275	283
Nebraska	157	190	246	298	339	345
Midwest*b*	122	133	145	158	172	181

SOURCES: Donald B. Dodd and Wynelle S. Dodd, *Historical Statistics of the South* (University: University of Alabama Press, 1973); *Historical Statistics of the United States, 1790–1970*, vol. 2, *The Midwest* (University: University of Alabama Press, 1976).
a Excludes Texas.
b Includes Illinois, Indiana, Iowa, Kansas, Michigan, Minnesota, Montana, Nebraska, North Dakota, Ohio, South Dakota, and Wisconsin.

made by historians is that "you can't generalize about the South," because the plantation areas of the deep South are so different in so many ways from the small farm and backwoods sections. They certainly were different, yet here we have a trend that seems to unify the South in contradistinction to the rest of the country. Farm size declined in Virginia and North Carolina as steadily as it did in Mississippi, while the rest of the country moved in another direction. Third, it is sometimes said that World War I marked the decisive beginning of the trend toward national convergence, but tables 3.1 and 3.2 indicate that divergence continued at least until the Great Depression.

A factor in the contrary trends of land and labor was the continuing high fertility of the southern population. A useful shorthand measure of fertility is the child-woman ratio, dis-

TABLE 3.3

Child-Woman Ratios, North and South, 1880–1930
(Children Aged 0–4 Per 1,000 Women Aged 15–44)

Year	South			Non-South		
	Total	White	Rural	Total	White	Rural
1880	741.5	711.4	—	545.9	547.5	—
1890	645.5	620.7	—	497.0	486.8	—
1900	636.0	638.1	—	467.7	460.6	—
1910	606.6	622.7	676.9	436.9	440.3	518.0
1920	537.2	546.9	615.9	445.6	446.1	533.4
1930	461.5	470.5	550.1	364.8	357.5	460.1

SOURCE: Dudley L. Poston, Jr., and Robert H. Weller, eds., *The Population of the South* (Austin: University of Texas Press, 1981), 7.

played in table 3.3 for the years 1880 to 1930. This indicator shows that the South had far higher fertility levels than the rest of the country, and the difference was not primarily a racial or rural-urban, but a regional, phenomenon. Southern white ratios were nearly as high as the regional average (and were in fact higher after 1900); and northern rural areas were well below those of the South for the years available.

One should not imagine, however, that the economy of the South was grinding deeper and deeper into poverty during this time, as each farmer scratched away at a progressively smaller plot of land. There is no question that productivity grew in southern agriculture, just as there is no question that per capita income grew for the South as a whole. An annual index of physical crop production per member of the rural population, for example, shows an increase of about 1 percent per year from the late 1870s to 1908.[1] Southern regional per capita income, though it stood at a level barely half of the U.S. average in 1880, nonetheless grew at about the national rate between 1880 and 1900, and faster than the national rate between 1900 and 1920.[2] If the rural population was steadily pressing upon the land, what then accounts for the observed economic progress?

What matters from an economic standpoint is not the physical ratio between land and labor, but the relationship between labor and the productive *value* of the land. This, in turn, depends upon the prices of commodities produced. In the case of cotton, however, the connection at the aggregate level was unique. American cotton so dominated the world market that the size of the U.S. crop (in conjunction with world demand) essentially determined the price. Econometric estimates of the demand for U.S. cotton show that the elasticity of demand (the percentage change in price divided by the percentage change in quantity) was very nearly unity (1.0) for as much as a century prior to World War I.[3] Though we should not exaggerate the precision of this estimate, the broad point is fundamentally important: over the range of observed variation, *aggregate incomes from cotton agriculture were limited by demand and not by productivity*. Though particular farms and particular regions might do better or worse, the aggregate growth of southern farm income per capita was primarily determined by the rate of growth of cotton demand relative to the growth of population.

This analysis broadly explains the timing of southern economic spurts and relapses prior to World War II. The rapid growth of the antebellum period was fueled by a 5 percent annual growth in cotton demand. Between 1860 and the late 1870s, cotton demand plunged and then stagnated. Figure 3.1 shows the clear inverse relationship between the recovery of production and the decline in the cotton price, over the years 1866–79. The mismatch between stagnant cotton demand and growing population (which increased by nearly 50 percent) accounts in part for the position of southern per capita income in 1880, barely half of the national level. From 1880 to 1900, cotton demand grew at an estimated 2.7 percent per year, while population grew at almost 2 percent. In the cotton states of the lower South, per capita growth was even less than this slender margin, because the output of other crops and livestock did not keep up. (The tobacco states of North Carolina, Virginia, and Kentucky, however, grew a bit faster because of the post-1880 tobacco boom, demand growing at close to 5 percent per year.) After 1900, cotton demand accelerated to 3.5 percent as textiles led the expansion of world trade, and the Southern economy picked up its pace. But after 1920, the chaotic state of international trade stymied cotton demand, which declined

FIGURE 3.1

Cotton Production and Price, 1867–79

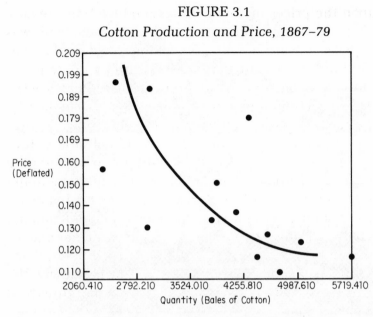

NOTE: Dots are annual price-quantity observations.

absolutely at .5 percent per year between 1920 and 1930.[4] As a result, even before the Great Depression, the South lost virtually all of the relative income gains achieved by 1920. Cotton production hit new peaks in the 1920s and 1930s (figure 3.2), but these did not correspond to peaks in the incomes of cotton farmers. Thus, claims for a long-term "convergence" process are not well-founded: the South was a largely separate population, with a distinctive demography and an economy dominated by a single commodity with a unique place in world trade.

Why couldn't southern farmers move into other crops or into livestock? The nineteenth-century South was heavily agricultural (table 3.4), but every agricultural option outside of cotton faced special difficulties. The other significant regional cash crops—tobacco, rice, and sugar—had narrow geographic limits. Across the broad center of the region from the Carolinas to Texas, cotton was the most profitable choice by a wide margin, as suggested in table 2.6. The acid soils and high early rainfall made it difficult to grow grains, grasses, and legumes in competition with temperate-zone states. Animal parasites and cholera killed hogs and cattle, and reduced body weight

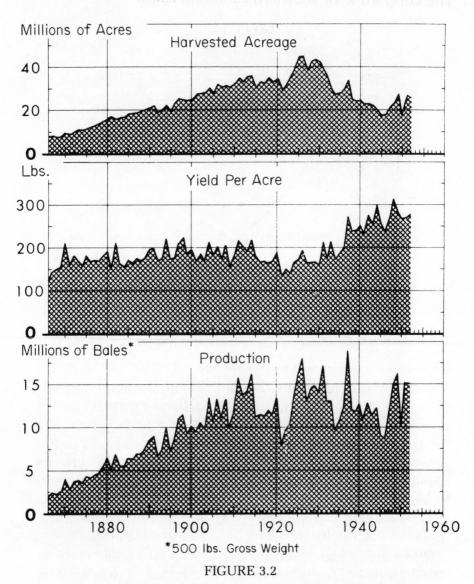

FIGURE 3.2

Cotton in the United States: Acreage, Yield, and Production

NOTE: U.S. Department of Agriculture, Agricultural Marketing Service, *Cotton and Cottonseed*, Statistical Bulletin no. 164 (Washington, D.C.: Government Printing Office, 1955), 3.

TABLE 3.4

*Agricultural Income as a
Percentage of Total Income,
1880–1900*

	1880	1900
Alabama	80	58
Arkansas	88	65
Florida	62	40
Georgia	78	62
Kentucky	64	52
Louisiana	66	53
Mississippi	89	76
North Carolina	82	63
South Carolina	84	67
Tennessee	73	54
Texas	69	68
Virginia	60	48
11 States	76	61
5 Deep South	79	63
10 States[a]	77	59

SOURCE: Richard Easterlin, "Interregional Differences in Per Capita Income," in Conference on Research in Income and Wealth, *Trends in the American Economy in the Nineteenth Century,* vol. 24, *Studies in Income and Wealth* (Princeton, N.J.: Princeton University Press, 1960), tables A-2, A-3.
[a] Excludes Texas.

and milk yields. Even raising mules, a work animal used more extensively in the South than in any other region, was found to be more cheaply done elsewhere.[5]

Though reformers favored diversification for decades, as late as 1926 an agricultural economist could accurately state that "nothing has been found to take the place of cotton on an extensive scale that would make the farmers as much money one year with another."[6] Corn and other crops for on-farm food and feed requirements could provide some insulation from market risks for those who could afford it, but they could not bring in money and they offered little hope as a source of progress. Cotton was not the totality of southern agriculture, but for most of the region it defined the opportunities and dictated the pace of economic life. Clarence Poe wrote in 1904: "When southern cotton prices drop, every man feels the blow; when cotton prices advance, every industry throbs with vigor."[7]

This story indicates that there is a kernel of truth in the idea that the South suffered from "poor soil." When times were good, the value of land yields in cotton was substantially higher than the value of land yields in other parts of the country. But when cotton prices fell, the southern "fall-back" options were distinctly inferior. The fact that moneymaking opportunities were unique but thin and specialized goes a long way toward explaining persistence in behavior that outsiders took to be ignorance, pathology, or traditionalism. Perhaps too there is an element of regional bias in the progress of agricultural science. Agricultural improvements tend to be geographically-specific, and to require a lengthy process of local adaptation when transported to a new place. To say that there were intrinsic limits to southern agricultural progress, given the limitations of nineteenth-century science, is, to some extent, merely a way of saying that the central concerns of the American agricultural research establishment were not southern.[8]

The Pace of Industrial Progress

Whatever truth there may be in the "poor soil" thesis, however, economists have understood for some time that soil quality in itself is not a cause of poverty.[9] There are much poorer soils in the frozen tundra and on the desert, but these are not causes of poverty because people do not by and large choose to live in those places. If a crop that is profitable for a time eventually "plays out" like a vein of ore, we would expect people to migrate from the area, unless alternative employment opportunities emerge, as they did in New England in the early nineteenth century, when farming in that region came under pressure. Perhaps the southern agricultural sector could not feasibly have done much better, but why didn't industrial demand take up the slack? Surely the slow growth of industry suggests an attachment to agrarian values or an absence of entrepreneurial vigor.

TABLE 3.5

Growth Rates of Real Value-Added
in Manufactures
1869–1929

| Year | South | | U.S. |
	5 States	11 States	
1869–99	7.2	7.8	5.8
1879–1909	7.4	7.3	4.9
1889–1919	5.3	5.2	3.4
1899–1929	4.5	5.0	4.4
1869–1919	5.9	6.1	4.8
1879–1919	6.3	6.4	4.5
1879–1929	6.2	6.6	4.9

SOURCE: Everett S. Lee et al., *Population Redistribution and Economic Growth: United States, 1870–1950*, vol. 1 (Philadelphia: American Philosophical Society, 1957), 694–95.

But the pace of southern industrial growth was not slow. The slave regime left an overwhelmingly agricultural economy as its legacy, but the figures in table 3.5 show that real value-added in southern manufacturing (the value of production less the value of materials used) grew at average rates of more than 7 *percent per year* for the forty-year period from 1869 to 1909. If we take the prosperity year of 1879 as perhaps a more reasonable base, we still find that growth rates of more than 6 percent were sustained for fifty years. This performance compares favorably with other historical examples of early industrialization.

It is true that southern industry tended to be labor-intensive, and labor productivity was well below the U.S. norm. But the growth rate of industrial labor productivity was as high as, or higher than, that of U.S. industry generally, between 1869 and 1939, and in every decade between (table 3.6). Its productivity growth at 2 percent per year is more rapid than that realized by New England industry during the first American industrial revolution, 1820–60.[10]

This is not an attempt to play tricks with numbers, to create statistically a thriving industrial South that every observer knows did not exist. Southern industry was indeed concen-

TABLE 3.6

Growth Rates of Real Value-Added Per Worker in Manufacturing, 1869–1929

Year	South 5 States	South 11 States	U.S.
1869–99	2.8	3.2	2.8
1879–1909	1.6	1.9	1.9
1889–1919	1.5	1.0	0.5
1899–1929	2.0	2.3	2.3
1869–1919	2.1	2.2	1.8
1879–1919	1.4	1.8	1.5
1879–1929	2.0	2.6	2.5

SOURCE: Everett S. Lee et al., *Population Redistribution and Economic Growth: United States, 1870–1950*, vol. 1 (Philadelphia: American Philosophical Society, 1957), 684, 694–95.

trated in low-wage, low-skill sectors, using imported technology and, usually, imported machinery. Industrialization in the South was not associated with spectacular technological breakthroughs or with numerous dynamic linkages to advancing sectors. The object of these tables is not to paint a glowing picture like those of the New South spokesmen, but to identify the economic forces at work. The reason for the persistence of "southern backwardness" was not that industrial growth was slow by historical standards, but that it was not fast enough *relative to the growing regional population*. In his justly celebrated *Origins of the New South*, C. Vann Woodward dismisses the New South movement as unsuccessful, not by proving that there was industrial stagnation but by citing statistics on urban population as a fraction of the total.[11] This criterion does not reflect the achievements of industry so much as the fertility of the countryside.

Southern industry could not have grown much faster without a massive inflow of outside capital—without, in other words, an expansion of the very "colonial" relationship that Woodward and many contemporaries decried. The capital stock of the South was not more but *less* subject to "outside" ownership than the capital of such growing northern states as

TABLE 3.7

Nonagricultural Wealth Owned by
State Residents as a Percentage
of Total Nonagricultural Wealth,
1880–1920

	1880	1900	1920
South			
Alabama	82	72	62
Arkansas	73	67	59
Georgia	88	81	72
Louisiana	114	101	85
Mississippi	84	63	42
North Carolina	94	75	54
South Carolina	87	75	58
Tennessee	90	75	59
Texas	81	107	126
Virginia	97	83	68
North			
Colorado	53	71	88
Indiana	79	70	59
Iowa	66	50	32
Kansas	54	61	65
Michigan	78	86	94
Minnesota	70	73	74
Montana	56	53	49
Nebraska	54	53	51
Ohio	103	95	85
Wisconsin	74	75	75

SOURCE: Everett S. Lee et al., *Population Redistribution
and Economic Growth: United States, 1870–1950*, vol.
1 (Philadelphia: American Philosophical Society,
1957), 729–33.

Iowa, Wisconsin, Nebraska, and Indiana. What set the South
apart from the rest of the country was not that capital came
in, but that elsewhere flows of capital were accompanied or
soon followed by flows of people, including bankers and busi-
nesspeople as well as farmers and laborers. In fairly short order,
the capital lost its "outside" identity; certainly this was so from
a regional if not always from a strictly local standpoint. But
not in the South. The steady decline between 1880 and 1920
in the fraction of nonagricultural wealth owned by home-state
residents is a distinctively southern regional trend (table 3.7).
The perception that the region was being taken over by outside
owners was not, therefore, a mere paranoid fabrication of

southern demagogues. But this way of looking at it confirms the arm's-length relationship between northern capital and the South. Ironically, the perception of a "colonial economy" relationship reflects the *limited* character of northern involvement in southern opportunities.

The Southern Labor Market

What these considerations point to is that the defining economic feature of the South prior to World War II was not poor performance or failure but isolation. Analytically speaking, the key was the isolation of the southern labor market from national and international flows.

Now the use of the term *labor market* with respect to the South is not without controversy. It is widely believed that labor in the post–Civil War South was economically immobile, held in place by "repression and enforced immobility," by debt peonage, and the crop lien system.[12] The most vivid accounts are about black plantation labor, but similar statements have been made about white labor in the mill villages, economists' favorite textbook example of labor monopsony (market power, but on the buyer's side). Jonathan Wiener writes:

> Sharecropping was established as a repressive system of labor allocation and control, based as it was on informal agreements among the planters to limit competition for labor, on state laws which established legal obstacles to the free market in labor, and on the intermittent use of terror against laborers. . . . Sharecropping was a form of "bound" labor, with restrictions on the free market in labor that did not prevail in fully developed capitalist societies such as that of the North.[13]

A study of an impoverished tobacco county in Virginia also reports that "no free market in labor actually functioned." Interpretations of twentieth-century institutions in the South continued to include such statements. For example: Croppers were "little more than serfs, held to the land by debt, ignorance, poverty and dependence on the landlord"; "The cheap-labor system was in reality a slave-labor system, perpetuated with minor changes after the Civil War."[14]

If we take these statements literally, they cannot be correct. For the immediate postwar period, the testimony is unanimous that freedmen moved from place to place in large numbers, driving hard bargains in an atmosphere of labor scarcity.[15] But on into the 1870s, when labor markets had softened considerably, labor turnover continued. A study of four Mississippi plantations during the years 1871 to 1874 shows that between 27 and 56 percent of the labor force was new in each year.[16] The picture was similar on the Hairston Farm tobacco plantation in Virginia between 1871 and 1877. Of the forty-five laborers who worked during this time, twenty-one stayed less than a single year.[17] Surviving records from plantations in Georgia and Alabama show not only that tenants frequently left, but that they were often more likely to leave if they were heavily in debt. Owners who wanted to retain a tenant were more likely to write off an end-of-year debt as an inducement to stay than to exercise legal compulsion to block mobility.[18]

Examination of payroll records for textile mills also makes it evident that workers were free to come and go, and frequently did so. Of the ninety-four workers on the January 1889 payroll of the Morgan-Malloy mill in North Carolina, for example, only one-quarter were still present two years later.[19] Oral histories of mill workers collected by a research team from Chapel Hill reveal a great deal of moving from firm to firm, many work careers spanning five or six different firms within a decade.[20]

Census figures indicate that state-to-state migration rates were high throughout the period, with net flows primarily from the low-wage Southeast to the high-wage Southwest. Louisiana reported a "constant immigration of colored people from the upper South, hunting lucrative jobs on the delta plantations." Blacks living outside their state of birth were more than two-and-one-half times as likely to have moved to another southern state than to a state in the North or West. For southern whites that ratio was nearly double.[21] A study by Steven DeCanio shows that intercounty mobility rates were high for both races,

FIGURE 3.3

Farm Labor Wage Rates Per Day Without Board (Deflated by WPI) in Selected States, 1866–1942

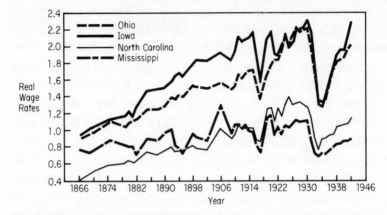

SOURCES: U.S. Department of Agriculture, *Crops and Markets* 19 (1942): 150–55; U.S. Bureau of the Census, *Historical Statistics of the United States*, part 1 (Washington, D.C.: Government Printing Office, 1975), 200–202.

the black rate being at least as high as the rate for whites.[22] Such aggregate indicators do not prove that no worker was "bound" (as of course could not be proved), and they do not say that southern laborers were treated fairly or munificently. But they do establish the proposition under scrutiny: there was a labor market in the South.

If there was a labor market, then we can analyze it according to the principles of markets, beginning with the price of labor or the wage. A useful index is the United States Department of Agriculture (USDA) series on farm labor wages by state, useful because the farm wage is a flexible market-determined rate for a reasonably homogeneous type of unskilled labor. Figure 3.3 displays the daily wage without board, deflated by the national wholesale price index, for four representative states, two northern and two southern. It is evident that there was a large gap between North and South. It is equally evident that the gap did not close. The absolute difference, what one might call the "cost of staying in the South," *widened* over time, from twenty cents per day around 1880 to fifty cents in 1902 and eighty cents in 1914 (Mississippi vs. Ohio). What is most notable for our purposes, however, is that both regions show convergence between low-wage and high-wage states;

that is, they behave the way market prices are supposed to behave, but they do not converge with each other. Labor markets existed in both North and South, but they were separate.

It is true that the largest fluctuations of the two series are similar, but this should not be taken as evidence that the labor markets were linked. There is bound to be some positive correlation, because the major events of war and the international business cycle (the depression of the 1890s, the panic of 1907, the Great Depression of the 1930s) affected both regions. If the wages were not deflated by the wholesale price index, the positive correlation would be even stronger, because the raw data reflect national and world trends in the general price level, declining from 1866 to 1896, rising thereafter until 1930. But the use of the same price deflator for both regions (necessitated by the absence of regional cost-of-living series) exaggerates the degree of correlation in real farm wages. The use of this deflator also raises the old question from the debates of the 1920s and 1930s: does the low southern wage merely represent low regional prices for items in the cost of living? The most careful historical studies, however, by Philip Coelho and James Shepherd, have found no evidence that the South generally (and especially not the low-wage South Atlantic section) was a relative low cost-of-living region at any time prior to the 1930s.[23]

Another reason we can be sure that the farm wage differences are not attributable to price differences is that the differential only occurs for unskilled labor. Though southern "common labor" wages were 30 to 50 percent below North Central levels in 1890, differentials for such skilled occupations as baker, bricklayer, carpenter, mason, painter, plumber, and stonecutter were between 10 and 25 percent for the South Atlantic, even less for the East South Central section. For some occupations (iron molder and machinist), wages were essentially equalized in all regions.[24] A similar pattern was observed in the textile industry of that period, where entry-level jobs like spinning and doffing paid 40 to 60 percent less in the South than in the North, while jobs that required more experience, like weaving, paid 10 to 15 percent less.[25] There are several ways to interpret these figures. One can view relative intraregional wages of skilled and unskilled labor as reflecting relative scarcities, the South having an abundance of raw labor and a scarcity of skill. Or one can view relative interregional differentials as indicators of the geographic mobility of different classes of labor, skilled labor moving more readily from South to North. For the present purpose, the contrast confirms that the large differences in farm wages were real, and that southern unskilled labor was largely isolated from unskilled labor markets elsewhere.

Some writers assume that the regional isolation of unskilled labor is essentially a racial phenomenon, which they attribute to segregation and discrimination. Brinley Thomas, for example, in his great work on the Atlantic economy of the pre–World War I era, writes:

> If by a miracle there had been racial tolerance, the black workers from the South could have played their full part, in common with immigrants from Europe, in meeting the labor requirements of the rapidly growing cities of the North after the Civil War.[26]

What this statement overlooks is that the southern unskilled *white* wage was almost as low as the wage for blacks. Planters told the Industrial Commission in 1900: "I think we give them about the same thing. . . . If there is any difference I don't know it."[27] USDA farm wage surveys taken between 1899 and 1902 confirm that racial differences were small, averaging 8 percent on a state basis.[28] An earlier survey by the Bureau of Labor Statistics of North Carolina (1887) posed the question of racial wage differences to landlords *and* to tenants and laborers in ninety-five counties. In ninety-four of the ninety-five counties, the landlords responded "no," and in seventy-seven of the ninety-five counties, the tenants and laborers also indicated that no differences prevailed in wages paid to whites and blacks.[29]

It is well-known that many southern industries excluded blacks, the prime example being the most rapidly growing industry, cotton textiles. Even here, however, we find that the wages paid to textile workers were closely linked to farm labor wages, which were accessible to blacks (figure 3.4). The most detailed industrial wage data available on a racial basis is for

FIGURE 3.4

Real Wages, Textiles, and Farm Labor, 1880–1916

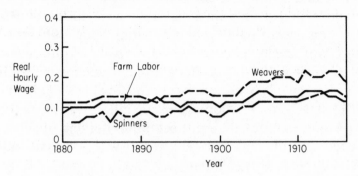

SOURCES: U.S. Bureau of Labor Statistics, Wages and Hours Series, nos. 65, 71, 77, 128, 150, 190, 239 (Washington, D.C.: Government Printing Office, 1906–18); U.S. Commissioner of Labor, *Fifteenth Annual Report: Wages in Commercial Countries* (Washington, D.C.: GPO, 1900); U.S. Commissioner of Labor, *Nineteenth Annual Report: Wages and Hours of Labor* (Washington, D.C.: GPO, 1904); U.S. Department of Agriculture, *Crops and Markets* 19 (Washington, D.C.: GPO, 1942): 150–55.

FIGURE 3.5

Aggregate Wage Distributions in Virginia, 1907

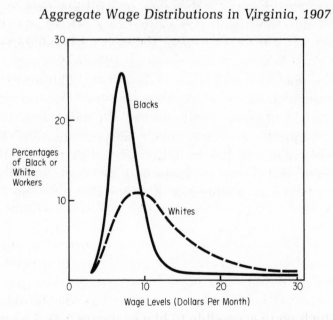

SOURCE: Bureau of Labor and Industrial Statistics for the State of Virginia, *Eleventh Annual Report* (Richmond: Davis Bottom Superintendent of Public Printing, 1908).

the state of Virginia between 1900 and 1909. Figure 3.5 displays estimated wage distributions for black and white workers for the year 1907. As the diagram suggests, the *modal* wage (the wage most commonly paid) was very similar for blacks and whites; in this example, indeed, there is virtually no difference. This is a stronger finding than the simple absence of explicit racial wages in specific occupations. At the level of an industry or an entire state, equalization of the unskilled wage was the rule more often than not, an equilibration reflecting the competitive pressures of a market. The racial wage gap was not always trivial, but it was substantially less than that between unskilled workers in the North and in the South.

This is indeed powerful evidence that an unskilled labor market was operating in the South, a market strong enough not just to generate western migration but largely to equilibrate racial wage levels, even in the midst of racial prejudice, racial legislation, and racial segregation. But it was a southern market and it did not promote equilibration with the North. It hardly needs to be said that this is not the full story of labor and the Southern economy. There was plenty of racial discrimination: figure 3.5 makes it clear that blacks had little access to advancement into the higher-paying jobs of a skilled or supervisory character. And sharecroppers, renters, and small farmers were not wage laborers; they were not involved, directly at least, in the market we have been describing. These matters are addressed in subsequent chapters. But the isolation of the southern unskilled labor market was a basic background condition for virtually the whole epoch between the Civil War and World War II, and the operation of this market affected the lives of all Southerners. The remaining questions for this chapter are how such a situation came to exist and what kept it in place.

National and International Labor Markets

Most economists would say that a persistent price differential between markets in the absence of legal constraints must reflect costs of transportation or barriers to the flow of information. From this standpoint, the logical interpretation of regional wage differentials is that they reflect the poor state of transport and communications of the pre–World War II era, the ignorance and poverty of Southerners, perhaps also their poor education and general unsuitability for the emerging industrial jobs of the North. Given this perspective, the breakdown of regional isolation is only a matter of time and the progress of civilization, the slow but cumulative spread of knowledge, the coming of the radio and telephone and automobile.

But there is a serious difficulty in applying this interpretation to the United States for the period prior to World War I, and that is that millions of Europeans with equally poor qualifications were coming much longer distances over oceans as well as land, to take the very jobs Southerners were supposedly ignorant of. Long-distance migration was vital to American industrialization. Table 3.8 offers some idea of the magnitudes as of 1907–8: in all but four of the nineteen industries listed, a majority of the male employees were foreign-born and more than 70 percent were either foreign-born or the sons of foreign-born. Not only were many immigrants at work in America in 1907, but, remarkably, there were large continuing transatlantic flows every year, *in both directions* (table 3.9). Fluctuations in the rate of net immigration, however, were clearly attributable to the growth of employment opportunities in America. Figure 3.6 shows the closeness of the association between immigration and pig iron production, basically a business cycle indicator. Immigrants came from many countries and for many individual reasons, but the *fluctuations* in the national flows were highly synchronized, and highly correlated with American demand.[30]

This evidence justifies the claim that there was a labor market, not just a northern market, but an Atlantic labor market

TABLE 3.8

Male Employees by Nationality and Industry, 1907–8

Industry	Percent of Total to the Nearest 1 Percent		
	Native-Born of Native Father	Native-Born of Foreign Father	Foreign-Born
Metal Manufactures			
Agricultural implements and vehicles	21	20	59
Car building and repairing	29	16	55
Foundry and machine-shop products	34	20	56
Iron and steel	29	13	58
Locomotive building	27	24	49
Sewing machine manufacture	16	26	59
Textiles			
Cotton goods	10	18	72
Silk goods	16	28	57
Woolen and worsted goods	13	20	66
Miscellaneous			
Boots and shoes	43	23	34
Cigars and tobacco	51	10	39
Clothing	4	14	83
Furniture	30	20	59
Glass	43	17	40
Leather	17	14	69
Oil refining	12	21	67
Paper and wood pulp manufacturing	42	17	41
Slaughtering and meat packing	25	13	61
Sugar refining	6	8	85

SOURCE: Daniel Nelson, *Managers and Workers* (Madison: University of Wisconsin Press, 1974), 80.

in unskilled labor. The evidence on wage rates suggests that the market worked well: U.S. wages were high, but the growth of real industrial wages over the half-century before World War I was very similar in all the countries of the Atlantic economy.[31] One recent study of the steel industry questions whether any significant differential existed in the unskilled wage between Pittsburgh and Birmingham, England.[32] Broadly speaking, we can characterize the unskilled labor market from the perspective of the United States, as in figure 3.7. The supply

TABLE 3.9

Arrivals and Departures of All Alien
Passengers to and from the
United States, 1870–1919
(in Thousands)

Year	Arrivals	Departures	Departures ÷ Arrivals
1870–74	1,970	278	.14
1875–79	956	431	.45
1880–84	3,201	327	.10
1885–89	2,341	638	.27
1890–94	2,590	838	.32
1895–99	1,493	766	.51
1900–1904	3,575	1,454	.41
1905–09	5,533	2,653	.48
1910–14	6,075	2,759	.45
1915–19	1,613	1,180	.73

SOURCE: Simon Kuznets and Ernest Rubin, *Immigration and the Foreign Born*, Occasional Paper no. 46 (National Bureau of Economic Research, 1954), 95.

of labor was extremely elastic, and fluctuations in demand were satisfied by fluctuations in net immigration. There was a domestic component to the industrial labor supply too (S_D), but employers would not pay domestic labor of equal quality much more than the immigrant wage, at least not indefinitely.

FIGURE 3.6

Cycles of Pig Iron Production and Immigration, 1860–1919

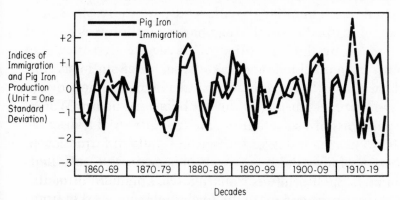

NOTE: Reprinted, by permission of the publisher, from Harry Jerome, *Migration and Business Cycles* (New York: National Bureau of Economic Research, Inc., 1926), 52, chart 11.

FIGURE 3.7

Labor Supply and Demand in Northern U.S. Industry

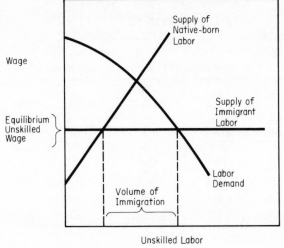

Unskilled Labor

The real wage certainly rose over time, but this was fundamentally a rise in the Atlantic wage rather than a unique accomplishment of the U.S. economy.[33]

The South was not linked to this international system, but it should be clear by now that the explanation lies in the realm of social institutions and social choice rather than in sheer barriers of distance and cost. To be sure, in agriculture and in farm labor markets, migration tended to proceed along east-west lines from early in the nineteenth century, for reasons having to do with familiarity with seeds, crops, livestock, and climate.[34] But this "natural" regional separation was ratified and extended by the institution of slavery, which insulated the South from outside labor flows. Then, the South was consumed by the turbulence of war and Reconstruction at the very time that mass immigration was becoming an established part of the northern social fabric. Such elements of timing are important because much of the actual flow of information in long-distance industrial labor markets operates through informal channels, such as letters from relatives and word-of-mouth talk within ethnic groups. Statistical studies confirm that the existence of a first wave of migrants from a country is the most important single factor in generating the second wave.[35] Unskilled workers rarely have specific prearranged jobs waiting for them, but rely on family and friends to put them up temporarily and assist them in finding work. As one Polish immigrant to Pittsburgh later recalled:

> The only way you got a job [was] through somebody at work who got you in. I mean this application, that's a big joke. They just threw them away ... to get a job with the railroad, my brother-in-law got it for me. My job at the hospital, my dad got it for me. I got the job at the meat place ... the boy I used to play ball with, he got it for me.[36]

Kinship networks allowed workers to go back and forth across the Atlantic numerous times before deciding where to settle.

But this does not mean that the overall migration is no more than the arbitrary sum of various rumors and kinship effects; as we have seen, the flow was highly sensitive to economic conditions. Rather than thinking of kinship, ethnic, and linguistic loyalties as market "imperfections," it is more appropriate to consider these forces as part of the way the market functions and expands. The trust among kinfolk is what ensures that reasonably accurate information is passed along concerning job openings, wages, working and living conditions. Indeed, as Michael Piore argues in his book *Birds of Passage*, long-distance migrants display a distinctively high responsiveness to pecuniary incentives, since many are trying to raise as much money as possible in a short time, and they do not have attachments to particular localities in the host country. Hence they are willing to work long hours, move from place to place, and accept demanding or even demeaning tasks that they would not consider doing at home.[37] Thus, there are strong tendencies to persistence of labor market flows and linkages, once begun. There are also strong elements of geographic *collective choice* in the economic sense of the term (adjustment in one direction that forecloses other possibilities), as jobs, communities, schools, and even technology itself came to be adapted to the characteristics of European immigrants.[38]

The South could not join in this expanding market for one decisive reason. As the optimistic hopes of the immediate post-

FIGURE 3.8

Southern Farm Wage as a Percentage of U.S. Average, 1818–99

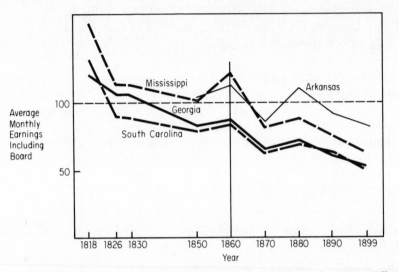

SOURCE: Stanley Lebergott, *Manpower in Economic Growth* (New York: McGraw-Hill, 1964), 539.

war years gave way to the declining cotton prices and stagnation of the 1870s, the South emerged as a low-wage region
in a high-wage country. Figure 3.8 shows that the relative farm
wage in all parts of the South declined sharply over the Civil
War decade; it is far from clear that the slave South was a low-
wage area, but from 1870 onward, the spread in the farm wage
widened, and carried wages in many other southern labor
markets with it.[39] In the circumstances, southern employers
found that they could not compete in the Atlantic market. Nor
could they initiate their own transoceanic labor flows because
the footloose "economic man" quality of the immigrants assured that they would not stay long in the low-wage South
once they arrived. Again and again, major initiatives by governments, planters, employers, or transport companies generated nothing but an evanescent pass-through. At the time
that blacks from the upper South headed southwest hunting
lucrative jobs on the delta plantations, the Chinese, who were
brought in for the same work, soon deserted; those who wanted
high-wage work could do much better in California.[40] When
a shipload of steerage passengers was brought to Charleston in
1904 by the North German Lloyd line, most of them quickly

moved on to the North and West, and the company refused to maintain a regular operation. The South Carolina labor commissioner complained: "The cry was, on the one hand, for only the highest type of immigrant; and on the other, to secure him at the scale of wages paid the Negro."[41] The frustrations are illustrated in this excerpt from a letter from the superintendent of a Virginia mining company, who was trying to recruit immigrants in New York:

> Tony arrived with 21 men last night. One got away in Jersey, two in Washington, D.C., 4 in Charlottesville. Some of the men are very good looking, but taken as a whole they are the worst lot I have ever seen. . . . Our New York transportations to this place have never been a success.[42]

By 1910 no more than 2 percent of the southern population was foreign-born.

Employers in the South made use of family and kinship ties in much the same way that their counterparts did in the North. One Alabama company official described it:

> We put the word out if we wanted employees to our own people that we are going to be hiring. And they'd go home over the week-end, and they'd put the word out at the country church. And along about Tuesday we'd have the finest-looking specimens out there you ever saw, and that's who we hired.[43]

But labor-hungry Southerners in Mississippi, Arkansas, Texas, and in the mines of southern Appalachia found that they could only recruit effectively in regions that had even lower wages than they did, which primarily meant the Southeast. The effects of their efforts in channeling migration is illustrated in these reflections by a black congressman from North Carolina:

> When the people have been left to themselves to emigrate, it has been largely to the North and East, and somewhat to the West; · but where the agents with oily tongues come about and offer flattering inducements, they have gone from one Southern state to another.[44]

Economists and philosophers may debate the precise meaning of being "left to themselves to emigrate," but it is clear from the description that it was much easier for a poor southern farm laborer to follow functioning market channels within the South than to set off on his own to an unfamiliar region. Recruitment thus reinforced the east-west lines of the labor market established under slavery.

Implications for the South

Because of their place in the national and world economies of the pre–World War I era, southern entrepreneurs could not play the dynamic, liberating role of their counterparts in the North. As low-wage employers in a high-wage country, they could not take vigorous steps to open communication and interaction with the outside world, without risking loss of labor. It was not just a matter of distance: an equally large wage gap between the East and the Far West closed with amazing speed between the 1860s and the 1880s. Whereas property owners in the western states had an unambiguous interest, both private and collective, in maximizing flows of both labor and capital from the East, Southerners had mixed feelings at best. Outside capital could also be threatening. Landowners may have been happy to sell their lumber, iron, and coal to outsiders, and mill owners were pleased to have northern investors and trade credit, but when it came to encouragement to new industries and new employers, the collective interest was often negative. Even in the 1930s, southern representatives in Washington did not use their powerful positions to push for new federal projects, hospitals, public works, and so on. They didn't, that is, so long as the foundations of the low-wage regional economy persisted. Thus, the isolation of the labor market was the basis for the isolation of the capital market.

Another implication was that the choice of techniques of production were different in both industry and agriculture, less mechanized and more labor-intensive. This is not in itself a sign of backwardness, since technology designed for high-wage workers is not intrinsically more "advanced," and labor-intensive technologies can be highly sophisticated and appropriate. But though it was a proto-country by many criteria, the South lacked a strong indigenous technological tradition and a "southern" technical community developing an advanced southern version of new innovations. In contrast to Japan, labor market isolation usually meant that the South was not operating at the American technological frontier, as it was not in a position to make use of the best products emerging from the American machine-tools industry, designed for the high-wage setting.

Like capital inflows, investment in education was a two-edged sword. Providing some elementary education facilities could be useful in recruiting workers with families to the mill village or the steel mills of Birmingham, and a literate worker was potentially more productive. But a high school diploma was as good as a ticket to leave the mill village. Similarly, rural landowners saw little benefit in providing education to their tenants, for it only had the effect of "making them discontented with farm work and not improving their morals." As an Arkansas planter put it in 1900:

> My experience has been that when one of the younger class gets so he can read and write and cipher, he wants to go to town. It is rare to find one who can read and write and cipher in the field at work.[45]

The inability of rural planters to capture returns to investments in education can in many respects be aggregated to the region as a whole. In the absence of established channels of labor market mobility for unskilled workers, education greatly increased the probability that a young person would leave both his home county and ultimately his home region.[46]

For reasons such as these, the South's investment in education was far below the rest of the nation (table 3.10), and this fact too served to preserve and maintain the separateness of the regional labor market. Expenditure figures like those in table 3.10 reflect many factors, such as the lower levels of southern per capita incomes and the politics of school segre-

TABLE 3.10

Per Pupil Expenditures as Percent of U.S. Average,
1890–1940

	1890	1900	1910	1920	1930	1940
Alabama	28	17	33	39	43	37
Arkansas	40	35	38	34	39	34
Florida	46	51	51	63	58	71
Georgia	24	33	38	33	37	42
Louisiana	50	38	70	65	56	63
Mississippi	32	32	31	32	43	31
North Carolina	20	21	28	38	49	49
South Carolina	20	22	24	30	46	42
Tennessee	27	26	36	35	49	46
Texas	63	56	65	67	63	73
Virginia	47	48	51	54	51	54

SOURCES: Leonard P. Ayres, *An Index for State School Systems* (New York: Russell Sage Foundation, 1920), 25, 31, 33, 35, 37; James C. Cobb, *Selling of the South* (Baton Rouge: Louisiana State University Press, 1982), 163; U.S. Office of Education, *Biennial Survey of Education, 1928–30*, vol. 2, Bulletin no. 20 (Washington, D.C.: Government Printing Office, 1932), 28–29.

gation. The record shows some evidence of some gradual relative progress in some states in the twentieth century. But taking a long view of the matter, the bottom line was that as late as 1940, the South's commitment to education was far lower than its relative income position can explain. The economic structure that supported this low priority was simply this: as a low-wage region in a high-wage country, the South had no expectation that it could capture the return on investment in its own people.

In any historical account blending geography, culture, technology, and economics, relationships are complex and it is risky to pick out one element for special emphasis. What we do know now in the case of the South, however, is that the heavy hand of history moved with remarkable speed when, beginning in the 1930s, the foundations of the low-wage economy were removed. That is a story for a later chapter. First, we need to take a closer look at southern agriculture and industry in the intervening years.

4

PLANTATION, FARM, AND

FARM LABOR IN THE SOUTH

FOR MOST of its history, the South has been a farming region. Before the twentieth century, of course, the same could be said of the whole country. But from the beginning, farming in the South was different. For over three hundred years, the prosperity of the South was tied to the performance of a handful of export staples—tobacco, rice, indigo, sugar, and preeminently, cotton. Each of these crops has geographic prerequisites. Cotton required two hundred frost-free days, a temperature of seventy-seven degrees Fahrenheit for three months of the year, and, prior to the rise of artificial irrigation, at least twenty-five inches of rainfall each year. The strictly climatic requirements for tobacco growing are less stringent, but the sweetness and flavor of tobacco from the upper South (Virginia, North Carolina, Tennessee, and Kentucky) are not easily matched elsewhere. Rice and cane sugar have been restricted to remote corners of the region, sugar to the Louisiana delta, while rice made a nineteenth-century migration from lowland South Carolina to Arkansas and Texas. Thus, the South has had a distinctive agricultural geography.[1]

But any regional unity the South might have is an artifact of history. On a purely geographic basis, one would be hard-pressed to find any basic common denominator joining the tidewater to the Appalachian highlands, the Piedmont to the

Gulf coast, or the pine barrens to the Black Belt prairies and the southwestern plains. Even the cohesion of cotton farming was only partial, as the cotton belt itself encompassed a remarkable variety of natural conditions in soils, rainfall, terrain, temperature, and much else. The distinctive unifying feature of southern agriculture was the simple historical fact that the Southern people intermingled less with outsiders than did the people of any other major American region. Economically speaking, the unity came from slavery before the war, from the regional labor market afterward.

Some geographic divisions within the South are too important to ignore, and these too are products of history rather than pure geography. The *plantation* belt provides a clear example. Though the census did not acknowledge the existence of large-scale units of landownership and organization before 1910, in that year a special survey found that plantations were the predominant form in a broadly contiguous belt of 325 counties.[2] The plantation area ran in a funnel up along the alluvial river basins of Mississippi, Louisiana, Arkansas, and east Texas, moved in an east-west direction across the Tennessee Valley and the black prairie of central Alabama, and then in a northeasterly direction across central Georgia and South Carolina onto the piedmont of North Carolina (see figure 4.1). The area resembles the cotton belt, but it fits even more closely the map of above-average soil and black-majority populations inherited from the age of slavery. Slavery was essential to the rise of these large-scale farming units, but they did not wither away when slavery was abolished. The plantations were linked to the regional labor market, but economic, political, and racial relationships were quite different in the plantation *counties* than they were outside.[3] Though there are some common elements, we really have to tell the story of southern agriculture twice, once for the plantation areas and again for the small farm sections.

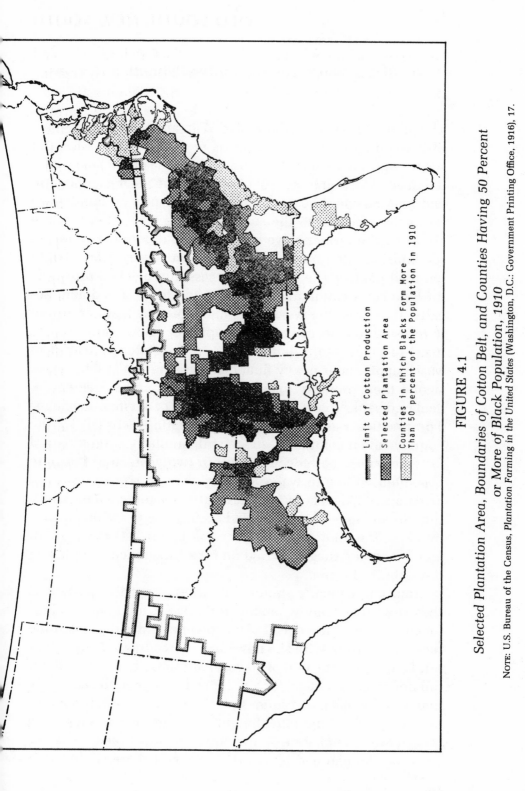

FIGURE 4.1

Selected Plantation Area, Boundaries of Cotton Belt, and Counties Having 50 Percent
or More of Black Population, 1910

NOTE: U.S. Bureau of the Census, *Plantation Farming in the United States* (Washington, D.C.: Government Printing Office, 1916), 17.

Limit of Cotton Production

Selected Plantation Area

Counties in Which Blacks Form More
Than 50 percent of the Population in 1910

The Rise of Sharecropping in the Plantation Regions

The plantations survived the Civil War, and their survival had little to do with their efficiency as producing units. Rice and sugar required large-scale plantings because of the heavy capital needed for water control or on-farm processing, but cotton and tobacco could be grown just as efficiently on family-size farms. No, the key to the survival of the plantation was the ability of the former slave owners to hold onto their land in the midst of intense legal and political struggles after 1865. In national politics, the planters successfully blocked proposals for land confiscation and redistribution to the freedmen. Locally, they used every social connection and legal strategem to forestall foreclosure for bankruptcy or seizure for nonpayment of taxes. Many landowners in the Natchez district of Mississippi, under heavy financial pressure in the late 1860s, signed their property over to their wives and subsequently declared bankruptcy, freeing themselves of outstanding debts. The practice was illegal, but sympathetic treatment by the courts made it commonly successful. Similarly, land forfeited for taxes could be redeemed within two years, and the state was often willing to waive penalty charges, sometimes even arrearages.[4] "Market forces" have little meaning when the ultimate sanctions of a propertied society are tested near their limits. In the immediate postwar South, one gets the sense of an elemental struggle carried on by a threatened class trying to retain its position.

From an economic standpoint, what is most important is that the large landownership units were maintained. This meant that the "new class" of landowners had to develop some new relationship with the new class of freedmen. They reluctantly accepted the end of slavery, but initially many of them did not accept the need for any radical change in the centrally managed, gang labor systems that they knew, nor in the methods of discipline and punishment. A planter in the Vicksburg area of Mississippi, for example, informed the Freedmen's Bureau that he planned to "work 100 Free Laborers," but that "it will be absolutely necessary to have some mode of punishment," which he apparently expected the Bureau to provide.[5] Encouraged by the Bureau, most planters reestablished the work gangs on a wage-paying basis. They also attempted to reestablish "plantation law," and regularly deducted penalties from wages for late starts after lunch, unexcused absence, or insubordination.[6] But these efforts to recreate slavery did not succeed, because they were unacceptable to the freedmen. Having been given nothing but the right to quit, the freedman had to work or starve, but they did not have to work for any one employer. And they did move, from plantation to plantation and from place to place, much to the consternation of the employers. Planters' organizations tried repeatedly to effect collusive agreements against "tampering" with each other's labor and undercutting standards of discipline, but almost invariably these failed.[7] In 1869 a Georgia planter contrasted the chaos of the plantation belt with what he took to be the prosperity of the up-country, asking rhetorically:

> And why is this? We answer: It is the unreliable and uncontrollable character of our labor in the first instance, their vagrancy and thievishness; and in the next place, a want of concert of action on the part of the landowners, in forming and carrying out a wise and uniform system of plantation discipline. At present, there is no uniformity in regard to the hours of labor or price of labor—hence there is no certainty of labor. A sort of grab game is the order of the day.[8]

It was a good description of a market in disequilibrium.

Thus the new labor systems, unlike the initial distributions of wealth, did emerge from a kind of market process. It was a process prolonged by political uncertainties and by inexperience and genuine ignorance about the reactions and priorities of the freedmen, but it was nonetheless a market process. Historians have often debated whether sharecropping was imposed by the planters on the freedmen or vice versa, whether one group or the other "instigated" the system, but to economists, once we know that the system emerged from a market process, we can be reasonably sure that the outcome represented a balance of forces. Sharecropping was a balance between the freedmen's desire for autonomy and the employer's interest in extracting work effort and having labor when it was needed. The freedman's aversion to gang labor discipline is often attributed to a resentment of anything that smacked of slavery. This motivation may be valid, but it is misleading to suggest that this was some special irrationality, a psychological association that only ex-slaves could feel. The freedom from minute supervision, orders, and punishment has always been a basic human goal and historically a dimension of economic class, just as it is a measure of social standing in our own day. We expect young people to submit to the tight regimentation of their time and to accept punishment for deviations or insolence, but for a mature adult to be treated this way is humiliating. For many slave owners, who had regarded slaves as children for generations, it was a major psychological struggle to accept the reality that they would have to accommodate to the freedman's preferences if they wanted to keep any labor.

So the market process was also a learning process, and in this case one can almost see the workings out of the logic of the market over the course of time. Many planters tried to hold on to a modicum of centralized authority by dividing the work force into smaller groups known as "squads," with foremen appointed on a subcontract basis to act as a buffer between employer and worker. This system had become common by 1870. An observer in 1869 wrote:

> When emancipation occurred the planters made great efforts to associate the laborers together on their large plantations, but the system has completely broken down and given place to the "squad system," where from two to eight hands only work together, in many instances a single family.[9]

The organization of squads around kinship connections foreshadowed the household-based system of sharecropping, but the process of decentralization went on through the 1870s. One problem was that the squads, begun as efforts to maintain some central direction, began to develop considerable autonomy in work norms and discipline. Another was the treatment of partial hands, women and children participating in field work but not entitled to a full share; the division of ultimate authority among husband, squad leader, and planter provoked continuing complaints and dissatisfaction. By 1880, most planters had come to agree with the one who wrote in the *Southern Cultivator*:

> I am satisfied from my experience and close observation . . . [that] there is but one correct mode of working our present labor (which I think is the best in the world), and it is simply this: Let each family work by itself, in separate fields or farms. This is much easier and I think far better than the old plantation style of working all together.[10]

The decentralization was virtually complete by 1880 and is vividly symbolized by the change in the physical layout of the plantation (figure 4.2).[11] Whereas in 1860 the slave quarters were adjacent to the master's house, in 1880 they were scattered across the subdivided fields. The transition of a nuclear household basis for labor was accompanied by a significant change in family labor force behavior that included a decline in the work week and in female field work. Economists Roger Ransom and Richard Sutch estimate that the net decline in black per capita labor supply was between 28 and 37 percent compared to the levels under slavery.[12]

To say that sharecropping emerged from a market process is not to say that a uniquely determined equilibrium arose solely from the balance between the freedmen's desires and the planters' demand for labor. Work routines, reliability, and even the special needs of family labor can be accommodated and balanced in various wage systems and other formulas. There was another element in the postwar situation, however, that severely constrained the choices of both employers and workers: the shortage of credit. This shortage was another direct effect of the abolition of slavery. One can find economists who say that the abolition of slavery did not destroy anything real for the Southern economy, but only transferred ownership of labor from one group to another. Don't believe it. Abolition destroyed the basis for credit in the antebellum economy. The movability of slaves and the well-developed slave markets made them highly attractive as collateral for loans, even at long distance. Land did not have these properties; prudent

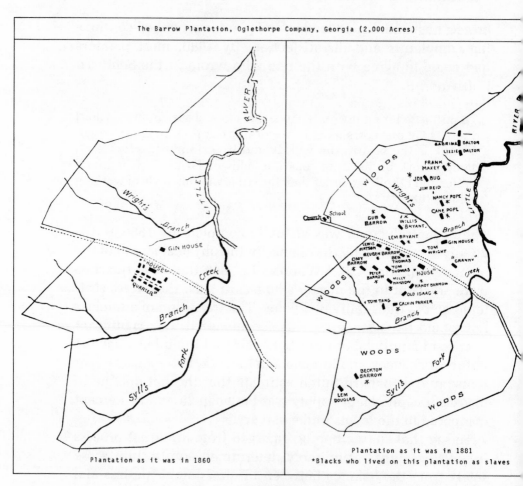

The Barrow Plantation, Oglethorpe Company, Georgia (2,000 Acres)

Plantation as it was in 1860

Plantation as it was in 1881
*Blacks who lived on this plantation as slaves

FIGURE 4.2

Plantation Layout, 1860 and 1881
NOTE: David C. Barrow, Jr., "A Georgia Plantation," *Scribner's Monthly* 21 (1881): 832.

nineteenth-century bankers did not consider real estate to be an acceptable backing for loans, and indeed such loans were prohibited under the National Bank System. The long-distance credit relationship between planters and factors in the port cities quickly declined after the war.[13] The problem of collateral alone would have strained credit supplies, but, in addition, many southern men of money were wiped out financially by the war, and many others suffered heavy losses during the first chaotic year of freedom.

The clearest symptom of credit shortage is that the overwhelming majority of the labor contracts recorded by the Freedman's Bureau in 1866–67 provided for a *postharvest wage*.[14] There were two main varieties: (1) the "standing wage," in which the laborer contracted for an annual wage but received only a portion of it (often only subsistence rations) on a monthly basis; (2) the share wage, in which the work force simply contracted for a specified share of the crop. The freedmen never did have the option of a periodic cash wage in return for their labor. It is not clear that many landowners could have paid on this basis even if they had wanted to. In fact, because of the rapid decline of the cotton price from its high 1865 levels, large numbers of employers could not even make good on their standing wage contracts. The standing wage quickly fell out of favor with the freedmen because of widespread employer default. Most of the so-called wage-labor contracts, therefore, were in reality collective share agreements. We cannot say that sharecropping arose over time because of the desire of both parties to share risk, because almost all contracts already provided for risk sharing from the beginning.

Once we know that collective share contracts were the rule, we can see that another force toward decentralization was at work. When a large labor force contracts for a fixed share of output, incentives are perverse. Each laborer knows that his own effort will have a minor effect on his own wage. In a phenomenon known in economics as the "free-rider problem," each individual has an incentive to shirk, relying on the effort of others. And those that do work hard will rightly come to feel that they are being exploited by their less industrious fellows. The northern missionary and idealistic planter Charles

Stearns described his own experience on a Georgia plantation:

> We found that a large portion of those engaged in this enterprise would inevitably shirk their portion of the work, leaving it to be performed by those less honest; and yet would claim an equal share in the profits with others. This, of course, created dissatisfaction among the industrious ones, and jangling and disputes followed; until it was apparent that those most needed in such an enterprise, preferred working for themselves.[15]

One can imagine, of course, settings with well-developed work norms and social sanctions that might maintain a high level of effort even on a collective share basis. On southern plantations in the 1860s and 1870s, it was far easier to decentralize from gangs to squads to the smallest social unit, the nuclear household.[16]

The Geography of Plantation Labor Markets

After 1880, as world cotton prices settled down near long-term levels, the institutions of southern agriculture settled into more stabilized patterns. The disequilibrium transition of 1865–79 gave way in later years to an equilibrium *coexistence* among different types of tenure. This too was a market phenomenon. Despite the tendency among contemporaries to debate the merits of wage labor, sharecropping, and rental as though they were absolute, unconditional alternatives, these choices depended on relative wage levels and rental rates. A factor driving freedmen away from wage systems between 1865 and 1868, after all, was the rapid decline in the level of wages. On the other side, where the advantages of centralized management really were substantial, as on the sugar and rice plantations of Louisiana, planters paid a wage sufficiently high to attract the wage labor they needed. Where those intrinsically large-scale units could not compete for wage labor, as in the old rice district of South Carolina, cultivation went into decline.

Through most of the plantation South, however, the coexistence of sharecropping and wage labor prevailed not just between districts but within each plantation. The typical planter divided his total acreage into portions assigned to sharecroppers, portions rented out to tenants, and a portion retained for himself and cultivated by wage labor, as on the plantation depicted in figure 4.3. Now there is no doubt at all that the decentralized sharecropping plantation emerged under the immediate pressures of the postwar situation; yet at the same time, there is something ancient about this picture, so reminiscent of the division of the medieval manor into tenant land and the lord's demesne. This familiarity suggests that the system was not just an expedient, but reflects some lasting underlying principles. Broadly speaking, the division of acreage corresponded to a division of the labor force into two types that corresponded, in turn, to the geographic scope of the labor market in which they operated. The markets for tenants and sharecroppers were local, while the markets for wage hands were long-distance. In determining the balance between the two, it helps to follow the economist's practice of dividing the elements into demand and supply.

On the demand side, an ever-present concern of the planter was the seasonality of his labor requirements and his vulnerability to loss of labor at the crucial times. Cotton has at least two peak periods, one early during the spring cultivation and a second for the harvest in the late fall. The precise dates were always uncertain, depending as they did on the weather and other accidents of plant growth. But when the plant ripened, the picking had a certain urgency because cotton on the boll could be ruined by rainfall, and, as a caption in an agricultural economics textbook put it, "delayed picking lowers grade and reduces return."[17] Much of the exasperation of planters over the poor work of their black laborers was closely linked to fears about seasonality. When John Dent of Georgia complained to one of his hands about "idleness," "his reply was 'I can leave and I will do so.'—and such all do who are hired for wages, leaving you at a time when their services are most needed."[18]

Economists recognize that this sort of situation will give rise to a demand for "labor-tying" contracts, in which the laborer agrees to stay for a specified period.[19] This was one of the things

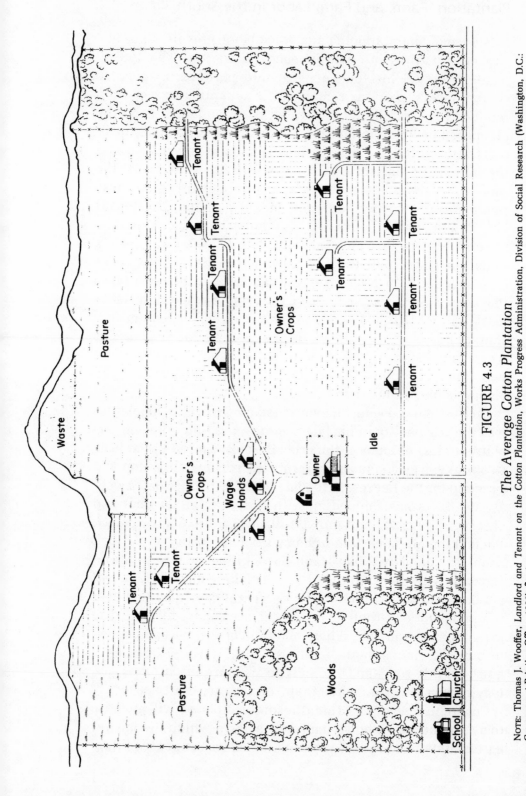

FIGURE 4.3

The Average Cotton Plantation

NOTE: Thomas J. Wooffer, *Landlord and Tenant on the Cotton Plantation*, Works Progress Administration, Division of Social Research (Washington, D.C.: Government Printing Office, 1936), fig. 1.

The figure is based on 646 typical cotton plantations having five or more families and a total acreage of 907

TABLE 4.1

Term of Occupancy and Tenure, 1910

	White Farmers			Black Farmers		
Years on Farm	Owners	Cash Tenants	Share Tenants	Owners	Cash Tenants	Share Tenants
South Atlantic						
Less than 1	3.8	29.0	37.9	2.2	17.6	33.9
1 year	4.4	17.6	17.8	3.0	13.5	17.4
2 to 4 years	16.4	31.8	28.1	16.1	34.7	31.5
5 to 9 years	19.0	13.0	10.0	20.9	18.2	10.5
10 years and over	56.5	8.9	6.2	57.9	15.6	6.6
TOTAL	100.0	100.0	100.0	100.0	100.0	100.0
East South Central						
Less than 1	4.7	36.7	45.6	2.5	19.1	38.9
1 year	5.1	17.1	17.8	3.4	12.4	15.9
2 to 4 years	18.8	29.8	24.8	16.4	34.5	28.1
5 to 9 years	20.2	10.4	7.5	21.9	18.4	9.7
10 years and over	50.9	6.0	4.1	55.7	15.6	6.2
TOTAL	100.0	100.0	100.0	100.0	100.0	100.0

SOURCE: U.S. Bureau of the Census, *Stability of Farm Operations*, unnumbered bulletin (Washington, D.C.: Government Printing Office, 1914).

accomplished by sharecropping. Such an arrangement might be mistaken for involuntary servitude, and in some measure it could even be involuntary if the laborer should change his mind during the course of the year. But we cannot equate this sort of contractual obligation with the lifetime "binding" of serfdom or slavery. It is the insurance against changing of mind that is precisely why the landlord agrees to the deal in the first place. The question is whether the sharecropping contract is voluntary *ex ante* to the laborer. Certainly the croppers had ample opportunity to move from place to place between seasons. Even in 1910, the evidence indicates that turnover among share tenants was remarkably high (table 4.1). What was in it for them?

As we have seen, the freedmen wanted sharecropping in the first instance as an escape from the oppressive overseers, work routine, and discipline of slavery and gang labor. Despite the lowly status of the cropper, and despite the continuing concern by the landlord about his performance, there is no doubt that sharecroppers were subject to less intense hour-to-hour and day-to-day supervision than were wage laborers.[20] An aspect of this autonomy was the desire of a head of household for full control over the labor of the members of his own family and a direct claim on their product. As a planter recalled in explaining the rise of cropping:

> The negro first became a cropper on shares as a step toward what you call in your inquiry "a more independent" position. Also largely due to the fact that if he hired himself out for wages he alone drew wages and his family such pay for day work as they might secure on the farm. By running the crop himself he could put his wife and children in his own crop.[21]

Implicit in this quotation is another feature of wage labor, the *uncertainty* of wage income to the worker. For the same reasons that planters could not be sure what wage labor they would need and when they would need it, laborers in this market could never be sure that their jobs would last from month to month. When the cotton was "laid by," the wage-labor force might be "laid-off" for two months in the summer, and again after the harvest in winter.[22] Of course, this risk would be much more serious to a married man with a family to support, especially one committed to a particular locality. A young unattached man, willing to move on to wherever work could be found whenever he had to, could undoubtedly earn much more over the course of the year than home-based family members looking for day labor on a particular plantation. The figures in table 4.2 make it clear that farm wage labor was composed predominantly of young unmarried males.[23] Sharecropping was fundamentally a family-based system. Plantation landowners struck a balance between the terms on which they could attract families from the vicinity (primarily by adjusting the size of the plots), and the wages they would have to pay for short-term labor, plus recruitment and transport costs. This is known as a "sorting equilibrium." Ideally, the balance would be struck so as to use all of the available acreage and equalize the marginal profitability of the two systems, as in the stylized diagram (figure 4.4). Where transient labor was abundant, as in the vicinity of towns, it was "esteemed a great advantage to farmers

TABLE 4.2
Male Farm Laborers, 1890

	Percent Black	Percent Married	Percent Under Age 25
Alabama	63.3	22.4	74.2
Arkansas	44.8	19.7	70.9
Florida	59.8	26.4	65.3
Georgia	63.7	25.7	72.0
Louisiana	74.3	34.4	61.1
Mississippi	75.9	22.9	71.3
North Carolina	49.6	26.0	69.4
South Carolina	73.1	28.1	71.1
Tennessee	37.0	27.0	66.4
Texas	31.9	15.9	70.6
Virginia	52.1	33.2	57.9
11 States	57.1	25.6	68.7

SOURCE: U.S. Bureau of the Census, *Population*, 11th Census (1890), part 2 (Washington, D.C.: Government Printing Office, 1895), table 116.

FIGURE 4.4
Allocation of Plantation Acreage Between Wage System and Tenants' Plots

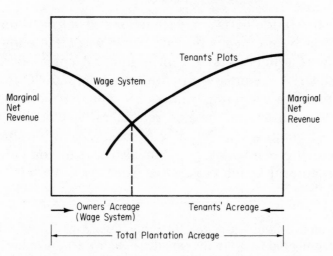

SOURCE: Warren Whatley, "Institutional Change and Mechanization in the Cotton South" (Ph.D. diss., Stanford University, 1982), 60.

and they always have a full supply of day labor to draw on without any charges for its keep," and so the size of the owner's plot increased.[24]

Surprisingly enough, those blacks who did enter the wage-labor market did about as well as the white laborers in the same market. Agriculture department wage surveys of 1899 and 1902 show racial differentials averaging less than 10 percent by state, and even those were probably attributable to geographic variations within states. Specific responses to the question of whether wages differed for blacks and whites in a given locality almost always were negative.[25] But why should this be surprising? In a real functioning market, where day labor is bought and sold like any commodity, the "law of one price" prevails. As R. J. Redding of Georgia explained:

> We have white men working on the farms. We frequently have applications every day. But when the white men come and are willing to work we have to say: We can not afford to pay you any more, because I can get a negro for 60 cents a day; if you are willing to work at that price the first vacancy we have you can have it. We occasionally put a white man in that way.[26]

The great majority of farm laborers were black, but even in the plantation states, as many as one-fourth were white in 1890.

The correlation between wage labor and young, unmarried males was by no means perfect, but it was close enough for many Southerners to take it for granted. A correspondent to the Industrial Commission in 1901 complained: "Our young negro men are becoming tramps, and moving about over the country in gangs to get the most remunerative work. The older men, with families, who live at one place, still crop on shares."[27] Planters who wanted wage labor also had to compete with nonagricultural employers. One Tennessee Valley planter observed:

> We employ families generally where we can. Those who are unencumbered with families are disposed to seek the public works. They have gone off to the Mussel Shoals from my neighborhood, and some have come down to Birmingham, and some have gone

elsewhere. It is usually those that are encumbered with families that stay at home.[28]

The expression "public works" is instructive. It was commonly used to refer to a job with minimal entry standards, like a mine or sawmill or blast furnace that would take any able-bodied male. These jobs paid well by southern standards and they were available to all comers; on a long-distance basis, the labor market worked well. But in 1890, the owners of the blast furnaces reported to the commissioner of labor that their employees were "mostly colored and the majority of them are single men or men living apart from their families." They usually clubbed together, ten or twelve in a room, sleeping on the floor.[29] The labor market was working, but what married man would want to take these jobs? Black single men did take them, however, presumably hoping that they wouldn't have to do it for a lifetime.

There was one more dimension to the market that sealed the matter: a sharecropping contract was also a credit transaction. In the plantation areas, the cropper normally borrowed for food and necessary supplies, the "furnish," from the landlord, though in some cases the landlord operated through a local merchant. Either way, a cropper had to borrow if he wanted even minimal security for his family's needs for the coming year, and he had to confront the basic fact of life that, in nineteenth-century America and well into the twentieth century, credit markets were intrinsically local. The very etymology of the word credit from the Latin for "believe" suggests that trust or believability is basic to a credit transaction. The local character of these relationships was not peculiarly southern. It was standard practice everywhere for farmers to return again and again to the same storekeepers, to establish and maintain credit; the need for credit exerted "a powerful bias toward continuing relationships."[30] The legal recognition of lien rights in a growing crop as a basis for credit originated as an effort to help planters borrow from distant merchants and is testimony to the difficulty of operating on credit without collateral. For poor farmers and laborers, the only way to establish creditworthiness was to stay in one locality and develop a track record of reliability. If they were black, the track record had to include not just productivity and attachment to a local area, but deference. No wonder W. E. B. Du Bois argued that young black men "sink to the class of *metayer*" when they married.[31]

It is ironic that historians should have tried to argue the exploitive nature of southern farming institutions by denying the existence of labor mobility, because contemporaries associated mobile labor with tramps and vagrants, people with no ambition. The Industrial Commission reported that "one of the most frequent complaints made against the negro laborers of the South is that they go about from place to place whenever they have an opportunity of bettering their condition."[32] One may say, of course, that these complaints merely represent the planters' view of things, the belief of every employer that his workers should stay put and be happy. Coming as they did from planters who in the same breath would describe blacks as lacking in ambition, energy, initiative, and desire for self-betterment, clearly these complaints cannot be taken at face value. But it is not the accuracy of their character analysis that is relevant, so much as their testimony to the traits that they themselves would value, because these are the traits that would be rewarded in terms of credit. P. H. Lovejoy, a planter and merchant from Hawkinsville, Georgia, was asked what profit margin he charged on goods, and replied:

> Size him up, and if he is pretty good, we sell him pretty cheap; and if he is a hard case, we just take what he makes and quit. . . . We generally put a pretty good margin on cheap men [25%] because we have to take chances on them. . . . We sell good men at 10 percent.[33]

It was this need to be known that kept black families in a local area; the great majority of family moves were to places in the same vicinity.[34] And many planters knew that the young men who went off to the mining districts "on account of higher wages" would "work a few months and generally drift back to the plantations."[35] Even sympathetic observers saw the promise of black progress as coming from "those Negroes who have been able to attach themselves to the land."[36]

The Agricultural Ladder

In reality, of course, plantation acreage was not divided simply between wage labor and tenancies, but also among several tenant categories in a fairly clear rank order known as the "agricultural ladder."

Farm families needed credit not just as insurance against destitution, but for access to these avenues of economic progress. Despite the accusation that blacks lacked ambition and energy, there is every reason to believe that they did desire advancement and worked hard at it. What they aspired to was not an ever-increasing wage as their productivity increased, because the labor market did not offer that, but accumulation of wealth leading to eventual farm ownership. The steps or rungs on the ladder of agricultural progress correspond closely to the phases of accumulation. The basic reasons for this are inherent in the operation of a credit market. For reasons that are fairly obvious, self-ownership in a nonslave society does not get you very far in a loan market. Just as a wealthless laborer has difficulty borrowing because he lacks collateral, a wealthless tenant farmer cannot offer a credible guarantee that he will pay a fixed rental fee. Theorists have built elaborate models around share and fixed-rent tenancies as functions of subjective individual risk preferences; but the objective fact is that a fixed-rent tenancy is not riskless to the landlord and cannot be made so. Concerns about risk and reliability permeated every arrangement. As one early writer on plantation tenancy pointed out in 1912 about cash rent:

> Since the cotton is sold through the planter, he is sure of his rent provided a crop is raised, but since he can not collect his rent if there is no crop, and since also the tenant is usually indebted to him for supplies advanced, the landlord exercises supervision over the cash renters, except in the case of renters whom he knows to be dependable.[37]

Another observer wrote:

> Landlords have to be very particular about renting outright because

99

they risk losing considerable sums on drifters, unsuccessful and dishonest tenants, and they also risk greater depreciation on their land.[38]

Intermediate forms of share tenancy, such as "thirds and fourths," were achieved when the tenant owned his own mule and implements, as described in this 1876 statement: "The idea with the laborer now is to try to buy some old horse or mule to claim ⅔ of all the grain he makes and ¾ of all the cotton."[39] But this was a stepping-stone to fixed-rent tenancy. Nate Shaw describes how he scraped together one hundred dollars for his own mule, borrowing the last twenty dollars from his father-in-law: "Got me a mule and gived up working on halves. . . . Paid cash rent and made a profit from my farmin."[40] The economist Benjamin Hibbard described in 1913 a "well-defined caste system among the tenants":

> The lowest class is represented by those who furnish little equipment and receive half, or less, of the crop; above this comes the group whose independence is measured by the possession of a mule and a plow and the means of subsistence till harvest time; the highest class consists of those who can be trusted to deliver a certain quantity of crop or possibly a sum of money, and who are by that fact emancipated in the main from the directing authority of the landlord.[41]

Note the blend of objective and subjective criteria. The basic issue was "who can be trusted," but the single most reliable rule of thumb for this assessment was ownership of assets, or wealth. Empirical studies confirm that tenants' wealth was strongly correlated with fixed-rent tenancy as opposed to shares.[42] A simulation exercise by economist Steven DeCanio indicates (as many historians have long argued) that the failure to distribute land or any other compensation to the freedmen was the single most important element in black-white income differentials before World War I. The advantages of wealth were such that blacks would have been behind for generations, even if there had been no discrimination.[43]

For blacks, it took an extra measure of proof even to gain the creditworthiness implicit in their accumulated wealth. It was a common saying that "the negro renters' foot is poison to the land." The responses to the 1910 plantation survey were filled with denunciations of the rise of black renting and statements of bitter resentment over the autonomy claimed by black renters. Accepting those views as authoritative, the Georgian R. P. Brooks wrote:

> The mass of the race are wholly unfit for independence. . . . [Planters] know that skill, industry, knowledge, and frugality are essential to successful farming, and they know that negroes in general lack these qualities.[44]

And yet, having made those derogatory generalizations, every single planter respondent could also list by name negroes who were successful and prospering as renters and landowners. As Booker T. Washington observed: "Everywhere I went, I found at least one white man who believed implicitly in one Negro, and one Negro who believed implicitly in one white man; and so it goes all through the South."[45] All things considered, blacks made remarkable progress in accumulating wealth in the postbellum South, yet even when they did so, it was not easy to translate this wealth into land ownership unless they were acceptable to the local white community.[46] As Arthur Raper concluded in his classic study of two Georgia plantation counties:

> Being acceptable here is no empty phrase. It means that he and his family are industrious and that his credit is good. It means that he is considered safe by local white people—he knows "his place" and stays in it.[47]

In what sense, then, can we say that sharecropping on the plantation was "institutionalized," and in what sense was it an exploitive relationship? Certainly it was not because there was only one rigid choice of contract, oblivious to market forces. No heavy hand of history prevented planter and laborer from changing their arrangement to mutual satisfaction, and tenure types did change and fluctuate over time. And it was not because croppers were bound to any one plantation, unable to vote with their feet. But there are two specific senses in which we may still say that sharecropping was "institutionalized." The first is that sharecropping became recognized by the law as a distinct category of labor, with specific rights and obligations. This status was distinctly inferior. As the Georgia Supreme Court stated in 1872:

> There is an obvious distinction between a cropper and a tenant. One has a possession of the premises exclusive of the landlord, the other has not. The one has a right for a fixed time, the other has only a right to go on the land to plant, work and gather the crop. . . . The case of the cropper is rather a mode of paying wages than a tenancy. The title to the crop subject to wages is in the owner of the land.[48]

The law in every southern state made this distinction, usually by the 1870s.[49] The economic importance of retaining title lay in the priority of claims on the crop in cases where the proceeds fall short—the so-called me-first provisions. Landlords and merchants continued to jockey for prior status in such cases, but the principle that the lien for advances and rent came ahead of any claim of labor emerged with bitter clarity.[50] Radical Republican legislatures made valiant efforts to rearrange those priorities, to put the "laborer's lien" at the top and guarantee the laborer a payment for his time; but these protections were all weakened or abolished when the so-called Redeemers came to power in the 1870s.[51] The effect was to transfer financial risk to the croppers, making it all the more difficult for them to accumulate the assets needed to climb the tenure ladder. This risk was not symmetrical, an unexpectedly good year likely to cancel a bad one, because the return on a surplus, even for a frugal family, could not possibly equal the high interest charges they had to pay for additional borrowing in the case of a deficit. The "homestead exemption" laws, designed to protect the homes and basic possessions of small holders, were of no help to the croppers. No wonder many blacks seemed to make little effort at self-advancement; if a small accumulation of savings was legally unprotectable, it made more sense to spend it when you could.

But there is another sense in which the market itself tends to "institutionalize" particular contract forms, a sense in which (as Brooks put it) "the law only crystallizes the actual economic facts as they have worked out."[52] There is an unfortunate intellectual tradition in economics that views "institutions" as things that stand in opposition to "market forces," and that impede their operation. But real, functioning markets are themselves institutions, and one of the ways in which markets deepen, expand, and improve is through emergence of well-known terms and categories, much the way trading communities tend to converge on a small number of instruments of payment. In this way, a bewildering array of contract forms in the immediate postwar years did give way to a much smaller number of reasonably standardized packages. And the distinctions that were important in these crystallizations were those that, in fact, were already in use before the war. The term *cropper* may be found in the 1860 census for the state of Georgia, and the distinction between croppers and tenants was recognized by the courts of North Carolina as early as 1837.[53]

It remains true that any two parties can negotiate any arrangement they wish. But most people have no strong basis for differentiating themselves from others, and instead adapt their own behavior to the market categories. Once it becomes known that wage laborers are young, footloose, and unreliable, anyone offering himself in that market will be taken to have those traits and will receive the corresponding wage. Men with wives and families could work as farm laborers (as a fair number of blacks did), but this would be taken, and with reason, as a sign of defeat, of low ambition and potential. Some planters actively preferred blacks in this market on the grounds that "the class of white men that offer for hire out there as a rule are a very sorry class of men."[54] If this is true for the labor market, how much more did it hold for credit markets, or markets involving labor-credit combinations in which trustworthiness was the central element? And how much truer was it for blacks, who had to overcome race prejudice and convince a landlord that they themselves were not like the other blacks? Thus, the contract forms seemed to reflect the characteristics of the different classes of workers, but some of the adjustment took the form of workers adapting to the categories rather than the other way around.

Despite, or perhaps because of, this increasing institution-

FIGURE 4.5

*Gross Farm Income by Race of Farm Operator
in the South Atlantic, 1900*

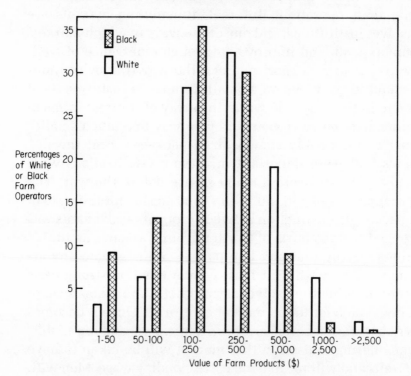

SOURCES: U.S. Bureau of the Census, *Agriculture*, 12th Census (1900), vol. 5, part 1 (Washington, D.C.: Government Printing Office, 1902), lx; U.S. Bureau of the Census, *Special Reports: Supplementary Analysis and Derivative Tables* (Washington, D.C.: GPO, 1906), table XXXVI.

alization of the agricultural ladder, blacks, it is important to note, were able to make substantial upward progress within the system. The distributions of farm output value (figures 4.5 and 4.6) do not show equality between the races, but they do show a significant range of opportunity for blacks who were fortunate enough to accumulate wealth and increase the share that they could claim. The number of black proprietorships did continue to grow (tables 4.3 and 4.4), many of them, to be sure, of small size and on inferior soil. This narrow range of opportunities may not have justified the extravagant claim that "farming is the open door to the negro race," but in comparison to the rigid assignments to dead-end jobs in nonagricultural pursuits (which we will examine in chapter 6), agriculture at

FIGURE 4.6

Gross Farm Income by Race of Farm Operator in
South Central United States, 1900

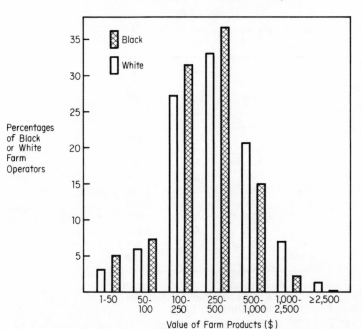

SOURCES: U.S. Bureau of the Census, *Agriculture*, 12th Census (1900), vol. 5, part 1 (Washington, D.C.: Government Printing Office, 1902), lx; U.S. Bureau of the Census, *Special Reports: Supplementary Analysis and Derivative Tables* (Washington, D.C.: GPO, 1906), table XXXVI.

TABLE 4.3

White and Black Proprietorships in
Thirty-one Georgian Counties,
1873–1902

	White		Black	
Year	Number	Average Acreage	Number	Average Acreage
1873	17,255	388.6	514	113.9
1880	20,725	339.5	1,865	93.8
1890	24,058	293.7	3,510	71.0
1902	26,957	264.8	5,221	64.3

SOURCE: Enoch Banks, *The Economics of Land Tenure in Georgia* (New York: Columbia University Press, 1905), appendix, table B.

TABLE 4.4

Acres Owned by Blacks,
Georgia, 1874–1903
(in Thousands)

Year	Acres	Year	Acres
1874	339	1889	877
1875	397	1890	976
1876	458	1891	1,004
1877	459	1892	1,064
1878	502	1893	1,044
1879	541	1894	1,064
1880	587	1895	1,039
1881	660	1896	1,044
1882	692	1897	1,058
1883	667	1898	1,097
1884	757	1899	1,062
1885	788	1900	1,075
1886	803	1901	1,141
1887	814	1902	1,175
1888	869	1903	1,252

NOTE: Enoch Banks, *The Economics of Land Tenure in Georgia* (New York: Columbia University Press, 1905), 69.

least offered some hope.[55] How then can we say that blacks were exploited?

Despite the tendency of economists to suggest otherwise, exploitation is not really an objective concept. A laborer may have earned the going market wage, yet that market may have been isolated from better markets in the same country. He may have earned the going wage for an entire lifetime, while others with no more talent or ability were able to accumulate their wages into property income by virtue of family connections, race, or good fortune. Or he may have committed himself to a local reputation early in life and missed out on better opportunities elsewhere. Since land owners had a class interest in perpetuating these barriers, there was an element of class exploitation even if every bargain was voluntary and every market competitive. But even for those blacks who did work their way up the ladder, there was a subtler but no less insidious exploitation in this need to be subservient, to know one's place, to differentiate one's self from one's race. They had to

TABLE 4.5

*Farm Tenure and Race in the South Atlantic and
South Central Regions, 1900*

	All Farm Operators		White Farm Operators		Black Farm Operators	
	Number	Percentage	Number	Percentage	Number	Percentage
Owners and Managers	1,389,247	53.0	1,200,978	63.9	180,979	24.7
Cash Tenants	458,790	17.5	187,088	10.0	271,522	37.1
Share Tenants	722,354	29.5	491,655	26.5	279,861	38.2

SOURCE: U.S. Bureau of the Census, *Agriculture*, 12th Census (1900), vol. 5 (Washington, D.C.: Government Printing Office, 1902), tables LXXIV, XCVIII, CIII.

be acceptable, nonthreatening, well behaved. They had to compromise their autonomy in order to gain it. Southern agriculture did offer some avenues of progress for "good blacks."

The Nonplantation Areas and the Small White Farmers

By 1900, two-thirds of the share tenant farmers in the South were white, and nearly half of the white farm operators were tenants (table 4.5). The major expansion of cotton acreage during the last third of the nineteenth century was primarily on the farms of white tenants and owners, not on the plantations. Prior to the war, the small farmers of the South had grown some cotton, but mainly on the basis of "safety-first" agriculture: "Raise our own supplies and let cotton be surplus"; "Be certain to make enough of bread and meat, and afterwards as much cotton as possible"; "Then cotton crop is extra, and what it brings we can keep in our pockets." These were the maxims and rules-of-thumb that prudent farmers lived by. We have to distinguish between the small farmers of the Cotton Belt, who limited their noncash crops to corn and who moved into cotton as they acquired slaves, and those of the up-country who practiced more diversified farming and traded mainly in local markets.[56] But as of 1860, neither made a major contribution to the national cotton crop, nor relied regularly on purchased food supplies. By 1880, however, large volumes of midwestern corn and meat were flowing into the South, from the Black Belt to the Upper Piedmont. One might think that some new wisdom or philosophy had swept across the South, that the logic of the marketplace had come to replace the old doctrine of self-sufficiency. But no, in the 1890s, prominent cotton growers and agricultural reformers were still preaching that farmers should "diversify their crops so as to raise their own supplies, and then raise all the cotton they can as a surplus crop."[57] How and why then did the small farmers of the South abandon their historic self-sufficiency in foodstuffs and move so strikingly toward production of cotton for the market?

Through the remainder of the nineteenth century, South-erners associated the decline of self-sufficiency with a fall in standards, a loss of prudence and thrift, or, at the very least, with an unfortunate falling behind financially. A reporter for an up-country Georgia paper wrote in 1878: "The majority of the farmers are going to plant largely of cotton, as most of them are in debt, and cotton is the only thing raised on the farm that will command ready money in the fall."[58] A correspondent to the Department of Agriculture reported in 1876: "People in debt must raise cotton till they break."[59] In prescribing for the "ills of the South" in 1894, Charles H. Otken wrote:

> The debts of the people . . . have been no small factor in bringing about the over-production of the great staple crop. Men in debt, want money. Farmers know that cotton is the only crop that will bring money . . . cotton brings the money, and money pays debts. What matters it if corn and meat raising is neglected, so a large cotton crop is made? This will deliver the man from his troubles. Thus reasons the average farmer.[60]

There is a whole aura of connotations behind statements like these, but the basic economic logic is simple. Farmers tried for self-sufficiency not in order to maximize annual profits but to protect their financial independence: to reduce the risk of having to borrow at what they knew would be exorbitant in-terest rates, and hence to guard against forced sale or foreclo-

FIGURE 4.7

The Choice Between Cotton and Corn

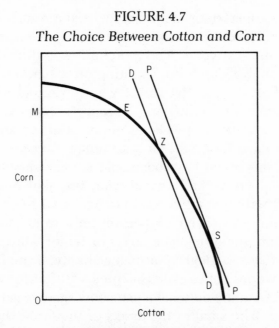

NOTE: Reprinted, by permission of the publisher, from Gavin Wright, "Freedom and the Southern Economy," *Explorations in Economic History* 16 (1979): 97.

sure on assets or the farm itself. An acre of cotton was clearly more profitable on average than an acre of corn, but it was also riskier, in the specific sense that basic food and feed requirements had to be met no matter what, and on-farm production was the surest way to meet these needs.[61] The problem for a small farmer was that once he fell into debt, he might not have the luxury of safety-first behavior anymore. Consider the farm depicted in figure 4.7, where the curve is the familiar production-possibility surface for a small farm, showing combinations of cotton and corn that may be grown with a given stock of land, labor, and equipment. Self-sufficiency is at point E. For given expected relative prices of cotton and corn, the expected profit-maximizing point is S. But if this farmer owed a debt D, and was required by law to pay it back, it meant that he had to raise at least enough cash to end up to the right of the debt line DD; that is to say, he had to be somewhere between Z and S on the production-possibility surface. Given the size of the farm, he could not do this and also be self-sufficient in corn. The reason that "only cotton will command ready money in the fall" was not that there was some quirk in the marketing system, nor a conspiratorial refusal by local merchants to buy corn, but that an acre of cotton was far more valuable than an acre of corn in most years. The merchant was thus, in effect, playing the role of landlord, insisting on a market-oriented allocation of acreage as the surest way to protect his claim. The institution of the "crop lien," a property right in the growing crop as security for the loan, merely ratified legally the only feasible basis for credit for poor tenant farmers.

Of course, this might have been only a temporary situation. The farm might have had a good year, the debt might have been paid off with enough to spare to finance a return to self-sufficiency and an orderly expansion on a safety-first basis. The majority of medium-scale farms or larger were still self-sufficient in foods in 1880.[62] But just as likely, if the farm was small, there would not be much surplus left after the debt was paid, and the farmer would have to borrow again to get through the next year. The smaller the assets of the farm, the poorer the credit risk and the higher the interest charges, hence the higher the debt burden for any given level of borrowing. So a small farmer who once slipped into debt might have had trouble ever returning to self-sufficiency, not necessarily because he was perpetually in debt but because he never got far enough out to get through a year without borrowing. He was always a year behind. Thus, from the individual small farmer's viewpoint, indebtedness could be a trap, a condition that a prudent and cautious farmer might be able to avoid but that with one slip could turn into an inescapable treadmill. By analogy, observers of southern agriculture often felt that events had just taken a wrong turn after the war, because of the wartime destruction of livestock, because of the temptations of high cotton prices, and because things would be better if they could just go back and start over.[63]

But while the loss of self-sufficiency might have seemed, from the individual farmer's standpoint, to be an accidental matter, a slippery slope that with luck could be avoided, from the regional perspective there were deeper pressures pushing more and more farmers into this position. One factor was the railroads, which came for the first time into many nonplantation areas after the war, and linked the interior directly to northern markets. Detailed study of the upper Piedmont region of northern Georgia shows that the rise of cotton growing came after 1870, when railroads came through, rather than right after the war.[64] A second, closely related, development was the rise of interior merchant stores, which offered to buy cotton locally and sell goods on credit. In earlier years, times of shortage might have been borne by severely depriving oneself, by moving in with kinfolk, or even by dying. Now there was a merchant offering goods on credit in exchange for a lien on a cotton crop. A third development was one of the goods on the merchant's shelf, commercial fertilizer, which fell dramatically in price after the war, and which expanded the feasible area for cotton and tobacco cultivation. Fertilizer manufacturers for the Piedmont could truthfully claim that "without commercial fertilizers few of us could afford to carry on cotton farming at all." The same could be said for the extension of bright-leaf tobacco into eastern North Carolina.[65]

For these reasons, commercial cotton and tobacco farming could spread without a revolution in farmer attitudes toward "market orientation." The reasonably substantial farmers were able to grow cash crops without giving up self-sufficiency in basic supplies. But smaller farmers and tenants could not have both, and the most basic continuing pressure toward commercialization at the expense of self-sufficiency was the decline in farm size, the pressure of population against the supply of farmland. While historians (echoing contemporaries) refer to the up-country as a "territory of the dispossessed," and suggest that white farmers "lost their land in large numbers," the actual loss of title by a farmer who had attained land ownership was relatively rare. Certainly some unfortunate families lost their land, like the father of the Populist leader Tom Watson, who forfeited the last acre of the old Watson farm in 1873. But on balance, for every farm that was lost, at least one new owner emerged. A study of white landownership in Georgia, using tax rolls for 1873, 1880, 1892, and 1902, shows that the number of white proprietors increased between every pair of dates and in almost every county.[66] But the increases were not great and the rise in tenancies was much larger. The average size of a white proprietorship declined from 388 acres in 1873, to 340 in 1880, to 294 in 1890, and to 265 in 1902. The number of white proprietorships of less than 100 acres tripled between 1873 and 1902, accounting for one-third of the total by that year. The problem of farm ownership was not primarily dispossession but lack of room for the young farmers coming up.

These small farmers, too, did not suddenly change their views about the desirability of safety-first agriculture, and they tended to blame the merchant for their plight. Respondents to an 1887 North Carolina survey excoriated the furnishing merchants for requiring that cotton or tobacco be planted as a condition for credit:

> As a rule, tenants are forced to make a certain amount of cotton in order to get their supplies furnished them, and they cannot, therefore, pay the attention to making their bread and meat that they ought. . . . We ought to plant less [cotton and tobacco] and more of grain and grasses, but how are we to do it; the man who furnishes us rations at 50 per cent interest won't let us; he wants money crop planted.[67]

But economically speaking, the merchant was just the messenger with the bad news. The real constraint was the fact of indebtedness itself. There is no doubt that interest rates implicit in the "credit prices" for goods were high, sometimes as high as 60 percent on an annual basis.[68] And there may have been an element of monopoly power in many localities. But interest charges were high even where merchants were competitive, as they are universally for small loans with limited backing.[69] Some merchants grew wealthy and became landowners, but the great majority were small, entry was common, and failure rates were high.[70] Commercial banks had no interest in these small loans and refused to take crop mortgages; bank loans to prosperous white farmers almost always required chattel mortgage security, the chief item usually being mules.[71] White tenants could often borrow from merchants on more favorable terms than blacks, but the fundamentals of credit and advancement were the same: the key questions were "character" and "do you have assets to pledge?"

Nor was it the case that tenants were typically held in place by an inability to "pay out" their debts at the end of the year.

Though failure to fully discharge a debt after the harvest was not rare, it was far from typical even in the plantation areas.[72] Terms like *peonage* and *debt slavery* were part of the metaphorical vocabulary of the day. The republican tradition in the North had long associated liberty with the ownership of productive property; hence lack of property was a form of slavery.[73] But by 1900 many Northerners had come to the more modern view that the freedom to choose one's employer was the only valid test. This difference in usage is illustrated in a remarkable exchange between two Industrial Commission members and O. B. Stevens, commissioner of agriculture for Georgia. The questioner suggested that "a man in continual debt, wearing out the land there for 10 or 15 years, is practically in slavery," and Stevens replied, "Yes; I think that is it." Again, the question was raised, "He is so tied up that it is impossible for him ever to escape it?" and the answer, "Yes; I think so." But the commission members thought this really meant that the tenant was bound to the land and could not leave. When Stevens says that many of them worked a place for five years, got discouraged, and then left, they were incredulous:

Q: At the end of any one year they do not have to work there the next year?
A: Oh, no.
Q: Is there any reason why a man should not take another place and make a new start?
A: Not at all. . . . There is nothing whatever to force a man to stay on a farm. They usually rent those lands from year to year.

The questioners were speaking literally, but Stevens was willing to say "practically in slavery" about a man discouraged after failure to advance in five years.[74]

This is not an attempt to dismiss these bitter complaints as groundless or "all in their heads," but only to understand them more fully in historical context. In blaming the merchant and railing against his constraints, small farmers were focused directly on some of the fundamentals of human interaction. The ability to "hold the crop," to bargain for better prices, to pick and choose at the time of the harvest—these were the fruits of independence. Of course there were some real economic benefits to "cotton unencumbered—which can be held for the best prices";[75] but these may not have been as telling as the raw humiliation of having one's cotton snatched by the merchants for debts as soon as it was ready. A sampling of contemporary perceptions is a newspaper comment from the 1870s:

> We can tell a man who has corn enough a mile off. The corn man cocks his hat one one side and swings along at an easy stride. The "no corn" man has his hat pulled over his eyes and shambles along with a slouching gait and a side-long look as if he expected every minute for someone to sing out, "I know what ails you, you haven't corn enough to last until May."[76]

Applying a labor market test to these farmers is entirely out of place. They were trying to escape the labor market, where they knew they would not do much better than blacks.

Another reason for the prominence of "holding the crop" in these discussions is that observers were drawing an analogy between an individual's strategy in taking advantage of fluctuations in a local market, and the low cotton prices received by the region as a whole. The loss of control felt by the tenant farmer who had to let his crop go at an unbearably low price was extrapolated to the aggregate, even by sophisticated observers. Self-sufficiency was advice "as to how to prevent the low price of cotton." The Selma, Alabama, *Times* argued in 1894 that "the only way to get out of debt and get a good price for cotton, is for every farmer to raise his farm supplies. Then he can sell his cotton whenever the price suits him."[77] The economist M. B. Hammond concluded in 1897 that "overproduction has actually taken place, and that the southern farmers are themselves directly responsible for the low price of their chief product."[78] To a modern economist this seems absurd. Self-sufficiency might bring greater independence, security, thrift, or peace of mind to an *individual*, but no individual could expect to influence the price of cotton in New Orleans, New York, or Liverpool. It may be true that an aggregate acreage reduction by all Southerners simultaneously would have pushed up the world cotton price, but it would have taken a lot more than holding the crop for a few weeks or months.

Plantation, Farm, and Farm Labor in the South

In retrospect, it is obvious that the low prices of the 1890s resulted from the demand-side effects of the worldwide depression. These opinions are noteworthy just the same, not for the accuracy of their implicit economics, but as testimony to the hold of the self-sufficiency standard and of the merchant-bargaining analogy in contemporary thinking. Many farmers, or at least the political leadership, seemed to feel that the real enemy was the merchant—that if they could all just hold on and stretch their savings a bit more, and refuse to accept unfair prices, they could turn cotton markets around.

Southern Political Economy and World Cotton Demand

Concern over terms of credit and the bargaining relationships implied by the expression "holding the crop" were the continuing themes and organizing points of the major farm protest groups in the South. Despite the penchant of most such movements for conspiracy theories, scapegoats, and farfetched economic doctrines, there was a hard core of logic and self-interest in the programs supported by the Southern Farmers' Alliance and other such groups, and in the political platforms that they developed and that were ultimately absorbed by the Populist party in the 1890s. The Alliance, which began as a frontier self-help organization in Texas in the late 1870s, spread rapidly both eastward and northward in the 1880s. Its central appeal, which "attracted farmers to the order in droves," was its system of cooperatives, or Alliance stores, which offered members discounts and reasonably priced credit on supplies, and the advantages of cooperative marketing of the cotton crop. However exaggerated the small farmer's views about the insidious local merchants may have been, the cooperatives nonetheless did address their most pressing practical problems, and they reflected the reasonable hope that scale economies in risk pooling, marketing, and bargaining could be realized and shared among the members. There were striking early successes in local areas, and a striking national success in 1888–89, when an Alliance-led boycott defeated a recently organized jute trust, bringing down the price of bagging to cotton farmers all over the South. A series of recent monographs has established the prominence of this organizational background in the Southern Farmers' Alliance as a forerunner to populism and as a stimulus to organizations in other states like Kansas and the Dakotas, where problems were similar.[79]

Why then did the Alliance and southern populism ultimately fail? A full answer to this question would go well beyond the scope of this book, but recent studies do offer us a menu of explanations, covering almost every logical possibility:

1. Populism was defeated by the full mobilization of threatened economic interest groups, from local merchants and bankers to the national and international cotton dealers.
2. Populism failed because it did not inculcate its analysis and ideology well enough among the membership, so that they were easily swayed by confusing appeals like those for free silver.
3. Populist leaders sold out, opting for fusion with the Democrats and the "quick fix" of electoral victories in 1896, abandoning the alliance program in favor of the free silver panacea (the "cowbird of the reform movement," in Henry Demarest Lloyd's phrase).
4. Southern populism was defeated by the race issue, the inability of whites to overcome racial prejudice and unify the farming classes in the South.[80]

Since any movement that fails provokes a thousand might-have-beens, it is possible that all of these analyses have some truth. The most plausible account of the immediate reasons for the Alliance's demise, however, is the one offered by historian Robert McMath: The co-ops that held the organization together had begun to fail under the pressure of falling cotton prices in 1891. Though they might offer modest savings to members in good times, like most other small financial intermediaries, they could not withstand the effects of a drastic price fall, much less the effects of the decade of depressed cotton prices that followed. According to McMath, the decision to "move into politics" in 1892 represented a "radicalization" of the leadership based on the obvious fact that the co-ops were no longer functioning. They *had* to appeal for a national program to have any hope of success, and the "subtreasury" scheme developed by Charles Macune was the natural successor to the co-ops at the new level. The plan proposed a system of warehouses and elevators, which would accept crops from farmers and issue treasury notes equal to 80 percent of the crop's value. The farmers would pay modest interest on the notes but could withdraw their crops for sale at any time. The system would offer cheap credit and unlimited ability to "hold the crop," the small southern farmer's psychological heaven.

Though the subtreasury plan was designed with the small cotton farmer in mind, it had serious shortcomings as the centerpiece of a national political strategy. Farmers in other parts of the country, who bought less fertilizer but more machinery, had quite different political priorities. Even in the South, farm laborers and sharecroppers had no real place in the plan, since they had no legal title to any crop in the first place. But even among the small white farmers of the South, populism was essentially defeated before it began because its institutional foundations in the Alliance stores were in ruins. Its membership had dissipated, and the Populists were never able to mobilize the potential voting strength that they seemed to have had in 1890.

To take a more positive view, however, one might ask not so much why populism failed in the 1890s but why there was no major resurgence of farm protest thereafter. One might invoke any number of political factors, but surely a fundamental reason was that world cotton demand surged forward for two decades after the political and economic disasters of 1891–98 (figure 4.8). It is not surprising that those who stress the exploitive, backward character of the Southern economy tend to write about the nineteenth century (when cotton demand growth was sluggish, and a catastrophic depression ensued), while those who press the revisionist case for progress tend to write about the first two decades of the twentieth century. The big jump in the tenancy rate during the 1890s slowed to a crawl after 1900 and stabilized between 1910 and 1920 (table

FIGURE 4.8

Annual Average Cotton Price Per Pound, 1879–1915

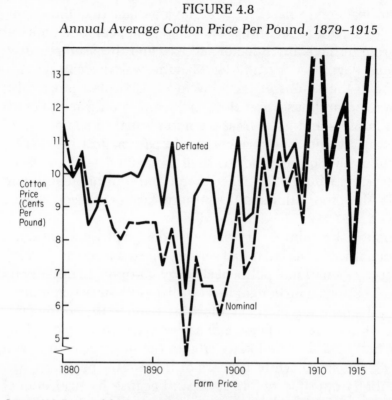

SOURCE: U.S. Bureau of the Census, *Historical Statistics of the United States*, part 1 (Washington, D.C.: Government Printing Office, 1975), 200–201, 517–18.

TABLE 4.6

Tenants, Including Sharecroppers, as Percentage of Farm Operators, 1880–1930

Year	South Atlantic	East South Central	West South Central	North
1880	36.1	36.8	35.2	19.2
1890	38.5	38.3	38.6	22.1
1900	44.2	48.1	49.1	26.2
1910	45.9	50.7	52.8	26.5
1920	46.8	49.7	52.9	28.2
1930	48.1	55.9	62.3	30.0

SOURCE: U.S. Special Committee on Farm Tenancy, *Farm Tenancy* (Washington, D.C.: Government Printing Office, 1937), 39.

TABLE 4.7

Farm Laborers ("Working Out"), 1910–20

	White		Black	
	1910	*1920*	*1910*	*1920*
Alabama	22,648	16,837	42,902	25,062
Arkansas	32,990	29,357	19,992	16,504
Florida	11,418	10,917	14,367	13,476
Georgia	28,663	23,442	68,559	50,267
Louisiana	25,198	23,982	59,916	38,515
Mississippi	12,903	9,821	40,070	22,364
North Carolina	33,483	27,880	40,472	25,732
South Carolina	13,314	9,477	52,834	32,461
Tennessee	50,466	38,863	22,256	15,381
Texas	98,889	103,652	37,186	33,693
Virginia	42,616	37,841	42,266	28,623
11 States	441,619	332,069	440,820	302,078

SOURCES: U.S. Bureau of the Census, *Occupations*, 13th Census (1910), vol. 4 (Washington, D.C.: Government Printing Office, 1914), table 7; U.S. Bureau of the Census, *Occupations*, 14th Census (1920), vol. 4 (Washington, D.C.: GPO, 1923), table 1.

4.6). Labor markets tightened and wages rose, for both blacks and whites. The expansion was not, of course, completely uninterrupted, but setbacks were brief; after the business contraction of 1908 ended the first wave of the boom, new records for the value of the cotton crop were set in 1909, 1910, and 1913. Tobacco demand was equally robust. Credit problems certainly did not disappear during these years, but the earnings from sustained prosperity reduced the threat of foreclosure or destitution for the small white farmers who had been the backbone of Alliance and Populist support. When wartime demands during World War I were added to the strength of the cotton economy, farmers worked their way up the ladder more quickly; the absolute number of farm laborers actually declined between 1910 and 1920 (table 4.7).

Not all rungs on the ladder became easier to reach. Though black wealth accumulation continued to be more rapid than that of whites, and even accelerated with the revival of the cotton boom, the relative growth of black landownership slowed down. Having risen from virtually zero to nearly 20 percent of farm operators in 1880, and to 25 percent in 1900, the rate of black ownership actually declined slightly to 24.7

FIGURE 4.9

Average Prices of Mules and Horses in the United States, 1866–1920

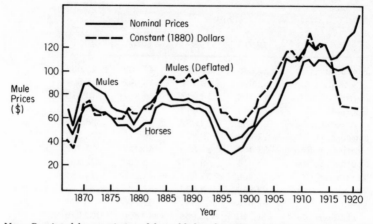

NOTE: Reprinted, by permission of the publisher, from Gavin Wright, "Freedom and the Southern Economy," *Explorations in Economic History* 16 (1979): 105.
Data compiled from U.S. Bureau of the Census, *Historical Statistics of the United States*, part 1 (Washington, D.C.: Government Printing Office, 1975), 200–201, 519–20.

percent in 1910, and to 23.8 percent in 1920. The obvious explanation is that land values were increasing just as fast as black wealth.[81] Another apparent anomaly is that the relative importance of sharecropping increased, as compared to cash rental. This was the case for both black and white tenants. If sharecropping and cash tenancy were rungs on a ladder of accumulation, and if incomes were growing at an accelerated pace, why should this be? Again, the likely explanation is that the price of the critical asset was also rising even faster. The price of mules doubled between 1899 and 1905, and tripled between 1899 and 1918 (figure 4.9). This pattern was not exclusively the result of cotton demand, since mules were raised primarily outside the South, but reflects also the general pressure on grain supplies and farmland during these decades. This may be seen from the fact that the price of horses (for which the South was a relatively small market) followed roughly the same path.

Racial equality also remained a distant prospect at best. If the average age of farm owners, renters, and sharecroppers represents a rough estimate of a young person's expectations for the future, the gap between blacks and whites had narrowed only slightly between 1880 and 1910 (table 4.8). A farm ladder

TABLE 4.8

Age and Tenure of Southern Farm Operators,
1880 and 1910

Tenure	Average Age, 1880			Median Age, 1910		
	White	Black	All	White	Black	All
Owners	43.6	45.5	43.9	46.3	48.5	46.6
Tenants	35.7	40.7	38.6	34.8	38.8	36.6
Renters	37.4	41.4	40.0	36.9	41.0	39.3
Share Tenants	35.2	40.5	38.1	34.2	37.0	35.1

SOURCES: Roger Ransom and Richard Sutch, *One Kind of Freedom* (New York: Cambridge University Press, 1977), 181; U.S. Bureau of the Census, Agriculture, 14th Census (1920), vol. 5 (Washington, D.C.: Government Printing Office, 1922), 353.

of sorts operated for both races, but white tenants averaged five years younger than black tenants in 1880, and the differential had fallen only to four years by 1910. The differential for share tenants had fallen to three years, but this may overstate the progress because black share tenants were twice as likely to be lowly "croppers," as opposed to true tenants. The census did not recognize this distinction until 1920, but in that year the difference in racial status was evident (table 4.9). Sharecropping was by no means an all-black category, however, as is often believed.

Despite those inequities and anomalies, it would be hard to dispute that the Southern economy prospered during the first two decades of the twentieth century, and that this prosperity was shared in some measure by both the black and white farm

TABLE 4.9

Tenure of Farm Operators by Race, 1920

Tenure	Percentage Owners	Percentage Cash and Standing Rent Tenants	Percentage Share Tenants	Percentage Croppers
All Operators	47.5	11.2	19.9	19.8
Whites Only	60.3	6.6	20.4	11.1
Black Only	22.4	20.2	18.9	36.9

SOURCE: U.S. Bureau of the Census, Agriculture, part 2, *Reports for 11 Southern States*, 14th Census (1920), vol. 6 (Washington, D.C.: Government Printing Office, 1922).

population. So preeminent was the role of cotton demand that the South as a whole did not suffer as a result of the boll weevil at this time, even though, beginning in the 1890s, it was working its way eastward from Texas. Though particular localities were devastated by infestation, and the pest had reached the East Coast by 1920, aggregate cotton earnings continued to grow robustly. Each new attack simply caused the price received by all the other areas to be raised, thus serving, if anything, to keep cotton culture strong in the older areas of the East longer than it otherwise would have been. And the attraction of cotton profits led to a mobilization of responses and adaptations, so that the decline in cotton acreage and production was transitory in most places.[82] Though the weevil had a lasting effect on cultivation practices, causing growers to change to early planting, different seed varieties, heavier fertilization, and the use of calcium arsenate, most parts of the South worked it into their routine and returned to "normal." What it did not do was to trigger a major diversification of southern agriculture or a new shift of resources out of agriculture into industry and other pursuits.

Though the cotton boom that occurred between 1900 and 1920 brought prosperity to the South, and a modicum of progress to most Southerners, ensuring an end to the despair and turbulence of the late nineteenth century, the political failures of the 1890s had an effect on the Southern economy that lasted far into the twentieth century. It was not that the Alliance or Populist programs could realistically have influenced the global forces that brought boom or bust to the South. But a by-product of the agrarian movement was disfranchisement of the black and much of the white voting population; between 1890 and 1903, every southern state adopted legislation limiting the vote. It was a "reform" demand that emanated from the black-majority plantation districts and was directed at blacks, but it also had the effect of reducing political participation by poor farmers generally. The resulting concentration of political power in the whites of the Black Belt had a critical effect on the social allocation of the earnings from the cotton boom. The allocation to education overall was quite modest, but the major new development between 1890 and 1910 was a virtual assault

TABLE 4.10
Per Pupil School Expenditures by Race,
1890 and 1910

	White Expenditures	Black Expenditures	Ratio
Alabama			
1890	3.14	3.10	1.01
1910	10.07	2.69	3.74
Florida			
1890	9.42	4.63	2.03
1910	11.58	3.11	3.72
Louisiana			
1890	5.85	2.92	2.00
1910	11.54	2.07	5.57
North Carolina			
1890	2.71	2.74	0.99
1910	5.20	2.52	2.06
Virginia			
1890	7.08	4.93	1.44
1910	11.59	4.10	2.83

SOURCE: Robert A. Margo, *Disfranchisement, School Finance, and the Economics of Segregated Schools in the U.S. South, 1890–1910* (New York: Garland Press, 1985), table I-1.

on the status of black schools (table 4.10). As J. Morgan Kousser and Robert Margo have demonstrated, discrimination in schooling closely followed the extreme new discrimination in voting, a correlation unlikely to have been coincidental.[83] Whereas the wave of Jim Crow legislation that also occurred during these years was a more urban phenomenon and of less clear-cut economic effect, the assault on black schools affected the lives of black Southerners directly for generations.[84]

A second consequence of lasting importance for the region was that state-level political power was now firmly lodged in the white minority of the plantation districts, which is to say, in the group with the least interest in promoting the integration of national capital and labor markets. Southern regional priorities and policies continued to be shaped by this class into the 1950s.

5

THE RISE OF

SOUTHERN TEXTILES

I T IS common knowledge that the American cotton textile industry migrated from New England to the South after the Civil War, and that the reason was "cheap labor." Stories like this one are familiar in the global history of the textile industry, which has been sensitive to locational labor costs over the past century and a half, if not longer. In world markets, Lancashire gave way in the first quarter of the twentieth century to Japan, which has now in turn largely relinquished the industry to South Korea, Taiwan, and Hong Kong. In the United States, cotton manufacturing arose in New England when that region was the labor-abundant region of the country, but began to grow in the Piedmont sections of the Carolinas, Georgia, and Alabama after 1875, when the Southeast emerged as the lower-wage region in a national context. Cost studies for the late nineteenth and early twentieth centuries confirm that cheap labor was the basis for the South's advantage.[1] But there is more to the story than that. It takes more than poverty to supply cheap labor to an industry, and more than cheap labor to ensure a sustained industrial growth. Even after the acceleration of the 1870s, it took at least a half-century for the South to gain the market position made possible by the labor-cost advantage. The fundamental reason for such protraction is that early industrialization is a matter of learning, in the broadest sense of that term: in management, in technology, in marketing, and certainly—though this is often underestimated—in learning on the part of the labor force. The cotton mill villages were the first exposure to town life for thousands of white Southerners, and the process of industrial development involved an extended period of adaptation by these people, not just to the factory and the tasks, but to the entire social setting, to industrial employment as a life's work and a way of life. This industry history is thus central to the South's postbellum economic experience.

The progress of textiles in the South was real, and was reflected in steady improvement in the productivity of its labor and in the quality and variety of its cotton cloth. But there were limits to the economic and social impact in the first fifty years. The industry did not provide the revolutionary regional dynamism of its New England predecessor, because the center of machinery production and associated technological development was still in the North. And because the advances in labor productivity came mainly from on-the-job experience rather than schooling, labor skills were narrow and not easily transferred to other kinds of work. Still, in its own terms, southern textiles was a success story, a growing industry that took over the national cloth market while improving the lot of its workers. If its progress had continued along the same lines, the limitations on its influence might gradually have been overcome. Instead, it began to stumble almost as soon as it triumphed, for it came under the influence of national political forces at the peak of its success.

The Abortive Antebellum Textile Boom

Who established the first American mechanized spinning mill in 1790, using technology pioneered by Arkwright, and where did this event occur? Every attentive schoolchild knows the story of Samuel Slater and his partnership with Moses Brown in Pawtucket, Rhode Island, but the correct answer is Hugh Templeton in Stateburg, South Carolina.[2] Unlike Slater's mill, however, Templeton's enterprise had no great success. It struggled for five years and then failed, largely because of the "unstable and costly labor supply"; Templeton employed slaves from nearby plantations, and several times he had trained them to run the equipment, only to have the owners withdraw the trained laborers from factory work.[3] It was an early illustration of the proposition that labor experience as well as labor costs matter for industrial success.

The major spurts in American textile history, however, do not date from 1790 but from the period of the Jeffersonian Embargo and war with England (1807–15), and the technological revolution of the power loom and the Lowell-Waltham mills after the war (1816–33).[4] During the first of these, the South's role as supplier of raw material was merely the mirror image of New England's industrial success. The United States was virtually a closed economy between the Embargo and the peace of 1815, and the hothouse boom of the cotton industry in the North allowed the cotton states to pull out of their depression even before the reopening of foreign trade. The notion that the South was on the verge of an industrial revolution in 1816 is a latter-day myth. When the young John C. Calhoun and other southern congressmen supported the protective tariff in 1816, it was not in the hope of encouraging southern cotton mills, but with an eye toward protecting the besieged northern factories that had been the main market for raw cotton during the previous decade. The atmosphere was infused with the fear of renewed warfare, but when Eldred Simkins of South Carolina endorsed the tariff "to give some protection to those establishments which had greatly helped to save us in time of war," it was undoubtedly economic as much as military salvation that he had in mind. With the coming of peace and the revival of foreign cotton demand, this southern interest in protectionism quickly evaporated.[5]

A generation later, however, Southerners did make a move into textiles, in the midst of the depressed cotton prices of the 1840s. The mills were small and scattered, but, as table 5.1 shows, the rate of growth of employment in southern textiles

TABLE 5.1

Employment in the Cotton Goods Industry, 1840–80

Region	1840	1850	1860	1870	1880
North					
Massachusetts	20,928	28,730	38,451	43,512	61,246
Rhode Island	12,086	10,875	14,077	16,745	21,174
New Hampshire	6,991	12,122	12,730	12,542	16,395
Connecticut	5,153	6,186	9,002	12,086	14,484
4 states	45,158	57,913	74,260	84,885	113,299
Average percent of growth		2.49%	2.49%	1.34%	3.89%
South					
Alabama	82	715	1,312	1,032	1,448
Georgia	800	2,272	2,813	2,846	6,215
North Carolina	1,219	1,619	1,755	1,453	3,232
South Carolina	570	1,019	891	1,123	2,018
Tennessee	800	891	899	890	1,015
Virginia	1,735	2,962	1,441	1,741	1,085
6 states	5,206	9,479	9,111	9,085	15,013
Average percent of growth		5.99%	−0.04%	−0.03%	5.02%

NOTE: Reprinted, by permission of the Economic History Association, from Gavin Wright, "Cheap Labor and Southern Textiles Before 1880," *Journal of Economic History* 39 (1979): 671, table 1. Data compiled from U.S. Bureau of the Census, *Compendium of the Sixth Census* (Washington, D.C.: Government Printing Office, 1841), 112, 124, 160, 184, 196, 208, 220, 256; Ernest Lander, *The Textile Industry in Antebellum South Carolina* (Baton Rouge: Louisiana State University Press, 1969), 79; U.S. Bureau of the Census, *Manufactures*, 10th Census (1880) (Washington, D.C.: GPO, 1883), 542–43. Discrepancies have been resolved in favor of the summary in the later census.

was much greater in this decade than in the North. Obviously the South had a long way to go in this industry, but the spurt was impressive enough to produce real concern in the North and a flurry of worried comments in such national periodicals as *Niles Register* and *Hunt's Merchant Magazine*. In 1850 the *Scientific American* wrote:

> Coarse goods can be manufactured cheaper at the South, and with the great number of factories now in operation [in the Southern states], how can it be expected that our northern manufacturers can long keep the field against them—they cannot do it.[6]

But the forecast was wrong; two or three years later, these fears were entirely forgotten. Table 5.1 also shows that southern textile employment made *no further gain* between 1850 and 1860. The same is true for invested capital, and output growth is only slightly more positive. What happened?

The fundamental change was the reacceleration of world

TABLE 5.2

Labor Costs in Textiles and All Manufacturing, 1850 and 1860

Region	Annual Wage Per Hand			Cotton Consumed by Mills: Percentage of Change
	1850	1860	Percentage of Change	
Cotton Textile Industy				
Alabama	$117	$151	29.1	123.9
Georgia	122	148	21.3	52.8
North Carolina	92	108	17.4	−9.6
South Carolina	126	138	9.5	−11.0
Tennessee	96	155	61.5	41.2
Virginia	100	181	81.0	−5.6
6 Southern States	99	146	47.5	12.2
Massachusetts	199	203	1.75	33.2
4 New England States	195	203	5.7	44.8
United States	167	196	17.7	46.5
All Manufacturing				
Alabama	$224	$270	20.7	
Georgia	204	253	23.6	
North Carolina	144	189	31.0	
South Carolina	161	197	22.6	
Tennessee	189	269	42.3	
Virginia	186	236	27.0	
6 Southern States	181	235	29.8	
Massachusetts	239	262	9.3	
4 New England States	239	268	12.0	
United States	243	289	18.8	

NOTE: Reprinted, by permission of the Economic History Association, from Gavin Wright, "Cheap Labor and Southern Textiles Before 1880," *Journal of Economic History* 39 (1979): 672, table 2. Data compiled from U.S. Bureau of the Census, *Compendium of the Seventh Census* (Washington, D.C.: Government Printing Office, 1854), 179; *Manufactures*, 8th Census (1860) (Washington, D.C.: GPO, 1865), 729. The 1850 monthly wage totals have been multiplied by 12.

cotton demand, which made the 1850s the most prosperous decade in history for cotton growing. The channel by which this change affected textiles, however, was the labor market. Table 5.2 presents evidence that the trends in wage rates were dramatically different in the North and in the South. Almost all of the slaves had been pulled out of the mills by 1860, because their labor was so much more valuable in the fields.[7] The poor whites, for their part, were in a much better position to exercise their "notable reluctance . . . to accept employment in the cotton mills."[8] Most remarkably, while one would expect a nongrowing labor force to "age" or mature over time, what evidence we have suggests that southern textile labor was even more youthful in 1860 than it had been in 1850.[9] The buildup of work experience is a basic part of industrial progress that the antebellum southern textile mills missed.

Many elements of this story are significant for understanding the slave economy, but for present purposes there is one main point: the isolation of the southern labor market dates back to antebellum times and was the main factor behind slow growth in textiles. In contrast to the North, upward pressure on wages did not produce a massive inflow of labor. The proposal to reopen the African slave trade was blocked by slave owners, who also displayed no interest in active recruitment of free labor from outside. The interests of the slave owners in maintaining high prices were well represented by this 1859 editorial in the *Southern Banner* of Athens, Georgia:

> One of the arguments . . . used in favor of opening the African slave trade is that it would give us cheap labor. If there were no other reason for opposition to it we would oppose it on that ground. We want to see labor high. . . . No country can be really prosperous and happy where it is otherwise. . . . Cheap labor is a curse to any country. We wish it was twice as high in the country as it is.[10]

They were not playing that tune in the manufacturing towns of the South, twenty years later.

The Era of Regional Coexistence

After the war, southern textiles did begin more than fifty years of sustained progress that culminated in the collapse of the historic New England industry in the 1920s. Figure 5.1 displays the trajectory of regional spindleage and cotton consumption by mills. Table 5.1 indicates that the advance began after 1870 but before 1880, so that the growth of employment was well underway by the time of the Atlanta Exposition of 1881, conventionally cited as the beginning. The timing is significant. The fact that cotton manufacturing took off only after the bottom had fallen out of the postwar cotton market confirms once again that conditions of labor supply were crucial to the in-

FIGURE 5.1

Northern and Southern Cotton Consumption and Spindles,
1880 to 1930

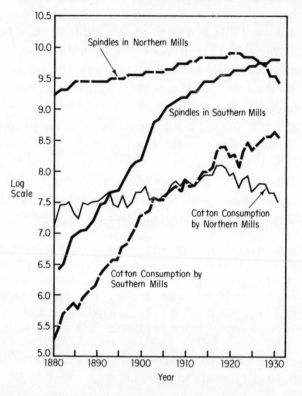

NOTE: Reprinted, by permission of the publisher, from Gavin Wright, "Cheap Labor and Southern Textiles, 1880–1930," *Quarterly Journal of Economics* 96 (1981): 606.
Data from U.S. Bureau of the Census, *Statistical Abstract of the United States* (Washington, D.C.: Government Printing Office, 1880–1930).

dustry's success.[11] Parallel to the decline in the relative farm wage, full-time earnings in cotton textiles fell in the South Atlantic by 17 percent between 1860 and 1870, and by 1900 were barely half the level of the New England states. Even these wage figures do not reflect the important new elasticity of labor supply, as the spread of tenancy and the decline in farm size increased the number of farm families to whom factory work seemed an acceptable alternative. From the 1870s to the end of the century, employment grew at nearly 10 percent per year with no detectable upward pressure on wages.

With hourly wage rates 30 to 50 percent below northern levels by the 1880s, one might ask why the southern success

was not faster than it was. One constraint was investment capital. Southern mills were small and scattered, initiated almost
entirely by southern money. It is as misleading to describe the
movement as a "revolution from above" by the planter class
as it is to label it a nationalist drive for regional "revenge."[12]
Investors and organizers came from a variety of backgrounds;
many of them, it is true, were land owners, but more often
they came from a commercial background. In South Carolina,
considerable financing came from Charleston, but in that state
and the others, membership on boards of directors was overwhelmingly local, reflecting the localized perspective and motivation behind the majority of projects.[13] "Every little town
wanted a mill," one industry man recalled. "If it couldn't get
a big one, it would take a small one; if not a sheeting, than a
spinning mill."[14] Stock was sold in small amounts on install-
ment, with payments as low as fifty cents per week without
interest. Though trade credit from northern marketing houses
was important, and machinery manufacturers occasionally
took partial payment in the form of shares, as late as the 1920s,
80 to 90 percent of southern spindles were southern-owned.[15]
Indeed, the term *migration* as applied to textiles is really inappropriate, and this industry has never fit very easily into the
conception of the South as a colonial economy. The *absence*
of a unified northern industrial class interest is in fact confirmed by the fact that what capital did come South was not
coming from the textiles industry but from the independent
textile *machinery* industry, which was already well represented at the Atlanta Exposition in 1881. The specialized machinery companies, offspring of the New England textiles par-
ent, played the role of aggressive propagators of grandchildren
who would ultimately destroy their own grandparents. In the
era of regional coexistence, however, northern interest in these
firms was fleeting, and most were left to accumulate their own
capital over time through reinvestment of profits.

But capital was not the only constraint. As shown in figure
5.1, the New England industry was able to continue growing
until 1920 in both output and capacity. Much more than they
used to, economists now appreciate that productivity growth
in early industrialization comes from *learning*. Technological

improvements came mainly from the machinery industry in the North, but the inexperienced owners, managers, machinists, and machine tenders of the South all had a lot to learn. "Looking back on them," one informant told industry historian Broadus Mitchell in 1916, "I can see that the first mill men were a set of blundering children, some a little more apt than others."[16] The labor force also learns. It is often said that skill requirements in the textile industry are minimal, that the work can be learned in a few weeks at most. This is highly misleading. Even in the simplest tasks, there is wide scope for variation in individual performance, and experience makes a big difference. Detailed studies of the early Waltham mills and the later Japanese industry show that the accumulation of worker experience is a major component of overall productivity growth, especially in the first decades of industrialization.[17] This "learning" may be more a matter of socialization and "getting used to it" than accumulating cognitive knowledge, but there is also a certain knack to piecing breaks in the yarn, a certain "feel" to identifying problems with the machinery, and a certain self-discipline to staying at the job dutifully through long hours. Throughout the period, mill owners continued to talk about the need for a "dependable" labor supply, for "the right class of worker."

One objective measure that is closely associated with experience is age, and there is no doubt that age made a difference. The mill job requiring the least skill was "doffing," the task of replacing full bobbins with fresh ones on the spinning machine. Table 5.3 shows the hourly earnings of doffers paid on a uniform piece rate at a representative mill in 1907, and indicates that seventeen year olds were 25 percent more productive than fourteen year olds, and 60 percent more productive than twelve year olds. Similarly, a study of productivity in weaving, a job given to both men and women and paid on a piece rate, show that adult male weavers on the average had a 15 to 25 percent productivity advantage over women.[18] Hence the gradual increase in the share of males in the labor force, from 43 percent in 1880 to 63 percent in 1920, constitutes a form of productivity gain. On several fronts, therefore, the

TABLE 5.3

*Hourly Earnings of Doffers Paid
by Uniform Piece Rate in a
Representative North Carolina
Mill, 1907*

Age in Years	Earnings	Number
Under 12	$0.074	4
12	.074	8
13	.082	11
14	.087	19
15	.092	11
16	.107	11
17	.119	7
18	.116	4

NOTE: U.S. Department of Labor, *Report on Condition of Women and Child Wage-Earners in the United States*, vol. 1 (Washington, D.C.: Government Printing Office, 1910), 230.

"maturing" of the work force was an integral component of southern textile progress.

Unlike those engaged in cotton agriculture, cotton manufacturers were able to capture some of the returns to increased production in the form of augmented regional income, even though wage rates showed little gain. (One might say, in fact, that it was the stability of wage rates that allowed the developmental process to continue, in contrast to the antebellum experience.) There were aggregate limits here too, in this case the limits set by the growth of national demand for cotton goods, which was just about as fast as the growth of U.S. national income between 1880 and 1930. Foreign demand was incidental, of interest to only a small number of firms with special connections, and constituting a small and declining fraction of total production.[19] But even while limited to the national market, the southern industry was able to grow at a rate faster than national demand so long as the southern market share was rising at the expense of New England. What form did this displacement take?

At each moment of time between 1880 and 1920, the northern and southern branches of the industry produced basically

TABLE 5.4

Average Yarn Number in Southern Cotton Mill
Production, 1879–1921

Year	Average Yarn Number	Production Year	Average Yarn Number
1879–80	13.00	1903–4	19.38
1886–87	13.67	1904–5	19.00
1887–88	13.50	1905–6	19.63
1888–89	13.88	1906–7	20.00
1889–90	14.60	1907–8	20.00
1890–91	14.81	1908–9	20.50
1891–92	14.75	1909–10	20.25
1892–93	15.44	1910–11	21.00
1893–94	15.80	1911–12	22.00
1894–95	16.25	1912–13	22.00
1895–96	17.00	1913–14	22.00
1896–97	17.75	1914–15	22.00
1897–98	18.25	1915–16	22.00
1898–99	18.00	1916–17	22.00
1899–1900	18.75	1917–18	20.00
1900–1901	19.00	1918–19	20.75
1901–2	19.00	1919–20	21.00
1902–3	19.50	1920–21	21.50

NOTE: Reprinted, by permission of John Wiley & Sons, from Gavin Wright,
"Cheap Labor and Southern Textiles, 1880–1930," *Quarterly Journal of Economics* 96 (1981): 614, table 4.
Data compiled from *Commercial and Financial Chronicle*, issues devoted
to annual cotton crop survey, August or September 1886–1921.

different products, with only a narrow "frontier" of goods persisting in each region simultaneously. Though even in 1880 the bulk of southern output came from mills that integrated spinning and weaving, the South did begin in product lines that were least capital-intensive and least demanding in terms of labor skills. A convenient illustration is the average count or "yarn number," a measure of the fineness of yarn spun.[20] Higher yarn counts are more capital- and skill-intensive than lower counts because the yarn spends more time on the spindle and breaks more frequently. Because the national average count changed little over the period, the rise in the southern figure displayed in table 5.4 may be read as a kind of scoreboard of southern market penetration. Thus we have a moving equilibrium, in which the South was gradually able to work its way up the product quality ladder by accumulating the necessary experience and capital, while New England was able to hold on for a long time on the basis of expertise in fine goods and because the overall market was growing.[21]

By this criterion the pace of the takeover was not uniform. The most rapid relative surge came in the depressed 1890s, as New England cut back production in response to weak demand only to see one product line after another fall to the South. The southern textile industry in the 1890s was in the position of Japan in the 1930s, barreling ahead with construction and production even in the midst of depression, taking advantage of the misfortunes of others, both its competitors in the North and the struggling tenant farmers in the South. It was a demoralizing time in New England. Between 1895 and 1900, a flurry of northern investments in southern branches were initiated, the one point in prewar industry history in which northern investment money was significant.[22]

Knowing as we do what the post–World War I era had in store for New England textiles, it is difficult for us today to appreciate how fully these fears dissipated after 1900, and how completely the interregional competitive atmosphere changed. As early as 1902, the English visitor Thomas M. Young was told at Lowell "that the Southern mills had already reached the limit of their advantage over the Northern mills in wages, that the 'mountain whites' were already fully employed, that the negro would never become an efficient machine-minder, and that whenever the South should come into competition with the North for immigrant mill labour the South would have to pay more than the North to get it."[23] Northern investments in southern mills ceased completely. When in 1912 Melvin T. Copeland completed his authoritative study of the industry he wrote:

No new southern branches have been established for several years, and one hears no suggestion that any are contemplated. On the contrary, one of the Lowell manufacturing companies which has a southern mill that is supposed to have yielded good returns chose to enlarge its northern plant in 1909, thus indicating that the prospects were better in Lowell than in the southern states. . . . That the fear of southern conquest has now almost entirely disappeared is attested by numerous fresh undertakings in New England.[24]

It is easy enough to indict Copeland and the New Englanders whose views he recorded for complacency and shortsightedness, especially since he concluded that on the international scene the English would be the main competitors and that "an actual decline or even cessation of expansion of the cotton manufacturing industry in any of the countries here considered is not to be expected."[25] But these opinions were derived from objective evidence, trends that lasted for two decades. What had happened?

The most immediate change was that the revival of the national economy had generated growth in demand for cotton goods, so that New England was able to increase production of the products it still controlled, even while the South continued to chip away at the margin. A deeper underlying change was that the revival of the *world* economy had accelerated demand for raw cotton, affecting the conditions of labor supply that were the key to southern textile progress. Complaints of labor shortage after 1900 were widespread and undoubtedly real. This time, in contrast to the 1850s, the industry did not shrivel up and contract. Instead, employers took active steps to recruit new workers; they were limited, however, by the racial barriers that had built up over the previous decades and by the geographic boundaries of the low-wage southern labor market.

Indeed, the term *southern labor market* is somewhat premature as applied to the textile industry before 1900. Most of the mills drew their first labor from the immediate vicinity, and in the 1880s and 1890s wage differentials between mills and local markets were often high.[26] But as employment expanded and labor markets tightened, mills attempted to slow the rise of wages by expanding their sphere of recruitment. As one millman recalled: "Labor for the early factories came from the localities—90 percent of it. But after 1900, when there was a madness of mill building, they began to pull labor from a

FIGURE 5.2

Real Wages, Textiles, and Farm Labor

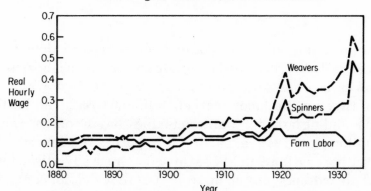

SOURCES: U.S. Bureau of Labor Statistics, *Wages and Hours of Labor*, Bulletin nos. 65, 71, 77, 128, 150, 190, 239, 262, 288, 345, 371, 446, 492, 539 (Washington, D.C.: Government Printing Office, 1906–31); U.S. Department of Agriculture, *Crops and Markets* 19 (1942): 150–55; U.S. Commissioner of Labor, *Seventh Annual Report: Wages and Hours of Labor* (Washington, D.C.: GPO, 1904).

distance of 250 miles."[27] During the severe labor shortage of 1905–7, Spartanburg mills sent agents into the mountains of North Carolina and Tennessee, advancing rail fares to bring labor to South Carolina. Companies accused each other of raiding their labor, and differentials narrowed.[28] In this way, labor mobility increased and a regional labor market was created. Surveys from the 1920s show that mountain people were a substantial minority of the labor force at representative Piedmont mills.[29]

Thus the industry continued to make progress at a slower pace after 1900, and the experienced labor force shared in this progress to some extent, as industry wage levels gradually inched up relative to farm labor (figure 5.2). The broader wage advance enjoyed by all the mill workers, however, resulted not mainly from the industry itself but from the trends in the regional labor market of which they were a part. It was inevitable that the southern industry would eventually overtake New England's; and given the confinement to the national market, it was inevitable that industry growth would slow down. But it was not inevitable that these things would happen in just the way that they did in the 1920s and 1930s.

The Family Labor System

The southern mill village has often been seen as a calculated exploitative device, designed to isolate and control a labor supply. But in its origins, the mill village was virtually forced on the industry by the labor market. William Gregg, the best-known founding father of southern textiles, began construction of dormitories in 1848, expecting to replicate the success of the "Waltham system" in Massachusetts. Gregg advertised for 400 female workers plus 30 matrons, but they did not come.[30] Then he began offering separate dwellings for whole families. At Graniteville and in other antebellum mills, employers had to offer heavily subsidized housing to entire families, even where only the young females were expected to work in the mill! These labor-supply conditions stand in contrast to those in Japan, the other great example of the triumph of cheap labor competition in textile history. Whereas Japan had a well-developed rural market in female farm labor, which textile firms were able to buy into with little difficulty, in the South, young girls worked only for their parents. It was cheaper to recruit the entire farm family than to bid separately for individual members.[31]

These considerations help to explain the remarkable imbalance in the demography of the work force in 1880 (table 5.5). The postbellum mills employed men, women, boys, and girls at all times, but in the age bracket between sixteen and twenty-four, there were nearly twice as many females as there were males. Almost all of the overall female majority may be found in this nine-year span of the life cycle. "Civil War widows" could not have been a major contributor to this situation in 1880, but selective migration undoubtedly was: families with large numbers of girls were much more likely to find the mill village attractive than families with teenage boys. The system may be thought of as a direct transfer of the family-farm work unit from the countryside to the factory, but the transfer radically changed the relative productivities of boys and girls. As one woman recalled years later: "Papa decided he would come

TABLE 5.5

Age-Sex Composition of Cotton Textile Labor Force,
1880–1920

Age in Years	Percentage of Operatives in the South[a]		Percentage of Operatives in New England[b]	
	Male	Female	Male	Female
1880				
10–15	13.9	14.0	6.4	6.6
16–24	16.9	29.4		
25 and over	12.1	13.8	44.3	42.7
	42.8[d]	57.2	50.7	49.3
1890				
10–15[c]	12.4	12.4	3.5	3.5
16–24	19.1	26.7	20.6	29.0
24 and over	18.6	10.8	25.8	17.6
	50.1	49.9	49.9	50.1
1900				
10–15	14.1	15.7	5.0	5.2
16–24	22.2	21.1	18.8	24.5
25 and over	19.4	7.3	25.8	20.7
	55.7	44.3	49.6	50.4
1920				
10–15[c]	2.5	2.5	2.5	2.5
16–24	24.7	19.8	13.9	18.8
25 and over	36.0	14.3	37.7	24.6
	63.2	36.7	54.1	45.9

NOTE: Reprinted, by permission of John Wiley & Sons, from Gavin Wright, "Cheap Labor and Southern Textiles, 1880–1930," *Quarterly Journal of Economics* 96 (1981): 611, table 3.
Data compiled from U.S. Bureau of the Census: on 1880 South from census sample, 10th Census, unpublished manuscript; on 1880 New England from *Manufactures*, 12th Census, part 1 (Washington, D.C.: Government Printing Office, 1905), table XXXI; on 1890 from *Population*, 11th Census, part 2 (Washington, D.C.: GPO, 1895), table 116, and from *Manufacture Industries*, 11th Census, part 3 (Washington, D.C.: GPO, 1895), 42; on 1900 from *Special Reports 1900: Occupations*, 12th Census (Washington, D.C.: GPO, 1904), table LXV and p. 41; on 1920 from *Population: Occupations*, 14th Census, vol. 4 (Washington, D.C.: GPO, 1923), table 1.
[a] Alabama, Georgia, North Carolina, South Carolina.
[b] Connecticut, Maine, Massachusetts, New Hampshire, Rhode Island.
[c] Male and female set equal by assumption.
[d] Due to rounding, percentages do not always add up to the totals.

because he didn't have nothing much but girls and they had to get out and work like men."[32] Thus, we have another sorting equilibrium, in which families with the fewest resources and poorest prospects in agriculture (tenants and marginal landowners) found that the family unit could do better in the mill village. Their calculation is expressed by the woman who said that she "would prefer to live in the country if conditions were favorable, and I owned my own home, with no rent to pay. But under present conditions and circumstances, owning no land, with rent to pay, I would rather live at the mills, where all of our family can work."[33]

But selective migration cannot explain the entire gap. If it did, we would expect to see a larger difference in the younger age bracket, where instead the proportions of male and female are essentially equal. Mill children typically began work somewhere between the ages of ten and fifteen, with little difference between boys and girls on this score.[34] The major difference was that young men in their late teens and early twenties were much less likely to stay on in the mill village because they had access to wage-paying jobs in agriculture, which the young women did not. We can be fairly sure this was happening because the average male wage began to pull ahead of the average female wage at sixteen years of age (table 5.6). It may perhaps be surprising that girls earned more than boys before age sixteen. But it is widely observed that girls mature faster than boys and display more physical dexterity (a phenomenon that may have social as well as physiological determinants), and it is certainly true that spinners' jobs assigned to the girls were much more demanding than the doffing work typically given to young boys. From about age sixteen onward, however, the boys began to catch up and develop higher potential productivity in the mill, but they also began to leave for better-paying job opportunities elsewhere. Their services had to be bid for in a competitive market.

This analysis shows that textile wages were indeed linked to the agricultural labor market, even if the links were sometimes indirect and loose. The family as a whole had only to receive a "family wage" that was better than their earning ability in farming, but the wages of young men could not be very different from the farm wage. Differentials above and below this level had to have at least some connection with relative productivities.

Despite this structural pattern, over the course of time the

TABLE 5.6

Hourly Earnings of Male and Female Employees in All Occupations in North Carolina Cotton Mills, 1907

Age in Years	Number of Employees		Earnings Per Hour		Female Earnings/ Male Earnings
	Male	Female	Male	Female	
Under 11	42	23	$0.044	$0.047	1.068
11	57	36	0.052	0.056	1.077
12	170	159	0.055	0.058	1.055
13	261	210	0.060	0.065	1.083
14	340	299	0.067	0.070	1.045
15	273	311	0.072	0.087	1.083
16	169	338	0.082	0.082	1.000
17	98	300	0.099	0.089	0.899
18	141	391	0.105	0.091	0.867
19	95	266	0.119	0.090	0.756
20	140	265	0.120	0.093	0.775
21	120	190	0.119	0.097	0.815
22	111	159	0.124	0.096	0.774
23	72	111	0.134	0.097	0.724
24	89	80	0.131	0.102	0.779
25 to 29	282	322	0.137	0.101	0.737
30 to 34	165	158	0.133	0.106	0.797
35 to 39	71	76	0.135	0.096	0.711
40 to 44	39	62	0.107	0.095	0.888
45 to 49	43	29	0.100	0.096	0.960
50 and over	47	20	0.099	0.088	0.889
Total who reported age	2,825	3,805	0.097	0.087	0.807

NOTE: Reprinted, by permission of John Wiley & Sons, from Gavin Wright, "Cheap Labor and Southern Textiles, 1880–1930," *Quarterly Journal of Economics* 96 (1981): 609, table 1.
Data compiled from U.S. Department of Labor, *Report on Condition of Women and Child Wage-Earners in the United States*, vol. 1 (Washington, D.C.: Goverment Printing Office, 1910), 314.

proportion of males over the age of sixteen in the industry labor force reversed itself almost completely, from less than 30 percent in 1880 to more than 60 percent in 1920. Much of this shift occurred not in the depressed years before 1900 but during the cotton-boom decades when young men were actively recruited by farm employers. The answer to this apparent paradox lies in another behavioral regularity of great importance to the family system: young men had more choices than anyone else, but a young man who was still in the industry at age twenty-five was *unlikely ever to leave.* It was not that they were trapped by debts or kept in ignorance of the outside world, but if they had no agricultural experience whatever by their mid-twenties, it was difficult to start anew at that age.

Even the so-called unskilled work of farm labor involved countless bits of knowledge and technique and familiarity, to say nothing of the need to establish credit connections if one hoped to work up the farm ladder. In contrast, a twenty-five year old who had grown up in the mill had ten to fifteen years of textile experience and was a valued worker who could look forward to some chance at promotion to top jobs like loom fixer or foreman. The young women who stayed on through their late teens and early twenties, however, began to drop out or move to an in-and-out work status as they married and had children.

Thus the swing toward older males over time was inevitable and was closely connected with the overall effectiveness of the family system in accumulating and retaining factory experience. Employers complained endlessly about "the moving disposition of mill people,"[35] but payroll studies show that within a few years of a mill's opening, average experience quickly exceeded levels under dormitory systems like Japan.[36] The Royal Cotton Mill of Wake County, North Carolina, for example, started from scratch in 1903, and by 1912 had exceeded average Japanese experience levels built up over a much longer industry history. Older mills like Alamance averaged over ten years of experience at this time. Extremely high turnover rates are often quoted for the southern textile industry, with the implication that the labor force was highly unstable and migratory. But most of this turnover was concentrated in a minority of families and unattached individuals who moved often, while the core of the labor force for a typical mill came from a group of families who were more-or-less permanent. From the standpoint of the industry as a whole, the accumulation of experience was even more rapid, because much of the turnover was from mill-to-mill rather than mill-to-farm and back.

A simulation model based on stable entry-exit behavior for males and females is able to track closely the change in the age and sex composition of the work force (see tables 5.7 and 5.8). The conception that the labor force "grew up" into its twentieth-century shape helps to unify several otherwise separate threads in industry history. One is the phenomenon of

TABLE 5.7

Age Distributions of Male and Female Southern
Textile Workers, 1890–1920 (Actual and Simulated)

Age in Years	Male		Female	
	Actual[a]	Simulated[a]	Actual[a]	Simulated[a]
1890				
24 and under	62.9	62.3	78.4	79.6
1900				
15 and under	25.3	27.4	35.5	35.7
16–24	39.9	37.1	47.7	47.5
25–44	27.2	30.4	14.5	15.1
45 and over	7.2	5.1	2.2	1.7
1907				
15 and under	—	—	26.7	27.6
16–24	—	—	52.6	53.9
25–44	—	—	18.6	16.5
45 and over	—	—	2.1	1.9
1910				
15 and under	18.6	18.6	26.5	27.2
16–24	22.4	20.0	35.7	37.8
25–44	47.5	52.0	34.7	32.6
45 and over	11.5	9.4	3.1	2.4
1915				
15 and under	14.4	15.4	17.4	24.9
1920				
17 and under	14.0	23.6	24.8	42.0
18–24	28.9	19.8	36.2	34.8
25–44	40.4	39.9	32.7	19.4
45 and over	16.7	16.7	6.3	3.8

NOTE: Reprinted, by permission of the publisher, from Gary Saxonhouse and
Gavin Wright, eds., Technique, Spirit, and Form in the Making of the Modern
Economies: Essays in Honor of William N. Parker (Greenwich, Conn.: JAI Press,
1984), 15.
[a] Actual means levels reported in the census or special survey. Simulated means
levels generated by assumed entry-exit behavior. Full details may be found in
the source.

the "tin-bucket-toters," or "cotton mill drones," indolent fathers who supposedly lived off the earnings of their children,
doing nothing more than carrying lunch pails each day.
Whether these cases were ever common is not known, but the
reports come mainly from the early days, when families came
to the mill after years of struggle to make it in agriculture.
Fathers with teenage children must have been in their thirties;
they may not have been lazy, but with no previous factory

TABLE 5.8

Sex Distribution of Southern Textile Workers
(Actual and Simulated)

	Percentage of Females			Percentage of Females	
Year	Actual[a]	Simulated[a]	Year	Actual[a]	Simulated[a]
1880	57.2	57.2	1910	37.0	45.1
1890	52.1	49.1	1915	35.0	42.6
1900	46.6	47.1	1920	38.2	41.3

NOTE: Reprinted, by permission of the publisher, from Gary Saxonhouse and Gavin Wright, eds., Technique, Spirit, and Form in the Making of the Modern Economies: Essays in Honor of William N. Parker (Greenwich, Conn.: JAI Press, 1984), 15.
[a] Actual means levels reported in the census or special survey. Simulated means levels generated by assumed entry-exit behavior. Full details may be found in the source.

experience they were not good workers and were not really wanted, except for help in monitoring the work performance of their children. When the investigators for the Report on Women and Child Labor surveyed the southern industry in 1907, they found virtually no cases of complete fatherly idleness. They did observe the following:

> The man who has worked upwards of twenty years on the farm soon discovers, however, that he is not adapted to cotton mill work. His fingers are too clumsy for the tasks requiring dexterity, and the number of common laborers required is limited. If he obtains work in the mill it is probably in the dusty picker room. After a short time his daughter, 12 to 14 years old, doing lighter work than he does earns as much or more than he. Having never been accustomed to indoor work, he tires of the confinement of the mill and seeks employment outside. He becomes a wood chopper or a carpenter, doing odd jobs, and soon joins the class that works only occasionally or not at all.[37]

It was entirely different with the young men who, having started as children and grown up in the mills, came into maturity after 1900. By the inexorable demography of the family system, this latter group predominated by 1910, if not earlier.

Another issue is the link between the labor force and the diffusion of such new technologies as the high-speed Draper automatic loom, which was rapidly adopted in the South after 1900.[38] Writers observing the rise of adult males and the relative decline of child labor seem to assume almost invariably that technology was calling the tune, that "the demands imposed by technical changes have called for more male labor."[39] Harriet Herring, the longtime student of southern mill workers, listed as one of the advantages of the mill village the fact that "cotton mills have jobs for men and women, and in the early days for children, in about the same proportion in which they are available for work in families,"[40] and suggested that the adult-male bias of new technology helps to explain the decline of the mill village in the twentieth century.

These interpretations have it backward. The family labor system would have made no sense unless the mills did all they could to design jobs so as to make use of all the family members. This was one reason why most production was in vertically integrated mills, even at the early phases of development, because combined spinning and weaving allowed the mills to make use of heterogeneous workers more effectively. The reason that job assignments became more demanding and more strenuous over time is that the system succeeded in cultivating a homegrown crop of adult male workers accustomed to indoor work and interested in routes for self-advancement within the industry. The reason for the relative decline of child labor, at least as of 1915 or so, is not that there was some built-in technological law to this effect (if it wanted to, modern technology could make much more effective use of children than nineteenth-century mechanics ever could), but that there was now a pool of experienced adults who could do the same jobs with higher productivity.

Can we say, then, that the southern mill village was fundamentally an exploitative device, a "vehicle perfectly calculated from all angles to restrict the development of the workers into independent free-acting citizens"?[41] Just as in the case of the plantation, this is not an objective economic question. In its origins, the system was more a market necessity than a calculated vehicle, and the bitter denunciations did not begin until the twentieth century (and then came mostly from non-Southerners). Child labor is intrinsically exploitative from a modern viewpoint, but this practice could be blamed as much on the parents as on the employers (as the mill owners always

145

did), and it was no more than what farm families had always done with their offspring. Families could and did move from one village to another if they were mistreated or underpaid, and young men could leave the industry entirely if they had better opportunities elsewhere. But calculated or not, the study of mill demography suggests that there was truth in reformer Frank Tannenbaum's lament, "once a mill-worker, always a mill-worker. Not only you, but your children and children's children forever and ever."[42] Young men were not likely to find good job opportunities elsewhere because they were poorly educated and were pointed toward mill work long before they reached an age of independence. Northern social critics have suggested that the public schools served to prepare students for factory labor, but the southern mills found that an even better preparation was mill work itself. Above all, the mill village system did little to widen horizons of the workers and integrate them into southern (to say nothing of national) society. Even, or perhaps especially, in the mills adjacent to cities, there was a social stigma to mill work and the mill village that recent oral-history projects vividly convey.[43]

Despite this indictment, it must also be said that within its own inward-looking terms, the mill-village, family-labor system did have a certain internal logic, a certain balance between effort and reward, a certain opportunity for individual progress and family stability, a certain sense of belonging and group support and fairness in labor relations—a certain "moral economy," if you like—in good times. An early Japanese visitor who worked in the southern mills for a year reported back to his countrymen that the southern system was much better than their own, noting particularly the high skill, diligence, and morale of the American workers, the quality of supervision, the absence of drunkenness, and the strong sense of mutual obligation between employers and employees.[44] But times did not stay good, and in the 1920s, the conjunction of market forces and the evolutionary tendencies of the family system produced a crisis that ultimately led to the system's demise.

The Crisis of the 1920s

The New England textile industry began a bitter, painful, and thoroughgoing collapse in the 1920s, and the eyes of the nation looked to the South for the culprit. Even the famous Harvard free trader Frank Taussig described the southern expansion as "a semi-artificial and almost insensate growth," and as early as 1926, a writer observed that "the columns of the textile press reporting the discontinuance and liquidation and abandonment of New England mills read like wartime casualty lists."[45] Most Northerners thought the enemy was the South. But those close to the industry knew that the southern mills were stumbling too. Conditions were by no means as drastic as in New England, but a glance at figure 5.1 will show that new investment slowed down markedly in the South as well. Statements that the South was "industrializing rapidly" in the 1920s are often misleading, because they are based on employment figures. The number of *workers* in southern mills did grow substantially, from 190,000 in 1919 to 270,000 in 1929, but many of these had trouble finding full-time work. Profits were low, and southern as well as northern firms took losses in bad years. Even large well-managed firms felt it. The famous Dan River Mills of Danville, Virginia, had established an elaborate system of welfare benefits and "industrial democracy" in 1919, complete with a "house of representatives," "senate," and "cabinet." But the system fell into disrepute and decline when the company was unable to pay the promised "economy dividend" regularly after 1923.[46] All of these difficulties were clearly visible before the Great Depression of the 1930s. The "migration" of northern capital into the South, which began in earnest in the 1920s, in fact reflected distress in both regions. A million spindles were literally carried South during the decade, a sign that the future in New England was utterly without hope. But southern firms also went under during these years, many of them falling into the hands of northern creditors in the process.

The underlying causes of the great textile depression were fundamental, but they were widely misperceived by contemporaries. The North blamed oppressive labor conditions and "unfair competition" from the South, which was of course partially true but by no means new in the 1920s. Industry spokesmen in both regions blamed "excess capacity," the competitive structure of the industry, and unfavorable trends in demand. But the textile industry had always been competitive, and demand estimates for textiles do not indicate that any major slowdown had occurred in the domestic market in the 1920s.[47] Capacity was "excess" only because the American industry had grown up behind a tariff wall since the Civil War, and had long since priced itself out of foreign markets. This long-term commitment to the domestic market did place limits on potential growth, but these constraints were exacerbated in the 1920s by the sharp increase in wage costs in both regions. The increase in real hourly wages of textile workers, relative to prewar levels and relative to farm wages, is plainly visible in figure 5.2, and, though it was rarely discussed explicitly at the time, it constituted the major new fact of economic life in the decade of the 1920s. The increase was not an artifact of geographic or compositional changes in the industry or the work force.[48] The very same relationships are observed for particular states and counties and even individual mills: Table 5.9 presents an illustration using the Royall Cotton Mill of Wake County, North Carolina, as an example.

The argument that weak demand caused the problem is really only valid for the South. Given that the competition was for the national market, it was inevitable that the growth of the southern branch would slow down, because the southern market share could not go on increasing. But the alacritous contraction in New England actually gave some temporary relief on this score; market simulations indicate that southern production and profits during the 1920s were somewhat better than an extrapolation of prewar trends would predict. The important point is that demand-side constraints might explain a gradual slowing of growth, a "soft landing" onto a sustainable path. They do not explain the emergence of "surplus labor" conditions in southern textiles in the 1920s. Before World War

TABLE 5.9

Mean Daily Wages, Royall Cotton Mill
and North Carolina Farm Labor, 1902–29

	Mean Daily Wages (in Dollars)		
Year	Royall	Farm Labor, North Carolina	Farm Labor, Wake County
1902	—	.66	—
1903	.77	—	—
1904	.79	—	—
1905	.83	—	—
1906	.87	.92	—
1907	.91	—	—
1908	.87	—	—
1909	.98	.89	—
1910	.93	.97	—
1911	.93	.99	—
1912	1.00	1.03	—
1913	1.03	1.06	—
1914	1.17	1.02	.82–1.32
1915	1.09	1.02	.87–1.19
1916	—	1.11	.83–1.24
1917	1.57	1.50	—
1918	2.02	1.97	1.00–1.52
1919	3.08	2.50	—
1920	4.01	2.85	2.00–2.75
1921	2.18	1.60	—
1922	1.92	1.75	1.79
1923	2.31	1.75	—
1924	2.50	1.88	1.56
1925	2.28	2.09	—
1926	2.23	1.90	1.91
1927	2.27	1.84	—
1928	2.32	1.88	—
1929	2.38	1.81	—

SOURCES: Royall Cotton Mill payroll records, Duke University Library; U.S. Department of Agriculture, Crops and Markets, vol. 19, no. 5 (Washington, D.C.: Government Printing Office, 1942); North Carolina Department of Labor and Printing, Annual Reports, vols. 28–35 (Raleigh, N.C.: State Printers, 1914–1926).

I, the southeastern white labor market was essentially equilibrated between sectors. After 1920, it was a dual economy, with a substantial "wage gap" between agriculture and the largest component of the industrial sector.

In the first instance, the wage increase was a legacy of the World War I boom time, which continued through to the Fall of 1920. Farm and industry labor markets were tight, production was strong, and inflation was rampant, so that nominal wages had to increase by two to three times, just to keep pace. By 1920, however, *real* wages were at a peak for both farm and textile labor. The difference was that farm wages were flexible downward while textile wages were "sticky." Though there was a nominal wage cut during the deflation of 1920–22, real wages stayed at their new plateau, now well above the farm wage.

All the symptoms that an economist would predict, given this information, began to appear in southern textiles at this time. Mills kept rolls of "spare-hands," who showed up each day hoping to fill a vacancy, and these lists grew longer and longer. One superintendent explained: "[We have] more than we want, but folks come from the farm and beg to be taken on, and if they can find a place in the village to live we give them a chance."[49] These "extras" were regularly sent home, and even regular employees were asked to "rest" frequently, to share the work among a larger number.[50] Access to the mill village came to be tied to extra stipulations, such as the promise to provide family workers for the night shift. Northern critics complained about weak regulations on work hours in the southern states, but, in fact, the standard workweek declined in the 1920s. Even with the shorter week, the percentage of full time actually worked was down (table 5.10). The high turnover rates reported by surveys in the 1920s are often cited as evidence of the persistence of rural folkways and premodern work habits, but this is a grievous misreading of the situation: textile workers moved around in the 1920s because at mill after mill they could not find steady work.[51]

This may seem to be an unsympathetic treatment, a case of blaming the victim. How could anyone claim that the southern mill workers, of all people, could have been overpaid? But it is not a question of blame, or of begrudging improvement in the workers' living standards, which were certainly low by national standards. Southern mill workers had reason to feel that they were not much better off. In the case of the Royall Cotton Mill, figure 5.3 shows that while hourly wage *rates* had risen dramatically, real weekly *earnings* had not, at least not for all workers. What is most striking, however, is the change

TABLE 5.10

Hours of Work in New England and Southern Textile Mills

	1907		1924		1928	
	New England	South	New England	South	New England	South
Percent of Full-Time Actually Worked						
Ring spinners[a]	83	82	78	73	81	65
Speeder tenders[b]	87	78	83	80	83	71
Spoolers[a]	86	78	83	77	85	71
Doffers[c]	82	81	81	75	82	71
Weavers[b]	88	80	84	79	86	71
Hours Actually Worked, Per Week						
Ring spinners	48.7	51.2	39.8	40.4	41.5	37.1
Speeder tenders	50.7	49.1	42.1	44.4	41.7	40.0
Spoolers	50.0	48.6	41.3	42.4	42.2	39.5
Doffers	48.0	51.0	40.9	41.8	42.3	39.3
Weavers	51.2	50.1	42.3	43.7	43.0	39.6

Full-Time Hours Per Week

Year	Spinners in S.C.	Weavers in S.C.	Slasher Tenders S.C.	N.C.	Ga.
1900	66	66	—	—	—
1902	66	66	—	—	—
1904	66	66	—	—	—
1906	65.7	65.5	—	—	—
1908	60.1	60.4	60	65.3	63.2
1910	60	60	60	62.5	62.2
1912	60	60	60	60	60
1914	60	60	60	60	60
1916	60	60	60	60	60
1918	56.5	59.9	60	60.2	60
1920	54.0	54.3	55	55.2	56.4
1922	54.2	54.9	55	55.2	56.8
1924	55	55	55	55.3	55.9
1926	55	55	55	55.5	56.3
1928	55	55	55	55.4	56.3

NOTE: Reprinted, by permission of the publisher, from Martha Shiells and Gavin Wright, "Night Work as a Labor Market Phenomenon: Southern Textiles in the Interwar Period," *Explorations in Economic History* 20 (1983): 346, table 2.

Data compiled from U.S. Department of Labor, *Report on Condition of Women and Child Wage-Earners in the United States*, vol. 1 (Washington, D.C.: Government Printing Office, 1910), 262–69; U.S. Bureau of Labor Statistics, Bulletin nos. 371 and 492 (Washington, D.C.: GPO, 1924, 1928).

[a] Females only.
[b] Both females and males.
[c] Males only.

FIGURE 5.3

Earnings Profiles, Royall Cotton Mill

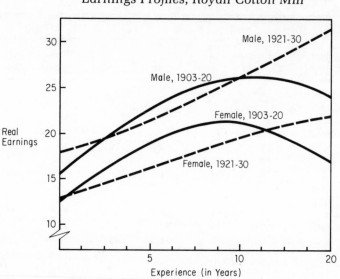

SOURCE: Royall Cotton Mill payroll records, Duke University Library.

in the shape of the curves relating earnings to experience. Before the war, the curvilinear shapes reflect the relationship between experience and productivity. After the war, the straight-line functions reflect the new reality that earnings were heavily determined by the rationing of jobs and work hours. The experience of one mill may not reflect the developments elsewhere, but the patterns displayed in figure 5.3 make economic sense: women were squeezed out much more than men, and the chief beneficiaries were the men with most years of experience. With labor in excess supply, it is no wonder that the industry acquiesced in the abolition of child labor in the 1920s, after having resisted this reform for years.[52] But for families who had previously depended on the earnings of every family member, it is by no means clear that they were better off on balance in the 1920s.

Wage stickiness is commonly observed in industrial labor markets, and, indeed, many other U.S. industries and countries had to deal with the dislocation of the wage scale in the wake of World War I. The observation that wage cutting is unrealistic as a remedy for unemployment is the starting point for Keynesian economics, which drew its inspiration not just from the Great Depression but from the chronic unemployment in British industry during the 1920s. What is distinctive about southern textiles was not wage stickness but the anomaly that this phenomenon occurred in the midst of a depressed, low-wage agricultural economy, an economy with virtually none of the institutions commonly held responsible for wage stickiness—unions, welfare, minimum wage laws, public-sector employment. What southern textiles did have by the 1920s, however, was maturity. The majority of workers were adult male heads of households, who had little formal education but had grown up in the mills and planned on staying. Most of the foremen, superintendents, and loom fixers were "career men."[53] These men and their families had developed a strong sense of community identity, of job hierarchies, and of the proper way for tasks to be performed. And like most Americans, they had a set of expectations about the individual progress they would make and the kind of jobs they could move into if they worked well and stayed on with an employer.

The problem was that the industry was top-heavy with older males. The mill village, which had functioned so well to retain workers and accumulate valuable experience, had overshot industry labor force requirements by the 1920s. Given the wage scale and given demand conditions, there was no way that the industry could provide enough top-of-the-line jobs for the men who thought they were entitled to them. The South in 1930 had one loom fixer for every three weavers, and even at this ratio, there was grumbling that these positions were passed out to company loyalists no more qualified than many other weavers. Doffing, which was performed by boys in 1900, was done by men in their thirties in 1930. Articles began to appear in the *Southern Textile Bulletin* on the need to turn down for promotions to overseer experienced, forty-year-old men in favor of younger men.[54]

As understandable as the workers' plight may have been, for the employers there were only two options: (a) aggressive wage cutting, or (b) active measures to raise worker productivity and take better advantage of the work force they had grown. The first was ruled out with few exceptions, as it was sure to trigger labor revolt, to say nothing of adverse outside attention. Even at earlier points in southern textile history, outright wage cuts had precipitated walkouts and turmoil in older centers of production.[55] Even the nominal wage cut of 1920–21, when the general price level fell by more than 35 percent, caused the "largest, bitterest strike" in southern textiles to that time, involving 9,000 workers in nine towns.[56] And replacing an older experienced group of workers with a set of new recruits off the farm was tantamount to throwing away fifty years of progress in labor skills and socialization. For these reasons, the employers opted for the second alternative, productivity change, but this did not save them from labor revolt.

In a series of strikes and walkouts that spread across the entire textile region between 1929 and 1931, southern workers resisted the "stretch-out," a program of increasing loom assignments for weavers and stepping up the work pace for many other tasks. Sometimes wage cuts were also involved, but nearly every strike demanded an end to the "stretch-out." The great majority were spontaneous actions at first (usually led by weavers and loom fixers), but they often became bitter and violent, and soon attracted national attention and the participation of outside labor organizations. The most spectacular and confrontational strikes (Elizabethton, Gastonia, and Marion) resulted in worker defeats, but many others won concessions and reversals. For example, in the Greenville, South Carolina, area it was reported:

> Of the fifteen strikes against the system in this region in three weeks all but four have been won, and the leaderless strikers have returned with flying colors. The truth is that not one of these strikes could have been won if conventional strike tactics and union organizers had been used. . . . For the time being the weakness of these leaderless strikers is their strength.[57]

The workers had a good deal of implicit power to block changes in 1930 "for the time being," but one could see in these events the beginning of the end for the mill village and the family labor system.

From this point forward, further industry progress took the form of installing ever-more-advanced high-speed automatic machinery, operated by ever-smaller numbers of workers.

The Rise of Southern Textiles

Though textiles had carried thousands of southern families into the modern era, and though many companies have managed to survive and grow through technological and managerial sophistication, the industry's role as a dynamic source of regional employment growth was essentially over by 1930. It was a regional triumph that never had a golden age, never a heyday of prosperity like that enjoyed by Lancashire and New England. The southern textile industry was unable to parlay its decades of progress into export markets; instead, having hardly had time to savor its victory in the national market, it found itself vulnerable to import competition. The fundamental reason for this state of affairs was that the industry was no longer able to buy its labor at the low wage levels of southern farm workers. The farm-factory wage gap that opened in the 1920s widened still further n the 1930s, until the southern industry was in effect paying a national wage and adopting a labor-saving technology intended for an embattled high-wage environment. This has been the industry story down to the present.

The political forces that brought about this redirection were not all clearly visible in 1930, but became so in the course of the next decade. We return to this narrative in chapter 7.

6

SOUTHERN INDUSTRY, THE COLONIAL ECONOMY, AND BLACK WORKERS

COTTON MANUFACTURING was not the only growing southern industry, but there were not many equally spectacular success stories before World War II. Most industries produced a narrow range of cheap, standardized, low-skill commodities that embodied relatively little processing and hence added relatively little value to the (southern) raw material. As more of the regional industrial capital stock fell into the hands of outside owners, while Southerners still had to look to the North to buy goods made with their own cloth or lumber or iron, it was understandable that they came to feel that they were part of a "colonial economy." And in the circumstances, perhaps it was inevitable that this colonial relationship came to be seen as not just a description but also an explanation for the regional plight. This analysis has been echoed by historians ever since. Sheldon Hackney, writing in 1972 about the enduring legacy of C. Vann Woodward's *Origins of the New South*, summarized the case this way:

> The reasons for the slow rate of industrial development are not far to seek. The South was a colonial economy. It remained overwhelmingly a region of staple-crop agriculture and extractive in-

dustries. This meant that southerners bought almost all their manufactured goods, and not a little of their food, from outside the region. Not only that, but southern railroads and other establishments in the modern sector were increasingly controlled by outside capital. Profits that might have been re-invested in southern enterprise or helped to stimulate the local economy were drained off to the North. More important, decisions affecting the economic health of the region were made by men in northern boardrooms who had a vested interest in maintaining it in its colonial status.[1]

On close scrutiny, however, these patterns cannot be blamed on the schemes and powers of outsiders. They reflect primarily the burdens of historical timing and the characteristics of the southern labor market.

Is it the case, therefore, that the "colonial economy" idea is simply erroneous, an example of scapegoating and demagoguery that should be demolished and buried once and for all? Not at all. We ought to do more than simply evaluate this argument within the same terms of reference that gave rise to it, fifty to one hundred years ago; we should also ask what it was about the South and its development that made the colonial economy idea seem so right to those generations. Southerners had a distinct enough heritage and culture and perspective for southern businessmen to feel part of a regional business community. The South remained separate enough, as a labor market and as a people, that Southerners continued to feel like citizens of a separate country. Yet it was a "country" that was not large enough or strong enough or cohesively organized enough to have its own technology, its own industrial standards, specifications, techniques. Southerners were continually having to adapt to what they took to be a "northern" approach. And given the fact that applied technology prior to World War II progressed in channels that had strong geographically- and culturally-specific components, these Southerners were often right. The standardization of the national railroad gauge at northern dimensions in 1886 was an appropriate symbol of their sense of regional subservience.

The preeminent distinctiveness of the southern context was the labor market. Americans presume that mechanized, labor-saving techniques are always more advanced because that has been the mainstream path of the high-wage American economy. But labor-intensive technologies can be advanced and sophisticated too, as the course of Japanese development shows. This is what the South was lacking, and this is what kept the image of colonial status alive and real. Southern industry did, however, have to develop its own ways of handling the problem of its nation-within-a-nation, the black population. Here too, Americans who take their own country's development path as the natural, self-evidently logical one have also believed that the process of industrialization would inevitably undermine and dissolve what they take to be "traditional" or "customary" relationships, such as southern race relations. One group of scholars writes:

> The industrial society tends to be an open society, inconsistent with the assignment of workers to occupations or to jobs by traditional caste, racial groups, by sex or family status.[2]

The logic of the marketplace and the pressures of competition are often portrayed in this way as social solvents, dissolvers of traditional prejudices and loyalties (albeit often all too slowly). But this is not what we see in the South. The southern industrial workplace was highly segregated, and its lines of segregation were remarkably persistent through good times and bad. This chapter rejects the view that the "forces of tradition" were more potent than the "forces of modernization" or the "forces of the market." What happened instead was that profit-seeking firms increasingly came to see their segregation patterns as "natural," dictated not just by racial norms but by the observable skills and qualities of black and white workers. Thus southern industrialization did not necessarily open doors of advancement for blacks, and may even have increased racial inequality, despite, and indeed because of, the existence and functioning of regional markets for industrial labor.

TABLE 6.1

Southern Labor Force in Mines, Forests, and Factories, 1870–1930
(in Thousands)

Year	Mining		Forest		Manufacturing	
	Number	Percentage of Total	Number	Percentage of Total	Number	Percentage of Total
1870	4	0.1	5	0.2	218	6.8
1880	7	0.1	9	0.2	320	7.0
1890	29	0.5	24	0.4	515	9.6
1900	59	0.8	44	0.6	747	10.4
1910	84	0.9	56	0.6	1296	13.5
1920	106	1.1	57	0.6	1665	17.7
1930	121	1.1	56	0.5	2117	19.3

SOURCE: Harvey S. Perloff, et al., Regions, Resources and Economic Growth (Baltimore: The Johns Hopkins University Press, 1960), 622–35.

Patterns of Southern Industry to 1930

With the redirection of southern economic life after the Civil War, a steadily increasing share of the region's labor force moved into nonagricultural wage-labor employment. Particularly after 1880, intensified exploitation of mineral and forest resources pulled workers into coal mines in Alabama, Tennessee, and southern Appalachia, and into logging camps in virtually all parts of the South. Though most regional industry had a regional resource base, manufacturing was at all times substantially larger than the "primary product" or extractive industries (mining and logging), and only manufacturing showed continuous growth in both employment and output in every decade after 1870 (table 6.1).

It may be surprising that until the 1920s, the largest southern manufacturing industry in both employment and value-added was not cotton goods but lumber and timber products (table 6.2). About two-thirds of the labor force under this heading worked at sawmills or some other phase of processing, rather than logging, so the industry is properly classified as manufacturing. But it is not surprising that lumbering has received far less attention from social and economic historians and critics than has textiles. It was a manufacturing industry with an

TABLE 6.2
Leading Southern Manufacturing Industries, 1880, 1910, and 1930

Industry	Employment	Percentage of U.S. Employment	Percentage of U.S. Value-Added
1880			
Lumber and timber products	27,690	17.0	13.5
Tobacco manufactures	23,068	26.4	16.2
Cotton goods	16,389	9.4	6.9
Iron and steel	8,094	5.9	3.0
Turpentine and resin	7,995	99.9	99.9
Foundry and machine shop products	5,317	3.7	3.4
Fertilizers	3,353	39.0	28.9
Cotton seed oil and cake	3,174	95.6	94.7
Printing and publishing	3,151	5.4	4.6
Boots and shoes	2,392	1.8	3.4
Men's clothing	2,369	1.5	1.3
1910			
Lumber and timber products	304,093	43.8	38.5
Cotton goods	145,589	38.4	30.8
Cars and general shop construction by steam railroad companies	49,499	17.5	15.8
Turpentine and resin	39,511	100.0	100.0
Tobacco manufactures	31,578	18.9	21.2
Foundry and machine shop products	23,313	4.3	3.6
Printing and publishing	19,765	7.6	6.5
Cotton seed oil and cake	15,798	92.5	96.6
Hosiery and knit goods	14,176	11.0	7.3
Furniture and refrigerators	12,436	9.7	7.3
Iron and steel	11,000[a]	3.9[a]	3.0[a]
Fertilizers	10,635	58.1	56.6
1930			
Cotton goods	269,991	63.5	58.3
Lumber and timber products	241,446	44.7	36.0
Car and general construction and repair by steam railroad companies	69,803	18.9	17.2
Hosiery and knit goods	53,502	25.7	17.1
Turpentine and resin	40,157	100.0	100.0
Tobacco manufacturers	37,000[a]	31.9	58.0
Furniture	32,487	16.8	11.5

TABLE 6.2, continued

Industry	Employment	Percentage of U.S. Employment	Percentage of U.S. Value-Added
Printing and publishing	25,129	8.9	6.9
Foundry and machine shop products	21,986	4.8	4.1
Men's clothing	19,021	10.1	4.4
Iron and steel	18,198	4.3	4.0
Cotton seed oil and cake	14,452	91.3	85.0
Fertilizers	13,298	63.5	57.5

SOURCES: U.S. Bureau of the Census, *Manufactures*, 10th Census (1880), vol. 2 (Washington, D.C.: Government Printing Office, 1883); *Population: Occupational Statistics*, 13th Census (1910), vol. 8 (Washington, D.C.: GPO, 1914); *Population: Occupations by States*, 15th Census (1930), vol. 2 (Washington, D.C.: GPO, 1933).
ᵃ Partially estimated.

extractive and nonpermanent base. The rapid growth after 1880 was clearly a "catching-up" after a long delay; in that year there was more than twice as much pine timber left in the South as in the rest of the nation.[3] Logging camps were isolated, temporary affairs, in which the great majority of the workers were "single, homeless, and possessionless."[4] The sawmills were somewhat more lasting, but even here the company's time horizon was usually no more than ten to fifteen years at a given site. As the secretary of a large sawmill company explained to a group asking about labor conditions in the 1920s:

> I do wish to state in connection with the sawmill operation that about 90 percent of such manufacturing projects are temporary establishments. In other words, a sawmill operation can last only as long as it has a timber supply. When this supply of raw material is exhausted there is little left to a sawmill operation that can be classified as much better then junk. In view of those conditions ... it is always a foregone conclusion when starting a sawmill operation that there is only a limited number of years during which it can be operated. Consequently, the program of constructions and development is governed accordingly. Therefore, you can readily realize that a sawmill operation having only a short life cannot very well construct expensive dwellings for its employees, or expand too much in the way of recreational work.[5]

Because the sawmills themselves were temporary, the work force was even more temporary and did not build up either the sense of self-identity or the social visibility of the cotton mill people. Also contributing to this invisibility was the fact that a majority of southern lumber workers were black, and many industry people found it easier to blame their low labor standards on race:

> The sawmill Negro is rather shiftless and is not inclined to stay long in one location and consequently there is little incentive on the part of the operator or owner to carry on welfare work in any extensive manner.[6]

In most areas, lumbering made no lasting contribution to local development, and for the South as a whole, employment and national market share peaked before World War I. By the 1920s, many areas were cut over and production was declining precipitously.[7] The turpentine and rosin industry (the old "naval stores" from colonial times) showed a similar kind of life-cycle trajectory. But there were some sustained developments linked initially to lumbering, most notably furniture manufacture. Beginning with the first southern furniture factory built at High Point, North Carolina, in 1888, products of this industry gradually displaced those made by northern producers in local and regional markets, and by the 1920s the industry was becoming a factor in national markets. The development of the furniture industry was similar to that of textiles; at the beginning, only the cheapest kinds of furniture were made, but gradually quality and variety were built up so that production in areas like High Point continued to grow even after the original local supplies of cheap timber were exhausted.[8] Even by 1930, however, furniture accounted for only one-tenth the employment and one-ninth the value-added of cotton textiles and related industries (hosiery and clothing).

Indeed, all other industries were small after textiles and lumber (table 6.2). Though particular areas of industrial concentration became large enough to affect labor market conditions in surrounding areas (such as textiles, tobacco, and furniture in North Carolina), the southern labor force as a whole remained overwhelmingly agricultural, and this was still true in 1930 and for some time thereafter. This fact is closely related

TABLE 6.3

Comparison of South and Non-South Value-Added
Per Worker, 1910

Type of Industry	South	Non-South
Lumber and timber products	820	1020
Cotton goods	544	764
Cars and general shop construction by steam railroad companies	657	746
Turpentine and resin	516	—
Tobacco manufactures	1615	1394
Foundry and machine shop products	1075	1307
Printing and publishing	1760	2100
Cotton seed oil and cake	1715	—
Hosiery and knit goods	461	724
Furniture and refrigerators	732	1052
Iron and steel	1182[a]	1433
Fertilizer	1833	1947

SOURCE: U.S. Bureau of the Census, *Reports by States*, 13th Census (1910), vol. 9 (Washington, D.C.: Government Printing Office, 1912).
[a] Partially estimated.

to another characteristic that southern industries, with few exceptions, had in common: they paid low wages and they added relatively little value to the raw materials with which they worked. Professor Vann Woodward was neither the first nor the last to lament that "the South seems to have had a fatal attraction" for low-wage, low value-creating industries, implying perhaps that the region's low wages were attributable to the low quality of its industries.[9]

It is much more likely that the industries that emerged in the South were those that could make effective use of the region's relatively cheap unskilled labor. Most of these were labor-intensive industries in general. A good indication that labor market features were determining is given in table 6.3, which shows that *within* industry categories, southern firms generated less value-added per worker than firms outside. In some cases the gap was as high as 40 to 50 percent. This reflects two general components: specialization in cheaper product lines within broad industry categories, and less use of labor-saving mechanized techniques in producing the same commodities. Examination of equipment inventories for Alabama iron-making firms, for example, shows that in the late 1920s, they were still using hand methods that had been phased out as early as the 1890s in the North.[10] Mechanization and productivity in the southern lumber industry remained far below standards set elsewhere. As one employer put it: "Instead of installing machinery to do the work, we always undertook to do it putting in another cheap negro."[11] The one exception, tobacco, does not really refute the rule. In 1880 southern tobacco manufactures were far below the national average in value-added per worker. The high levels of value-added over the period 1890–1910 reflect primarily the cigarette profits of the American Tobacco Company (ATC), a monopoly in which southern production predominated. Cigar production in the North remained decentralized and competitive. Subsequently, after the dissolution of the ATC in 1911, the high profits were transmuted into high selling costs from advertising and brand name promotion.[12] Whatever else they might represent, high levels of value-added per worker in the southern tobacco industry did not represent high wages. As of 1907, the median weekly earnings of males in the cigarette industry of North Carolina were only $7.35, a figure 37 percent below the New York equivalent. In the North Carolina smoking, chewing, and snuff division, weekly earnings for males were only $5.55, for females only $3.47.[13] It is true that an early commitment to the Bonsack cigarette-making machine was the key to the success of the Dukes and the American tobacco industry, but the precigarette phases (stemming, stripping, and other leaf-handling tasks) remained almost completely unmechanized until the 1930s.

Labor-intensive industries are not necessarily backward and slow growing. As in the case of farming, much of the perception of southern technological backwardness reflects the labor-saving, high-wage bias of the northern milieu. The examples of furniture and textiles show that a learning-and-development process could take place even in a low-wage, low-skill industry, and the example of cigarettes shows that even a sophisticated corporate enterprise of national and international stature could emerge in the low-wage labor market of the South. If the South specialized in making simple, cheap, undifferentiated items that may have required further processing elsewhere, surely this pattern was no more than the most promising bootstraps approach to economic progress, given the region's resources and relative advantage. And yet the feeling persists that these factors are not enough; that the South was a colonial economy in the deeper sense that development was actively discouraged and even actively suppressed by northern capital. The prime example is Birmingham steel.

IRON AND STEEL

The iron and steel industry was the biggest disappointment of the New South. It had such promise in the beginning. The old charcoal-burning industry in Virginia, Tennessee, Alabama, and several other states quickly revived and expanded after 1865. The real boost came with the first use of coke as a fuel for making pig iron in Rockwood, Tennessee, in 1867. This success launched the rapid growth of Chattanooga as an iron-making center in the 1870s; by 1885 the city boasted nine furnaces with seventeen foundries and machine shops. Iron industry growth spread through the entire southern mineral belt, and was uninterrupted until the depression of the 1890s (table 6.4). Birmingham, Alabama, established in 1871 as a real estate speculation at the anticipated intersection of two railroad lines, was only one of dozens of such towns attempting to capitalize on the combination of cheap coal, coke ovens, blast furnaces, and railroads.[14]

Even when production in the other states faltered in the 1890s, Alabama's, especially Birmingham's, continued to surge ahead. That city's unique locational advantages are obvious from the map (figure 6.1). No other site in the nation was so well located with respect to both iron and coal deposits. What industry men refer to as "assembly costs" (the costs of bringing coal and iron to the same location) were lower there than in any of the other national centers of production. Though as late as 1886, Chattanooga was still regarded as "the centre of iron-making in the South," in that same year the Tennessee Coal Iron and Railway Company (TCI) bought its way into the Birmingham area, and over the succeeding years, TCI and Birmingham came to dominate the southern industry. With his eye on the mineral maps and observing that the South was

TABLE 6.4

Pig Iron Production by State, 1856–1900
(in Thousands of Tons)

Year	Va.	Ga.	Tenn.	Ala.
1856	6		71[a]	1
1872	21		110[a]	12
1878	17	16	28	41
1879	19	20	41	50
1880	30	27	71	77
1881	84	37	87	98
1882	88	42	138	113
1883	153	45	134	172
1884	157	43	135	190
1885	164	33	161	227
1886	156	46	200	284
1887	175	41	250	293
1888	197	39	268	449
1889	224	25	267	707
1890	293	29	—	817
1891	295	50	292	796
1892	343	10	300	915
1893	303	40	208	727
1894	298	40	213	592
1895	347	31	248	854
1896	386	15	248	922
1897	308	17	272	948
1898	283	14	263	1,034
1899	365	18	346	1,084
1900	491	29	362	1,184

SOURCES: Kenneth Warren, The American Steel Industry, 1850–1970 (Oxford: Clarendon Press, 1973), 67; U.S. Bureau of the Census, Statistical Abstract of the United States, vols. 9–23 (Washington, D.C.: Government Printing Office, 1879–1901).
[a] Includes Kentucky.

supplying the bulk of the cast iron pipe for the new water and gas lines going in around the country, Andrew Carnegie declared in 1889 that "the South is Pennsylvania's most formidable industrial enemy."[15] Even in 1906, the southern industrial journalist Richard Edmonds noted that regional pig iron production had doubled every ten years since the war, and predicted that production would surely reach 7,500,000 tons by 1916.[16] It didn't come close, and the problem was steel.

Although the South was a great success in the cast iron pipe market, demand was increasingly shifting to steel. When a TCI representative discovered in 1896 that Alabama pig iron was

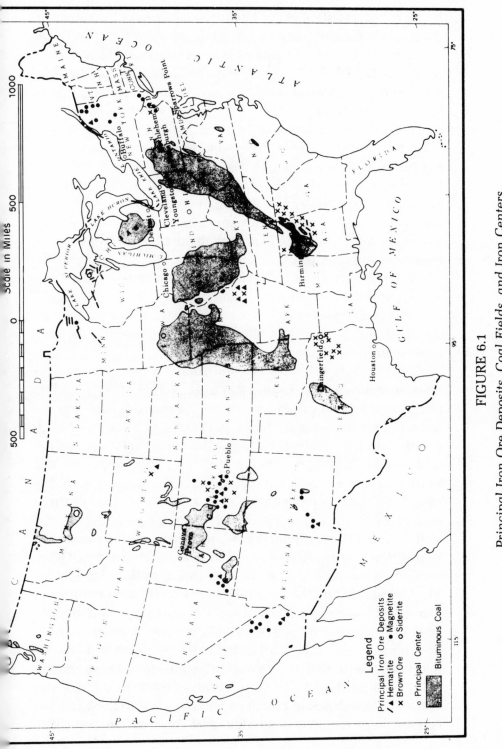

FIGURE 6.1

Principal Iron Ore Deposits, Coal Fields, and Iron Centers

NOTE: Reprinted, by permission of the publisher, from Herman Hollis Chapman et al., *The Iron and Steel Industries of the South* (University: University of Alabama Press, 1953), map 5.

being made into steel at the Homestead Works of the Carnegie Company, the company began basic open-hearth steel production in 1898 at its Ensley plant. A sequence of technical problems held back the early expansion of steel production, and having committed itself to a large expansion with little to show for it, the company found itself in severe financial straits even before the business contraction crisis of 1907. It was purchased by the U.S. Steel Corporation in that year, much to the joy of the local press, which praised the buy-out as "enough to cause sincere public thanksgiving," a "fulfillment of promise" that would "make the Birmingham district hum as it has never hummed before." One paper predicted that the new owners would "make the Birmingham district the largest steel-making centre in the universe."[17] The subsequent growth, however, was agonizingly slow, inching up to no higher than 4 percent of the national steel market forty years later (figure 6.2). It seemed clear in retrospect to many historians and economists that U.S. Steel had bought up a threatening rival only to slow its growth.

Not only does this mystery story have a prime suspect, it has a weapon as well. From 1900 to 1924, U.S. Steel priced its products using a formula known as "Pittsburgh Plus": the delivered price at any point was equal to the price in Pittsburgh plus freight from Pittsburgh, regardless of actual costs and actual freight. When the manager of the newly acquired TCI branch protested that this system unfairly handicapped Birmingham, the company changed to a flat differential of three dollars a ton above the Pittsburgh price for plates, bars, and shapes. This "Birmingham differential" remained in force until World War I, when it was raised to five dollars per ton. Other products continued to be priced at Pittsburgh Plus. When U.S. Steel was forced by the Federal Trade Commission to move to a multiple basing point system in 1924, the company still managed to freeze some "phantom freight" into the Birmingham base price, so that it was not until 1938 that the discriminatory handicap was actually removed. The effects of these pricing policies, according to industry critics, were to restrict the growth of Birmingham's steel production, and to deny the entire southern region the benefits of its abundant minerals.[18]

FIGURE 6.2

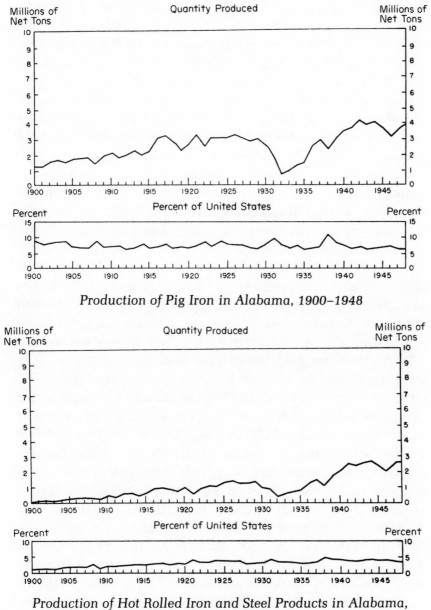

Production of Pig Iron in Alabama, 1900–1948

Production of Hot Rolled Iron and Steel Products in Alabama, 1900–1948

NOTE: Reprinted, by permission of the publisher, from Herman Hollis Chapman et al., *The Iron and Steel Industries of the South* (University: University of Alabama Press, 1953), 124, chart 12. Data from American Iron and Steel Institute.

As powerful as this circumstantial case may appear to be, on close examination of the evidence, the sluggish performance of southern iron and steel cannot primarily be blamed on the policies of U.S. Steel. The problem with the "colonial economy" diagnosis is not necessarily with the motive, but with the effects. In other areas of the country, the very same pricing formula is given credit for encouraging the geographic dispersion of steel production. In Pennsylvania, Ohio, Illinois, and Michigan, the "price umbrella" generously provided by U.S. Steel allowed old firms to survive and expand, and new firms to appear and grow.[19] It is a familiar proposition in international trade theory that so long as a region remains a deficit-producing area, local firms will not charge less then the import price (in this case, Pittsburgh Plus). If U.S. Steel had aggressively sold cheap Pittsburgh steel in the South (as the German iron and steel cartel did in many countries), they could plausibly have been accused of "dumping" with the motive of destroying southern competition. Instead, the company's conservatism held open the umbrella of protection to southern firms, yet few of them emerged, and those that did had no great success.

In many ways the Birmingham location was not really as good in practice as it seemed in theory. U.S. Steel did in fact pour $23.5 million into improvements and expansion at Birmingham between 1907 and 1913, yet encountered a continuing series of problems in labor costs, product quality, and marketing. Southern labor was industrially inexperienced and turnover and absenteeism were high; these problems were serious enough to lead U.S. Steel, beginning in 1915, to undertake an ambitious program of "welfare capitalism" in an effort to stabilize and improve the work force. Extraction costs were high for both iron ore and coal because the mines were all underground, rather than open-pit, and the terrain is irregular and full of seams. Alabama mines made no gains in labor productivity relative to the national average between 1912 and 1945. Most important, the Alabama red hematite ore is relatively low in iron content and unusually high in phosphorus, qualities that raised costs and presented special problems in technological adaptation.[20] Americans do not fully appreciate the extent to which our country's rise to world leadership in

TABLE 6.5

*Harper's Calculated Optimum Output,
Steelworks and Rolling Mills, 1879–1919
(in Thousands of Tons)[a]*

	Birmingham		All Other Centers	
Year	Optimal	Actual	Optimal	Actual
1879	2,643	1	0	2,805
1889	4,730	52	1,031	7,672
1899	7,995	108	1,204	15,283
1909	7,893	300	9,180	18,041
1919	2,171	689	19,517	28,868

SOURCE: Ann Harper, *The Location of the United States Steel Industry,
1879–1919* (New York: Arno Press, 1977), 165–67.
[a] The results reproduced here do not allow for differences in input
requirements (see Harper, p. 172).

steel after 1870 depended on the unusually rich iron ore fields of the Mesabi range.[21] It was not just that northern resources were "better," however, but that this unique resource base served as the foundation of advanced national technology and applied science oriented toward developing the potential of *these* resources. By 1900 Andrew Carnegie's fears of southern competition had receded, and he taunted the people of Birmingham: "You have all the elements but you cannot make steel."[22]

Furthermore, the southern market may not have been growing rapidly enough to justify major expansion of steel-making capacity. This possibility is vividly illustrated in a linear programming calculation carried out by economist Ann Harper. Harper proposed to test the locational rationality of American steel production by comparing actual location to the "optimal" location, defined as that pattern that would minimize total transportation costs (assuming the location of *demand* to be unaffected). She obtained the astounding result that *all* of American steel and rolling mill output in 1879 should have been produced at Birmingham (table 6.5)! Though Birmingham continued to produce far below its optimum level through the period of Harper's study (1879–1919), her calculations show that the level of "optimal" production in that city reached a peak in 1899 and had declined to a mere 7 percent of the national total by 1919. As fanciful as these counterfactuals may be, they underscore a point that is undeniably real: U.S. Steel bought into Birmingham in 1907 at a time when its locational luster had already begun to fade. Such developments as the tractorization of northern agriculture and the rise of the automobile industry in Michigan exerted a continuing northward pull on the location of iron and steel production. These pressures would have been unfavorable for Birmingham steel even if the U.S. Steel Company and Pittsburgh Plus had never entered the picture.[23]

THE REAL BARRIERS TO SOUTHERN INDUSTRIALIZATION

Other southern industries did better than iron and steel, but most of them were similarly limited to cheap, standardized, low-skill, relatively unprocessed commodities. This industry case study does illustrate each of the major elements in the regional situation that made expansion and diversification slow and difficult. These are:

1. the late start of southern industry,
2. the absence or small size of the indigenous regional technological community,
3. the isolation of the southern labor market.

Because industrial development involves a set of learning processes in technology, management, and labor, early leadership often generates cumulative advantages for long periods of time. This is especially so where scale economies are significant, as in steel. If Alabama's mineral resources had been developed from the 1830s, like those of Pennsylvania, the South might have participated fully in the first industrial revolution in iron-making, and Alabama might have been in a position to dominate steel production by the 1870s and 1880s. Harper's calculation that Birmingham was ideally situated in terms of transport costs in 1879 suggests that the optimal time for local industry development was much earlier than the late nineteenth century. If the area had exploited its geographic advantages when they were ripe, sophisticated foundry and machinery-products industries might have sprung up, providing locational staying power that would have survived the depletion of high-quality ores.

The catching-up process might have occurred much more quickly, however, if the South had had its own regionally based technological community. The establishment of a specialized machine-tool industry, actively engaged in adapting European innovations to the American setting, was the crucial development that set the United States apart from the other growing regions-of-recent-settlement around the world.[24] Having missed the formative phases of the "American system," the South was lacking a machine-tools and capital-goods sector almost entirely, and therefore was bypassed by the kind of adaptive, dynamic, path-breaking series of technological breakthroughs that made "the American system" distinctive.[25] Because the inflows of northern capital were not associated with permanent migration of people, the South did not develop a large, indigenous community of engineers and mechanics adapting advanced technology to the southern situation. Instead, most southern industries continued to rely on imported machinery that embodied an imported technology adapted to northern, not southern, conditions.

Here is the element of truth in the "colonial economy" thesis, and it is no small matter. From the time of the great innovations of Bessemer and Kelly in the 1850s, the evolution of steel-making technology involved a continuing interactive process of adapting techniques to the peculiarities of national and regional iron ores. The early success of Bessemer (unbeknownst to the inventor) depended on an iron ore unusually low in phosphorus. British, French, German, and Belgian ores all shared the high-phosphorus problem, and the efforts at solution led to the Basic Bessemer process in the late 1870s. By perverse fate, the new process required an ore *higher* in phosphorus content than the ore indigenous to the Birmingham district. Only the emergence of the Basic Open Hearth process allowed successful steelmaking at the Ensley plant in 1898, but even then, economical use required larger amounts of iron and steel scrap than Birmingham could command. The introduction of the duplex process (an amalgamation of Bessemer and open-hearth principles) in 1906 solved this problem, but by this point steelmaking in the North had been well established for nearly forty years. At every step along the way, the South had to wait for the emergence of a new technique somewhere else in the world.[26] And when a bright young engineer from Georgia, George Gordon Crawford, wanted high-quality training after his graduate work in Germany, he quickly found that he could not get it in Birmingham. Instead, he took a position as a chemist in the Edgar Thomson works of the Carnegie Steel Company in Pennsylvania, and spent fifteen years thoroughly mastering technical aspects of the *northern* industry, before being chosen by U.S. Steel to direct its new TCI operations in Alabama.[27]

When U.S. Steel came in, TCI had access to capital and technological expertise, but TCI was only one part of a large corporate portfolio of holdings and interests, not a very typical component at that. U.S. Steel did not have to suppress incipient industrial expansion in Birmingham, but there is reason to think that the company did not appreciate the potential uses of its southern properties. U.S. Steel did not undertake tinplate production in Birmingham until an exhaustive, three-year engineering study in the 1930s demonstrated that its failure to do so was costing the company one million dollars per year! G. W. Stocking, the most vigorous critic of U.S. Steel's pricing policy, suggested that the company had been "blinded . . . to the profit potentialities of its Birmingham properties," and that "out of concern for its northern plants carried the principle so far as to defeat its ends."[28] In effect he conceded that U.S. Steel had no strong economic *interest* in stifling Birmingham. U.S. Steel's real crime was not suppression but neglect. The steel case stands in marked contrast to tobacco manufacturing, in which the Duke family maintained a North Carolina base and a regional perspective on subsequent investments, including many well removed from the original industry. Eschewing investments that were "too far from home," the Dukes promoted textile mills, banks, and railroads, and eventually led the region into the development of hydroelectric power.

Whether the early emergence of a southern-oriented technological community might have successfully developed an "appropriate technology" for Birmingham steel, we cannot say. But the basic lack of an indigenous technology is observable in many other areas. In the paper industry, for example, prewar processes were not well suited to resinous woods like southern pine. Only the introduction of a German/Swedish sulfate process (adapted by experiments in Wisconsin and Canada) allowed the production of brown kraft wrapping paper from southern trees in the 1920s.[29] More broadly, the new technologies turning up in the North had a persistent *labor-saving* bias that was not ideal for southern conditions. Labor-saving technologies are not intrinsically superior to labor-using techniques, but the South lacked the capacity to generate its own *advanced* forms of labor-using methods, in contrast to the pattern in Japan.[30] This was true even in the textile industry, except that beyond a certain point, the South's homegrown success made it the most attractive market for the northern textile machinery producers, who began to court the southern firms actively.[31] In this one case one can see the outlines of something like an indigenous development path. In the twentieth century, southern engineers began to take the lead in such new areas as humidity control and air conditioning (where climatic elements are obviously essential), and after World War II, the textile machinery industry itself moved South. By the time that happened, however, the South was well on the way to losing its distinctive regional economic identity, and technological leadership in textile technology has since slipped away to other countries.

If the technology could not readily be adapted to southern labor, why not upgrade the labor to fit the technology? The iron and steel industry also illustrates the shortcomings of this strategy. Indeed, Birmingham might be called the exception that proves the rule. Schools in Birmingham were substantially better funded than schools in rural areas, for *both* whites and blacks. Despite continued racial inequity, it was one place in Alabama where the practice of diverting state funds from black to white schools did not occur. The motives were clear: the city boosters wanted to attract a high-quality population and the industrial employers wanted to attract and retain stable, family-based workers. U.S. Steel itself played an active role in promoting schooling, supplementing state funds and administering schools in several planned communities. Well-funded

FIGURE 6.3

Alabama Wages in Agriculture and Blast Furnace,
1890–1930 (Deflated)

SOURCES: U.S. Bureau of Labor Statistics, Bulletin nos. 59, 65, 71, 77, 137, 151, 168, 218, 265, 305, 353, 381, 442, 567, 573, (Washington, D.C.: Government Printing Office, 1914–1931); U.S. Commissioner of Labor, *Nineteenth Annual Report* (Washington, D.C.: GPO, 1904); U.S. Department of Agriculture, *Crops and Markets* 19 (1942): 150–55.

education attracted families with children and improved the quality of the next generation of workers.[32] But when World War I cut off the flow of European immigrants into America, the educated, experienced miners and steelworkers of the Birmingham district were among the first ones to leave for the better-paying jobs in the North.[33] By the 1920s, Birmingham company reports reveal a "pervasive and consistent concern for the problem of labor supply."[34] The effect is visible in the wage data (figure 6.3). In the 1920s, despite the depressed state of southern agriculture, southern iron and steel wages were far higher than wages in agriculture and lumber, especially for skilled labor. Even before unionization and the New Deal, the southern iron and steel industry was well on its way to losing its wage advantage over the northern competition.

The belief that the South as a region would not capture the returns on investments in education, especially for blacks, was one reason why industrial employers so often joined planters in opposing increases in spending on schools. Perhaps the mine operator who actively tried to avoid hiring workers who could read was an extreme case. He complained in 1912: "There aren't enough illiterate niggers to go around. They're spoiling them now-a-days by educating them."[35] But many employers of black labor in mines, sawmills, and lumber camps agreed that there was little return for them in black schooling. They could not block the mobility of workers determined to leave, but they did not have to spend their money on an educational process likely to raise the probability of departure. In many ways the isolation of the southern labor market stood behind all other isolations, since it led the Black Belt planters to be hostile to outside influences, outside people, outside capital, even to education itself. They must have thought Birmingham educational policies were ultimately suicidal, and in a sense they were right. As the political implications of disfranchisement unfolded in the early twentieth century, blacks bore the brunt of this effort to keep the low-wage labor force in the South. But their situation was not fundamentally different from that of unskilled whites, like the cotton mill workers of the Piedmont. The millowners' commitment to the education of their work force was no more wholehearted than that of the planters.

Racial Segregation in Southern Industry

Both economic and social theorists have advanced the view that industrialization and the operation of competitive labor markets are fundamentally hostile to discrimination and the use of racial categories. In economics, the basis for this belief is the view that firms will gain a competitive advantage by using efficiency rather than racialist criteria in hiring and assignment decisions. Thus market pressures will tend to drive out unjustified racial distinctions, unless these distinctions are enforced by such institutional barriers as segregation laws or trade union rules. Echoing W. H. Nicholls's view that the South faced a choice between "tradition" and "regional progress," economist Robert Higgs analyzes the treatment of blacks as a struggle between "competition" and "coercion," the forces of the market and the forces of prejudice and repression. He writes that "the region's economic development increasingly undermined the foundations of its traditional race relations."[36]

Despite the progress of southern industry, however, many southern employers maintained firm racial barriers and segregation systems for generations. Table 6.6 presents census information on employment by race for five major southern industries between 1890 and 1930. Though cotton textiles was the extreme case, racial distinctions are evident in almost all cases. And it does not seem prima facie that those practices were economically damaging. The most successful southern industry, cotton textiles, was the most lily-white of them all; the biggest disappointment, iron and steel, was a major employer of blacks. Either something is wrong with the theory, or else the premises do not apply in the South.

It might be conjectured that the patterns merely reflect the racial percentages in the industry locations, but this is not so. Segregation followed industry lines rather than geography. The state of North Carolina contained all-white cotton mills and nearly-all-white furniture factories, along with heavily black tobacco factories and mixed saw and planing mills (table 6.7). Tobacco manufacturing was a major black employer even though it was concentrated in white-majority states like North Carolina, Tennessee, and Kentucky. This regularity held even down to the level of particular towns. White cotton and black tobacco coexisted in places like Danville, Virginia, and Durham, North Carolina. In Birmingham, where two-thirds of the iron and steel workers were black, the Avondale cotton mill was 98.1 percent white.[37]

Two factors that were not responsible were legal restrictions and trade unions. This point deserves to be emphasized, because many volumes have been written on the rise of "Jim Crow" laws at the end of the nineteenth century. The unwary reader might read them all and not quite know that racial practices of employers were almost completely unregulated by law in the southern states. Explicitly racial laws enforced segregation in public conveyances, marriage, schools, places of

TABLE 6.6

Black Workers in Selected Southern Industries, 1890–1930

Industry	White		Black		Percent Black	
	Male	Female	Male	Female	Male	Female
Cotton Textiles[a]						
1890 Operatives[b]	15,966	17,882	2,648	545	14.2	2.96
1900 Operatives	47,654	38,653	958	317	1.97	0.81
1910 Laborers	11,454	2,459	3,900	342	25.7	12.2
Operatives	55,323	43,849	749	335	1.33	0.76
Loom fixers	2,217	0	4	0	0.18	0
1920 Laborers	26,147	8,326	9,201	2,385	26.0	22.3
Operatives	68,119	51,725	1,124	638	1.62	1.22
Loom fixers[c]	2,043	0	6	0	0.29	0
1930 Laborers	22,469	4,042	8,114	1,667	26.5	29.2
Operatives	102,437	85,391	1,580	529	1.54	0.62
Loom fixers[d]	5,602	0	4	0	0.07	0
Saw and Planing Mills[e]						
1890 Employees	12,977		12,852		49.8	
1900 Employees	21,836		25,171		53.5	
1910 Laborers	43,573		73,612		62.8	
Semiskilled	11,377		7,562		39.9	
Sawyers	7,642		2,361		23.6	
1920 Laborers	45,533		77,515		63.0	
Semiskilled	10,206		5,242		33.9	
Sawyers	7,327		2,041		21.8	
1930 Laborers	48,740		79,267		61.9	
Semiskilled	8,778		4,753		35.1	
Sawyers	9,020		2,805		23.7	
Furniture[f]						
1900 Employees	627		77		10.9	
1910 Laborers	2,691		575		17.6	
Semiskilled	1,815		160		8.1	
1920 Laborers	3,750		974		20.6	
Semiskilled	2,348		212		8.3	
1930 Laborers	6,198		1,229		16.5	
Semiskilled	5,171		428		7.6	
Tobacco[g]						
1890 Operatives	4,622	1,795	8,055	4,320	63.5	70.6
1900 Operatives	4,987	3,200	7,858	4,698	61.2	59.5
1910 Laborers	1,796	719	5,343	2,279	74.8	76.0
Operatives	3,692	4,938	5,621	6,892	60.4	58.3
1920 Laborers	4,478	2,519	12,242	7,549	73.2	75.0
Operatives	6,013	6,693	8,012	10,232	77.8	78.7
1930 Laborers	2,129	1,236	8,127	2,906	79.2	70.2
Operatives	2,966	7,174	4,212	11,678	58.7	61.9
Iron and Steel[h]						
1890 Employees	2,476		2,731		52.4	
1900 Employees	3,748		5,681		60.3	

TABLE 6.6, *continued*

Industry	White		Black		Percent Black	
	Male	Female	Male	Female	Male	Female
1910 Laborers	2,959		8,412		74.0	
Semiskilled						
Blast furnace[i]	768		635		45.3	
Car and railroad shops	1,417		177		11.1	
Furnacemen, etc.[i]	255		1,045		80.4	
Molders, etc.	2,429		774		24.2	
1920 Laborers	6,061		18,475		75.3	
Semiskilled	5,695		3,112		35.3	
Furnacemen, etc.[i]	169		666		79.8	
Molders, etc.	2,745		1,105		28.7	
1930 Laborers[i]	2,574		11,563		81.8	
Semiskilled	4,605		3,250		41.4	
Furnacemen, etc.[i]	445		287		39.2	
Molders, etc.	2,860		1,257		30.5	

Sources: U.S. Bureau of the Census, *Report on Population,* 11th Census (1890), part 2 (Washington, D.C.: Government Printing Office, 1900), table 116; *Special Reports: Occupations,* 12th Census (1900) (Washington, D.C.: GPO, 1904), table 41; *Population: Occupational Statistics,* 13th Census (1910), vol. 4 (Washington, D.C.: GPO, 1914), table VII; *Population: Occupations,* 14th Census (1920), vol. 4 (Washington, D.C.: GPO, 1923), chap. 7, table 1; *Population,* vol. 4, *Occupations by States,* 15th Census (1930) (Washington, D.C.: GPO, 1933), table 11.
[a] Alabama, Georgia, North Carolina, South Carolina, Tennessee, and Virginia.
[b] In 1890, figures are for cotton, woolen, and other textile mill operatives.
[c] North and South Carolina only.
[d] Georgia, North and South Carolina only.
[e] Alabama, Florida, Georgia, Louisiana, Mississippi, North Carolina, South Carolina, Tennessee, and Virginia.
[f] North Carolina and Tennessee.
[g] Kentucky, North Carolina, Tennessee, and Virginia.
[h] Alabama and Tennessee only.
[i] Alabama only.

TABLE 6.7
Black Workers in North Carolina Industries, 1900

Industry	White		Black		Percent Black	
	Male	Female	Male	Female	Male	Female
Cotton textile	16,556	14,019	109	33	0.65	0.23
Saw and planning mills	2,598	0	1,691	0	39.4	
Furniture	333	0	25	0	7.0	
Tobacco	866	616	2,411	1,611	73.6	72.3

Source: U.S. Bureau of the Census, *Special Reports: Occupations,* 12th Census (1900) (Washington, D.C.: Government Printing Office, 1904), table 41.

public accommodations, amusement, and burial, but not employment.[38] (The only significant exceptions are the North Carolina statute requiring separate toilets in manufacturing plants, and the South Carolina law requiring segregation in cotton textiles; these were not passed until 1913 and 1915, respectively, and were not imitated in other equally segregationist states.)[39]

Trade unions were not entirely absent from the South, especially in skilled crafts in the cities after 1900, and they were often highly exclusionist on a racial basis, like their counterparts in the North. The printing industry, for example, with the longest and strongest tradition of craft unionism in the South, hired virtually no blacks. Many of the building trades unions were openly hostile. Yet the southern unions were by no means worse offenders than those in the North, and were often better. Where there were large numbers of skilled blacks, as in carpentry and bricklaying, the unions often had to find some way to include them, as argued by the executive board of the Virginia Bricklayers and Masons in 1903:

> The colored bricklayer of the South is going to lay brick, whether we take them under our care or not, and this fact being conceded, the Board maintains that his proper place is within our fold.[40]

Even though blacks had a hard time breaking into the newer trades like plumbing and electrical work, the absolute and even the relative numbers of black craftsmen actually crept upward in the South until 1920.[41] Where industrial unions enjoyed periods of success (usually brief), their interracial quality was often remarkable.[42] Whatever the net effect of unions may have been, they were largely peripheral to the industrial story in the South. The great majority of the new industrial wage earners were not unionized, yet segregation persisted.

How can this persistence be explained in terms of economics? The theory of racial discrimination is not one of the more firmly grounded branches of economic analysis, but the last twenty-five years of discussion has established one point with clarity: the motives that give rise to racial distinctions are much more likely to generate job segregation than wage discrimination in a competitive market setting. If white employees refuse to work with blacks, the prudent employer will divide the jobs into separate rooms or buildings, white and black. If some employers prefer to have nothing but white workers, other more money-conscious employers will find it in their interests to hire nothing but blacks. There are so many ways to segregate—by room, by job, by location, by firm—that it would not require any very large number of profit-seeking employers to drive the black wage up to the level of the white wage.[43] Even if whites as a group have a low opinion of blacks as workers, those employers who know better or are willing to take a chance (and again, it need not take many) should gain a competitive advantage that will quickly drive out an unwarranted evaluation of black capabilities. If these propositions seem more like abstract possibilities for the classroom than likely descriptions of the real world, consider the case of agricultural wage labor, a large, diverse competitive market in a region where racism was rife. Many landlords hired only blacks or only whites, but overall wage differentials were small.

There is ample evidence that these competitive pressures were felt in industrial labor markets as well. The prevailing practice was summarized by a Chattanooga iron company official in 1883: "I have made it a rule to pay colored men the same as we pay white men for the same kind of labor. . . . We pay the men according to the positions they occupy." The same was reported from a brick-making firm in Columbus, Georgia: "This is about the cheapest field for labor that I have ever found anywhere . . . white labor of the same class is equally cheap. We pay the same to whites as to blacks, when we employ them."[44] A study of wages in Virginia by Robert Higgs found that wage differentials by race within firms were rare, even though segregation was common.[45]

More important than the policies or attitudes of individual employers was the effect of the market. So long as both blacks and whites had relatively open access to the farm labor market, and so long as labor flowed freely between sectors, industrial wages for unskilled labor could not deviate widely from the farm wage. Of course there were differentials by age and sex, and differentials between older and newer areas, and possibly differentials for unusually strenuous or dangerous jobs—as there are in any competitive market—but by and large the evidence indicates that farm and industrial unskilled labor markets were closely linked (see figure 5.2 for textiles, 6.3 for iron). The equilibrating pressures of a competitive labor market were vividly illustrated by the convergence of wages for white males in cotton textiles and black males in tobacco manufacturing, despite the radically different racial employment policies of those two industries. In Virginia, in 1907, the median white male wage in cotton manufacturing was $6.78 per week, while the median black male wage in tobacco was $6.44. The *modal wage* (the wage paid to the largest number) was actually higher than that of white males, $7.00 to $6.00. (In contrast, for females, who did not have ready access to jobs in farm labor, a gap in median wages of 25 percent persisted between whites and blacks in the two cases.) This tendency to equalization is the grain of truth in the statement often heard that the wages of white cotton mill workers were held down by the "threat" of replacing them with blacks. Mill owners voiced such threats only rarely, and lacked all credibility when they did (as the handful of attempts at integration or all-black mills demonstrated). But, in effect, the labor market accomplished the mill owners' goal: obtaining white labor at the black wage. In this way, industrialization and competitive profit-seeking firms were perfectly consistent with continued segregation by race. The system generally had enough flexibility to avoid severe shortages and constraints. For example, in textiles, blacks could be used in "outside" jobs or in laboring jobs isolated from the operatives (such as the picker room), but these jobs were not *reserved* for blacks, and the majority of workers in them were white. Segregation of this sort, which divides the labor market without affecting the wage, is called "horizontal" segregation, and may at first glance appear to be innocuous.

With the passage of time, however, horizontal segregation ceased to be innocuous because it served to reinforce the "vertical" segregation that prevailed in all southern industries, the unequal access by blacks to higher-paying jobs of a skilled, supervisory, or administrative character. The unique wage data collected after 1900 by the commissioner of labor for the state

FIGURE 6.4

Aggregate Wage Distributions in Virginia, 1907

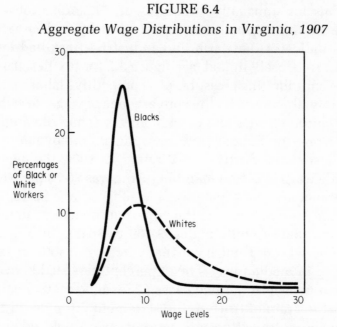

SOURCE: Bureau of Labor and Industrial Statistics for the State of Virginia, *Eleventh Annual Report* (Richmond, Va.: Davis Bottom Superintendent of Public Printing, 1908).

of Virginia allow us to estimate the overall *distribution* of wage levels for black and white workers, graphed for 1907 in figure 6.4.[46] It is a picture worth a thousand words, showing that market equilibration of the unskilled wage was only one part of the story. Though the *modes* or peaks of the two curves are almost identical in 1907, the means and medians show a 30 to 50 percent advantage for whites over blacks (see also table 6.8).

TABLE 6.8

Aggregate Statistics of Male Wage Earners in Virginia, 1907

	White	Black
Number	22,914	13,765
Mean Wage	$11.92	$7.68
Modal Wage	8.00	8.00
Median Wage	10.01	7.71
Standard Deviation	5.61	1.90
Standard Deviation (LOG)	0.438	0.241

SOURCE: Bureau of Labor and Industrial Statistics for the State of Virginia, *Eleventh Annual Report* (Richmond, Va.: Davis Bottom Superintendent of Public Printing, 1908).

184

TABLE 6.9

Percentages of Upward Occupational Mobility by
Race, Birmingham, 1880–1914

	1880 Group	1890 Group	1899 Group
Five Years			
White	19%	29%	23%
Black	14	9	14
Ten Years			
White	31	33	40
Black	13	8	17
Fifteen Years			
White	34	34	43
Black	14	13	18
Twenty Years			
White	48	34	
Black	18	16	
Twenty-five Years			
White	48	39	
Black		18	

NOTE: Paul B. Worthman, "Working Class Mobility in Birmingham, Alabama, 1880–1914," in Anonymous Americans, ed. Tamara Hareven (Englewood Cliffs, N.J.: Prentice-Hall, 1971), table 9. Copyright © 1971. Reprinted by permission of Prentice-Hall.

Job discrimination in the better-paying positions was far more important than wage differentials for the same job. Blacks could get the going wage in the unskilled market, but there was a virtual upper limit to their possible progress above that level. The contrast with the agricultural distributions is clear. Blacks were not "confined to agriculture," but, all things considered, the prospects for "good blacks" were much more inviting on the farm ladder.

Studies of occupational mobility by social historians confirm this picture. In Birmingham, for example, with one of the largest concentrations of black industrial labor, more than 80 percent of black workers who stayed for ten years made no upward progress at all toward better jobs during this time (table 6.9). By contrast, half of the white workers moved up after ten years; half again of this number actually moved into white-collar jobs (table 6.10). In a nutshell, the typical white unskilled worker could expect to move up over time, the typical black could expect to go nowhere. Separate studies of Atlanta, Georgia, and Washington, D.C. show depressingly similar patterns.[47]

TABLE 6.10

Occupational Mobility for Selected Groups by Race, 1890–1909

	Number Persisting, 1890–1899	Percent Climbing to White-Collar Jobs	Number Persisting, 1890–1909	Percent Climbing to White-Collar Jobs	Number Persisting, 1899–1909	Percent Climbing to White-Collar Jobs
White						
Building trades	25	20%	10	40%	40	37%
Railroad	33	12	16	25	28	25
Mechanics	28	32	16	63	48	37
Service	8	63	8	75	14	35
Unskilled	30	23	13	62	48	25
TOTAL	124	24	63	51	178	31
Black						
Building trades	16	0	8	0	20	5
Railroad	14	0	4	0	21	4
Mechanics	14	0	8	0	24	5
Service	42	37	20	50	14	21
Unskilled	30	10	13	38	49	4
TOTAL	116	6	53	18	128	5

NOTE: Paul B. Worthman, "Working Class Mobility in Birmingham, Alabama, 1880–1914," in *Anonymous Americans*, ed. Tamara Hareven (Englewood Cliffs, N.J.: Prentice-Hall, 1971), table 10. Copyright © 1971. Reprinted by permission of Prentice-Hall.

The human reality of figure 6.4 was recounted in unexpected fashion to the 1883 Senate Committee on Relations between Capital and Labor. Relaxing on the train en route between their very formal hearings in various cities around the country, committee members fell into conversation with the train porter, Mr. Floyd Thornhill, of Lynchburg, Virginia. Learning that Thornhill had an interesting work history, the committee called an impromptu session officially recorded "on the train, near Bristol, Tennessee," possibly with some bemusement. Thornhill had been a slave, and after staying with his owner for one year after emancipation, he moved to Lynchburg, where he worked for twelve years in a tobacco factory. He became a "boss hand," and said: "I have done more than anybody else in that business." And yet, according to his testimony, Thornhill's earnings at that point were still barely higher than the local farm wage. After twelve years, he left the factory and became a porter. Thornhill doubted that education would have been of any great help to him or to his family.[48]

THE DYNAMIC EFFICIENCY OF VERTICAL SEGREGATION

The white domination of the upper end of the wage distribution reflected many possible effects: craft union exclusion, unequal education and skills, the resistance by white workers to black foremen, and employer prejudice, to name a few. The key questions are, did vertical segregation represent the strength of tradition or prejudice over profit motives; was vertical segregation therefore a drag on southern progress; were market pressures therefore ultimately hostile to segregation and discrimination by race? Anyone acquainted with economists knows that, in theory, the answers are "definitely maybe." In practice, in the American South the answers were all no. The crucial ingredient was on-the-job experience as a component of economic progress.

In the testimony offered to the Senate Committee by southern employers in 1883, there was a remarkable discrepancy in the opinions about black laborers coming from the iron industries of Alabama and Tennessee, on one hand, and from the Georgia cotton textile industry on the other. The iron men, who employed large numbers of blacks, extolled the quality of black workers, arguing that there would be no racial difference "with equal training." Many actually preferred blacks even if whites were available. The cotton manufacturers, who employed no black operatives, made statements like: "I don't think the negro would be fit to work in a cotton factory"; "He is not adapted to the management of intricate machinery . . . their fingers are too stiff."[49] It is possible that the iron masters were merely enlightened while the cotton mill men were merely ignorant and prejudiced. More likely, blacks really were good iron workers because they had experience. They were or would have been poor cotton mill workers because in 1883, blacks had virtually no experience in that line of work. Nor did they gain any in subsequent years. When the use of blacks in the mills came under discussion in the 1890s, the debate was abstract and speculative, as though no one could really imagine what black textile workers would be like.[50]

How did this situation come about? Paul Norgren, in his

historical appendix to Gunnar Myrdal's 1944 classic, *An American Dilemma*, noted that it could not have been a simple absence of potential black workers, because blacks were about one-third of the population in the Upper Piedmont. He attributed the exclusion to the fact that the industry was a new one "not a descendant of pre-war plants."[51] On this point, Norgren had it wrong. We now know that the postwar industry *did* descend from the prewar plants; in many cases, the factories themselves survived the war, but even where this was not so, the antebellum locations (and often management) formed the nucleus of the early postbellum industry.[52] Before 1850, southern cotton mills made heavy and successful use of slaves, but by 1860, for reasons having to do with the interaction between the cotton boom and the markets for free and slave labor, the mills had become almost entirely white.[53]

Given this background, whites had an "initial advantage" over blacks in textile work after the war. If labor markets are competitive, and if the economic advantages of segregation are compelling, even a small margin may be enough to swing the entire factory labor force. To be sure, most of the textile workers were new to industrial life, but the core of experienced workers were white, so it made economic sense for the new workers to be white too. Since the industry was only a small part of a larger agricultural economy, the wage scale was basically set by the farm wage, and segregation was mainly horizontal, neither inequitable nor inefficient in any major way.

As the industry developed, however, this initially innocuous picture began to change character. The key point is that the operative jobs were the ones for which experience mattered. As we saw in chapter 5, the maturing of the labor force was an integral part of the development process. Spinners learned to tend more sides, doffers became weavers, weavers became loom fixers and section heads. Under the mill-village system, new generations of workers actually grew up in the mill, becoming socialized to the routines, the noise, and the machinery at early ages. Gradually the average wage drifted up relative to farm labor, but so long as the wage structure matched the structure of useful experience, this increasingly "vertical" segregation was no more inefficient from the employers' standpoint then was the original type. The wage paid to these all-white workers was still no more than they were worth. The important point, though, is that the prospects for black textile jobs became more remote over time. How could completely inexperienced black workers compete with whites who had been born and raised in a mill village? By 1910 or so, it would have seemed like turning the clock back half a century, starting from scratch. It is a good example of what is known in economics as "increasing returns," in which relatively small initial advantage produces a result that becomes more compelling and less arbitrary over time. A close analogy is the case of the QWERTY typewriter keyboard, in which an early choice became embedded in the training of the labor force, and subsequently dictated the design of the instrument right on into the age of computers.[54] In both examples, the labor market was the vehicle. The advantages of identifying and using workers with established skills in relationship to particular tasks and particular machines were so great that new firms quickly followed the prevailing racial practices. Though generations of critics have asserted that the threat of black labor was used to keep white mill workers "in line," when a strike did actually occur in Augusta in 1886 the owners imported *white* strikebreakers from surrounding counties and even from Paterson, New Jersey, rather than employ blacks.[55]

The best evidence that segregation in textiles did not run counter to economic pressures is what happened when black mills were tried. Perhaps as many as a dozen attempts at the use of black labor occurred between 1895 and 1905 in Georgia and the Carolinas, and all were failures. Sometimes, it is true, the opposition of white workers was decisive, especially when the owners tried to integrate blacks into an existing plant. When 20 Negro women were employed in the folding department at Atlanta's Fulton Bag and Cotton Factory in 1897, 1400 white workers refused to enter the factory. They gathered in an angry rock-throwing crowd, heard inflammatory speeches against the "nasty, black, stinkin' nigger wimmin," and forced the dismissal of the black women and the transfer of all blacks from direct contact with whites. In 1898 at the Kincaid Mills in Griffin, Georgia, the white workers flogged the black employees, beat up blacks who had no connection with Kincaid, chased the mill superintendent out of town, and had to be restrained by the state militia. Thus there is no doubt that many whites viewed black exclusion as an issue of "moral economy," that the cotton mill was an institution "held in trust for the white toilers of the fields," and, hence, that a strategy of gradually blending black labor into existing mills was unpromising.[56]

But there were several other examples in which all-black mills were established and carried on operations peacefully, and these too all failed. Two of these "experiments" were closely watched by people in the industry. In the case of the Charleston Cotton Mill, purchased and renamed the Vesta Mills in 1899 by prominent South Carolina manufacturer John Henry Montgomery in association with the head of a New York commission house, the project had experienced managers, substantial capital, a strong local reputation, and careful advance planning. Early reports were positive, though expressing concern about the tendency to absenteeism for such reasons as a meeting, a "frolic," or a funeral. When the mill closed in 1901, the manager concluded:

> We had the best management and fine machinery, and all the money necessary. It was the labor. I am absolutely convinced it was the labor.

Montgomery himself strongly challenged these statements, noting that the labor problems were no different from those experienced with a "green white labor force" in the up-country, and that the problem with Vesta was its location (where there were competing employment opportunities in the city and in the surrounding country during the harvest season). Most observers and most of those involved blamed the labor, but even Montgomery's plausible analysis underscores the disadvantage that any all-black mill faced in any location in 1900: they could not hire experienced workers away from other mills because there were no experienced black textile workers. The availability of a pool of such workers was a major reason why mills tended to locate in established textile centers or adjacent to them, and the industry became more concentrated geographically over time. Indeed, around the world, cotton textiles was said to be "naturally gregarious."[57]

Another instructive example was the Coleman Manufacturing Company of Concord, North Carolina, launched in 1899 by a group of black businessmen with the financial support and sympathetic encouragement of Washington and Ben Duke of the Duke tobacco family. The Dukes even advanced a second loan of $10,000 two years later, though no interest had been paid on the original loan of the same amount. Even after the black manager, W. C. Coleman, was replaced by a white man in 1903 in hopes of obtaining a better insurance break, no interest was paid. Finally B. N. Duke filed foreclosure papers in 1904, writing:

> I have never had any disposition to have mortgages I hold foreclosed, as you might have been aware from what has been stated to you, but it has become necessary for me to have this step taken out of sheer necessity to protect my interest.

The black supporters argued that the problem was "lack of adequate capital," as struggling small businessmen always believe, and that with more time they would succeed. In this, of course, they were absolutely right; with enough time and money blacks could learn cotton mill work as well as anyone else. But would this investment look attractive to any lender when other cotton mills were paying handsome returns in short order?[58]

Every specific failure may be laid to management, capital, location, white opposition, or bad fortune, as well as to labor experience. But the special importance of labor is supported by the contrast between textiles and tobacco manufacturing, which overlapped the textiles region geographically, and which had labor requirements for male, female, and child labor that were in many ways similar. An essential difference was that the antebellum tobacco industry had used mainly slave labor.[59] Many freed blacks continued to work for years afterward in the same establishments where they had been slaves, and as late as 1930, black women still dominated the same phases of work—sorting, picking, stemming, hanging—that black slaves had done.[60] Like the iron masters, tobacco manufacturers praised the qualities of black workers. Though the tasks were commonly labeled "unskilled," they required dexterity and diligence; they certainly required accustomation to the smell and the atmosphere of the tobacco rooms. For these reasons, southern tobacco manufacturers clung to black labor as tenaciously as cotton millowners stayed with white, but they were firmly segregated, so that blacks had experience that whites did not, and vice versa.

The effects of labor experience in these jobs must surely have been of some importance if we are to explain the otherwise extraordinary behavior of manufacturers in new centers of production, who recruited and paid the transport costs of black workers with previous experience. An episode recounted by Nannie Tilley is enlightening:

> With the rise of the industry in the coastal plain and the absence of labor accustomed to the work of redrying plants, operators solved the problem by collecting employees in old tobacco centers and paying for their transportation to the new plants. One such employer, Hoge Irvine, experienced considerable inconvenience in 1900 with a group of stemmers transported from Danville to Kinston. Amusement at Irvine's predicament from fellow tobacconists indicates a situation not unusual. "After paying their way here, he was very much chagrined to find that fourteen of them had skipped. He sent over to Greenville in search of his stemming tourists, and returned last night with eight of them, as happy as distillery hogs and in no wise ashamed of seeking to leave him in the hole. Hoge is wrathy, and says he will get the others."[61]

Is it surprising then that segregation persisted on an industry rather than a geographic basis? Though the story suggests the difficulty of working on the fringes of an established market over time, mobility through the labor market merely served to reconfirm the existing segregation. In both textiles and tobacco, if firms had had to draw their labor solely from their surrounding communities, much more diversity would have been observed. But the process of *labor market development* tended to spread and reinforce an initial association between race and particular skills.

Sociologist Dwight Billings has recently portrayed the tobacco manufacturers as purely profit-seeking, modern businessmen because of their willingness to use black labor, as
contrasted with the more traditional cotton mill men who used
white labor and accommodated to the norms of the white community against race mixing.[62] From the accounts just given,
one can see the basis for this view; but it was the conditions
of the labor market that gave the management its character,
and in both cases, they were not fighting market pressures but
moving with them. Tobacco manufacturing employed black
workers, but they also employed whites, in separate buildings
and doing entirely different machine-tending jobs. For seventy-
five years, these segregation lines were firm.[63] When money-
hungry tobacco manufacturers like Julian Carr expanded into
cotton textiles, they employed white labor. (The handful of
successful textile-related black-labor plants were outside the
main line of jobs and experience, for example, knitting or hosiery mills.) And when northern manufacturers did begin to
come South in the mid-twentieth century, with few exceptions
they followed local segregation practices until strong political
pressures forced a change. Competitive pressures were extremely powerful in forcing wage equality in the open market
for unskilled labor, but neither competition nor any other "iron
law of industrialization" had any tendency to dissolve racialist
criteria for job assignments and advancement, usually to the
detriment of black workers.

Why is it that markets were so effective in equalizing returns
to unskilled labor, yet so ineffective at opening opportunities
for black advancement? There were markets for skilled and
experienced workers too, but *acquiring* skills or useful experience is not intrinsically a market process. Whereas progress
in agriculture could be shown by the more-or-less objective
measuring rod of wealth, advancement in industry is a social
affair, with all the subtleties of interpersonal relationships, such
as supervision of one person by another, or identifying the
most promising candidate for advancement from the ranks of
the unskilled. Since most of the important skills were learned
on the job, and there were few true individual differences in
aptitude, there was no great loss of efficiency in passing over

blacks for promotion indefinitely, so long as a substantial representation of whites persisted on the lower rungs. Why should we believe there are any great costs to following an arbitrary racial advancement rule, when even sophisticated modern tests have little objective value in predicting job performance? Furthermore, any such rule consistently followed will tend to be self-confirming, as blacks had little reason to acquire skills that they would never be able to use. Thus, on reflection, there is little reason to think that industrialization should always tend to undermine racial inequities or promote relative minority advancement.

This argument suggests that black upgrading would begin to occur only when blacks became the overwhelming majority in the lower ranks, so that few qualified whites were available. This did occur in various localities in an industry like lumbering. In Virginia sawmills as of 1900, for example, fourteen of the fifteen black foremen were in firms reporting virtually no white laborers; and of the thirty-seven black sawyers, twenty-three were in firms at which the loggers and laborers were 80 percent black or more. Perhaps a more important example is the iron and steel industry of Alabama and Tennessee, which drew its workers from a heavily black Deep South population. By 1910, three-fourths of the iron and steel laborers were black, and many semiskilled and skilled jobs came to have heavy black representation. TCI, for example, came to employ black workers as motormen, blacksmiths, masons, machine runners, linemen, rockmen, machinists, pipe men, and so on, even as supervisors. It is perfectly true that the desire to discourage or defeat unionism was a key part of this policy. But this is simply another way of saying that the company was able to utilize the southern labor market. Located in a black-majority state, in an industry in which blacks had acquired the bulk of the useful industry experience, they could only take full advantage of the labor market by upgrading blacks. In such an environment, resistance by skilled workers to this policy was usually ineffective.[64] Even in this case, however, explicit racial segregation in job progressions prevailed, even in branches of large national corporations, until court orders and threats of federal sanctions forced change in the 1950s and

FIGURE 6.5

Aggregate Wage Distributions in Virginia, 1926

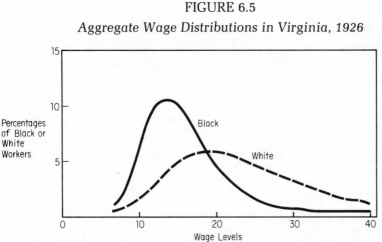

SOURCE: Bureau of Labor and Industry of the State of Virginia, *Twenty-Ninth Annual Report* (Richmond, Va.: Davis Bottom, Superintendent of Public Printing, 1927).

1960s. A study of firms throughout Alabama could not identify a single example of a company moving voluntarily towards nonracialism as a result of a profit calculation or for any other reason.[65]

The Emergence of Wage Differentials after World War I

If market pressures to upgrade black workers were powerful, we ought to be able to see substantial black progress when we come to look at the wage structure some decades later. The Virginia wage data give us this opportunity for the mid-1920s for one state, after the high-pressure times of the war and accelerated out-migration to the north. Virginia is by no means a typical southern state, but we know that segregation ran along industry lines, and Virginia had a sampling of almost every important southern industry—cotton, tobacco, iron, sawmills, printing, building, shipbuilding, mining, and many smaller ones. Comparing the picture in 1926 (figure 6.5) with that of 1907 (figure 6.4), we certainly do see change, but in the opposite direction. The black curve does begin to show a right-hand tail, which may reflect a slow upgrading. A much more visible change is the wide 40 percent wage differential between the peaks of the two curves. In Virginia during the 1920s, an explicitly racial wage differential had emerged, in clear contrast to the prewar relationship.

How can we explain this development? Research on this topic is too new to provide definite answers, but some elements may be identified. The widest gap is in the building trades, which were heavily unionized by the 1920s by unions that had become more, rather than less, racially exclusive. Increasingly, "black jobs" and "white jobs" were coming to be associated with "low-wage" and "high-wage" employment. But similar tendencies may be seen in many other industries that had never seen a successful union. For example, another component of the emerging gap is explained by cotton textiles, an all-white industry that by the 1920s paid wages well above black levels. Even in tobacco, traditionally the industrial employer of blacks, a noticeable spread could now be seen between wages for "white" and "black" jobs. In industries that continued to employ large numbers of undifferentiated laborers, however, the wage gap remained small and discrimination was less severe.[66]

Economists will be inclined to explain the new racial wage gap as a delayed effect of the assault on black schools begun in the 1890s.[67] It is certainly true that by the 1920s, blacks and whites were coming onto the labor market with increasingly dissimilar educational backgrounds, and this fact must have made it easier to separate pay as well as jobs in the workplace. In the tobacco industry, for example, interviews and personal references were required for white women but black women were hired by number.[68] But it should not be thought that the racial differences in work status and pay even among unskilled workers were directly linked to skills learned in schools. In most of the largest industries of the South, schooling had little to do with job requirements. Textiles is a clear example: the better-paid white mill workers in the 1920s had limited schooling, but great familiarity and experience with industrial work. Thus the racial divergence in work histories and job experience was just as much a part of the emerging dualistic labor market pattern as was public education, and it is probably more appropriate to think of both of these developments as symptoms of the larger historical process of creating a segregated society.

The important point is that dualism in the southern labor market, a pattern in which black and white workers not only had different jobs but noncompeting jobs at different base pay rates, was *newly* emerging in the 1920s. Market pressures and industrialization did not spread convergence and equalization, but the opposites. The trend became worse during the 1930s. Observers during this era described large racial wage differentials for similar work, and tended to assume that this was the "traditional" system, that these wage gaps had always been there. Charles S. Johnson, for example, wrote in 1943 that racial wage differentials were "now so well established in custom that they are frequently maintained where work is identical. . . . Separate wage rates for Negros are thus in a sense a fixed tradition."[69] *Segregation* was indeed a long tradition, but "separate wage rates" were part of a new tradition, created by more than a half-century of southern industrialization on a segregated basis.

7

THE INTERWAR YEARS:

ASSAULT ON THE

LOW-WAGE ECONOMY

WORLD WAR I was a turbulent time in southern economic life. Cotton prices soared, debts were cleared, and jaundiced landlords complained about "Negro tenants rolling in wealth." Military demands for lumber, cloth, explosives, and labor pushed production and wages to all-time highs, creating a tight, high-turnover labor market that was often chaotic. Many of these developments had lasting consequences. George Tindall has written that the war served "to create situations of dynamic change in an essentially static society."[1] Most portentous was the accelerated migration of black Southerners to the North. Faced with the sudden cutoff of European immigration, northern employers flooded the South with labor agents offering free transportation and assurances of jobs. Perhaps as many as a half-million southern blacks went North between 1915 and 1920.

It is tempting to see the wartime migration as the pump priming that set in motion equilibrating labor flows over the next half-century. This metaphor is misleading, however, because northern and southern labor markets were farther apart than ever after the war. As this chapter will show, during the 1920s, most southern employers were not paying higher wages forced up by outside demands: unskilled wages in the South were actually lower in that decade than before the war. Where wages did not come down, as in textiles, labor was in surplus, changing the nature of labor relations and making it economical for many firms to add extra production shifts at the same time that they were cutting back on hours of work. The resulting national outcry against night work tended to confuse effects with causes, blaming round-the-clock operations for depressed conditions and the miseries of southern mill workers, when the true causation was more nearly the opposite. The continuing separateness of the southern labor market during the interwar years may be seen most plainly in the priorities of southern representatives, who were more concerned with maintaining isolation than with bringing federal money into their districts. Despite their political power, and despite the impoverished conditions of the region, the South received less federal spending under the New Deal programs of the 1930s than any other part of the country.

But the effort to protect the isolation of the southern labor market ultimately failed. The night-work campaign was only one early example of political pressure directed against the symptoms of the low-wage southern labor market. The unification of national labor markets might ultimately have occurred through the gradual cumulative influence of market forces. Instead, it happened much more rapidly through the instrumentality of the federal government. At the end of the 1930s, regional labor markets were as separate as they had been in the 1920s. But the institutional bases for maintaining that separation had been thoroughly undermined. Under the incentives established by the New Deal farm programs, plantation tenancy was disintegrating, and sharecroppers were being turned into footloose wage laborers. At the same time, federal labor policies had sharply raised the level of base wage rates in the South, effectively blocking the low-wage expansion path for regional industry. By the time of World War II, the stage was set for a rapid transformation.

World War, Migration, and Labor Markets

Under the pressures of wartime demand and labor shortage, many northern employers radically altered their policies toward black workers. Whereas they had been previously excluded or restricted to menial tasks, blacks were openly recruited in the South by paid labor agents and by enthusiastic ads promising good wages and steady work. The *Chicago Defender*, a black newspaper widely circulated in the South, contained such items as:

> Men wanted at once. Good steady employment for colored. Thirty and 39½ cents per hour. Weekly payments. Good warm sanitary quarters free. Best commissary privileges. . . . For out of town parties of ten or more cheap transportation will be arranged . . . 3000 laborers to work on railroad. Factory hires all race help. More positions open than men for them.[2]

Ads often made it clear that they were looking for blacks by writing: "Apply Chicago League on Urban Conditions among Negroes." Once the first wave of black migrants had gone North, their letters and their presence as helpers served to keep the flow going. One contemporary survey reported:

> The universal testimony of employers has been that after the initial group movement by agents, Negroes kept going by twos and threes. These were drawn by letters and actual advances of money from Negroes who had already settled in the North.[3]

The sudden influx of southern blacks generated tensions and hostilities in many places, including bloody race riots in East Saint Louis (1917) and Chicago (1919). The visibility and controversy over black migration have led some writers to interpret the entire episode in racial terms. Robert Higgs, for example, has written that open foreign immigration had "allowed industrial employers simultaneously to satisfy their various appetites for labor and to gratify freely their tastes for racial discrimination." Cut off from this source during the war, however, employers "opened their doors wide to black workers," the result being that "by the late twenties a large and steady

TABLE 7.1

Net Migration from the South
1870–80 to 1940–50
(in Thousands)

Decade	Native White	Black
1870–80	91	−68
1880–90	−271	88
1890–1900	−30	−185
1900–1910	−69	−194
1910–20	−663	−555
1920–30	−704	−903
1930–40	−558	−480
1940–50	−866	−1,581

Source: Hope T. Eldridge and Dorothy S. Thomas, *Population Redistribution and Economic Growth*, vol. 3 (Philadelphia: American Philosophical Society, 1964), 90.

movement of blacks to the North had, like the weevil, become institutionalized, an established fact of American social life."[4]

The problem with accounts like this is that they do not treat the labor market as a market. Racial discrimination was certainly an aspect of southern regional isolation, but it was not strictly a racial matter because southern *white* wage earners also earned wages well below national norms. What happened during the high-pressure years of 1916–19 was not simply a change in racial employment policies but a redirection of the geographic scope of unskilled labor markets. This proposition is revealed most clearly by a single fact: the wartime out-migration of native southern whites was actually larger than the out-migration of southern blacks (table 7.1). The job opportunities, recruitment incentives, and premium unskilled wages were attractive to whites as well as blacks, and the labor market effects were felt in many parts of the South, even where out-migration was small.

It might seem that this insight makes the problem simple. The southern labor market was isolated before the war; afterward, as a result of the flows initiated during the war, a truly *national* labor market was established or at least was in the process of being established. As one recent writer puts it: "Landlords were forced more each year of the exodus to compete with northern employers, and to treat black croppers and

TABLE 7.2

Farm Wage Rates (Daily, Without Board) Deflated by
Cost of Living Index for Unskilled Labor

Year	Va.	N.C.	S.C.	Ga.	Ala.	Miss.	Ark.	La.	Tex.	Tenn.
1889–90	.82	.68	.69	.80	.81	.87	1.02	.97	1.07	.78
1899	.86	.73	.62	.72	.76	.85	.95	.95	1.10	.87
1902	.87	.78	.65	.76	.85	.88	1.09	1.11	1.18	.87
1906	1.15	1.03	.91	1.10	1.11	1.30	1.27	1.30	1.37	1.10
1909	1.05	.98	.78	1.00	.96	1.05	1.15	1.10	1.27	1.01
1910	1.07	1.03	.96	1.01	1.12	1.17	1.28	1.09	1.40	1.09
1911	1.07	1.04	.93	1.08	1.04	1.06	1.23	1.12	1.34	1.06
1912	1.08	1.06	.93	1.05	1.07	1.07	1.23	1.11	1.36	1.04
1913	1.17	1.08	.93	1.06	1.06	1.10	1.20	1.12	1.36	1.05
1914	1.09	1.02	.82	.94	.95	.98	1.12	1.04	1.34	1.00
1915	1.09	1.00	.74	.91	.92	.96	1.08	1.04	1.32	.96
1916	1.08	.96	.76	.87	.84	.90	1.04	1.02	1.22	.92
1917	1.20	1.09	.84	.95	.91	.92	1.14	1.01	1.20	.98
1918	1.35	1.18	.84	1.09	1.05	1.10	1.28	1.20	1.26	1.05
1919	1.27	1.32	1.11	1.13	1.10	1.22	1.29	1.27	1.66	1.12
1920	1.49	1.49	1.20	1.26	1.26	1.39	1.44	1.44	1.70	1.23
1921	1.07	.95	.69	.71	.74	.80	.89	.85	1.05	.87
1922	1.07	1.07	.66	.68	.79	.88	.93	.98	1.01	.85
1923	1.12	1.04	.66	.68	.78	.83	.90	.85	1.07	.90
1924	1.26	1.12	.79	.75	.85	.90	.97	.90	1.21	.95
1925	1.17	1.19	.79	.75	.82	.88	.95	.88	1.08	.87
1926	1.18	1.10	.77	.80	.85	.91	.93	.97	1.13	.90
1927	1.26	1.09	.78	.80	.87	.92	.95	.93	1.09	.90
1928	1.26	1.12	.77	.80	.86	.93	.93	.90	1.12	.88
1929	1.19	1.07	.72	.77	.86	.92	.95	.91	1.11	.90

SOURCES: Nominal farm wages from U.S. Department of Agriculture, *Crops and Markets*, vol. 19, no. 5 (Washington, D.C.: Government Printing Office, 1942); cost of living index from Jeffrey G. Williamson and Peter Lindert, *American Inequality* (New York: Academic Press, 1980), 319–20.

laborers as valued employees rather than as a child race."[5] But was this really true for the interwar years? Economic theory implies that if, in the wake of the wider horizons and labor market pump priming of the world war, southern landlords were increasingly in competition with northern industrial employers, southern farm wages should have risen, and the gap between northern and southern wages should have closed. Instead, real farm wages *declined* in nearly every southern state to levels no higher than those prevailing before the war (table 7.2). Comparisons between real wage levels across long time periods should not be taken literally, but it is still remarkable that across the Deep South from South Carolina to Texas, re-

TABLE 7.3

Southern Lumber Wage Deflated by Cost of Living Index (1914 = 100)

Year	Laborers	Doggers	Setters	Edgermen	Sawyers, Head Band
1912	.146	.163	.226	.236	.568
1913	.150	.168	.234	.245	.572
1915	.136	.152	.213	.221	.519
1919	.147	.188	.196	.197	.331
1921	.114	.136	.180	.196	.437
1923	.136	.164	.220	.227	.489
1925	.136	.159	.216	.221	.489
1928	.136	.163	.227	.223	.496

SOURCE: Abraham Berglund, George T. Starnes, and Frank T. de Vyver, *Labor in the Industrial South* (University, Va.: Institute for Research in the Social Sciences, 1930), 41.

ported real wages of farm labor were no higher in 1929 than they had been in 1890.

The wage decline was not limited to agriculture. In the lumber industry, the next most important employer of black and white unskilled labor, the picture was the same: the real wage increase during the war did not last, and wages were not pulled up by outside demands; instead they fell (table 7.3).

The important point about these developments was not the fact of decline, which reflected primarily the stagnation of the world cotton economy, but the fact that southern wages declined while the *northern industrial wage was rising*, a clear sign of the continued separation of regional labor markets. Table 7.4 presents indices of the gap between the southern farm wage and the northern industrial wage, showing that the spread was wider in 1929 in every southern state than it had been in 1914. In every state but Virginia and North Carolina, the gap was wider in 1929 than in 1899. These facts do not result from differences in the regional cost of living, as the table shows.

What then did happen during the war? How was it possible that such massive upheaval had so little effect on southern labor market institutions? There were a number of elements in the wartime migration that made it less revolutionary than the figures may suggest. The migrants were by no means typical southerners. Perhaps half or more came from towns and cities,

TABLE 7.4

Indexes of North–South Wage Gap: Southern Farm Wage/
Urban Unskilled Wage (1914 gap = 100)

Year	Va.	N.C.	S.C.	Ga.	Ala.	Miss.	Ark.	La.	Tex.	Tenn.
1899	84.0	76.3	80.5	81.6	85.2	92.3	90.3	97.2	87.4	92.6
1914	100.0	100.0	100.0	100.0	100.0	100.0	100.0	100.0	100.0	100.0
1915	98.0	96.1	73.5	94.1	94.9	96.1	94.5	98.0	96.6	94.1
1916	100.3	95.2	75.4	93.7	89.5	92.9	94.0	92.2	92.1	93.1
1917	112.2	109.0	83.6	103.1	97.7	95.7	103.8	91.8	91.3	100.0
1918	110.2	102.9	73.3	103.2	98.3	99.8	101.7	95.3	83.6	93.4
1919	106.7	118.5	99.6	109.9	106.0	114.0	105.4	103.8	113.5	102.6
1920	116.9	125.0	100.6	114.6	113.4	121.3	109.5	110.0	108.6	105.2
1921	95.3	90.4	65.6	73.3	75.6	79.2	77.2	73.7	76.1	84.5
1922	95.8	102.4	63.2	76.6	81.3	87.7	81.1	85.4	73.6	83.0
1923	90.9	90.2	57.2	63.9	72.6	74.9	71.1	67.1	70.6	79.6
1924	100.0	95.0	67.0	69.0	77.3	79.4	77.5	69.6	78.1	82.2
1925	94.9	103.2	68.5	70.6	76.3	79.4	75.0	69.5	71.3	76.9
1926	93.2	92.8	65.0	73.2	77.0	79.9	71.4	74.5	72.5	77.5
1927	96.3	89.1	63.8	70.9	76.3	78.3	70.7	69.2	67.8	75.0
1928	93.8	89.1	61.3	69.1	73.5	77.0	67.4	65.3	67.9	71.4
1929	87.5	84.1	56.6	65.6	72.5	75.2	67.9	65.1	66.3	72.1

Corrected for Regional Cost-of-Living Differences

Year	Va.	N.C.	S.C.	Ga.	Ala.	Miss.	Ark.	La.	Tex.	Tenn.
1899	86.7	80.2	85.1	85.9	94.1	103.4	103.8	110.5	100.4	101.7
1920	116.7	126.1	102.1	115.9	116.9	125.9	117.4	115.8	114.6	108.0
1929	94.0	95.8	67.1	67.1	88.8	86.9	85.8	72.4	76.4	83.2

SOURCES: Urban unskilled wage and cost of living index from Jeffrey Williamson and Peter Lindert, *American Inequality* (New York: Academic Press, 1980), 319–20; nominal farm wages from U.S. Department of Agriculture, *Crops and Markets*, vol. 19, no. 5 (Washington, D.C.: Government Printing Office, 1942).

and had long since left agricultural work. The great majority of departures from the Alabama steel towns of Birmingham and Bessemer were experienced miners heading for the coal fields of Kentucky, West Virginia, and Pennsylvania. Most of the migrants were single men with no responsibilities, and such long-distance moves had long been accommodated and even expected within the southern institutional system.[6] Virtually all of the decline in farm labor came from the wage-labor class, which had always been much more "floating" and long-distance than the croppers and tenants. Certain developments in the immediate prewar years had also tended to increase the "floating" element of the farm population. Though the boll weevil had little effect on aggregate cotton profits, it was devastating in some areas even before the war. The heavy out-migration of blacks and whites from Mississippi after 1910 was clearly related to weevil encroachment.[7] In addition, the initial effect of the war was not to stimulate but to disrupt cotton markets, forcing an actual closing of exchanges for three months in 1914. Severe floods in 1916 added more refugees to the number of rootless people flocking into the towns where northern agents were active.

Thus, much of the migration stream consisted of unrepresentative southern workers with industrial experience that could not readily be replicated by others, and another component was refugees whose departure did not disrupt established tenancy systems elsewhere. The latter class was of course not in such great demand. Labor agents were considered highly unscrupulous if they misrepresented a "boll weevil negro" as an experienced miner.[8] Undoubtedly many managed to do so anyway, but the distinction and the disputes about it tell us something basic about the nature of the migration.

What is quite clear is that established tenants did not leave in any great numbers. A survey of plantation tenants in the western cotton states during 1918 and 1919 found that 21 percent left their farms between years, but only 8 percent of these (1.6 percent of the total) went North. In the Southeast, the numbers may have been higher, but many of these were former tenants who had lost their tenant status.[9] This does not mean that tenants were unaffected by labor market conditions. The plantation regime accommodated the out-migration by expanding the tenancy and cropper acreage relative to the wage acreage. But the majority of southern farm laborers were also still tied to the region by the prospects of moving up the tenure ladder in the traditional fashion. Except for the distressed localities, these prospects never looked better than during the wartime prosperity. For these reasons, despite appearances, the war did not produce fundamental change in southern agricultural institutions, nor in the regional character of most labor markets.

Analysts have been misled in part by their focus on migration rather than labor market indicators. Out-migration continued high in the 1920s (see table 7.1). But "migration" is not a single human phenomenon subject to stable "laws." It may reflect the *functioning* of labor markets in one period, the active bidding among employers for a pool of mobile workers. But in another period, migration may result from the *malfunctioning* of labor markets, the failure of "market clearing" to occur because of local crises or inflexible wages. The labor flows of the 1920s were a mixture, but with much more of the latter than the former. The most sophisticated econometric analysis of this period finds a clear distinction between the determinants of migration before and after 1920: incentives were decisive in the first period; constraints were dominant for the next two decades.[10] "Constraints" include information, finance, and job availability. Black migration, which has been much more thoroughly studied, followed distinct grooves from particular areas in the South to particular communities in the North. Dislocation caused by the boll weevil in the early 1920s was far more extensive and catastrophic than it had been earlier. Quite in contrast to the boom years, blacks and unskilled white Southerners generally had no assurances of jobs waiting in the North. More often at this point the moves were mere shots in the dark, made possible by the presence of friends and relatives in northern cities, but with no clear access to the mainstream of national labor markets.

The 1920s were not good times for unskilled, inexperienced, poorly educated Southerners to break into American industrial employment. Employment trends were going just the other way. The cutoff of foreign immigration was confirmed and made permanent, and wages were high, but in response to these conditions, mechanization and rates of productivity growth accelerated. As a result, there was almost no growth in industrial employment. Even more important, many northern employers were changing their basic approach to the labor market. By establishing personnel departments and offering longer-term inducements to workers (such as internal promotion plans, insurance schemes, and other fringe benefits), employers were, in effect, accommodating high wages by being more selective (qualitatively and quantitatively) in the labor market. The triumph of "high-wage" thinking represented a culmination of long-term trends in business thought and social policy that paralleled the slow maturation of an experienced industrial labor force with lasting attachment to their jobs and communities. But these trends were accelerated during the war and institutionalized in many industries during the 1920s. If these alternative policies had not been available, it is doubtful that employers would have accepted the end of immigration with as little protest as they did. For these reasons, the long isolation of the South had lasting costs, even for those who did go North after 1920, only to find themselves unqualified for anything but menial jobs. In the absence of a strong pull from the North, the fortunes of the great majority of Southerners were still determined in the labor markets of the South.[11]

The Textile Industry and the Night-Work Issue

It would be quite wrong, however, to say that nothing important had changed in the South. The establishment of black footholds in northern industries, however precarious, was a new element in the postwar situation, creating a potential for out-migration that had not been there before. The steel industry, for example, a real holdout against the immigration cutoff and the new labor policies of the 1920s, continued to recruit in the South. The outflow of experienced black workers from Birmingham was a continuing problem there. With the aid of hindsight, it might seem that the ultimate unification of the national labor market was inevitable. The diffusion of the radio and the automobile, the gradual broadening of horizons and knowledge of the outside world, it would seem, might eventually have forced the South to pay a competitive wage to hold its labor. Perhaps it was inevitable, but this is not the way it actually happened.

Strictly as a matter of economics, it is just as imaginable that low-wage labor displaced from cotton agriculture might have been absorbed in a growing industrial sector within the South. As the South moved from agricultural production for the world market to industrial production for the national market, the conditions for what is known in economics as "factor price equalization" increasingly came into play. But wage convergence might have operated through the product market rather than through the labor market, and it might have been an equalization downward toward southern levels rather than upward toward northern standards. As the New England textile industry staggered in the face of southern competition, and as rayon, paper, rubber, furniture, tobacco, and other industries began to trickle south in the 1920s, this was indeed a pressing fear, taken seriously by both labor and capital in the North. There were many reasons why it did not quite happen this way either, but one of the clearest is that political pressures blocked the way. It was not primarily *market* forces that forced convergence through migration of labor and capital, but *political* pressures on the labor market that imposed wage convergence well in advance of the market out of fear of southern competition. The campaign against night work in the textiles industry was an early example.

The night-work problem was so widely misunderstood at the time that some background is needed. Among textile industry historians, the prevailing view has been that the rise of night work in the 1920s was a legacy of wartime experience with double shifts. They apparently believe that night work was an innovation that had not been feasible earlier, or that attitudes had changed so that (as one writer put it) "night work became socially acceptable for the first time" after the war.[12] Industry leaders as well as reformers did see night work as something new and insidious during the 1920s; they often viewed multiple shifts as the root cause of overproduction problems in textiles. Northerners saw night work in the South as another aspect of cheap-labor competition. The well-known Harvard free-trade economist Frank Taussig described southern textile expansion as "an artificial and almost insensate growth, much promoted by the use of nightwork so widespread as to shame our civilization."[13] But many southern industry men also came to see "the unrestricted night operation of plants" as "the most menacing factor of excess productive capacity."[14] It seemed that some new competitive force of self-destruction had been unleashed. The North Carolina textile economist Claudius T. Murchison wrote a book entitled *King Cotton Is Sick*, which stated:

TABLE 7.5

Percentage of Firms and Percentage of Labor
Force at Firms Reporting Night Shifts,
North Carolina, 1905–26

Year	Firms	Workers	Year	Firms	Workers
1905	23.0%	34.0%	1913	23.3%	24.1%
1906	21.4	31.6	1914	24.0	21.5
1907	18.5	27.7	1916	26.1	24.5
1908	15.3	23.0	1918	40.5	36.7
1909	14.1	14.3	1920	11.9	10.5
1910	16.9	15.2	1922	36.0	38.1
1911	17.3	14.9	1924	43.5	42.6
1912	19.0	15.6	1926	52.7	57.2

NOTE: Reprinted, by permission of the publisher, from Martha Shiells and Gavin Wright, "Night Work as a Labor Market Phenomenon: Southern Textiles in the Interwar Period," *Explorations in Economic History* 20 (1983): 343, table 1.
Data compiled from North Carolina Bureau of Labor and Printing, *Annual Reports* (Raleigh: State Printers, 1905–1926), 17–35.

The behavior of the textile industry is spangled with astonishing inconsistencies and incredible paradoxes . . . but none will seem more beyond understanding than that while 12 percent of the industry's equipment is being junked because of lack of orders, the other 88 percent should be lashed into an artificial fever of excitement to keep from suffering the same fate.[15]

As Murchison noted, "Many mills which run at night openly condemn the practice."[16]

But night work was not a new invention in the 1920s. There are numerous reports, in such journals as *Manufacturers Record*, of mills running "day and night" during the 1890s, and notices of mills using electric lighting at that time.[17] As early as the 1880s, virtually all Japanese cotton spinning mills were run on a twenty-four-hour basis. Closer to home, a 1909 study of the Mexican cotton industry reported that mills in that country "run night and day, and usually figure on 135 hours a week," more than twice the average for the South as of the early 1920s.[18] Table 7.5 presents evidence from North Carolina indicating that night work was by no means rare as of 1905, and did not suddenly become standard at the time of the war. Instead, the practice gradually grew over the course of the 1920s. This was the general pattern. In 1926, 41 percent of southern mills reported night shifts, 42 percent in 1928, and 64 percent in 1930.[19]

If night work was not a new innovation, then how do we explain its spread in the midst of depressed demand conditions? To understand night work, we really have to understand the *absence* of night work. Why would firms let plant and equipment sit idle overnight? The testimony of employers always emphasized one key factor: labor scarcity. In 1919, when the U.S. Housing Corporation asked textile firms in Charlotte, North Carolina, how many shifts they ran and why, only two of twenty reported more than one, and virtually every one of the one-shift firms gave "scarcity of help," "lack of labor," or "labor shortage" as the reason.[20] Respondents indicated that night work had come and gone over the years according to the availability of labor. In an interview conducted in 1907, a prominent cotton manufacturer stated:

> When labor was plentiful, in the early days of the cotton industry in the South, people came from the farms begging for work. They were so anxious to secure employment that the fact of its being night work did not matter. Then the mills were sure of securing as good a class of operatives for night shifts as for day shifts and night work was as profitable as day work. But from 1900 on, when labor began to be scarce, this condition vanished. The better class of operatives could always get day work. This left the least intelligent to do night work. Hence the product of such work was of inferior quality and less profitable than the product of day work.[21]

This earlier history points to the view that the spread of night work in the 1920s resulted from the emergence of labor surplus conditions, a situation that was itself the product of agricultural depression and sticky industrial wages.

Figure 7.1 may help to clarify the economics of night work.[22] The firm allocates its workers between two shifts on the same equipment. It would prefer to balance the shifts equally so as to get the most out of its capital, but it is prevented from doing so by the reluctance of labor to work at night. This reluctance is reflected in the "night work premium," which may be an explicit premium in cents per hour or (more commonly) an *implicit* premium, that is, the knowledge that a worker with

FIGURE 7.1

Disequilibrium Wage and the Expansion of Night Work

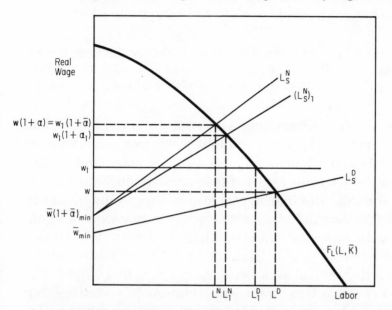

NOTE: Reprinted, by permission of the publisher, from Martha Shiells and Gavin Wright, "Night Work as a Labor Market Phenomenon: Southern Textiles in the Interwar Period," *Explorations in Economic History* 20 (1983): 338.

limited experience (one not considered part of the "good class of help") could get better pay if he accepted a job on the night shift than if he insisted on daytime work. At a small South Carolina mill in 1902, for example, the manager disliked night work because

> . . . apart from the cost of lighting the mill, the night shift had to be paid more than the day shift, he said, and no amount of driving would get equally good work out of them. The manager seemed to think that the main objection to the employment of very young children at night was their inability to keep awake. "They are always falling asleep," he said, "so we have as few of them as we can."[23]

When labor is in surplus, however, workers have to accept the night shift if they want any job at all; the company is only too happy to put them on the higher-productivity night jobs, and the premium declines. This is just what happened during the 1920s. Where premiums had been paid, they declined or disappeared. Families were required to supply night workers as a condition for obtaining a place in the mill village.[24] And exactly as figure 7.1 suggests, night work expanded even while the day shift contracted. As a 1928 observer remarked:

> A strange comment on shift work is offered by the combination of night work with short time. In many places, even with the mills running three or four days a week, the night shifts still continued.[25]

In other words, overproduction was not just another aspect of low southern wages. Instead, night work was a symptom of surplus labor conditions that arose because wages did *not* fall to the market-clearing level of the depressed southern market.

Why then did the industry choose to look at the matter in the way that they did? As practical people, they were less concerned with historical understanding than with doing something about their plight. They could not do much about the wage, but they hoped to raise prices by restricting output. The night-work issue was strategically chosen to mobilize labor and reform groups on the side of output reduction while avoiding antitrust prosecution. By defining the issue in terms of night work for women and children, the Cotton Textile Institute (CTI) managed to bring to its support such unlikely bedfellows as the National Consumers League, the Southern Council on Women in Industry, and the League of Women Voters. The concerns of the Women's Bureau about suffering from loss of sleep, deprivation of sunlight, accident rates, and neglect of families were undoubtedly genuine; but it is equally clear that the campaign did not emanate from the southern women mill workers themselves.[26]

The night-work issue was strategic in another and even more fundamental way. By defining the problem as "overproduction" rather than wage rates, the Cotton Textile Institute was able to unite northern and southern producers who would otherwise have been political adversaries. Though the opposition within the industry was mostly southern, many of the larger companies and perhaps a majority of the southern producers were won over to the scheme by 1931–32. In the absence of enforcement machinery, however, the problem was getting worse even while support for night-work prohibition was growing, for reasons any economist can understand. Manufacturers would not agree to cut out night work *voluntarily* unless assured that all competitors would have to do the same. In fact, what happened in 1931 and 1932 was that firms were able to declare that they *had* voluntarily eliminated night work for women and children, because the deepening depression allowed them to fill their night shifts with adult men desperate for work. Thus, the night-work campaign never actually succeeded in its original form, but it laid the groundwork for the industry's response to the National Industrial Recovery Act (NIRA) in 1933.

The NIRA was the first major legislation of Roosevelt's New Deal, and was an ambitious experiment in "industrial self-regulation" in which industries were empowered to establish "codes of good behavior" covering prices, wages, hours, and other relevant variables, the codes to be enforced by governmental authority. The NIRA provided exactly the kind of enforcement the industry associates had been looking for, and the cotton textile industry was, in fact, the first in the nation to jump on the bandwagon. The code enacted a strong version of night-work prohibition; it went further, indeed, to limit the work week to forty hours for labor and a total of eighty hours for machinery (the so-called forty-forty plan). The effects may be seen in the figures on spindle-hours per spindle (table 7.6), which fell back sharply between 1933 and 1935, the two years during which the NIRA survived. When the NIRA was declared unconstitutional by the Supreme Court in 1935, however, spindle hours jumped to new highs in 1936–37, 1938–39, and 1939–40. A 1937 survey reported that the second shift had become "all but universal," with 35 percent of southern firms making use of a third shift.[27] Night work never returned to political prominence thereafter.

Why was a reform with such a broad potential range of support unsuccessful? For the simple reason that the southern labor surplus conditions that encouraged night work grew more severe over time, so that the system came to be embedded in the routine of the industry and abolition became hopeless. The reason behind the reason was that southern textiles experienced continuing upward pressures on wage rates from 1933

213

TABLE 7.6

Spindle Hours Per Spindle, Southern States,
1921–57 (Years Ending 31 July)

Year	Spindle Hours Per Spindle	Year	Spindle Hours Per Spindle
1921–22	2,976	1939–40	4,232
1922–23	3,389	1940–41	4,920
1923–24	2,937	1941–42	5,855
1924–25	3,171	1942–43	6,042
1925–26	3,274	1943–44	5,590
1926–27	3,625	1944–45	5,352
1927–28	3,527	1945–46	4,882
1928–29	3,627	1946–47	5,275
1929–30	3,236	1947–48	5,425
1930–31	2,851	1948–49	4,574
1931–32	2,801	1949–50	5,084
1932–33	3,483	1950–51	5,795
1933–34	3,067	1951–52	5,040
1934–35	2,825	1952–53	5,509
1935–36	3,431	1953–54	5,141
1936–37	4,111	1954–55	5,423
1937–38	3,180	1955–56	5,609
1938–39	3,779	1956–57	5,536

NOTE: Reprinted, by permission of the publisher, from Martha Shiells and Gavin Wright, "Night Work as a Labor Market Phenomenon: Southern Textiles in the Interwar Period," *Explorations in Economic History* 20 (1983): 348, table 3.
Data compiled from U.S. Bureau of the Census, *Statistical Abstracts of the United States*, (Washington, D.C.: Government Printing Office, 1923–1958).

until the early 1950s. Not only were wages not allowed to fall to a market-clearing level, but they were raised still further. When the NIRA code cut the workweek, it also nearly doubled the hourly wage in the southern branch. Figure 7.2 shows the dramatic change between July and August of 1933. With the demise of NIRA, southern wages began to slide somewhat, but the enactment of the Fair Labor Standards Act of 1938 re-established the minimum, which subsequently increased in steps to a level of forty cents per hour by 1941. In effect, national wage standards were imposed on southern textiles, and the successful implementation of this policy ensured the failure of the crusade to abolish southern night work. By far the largest increases in weekly plant hours since 1929 have occurred in

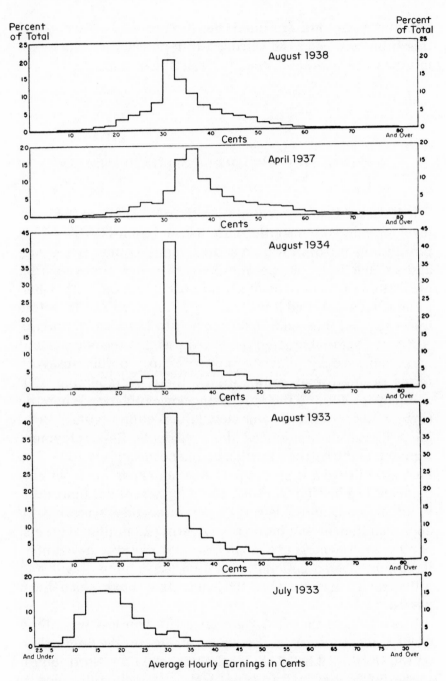

FIGURE 7.2

Percentage Distribution of Average Hourly Earnings in the
Southern Region of the Cotton Textile Industry

NOTE: U.S. Bureau of Labor Statistics, Bulletin no. 663 (Washington, D.C.: Government Printing Office, 1938), 118.

two low-wage southern industries (textiles and tobacco), and this transition occurred during a time when shift work premiums were small and steadily declining in real terms.[28]

New Deal Wage Policy and Southern Industry

The National Recovery Administration (NRA) raised the wage level for many other southern industries besides textiles. This tumultuous program was so short-lived (less than two years) and so chaotic in its operation, and is so far removed from present-day conceptions of sound economic policy, that historians have assumed it was merely a fiasco with little lasting influence. But this is not so for the South. The idea behind the NIRA (the act that created the NRA) was that recovery would be encouraged by allowing industries to prohibit unsavory forms of "cutthroat competition," thereby stabilizing both company profits and the purchasing power of labor. When the early industry response was slow (after cotton textiles), President Roosevelt announced the President's Re-employment Agreement (PRA), the so-called blanket code, in July 1933. The PRA established a limit of thirty-five hours per week per employee for industrial workers, and a forty-cent per hour minimum wage. Under this sort of pressure, codes were hastily approved in over 450 industries covering 23 million workers, or more than 90 percent of all industrial workers in the country. It was, in effect, a national minimum wage, more drastic and universal in its coverage than any that have since been passed.[29]

The effects of the NRA were far greater on low-wage than on high-wage industries, hence far greater on the South than on the North. Table 7.7 shows the impact on the North-South wage differential in furniture, iron and steel, cotton goods, paints and varnishes, and tobacco. The overnight increases in the southern hourly wage ranged from 21.5 percent in paints and varnishes to more than 70 percent in lumber. These figures

TABLE 7.7

Effects of the NRA on Regional Wage Differentials

Industry	Pre-NRA Average Hourly Earnings			NRA Average Hourly Earnings		
	South	North	South ÷ North	South	North	South ÷ North
Furniture	28.4	44.9	.633	38.7	44.8	.864
Iron and Steel	28.3	45.9	.617	42.5	59.4	.715
Cotton Goods	23.9	32.4	.738	34.3	42.0	.817
Paints and Varnish	37.1	47.2	.786	45.1	54.3	.830
Lumber	17.0	38.9	.437	29.0	53.0	.547
Tobacco	27.9	38.0	.734	41.4	47.1	.879

SOURCES: Charles F. Roos, *NRA Economic Planning* (Bloomington, Ind.: Principia Press, 1937), 159; Harry Mortimer Douty, "Recovery and the Southern Wage Differential," *Southern Economic Journal* 4 (1938): 319–20.

are averaged over all workers in an industry, skilled and un-skilled; hence they understate the increase for southern un-skilled workers, on whom the codes had their biggest effect. The industry cases vary considerably. In lumber and furniture, the NRA reversed a three-year downward slide in money wages; in cotton goods and in iron and steel, southern wages were already quite sticky. In every case, however, the NRA significantly reduced the North-South differential, and the im-portant point is that these reductions were never really reversed.

Wages did begin to slip in some industries with the demise of NRA in 1935. Plans to continue the NRA standards volun-tarily were announced by some businesses, such as Dan River Mills, the Virginia-Carolina Chemical Corporation, and the American Tobacco Company. By contrast, most firms in lumber and furniture beat a quick retreat.[30] But the retreats were lim-ited for several reasons. Wage increases are often difficult to reverse for firms with experienced employees. In this instance, the federal government supported higher southern wages in another way, through the policies of the work-relief programs, especially the Work Projects Administration (WPA). Originally mandated to pay local "prevailing wages," the WPA minimum rates in the southern states were only half the levels for the northern states. But between 1935 and 1939, the southern rates

TABLE 7.8

WPA Minimum Monthly Wage Rates, 1935–39

	May 1935	June 1938	August 1939
North			
Massachusetts	$40	$40	$39
Pennsylvania	40	40	39
Michigan	40	40	39
Illinois	40	40	39
Nebraska	32	40	39
South			
Virginia	21	26	31.20
North Carolina	19	26	31.20
South Carolina	19	26	31.20
Georgia	19	26	31.20
Alabama	19	26	31.20
Mississippi	19	26	31.20
Arkansas	21	26	31.20
Louisiana	21	26	31.20

SOURCE: Donald S. Howard, The WPA and Federal Relief Policy (1943; reprint, New York: Da Capo Press, 1973), 160.

steadily increased while the northern rates were unchanged (in some cases they actually fell). By 1939, WPA minimums in the South were up to 80 percent of northern minimums (see table 7.8). These rates were often more than double the farm wage, perhaps more cash money than southern workers had seen before. The WPA certainly did not employ all people who might have wanted to work at these wages. Indeed, there were cases in which whole classes of workers were dismissed from WPA jobs to work on the cotton or sugar harvest, even at lower pay.[31] But the work-relief wage set a standard that workers could hope to get if they waited their turn; this must surely have affected wage rates in other jobs.

A second way that the federal government raised southern wages in the 1930s was through the encouragement to unionization and liberal labor legislation. The unionization rate was still far lower than that of the rest of the nation in 1940 (10.7 percent compared to 21.5 percent), but even this figure was a significant increase, and in some industries, the effect was important. Though the textile strike of 1934 was decisively defeated, when the National Labor Relations Act (NLRA) of 1935 put the federal government firmly on the side of organizing, some millowners simply accepted their legal obligation to bargain and desist from "union busting."[32] In other cases, such as where unions would have had no chance given the balance of local power in depressed conditions, unionization was achieved only with the support of federal authorities.[33] National unions like those of the steel and rubber workers were important forces in bringing about the full equalization of industry wages in subsequent decades. For the most part, the South remained nonunion, but the organizational efforts focused national attention on southern conditions, and the state labor departments established under New Deal pressure were a continuing presence.

In the 1930s, however, the most direct federal effect on southern wage levels came through the minimum wage provisions of the Fair Labor Standards Act (FLSA) of 1938. Though southern industries may have been of incidental concern to the drafters of the NIRA and the NLRA, the FLSA was clearly passed by congress with its eye on the South. The act provided for an initial floor of twenty-five cents an hour, to be increased by steps of five cents a year to a limit of forty cents. Few employers outside the South were affected by these rates. Of the 690,000 workers earning less than thirty cents an hour in the spring of 1939, fully 54 percent were southern.[34] The thirty-two and one-half cent law which went into effect in October 1939 affected 44 percent of textile workers in the South, but only 6 percent in the North. The average percentage wage increase in the southern seamless hosiery industry between 1938 and 1940 was three times as large as that in the North. The hourly wage of black workers for independent leaf-tobacco dealers actually doubled between 1935 and 1940. Certainly most of the opposition was southern and was spearheaded by the Southern Pine Association, which considered the bill "by far the most important question facing our industry."[35] Cotton Ed Smith spoke for many employers when he told congress:

> Any man on this floor who has sense enough to read the English language knows that the main objective of this bill is, by human legislation, to overcome the splendid gifts of God to the South.[36]

It is pretty good evidence that a minimum wage is effective, when the wage frequency distribution shows a marked "heap-

FIGURE 7.3

Wage Distribution, Southern Lumber and Timber Products Industry,
1939–40

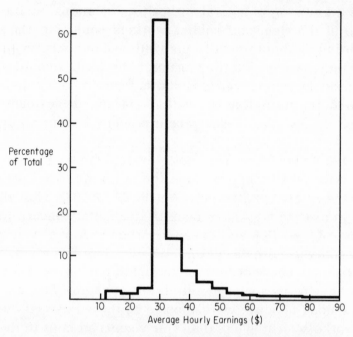

SOURCE: *Monthly Labor Review*, July 1941, p. 203.

ing" at or near the legal minimum. Many southern industry
distributions came to look just this way. In lumber and timber
products, half the workers in 1939–40 earned exactly the national minimum wage of thirty cents per hour (figure 7.3). The
southern lumbermen had good reason to lead the fight against
the FLSA.

Why was the New Deal administration so determined to raise
southern wage levels? Certainly "high-wage" thinking was in
the air in the 1930s; many, and perhaps most, supporters simply
felt that industry should be required to pay a decent wage,
and that was that. The WPA, for example, was not defensive
about paying wages above local levels. Its spokesmen argued
that "if any industry is paying less, somebody should investigate that industry," and that raising wage levels was "good
public policy in areas of extremely low living standards."[37] For
many advocates, the ideas that higher wages might stifle the
progress of southern industry or reduce the job opportunities

open to unskilled workers by stimulating mechanization were merely remote theoretical possibilities they would rather not confront. At the 1938 session of the Southern Regional Conference on Labor Legislation, a lone economics professor finally protested: "I have been profoundly impressed with the fact that you people do not answer the arguments that are brought against you."[38]

But if many people were unconcerned about possible economic repercussions of higher southern wages, it is equally clear that many others were looking closely at these effects, and that slowing the progress of low-wage southern industry was precisely what they wanted to do. The concerns of northern labor and industry groups about cheap labor competition from the South were of course not new, particularly in textiles. Between 1900 and 1903, the American Federation of Labor (AFL) had employed a young Englishwoman named Irene Ashby (later Mrs. Macfadyen) in a campaign for child labor laws in Alabama, Georgia, and South Carolina.[39] At the time of the debate over the Federal Child Labor Act of 1916 (which sought to prohibit the interstate shipment of goods produced by workers under sixteen), southern textile interests were firmly opposed but many northern producers were in support.[40] The widespread depression and suffering in New England textiles in the 1920s led the AFL to give some priority to southern organizing by the end of that decade, and as we have seen, industry groups gave implicit or explicit backing to efforts to raise labor standards in the southern mills. But all of these efforts intensified during the 1930s, precisely because the forces of labor were pushing wages up in the North and feared that southern competition would undermine all of their achievements.

The NRA, for example, did not question the opinion it received from the Department of Labor in 1933 that "there were no economic reasons for wage differences between regions and that these should be eliminated as soon as feasible," despite the fact that wage differences in excess of 50 percent for unskilled labor had lasted for more than a half-century at that point.[41] Once wage rates became direct objects of national decision, the inclination to move toward this conclusion was dif-

221

ficult to resist. John P. Frey, vice president of the AFL, observed in 1934:

> There are a large number of manufacturing industries bordering on the Ohio River. To give those on the southern side the 15 percent wage differential, results in lowering employment standards on the northern side of the river and taking away much business formerly done on the northern side and transferring it across the river into another state. These differentials create a problem as vital to the manufacturer's welfare as to the wage earners.
>
> The International Unions affiliated with this Department have no desire to place any handicap upon southern industries. But where southern manufacturers, because of much lower wage rates and lower standards of living invade other states with their cheaper products, and as a result tend to lower conditions of labor in states where higher standards of labor have been established, then the policy to be pursued becomes clearly evident.[42]

Once the higher standards had been accepted as a fait accompli in the North, many northern businessmen did come to see that they too had an interest in the matter. When H. C. Berckes, chief officer of the Southern Pine Association, canvassed business contacts in preparation for the fight against the FLSA in 1937, be found "very little sympathy among a number of those contacted toward our problem in the South." He reported to his subscribers:

> Frankly, I have found most of these businessmen anticipating a larger degree of influence by labor in their business, and the attitude of many of them would not be appreciated by the members of our industry. Much of this comes from the fact that there is plenty of agitation with respect to the necessity for curbing the trend of industry southward. A great many industrialists in the North, and especially politicians, believe that the South has an undue advantage and that labor is being sweated to the extent of destroying entire Northern industrial communities, which are already moving South because of wage differentials and agitation from foreign labor elements in the North.
>
> Many of the arguments that are being advanced for New Deal legislation are based on this premise.[43]

Thus, when Walter Lippman called the FLSA "in truth a sectional bill disguised as humanitarian reform," he exaggerated but not by much.[44]

It is also interesting to ask, however, why southern industrialists did not put up a better fight. In part, they simply lacked unity and regionally based organization. Southern textile men were lured into the *national* industry association by the night-work issue, and many of them seemed to discover only belatedly that the NRA cutbacks and wage hikes would apply disproportionately to themselves. Though southern industrialists later argued that "the NRA was devised, to a very large extent, to reform the South," it was only the following year that a concerted regional interest began to be expressed by the Southern States Industrial Council. By then, many of the changes were hard to reverse. In another dynamic that has frequently played a role in the extension of labor legislation, some *southern* firms found themselves paying high wages for one specific reason or another, and wanted to make sure that they were not undercut by "wage chiselers."[45]

But there was another, deeper, reason why southern industrialists were defeated, namely that the political forces of the New Deal were able to mobilize a *southern* labor and voting constituency in favor of these measures. Though the secretary of the Southern States Industrial Council claimed that "practically every one" of his organization's seventeen thousand southern industrialist members opposed the Black-Connery labor standards bill (forerunner of the FLSA), the Gallup poll reported in the same year that 56 percent of Southerners were in favor.[46] The decisive turning point in the legislative history of the FLSA came after two strong southern supporters were decisive winners in the 1938 primaries: Claude Pepper of Florida, and Lister Hill of Alabama; the latter had run for the seat vacated by the Supreme Court nomination of Hugo Black, himself the coauthor of the original bill.

It must be said, however, that not many blacks were voters in southern Democratic primaries in 1938, and black industrial workers were among the casualties of this line of policy. Just as an economist would predict, when jobs were made scarce by upward pressure on wages, racism became easier to indulge, and blacks were the first to be laid off. This tendency was unquestionably present in the interwar South well before the New Deal arrived, as demonstrated by the 1930 campaign slogan of the Atlanta Black Shirts: "Niggers, back to the cotton fields, city jobs are for white folks."[47] But the severity increased after 1933. Black spokesmen in Washington faced a cruel choice when the proposal for a racial wage differential was advanced in the early debate over the NRA. Recognizing the risks involved, the majority felt they could not support such an "official stamp of inferiority" and worked actively against the differential.[48] As right as they may have been for the long haul, the short-term consequences were severe. The Cowles Commission estimated that "directly or indirectly because of minimum-wage provisions of codes, about 500,000 negro workers were on relief in 1934."[49] Even for those still working, the cuts in hours stipulated or induced by the NRA often resulted in little or no increase in weekly pay. Black newspapers derided the NRA as the "Negro Removal Act," and it is easy to understand the source of this attitude when reading the bitter complaints expressed by black tobacco workers:

> I just haven't been able to see too much good in this NRA business. I don't believe its their [the Government's] fault either. I believe its just that the employers don't do what they ought to do. They say they are under the code and they don't act like it. They try to have you think you got a raise but they cut your hours and days down so much you don't draw what you think you should draw. You don't get any more money.
>
> I was raised twice under the NRA. I worked 10 hours and 5½ days a week before the NRA and I got less money. Then they put in machines to stem since the NRA and they put me on the machines. They laid off a hundred people when that NRA come in, and they put in that machine.
>
> They made us work harder now because they takes one or two hands and tries to make them work for four or five hands. I got raised under the NRA once and then got put off because of the machines they put in.[50]

The trend toward eliminating black jobs through mechanization and replacement by whites continued long after the NRA, under the FLSA and other sources of upward pressure

224

TABLE 7.9

Black Employment in Tobacco Manufacturing, 1930–60

Year	Total	Black	Percent Black
1930[a]	37,866	25,725	67.9
1940[a]	33,179	18,164	54.7
1950	40,663	15,119	37.2
1960	48,910	13,130	26.8

SOURCE: Herbert R. Northrup, "The Negro in the Tobacco Industry," in *Negro Employment in Southern Industry*, ed. Herbert R. Northrup and Richard L. Rowan (Philadelphia: Wharton School of Finance and Commerce, 1970), 29, 31.
[a] Figures for 1930 and 1940 are for laborer and operative employment only.

on the unskilled wage. A 1941 survey found that 95 percent of new job openings in Georgia were reserved for whites.[51] In the tobacco industry, where in 1930 two-thirds of the workers were black, the labor force was only one-fourth black by 1960 (table 7.9).

The fact that the burdens of displacement could be largely shifted onto blacks has to be counted as an additional reason why the South succumbed to the "Yankee plot" to impose northern wages. At the 1938 Southern Regional Conference on Labor Legislation, speakers objected to the whole idea of a "southern wage differential," saying that the apparent gap was merely due to the "abundance of colored labor." The representative from Mississippi commented:

> There are industries who pick the most unskilled labor and the people that can do the least work and put them on jobs that somebody else should be doing. . . . We should try to get these people to employ more competent workers.[52]

It does not take much reading between the lines to see the implication for black workers. Yet not much more than a decade later, a reputable economist could write that "it is unlikely that minimum wage legislation in the United States has had much effect," and that the North-South differential was largely attributable to the high percentage of nonwhites in the South.[53] What a complete misreading of cause and effect.

225

Federal Farm Programs, Mechanization, and the South

Yet another reason why low-wage southern industrialists were defeated in the South was that their natural political allies, the cotton planters, were going their own way in the 1930s. In contrast to the manufacturers, who struggled against more powerful northern adversaries and breaks in their own ranks, southern planters and their representatives were extremely powerful and cohesive in shaping agricultural policy. The chairman and ten of the twenty-four members of the House Agricultural Committee were southern; the chairman of the Senate committee was "Cotton Ed" Smith of South Carolina; the new head of the influential American Farm Bureau Federation was a northern Alabama planter named Edward A. O'Neal; and Oscar Johnston of Mississippi, owner of the largest plantation in the country, was perhaps the single most powerful person in the Agricultural Adjustment Administration. Not only was the legislation written from the planter's perspective, but at key points, discretionary powers were left to landlords and to local agents closely allied with landlords. This does not mean that the events of the 1930s were foreseen and tightly controlled by the "landlord class," but their position was a marked contrast to the fragmented and ineffective one of the southern industrialists.

The first policy steps, however, did not seem to be exploitive or biased, but directed toward the general benefit of the region. The deteriorating cotton prices hurt everyone, and the situation had reached a crisis two years before the New Deal: cotton prices had fallen from twenty cents per pound in 1927 to five cents in 1931; tobacco prices from twenty cents to eight cents. The Federal Farm Board, established by President Hoover in 1929 to stabilize commodity prices, had quickly exhausted its funds and turned to exhortations against excess cotton planting. Governor Huey Long of Louisiana proposed that 1931 be declared an extraordinary "Cotton Holiday"—an entire year with no cotton production at all—a plan that was approved by a conference of delegates from all the cotton-growing states.

The campaign failed, but not because it lacked broadly based political support in the South. An Alabama state representative wrote to Long: "Your great fight for the downtrodden cotton farmers of the South has made you the idol of 95% of our people. I mean, of course, the common people, and not the cotton gamblers, cottonseed oil kings, grafters and parasites who live by fleecing the common folks."[54] Southern political leaders had come to understand that raising cotton prices would require restriction of production, but these measures, which culminated in the Agriculture Adjustment Act (AAA) of 1933, were seen as a matter of economic justice for the entire region, not an enrichment of one class of Southerners at the expense of another.

No sooner was the legislation passed, however, than the elements of internal conflict emerged. The first AAA was not passed until May 12, 1933, well into the growing season. With an enormous carryover of twelve million bales hanging over the market, the administration determined that the only way to raise the cotton price substantially was to destroy a quarter of the crop, in other words to plow up more than ten million acres. The inducement took the form of a benefit payment of between seven and twenty dollars per acre released (depending on the estimated yield). Alternatively, farmers could take a smaller cash payment, plus an option on an amount of cotton equal to that destroyed, at six cents a pound. The benefits were to come in part from the direct payments, in part from higher cotton prices in the market. This latter goal was in good measure achieved, as the price rose from an average of six and a half cents in 1932, to over ten cents in 1933, and still higher levels in 1934–36. After 1933, the voluntary inducements were replaced by more compulsory controls under the Bankhead Cotton Control Act.[55]

The problem was, how should the benefit check be distributed among landlords, tenants, croppers, and laborers, and who should administer this distribution? The 1933 plowing in of the cotton crop provided that the benefit be shared *according to the tenant's share of the crop*, and in the haste of the emergency, the AAA relied heavily on the existing agricultural extension services, especially county agents, and on local committees dominated by landlords. The checks were mailed to the landlords, who were left to distribute the money appropriately, with virtually no effective federal enforcement. The 1934–35 contracts provided more explicitly for tenant participation, but only for cash tenants and "managing sharetenants," and this determination of status was again left to the discretion of local committees. At that point, the payment was divided into "parity" and "rental" components, tilted even more toward the landlord. In preserving and even worsening the preexisting distribution, the payment scheme was highly unequal on its face, but in addition, reports of cheatings, fraud, and illegal evictions by landlords were widespread. The "plight of the tenant farmer" became an object of national reformist concern, and a steady stream of journalistic exposes and surveys (and rebuttals) issued forth. The matter came to something of a head when a group of "New York liberal lawyers" in the AAA were "purged" in 1935, for their efforts to tighten safeguards against tenant evictions. Recent historical reconsiderations of this event have echoed contemporary assessments that these liberals simply did not understand "the art of the possible," that they failed to appreciate the difficulties of "forcing a new social order" on the South, that they were less prudent than FDR, who allowed: "I know the South and we've got to be patient." Taking a long historical view of the matter, however, we can see that it was not the northern liberals but the southern planters who were perpetrating revolutionary changes in southern institutions.[56]

To an economist, the honesty of the landlords is less important than the incentives created by the AAA system.[57] The AAA seemed to imagine that the plowing up of the crop, and later the cutback, would come proportionately from the entire plantation acreage, the wage-labor section and the tenants' plots. But the benefits from reductions in the tenants' acreage (including croppers) had to be shared, while those coming from the landlord's did not; any landlord pondering his options would quickly see that proportional cuts were not his most favorable choice. The *best* option from the landlord's standpoint was to take the reduction from the tenants' acreage but *report* it as coming from the wage-labor section. That way, the

FIGURE 7.4

The Allocation of Plantation Acreage Before and After the AAA

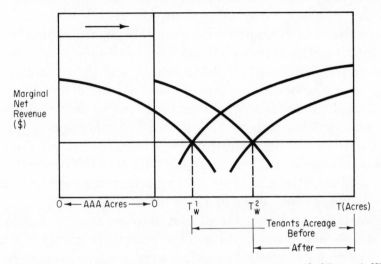

NOTE: Adapted from Warren Whatley, "Labor for the Picking," *Journal of Economic History* 43 (1983): 919.

landlord got the entire benefit "off the top" and reallocated the remaining acreage so as to equalize marginal net revenue between the two systems (figure 7.4). In the summer of 1933, this would have been "cheating," and landlords might have been restrained not just by the local committees but by the fear of losing their reputation in the market for tenants. By sending the check to the landlord, however, the AAA was surely dangling temptation before him, and undoubtedly many succumbed. Beginning in 1934, however, landlords did not have to engage in chiseling or fraud to gain these benefits, they merely had to reallocate the plantation acreage and the tenancy offers for the new season. Since the incentives pushed toward reducing the acreage assigned to tenants and croppers, worries about labor market reputations were not very constraining.

It is not surprising that there were widely varying claims and counterclaims about the number of evictions. Many Northerners thought of sharecropping as a "form of slavery," an opinion often echoed by historians, and they viewed the problem as croppers being turned away from ancestral plots and homes. But as we have seen, sharecropping had always been a high-turnover system; from year to year, croppers had never had any more security than the local market could provide. The real problem was not "eviction" but simply not adding new tenancies. No wonder there was such a sharp clash between the liberals who saw that landlords were evading the clear intent of Congress to extend help to all cotton farmers, and southern planters who felt that requiring them to maintain the very same group of tenants every year would have involved a more rigid and extensive bureaucratic control then that imposed on any other employer. Certainly it didn't happen, and it is hard to see how such controls could have been maintained in the face of powerful economic incentives to the contrary.

The decline of tenancy and the expansion of wage labor in the 1930s may be seen in many ways. In two Black Belt counties of Georgia, Arthur Raper found that between 1927 and 1934, the percentage of black farm families who were croppers fell from 45.8 to 31.1, while the percentage of wage hands and laborers rose from 20.5 to 34.5.[58] In the Mississippi Delta area, many planters switched to a wage system almost completely. As one of them told an interviewer in 1935: "Sure I'm going to shift to farming entirely by day labor next year. It's the only way a landlord can make money now."[59] To be sure, much of the "displacement" and "demotion" of tenants had occurred before the AAA, during the downward slide of 1930–33, just as it happened in the 1890s. What was new in the 1930s was that the downgrading was not reversed with the return of normal cotton prices; for farm laborers, things kept getting worse. The decisive effect of the AAA may be seen in the course of farm wages, which *declined* in 1933–35, from what were already depression levels (table 7.10). Even the recovery of the late 1930s did not bring farm wages back to the rates of the 1920s. These figures should be contrasted with the course of industrial wages, which was sharply upward (table 7.7).

The official surveys of the mid-1930s do not show a major absolute reduction of croppers and tenants between 1932 and 1935, suggesting that cases of outright abuse may have been exceptional. But because of the incentives created by the AAA, the recovery of cotton prices was not accompanied by any reinstatement of tenants; a survey of forty plantation counties between 1930 and 1935 showed virtually no net change in

TABLE 7.10

Southern Farm Wages, 1925–40

Year	Nominal Daily Wage[a]	"Real" Daily Wage[a] (1926 = 100)
1925	$1.65	$1.59
1926	1.66	1.66
1927	1.61	1.71
1928	1.60	1.65
1929	1.58	1.66
1930	1.41	1.63
1931	1.06	1.45
1932	.78	1.20
1933	.76	1.15
1934	.89	1.19
1935	.94	1.18
1936	.98	1.21
1937	1.09	1.26
1938	1.05	1.34
1939	1.07	1.39
1940	1.09	1.39

SOURCE: Herman Jay Braunhut, "Farm Labor Wage Rates in the South, 1909–1948," *Southern Economic Journal* 16 (1949): 195.
[a] Table shows annual average rates per day without board. Wages are deflated by the all-commodity wholesale price index.

croppers and share tenants, but a 20 percent increase in the number of wage hands. In the Red River and Arkansas River areas, the increase in wage hands was as high as 40 and 50 percent over five years.[60]

The elements of extreme inequity in the farm program have been recounted by historians many times: the enormous government payments to wealthy landlords, the domination of local administration by the planters, the evictions and displacements and the feeble efforts by the harassed and under-funded Resettlement Administration (later the Farm Security Administration) to resettle tenants on land of their own.[61] The three liberal Southerners who wrote in 1935 that "the landowner is more and more protected from risk by government activity, while the tenant is left open to risks on every side," were surely right.[62] What has not been sufficiently acknowledged, however, is that despite the "purge" of 1935 and the effective scuttling of the resettlement program, the farm pro-

TABLE 7.11

Landlord's Benefit Payments Per Acre
(on Acres Yielding 350 lbs. Lint)

Year	Managing Tenant	Share Tenant	Sharecropper	Wage Laborer
1933	$ 5.25	$ 5.25	$10.50	$21.00
1934	11.38	21.88	22.75	24.50
1935	6.22	13.34	14.44	16.63
1936	9.00[a]		13.63	18.50
1937	9.87[a]		14.94	20.25
1938	6.46[a]		12.92	25.85
1939	6.39[a]		9.77	25.55

SOURCE: Warren Whatley, "Labor for the Picking," *Journal of Economic History* 43 (1983): 915.
[a] Figures apply to managing tenant and share tenant; since 1936 there has been no distinction between managing and share tenants.

grams of the late 1930s were significantly improved as far as protecting the rights of tenants and raising their share of benefit payments were concerned. When the AAA was abolished by the Supreme Court in January 1936, Congress reenacted the same policies under another name, the Soil Conservation and Domestic Allotment Act. Under this legislation, share tenants and croppers received a share of the land rental (now called soil-building payment) for the first time. Significantly, checks were mailed directly to the tenants, a real break with plantation-area traditions. When total benefit payments were increased after the economic relapse of 1937, the landlord's share was steadily reduced (table 7.11). As unequal and unfair as the system continued to be, these benefits were of more value to more people than the lamented land distribution schemes could ever have been.[63]

This sort of moderate incremental success merely pressed the underlying contradiction more quickly: the more the status of the tenant was enhanced, the more the planters were induced to move to the wage-labor system. Rates of displacement accelerated; in fact, the absolute number of tenants of all kinds, which increased slightly between 1930 and 1935, declined by more than 25 percent between 1935 and 1940, while the number of hired laborers increased.[64] The effects were even more extensive when measured in terms of shares of acreage. In the Mississippi Delta region, the percentage of cropland harvested under the tenant system declined from 81.9 percent in 1930 to 58.2 percent in 1940.[65] In other words, while the tenants' plots remained small (and the allowed cotton acreage on each one declined), the size and production of the wage-labor acreage was rapidly growing. The means to this end was mechanization.

It is such a deeply embedded part of the American tradition to equate "mechanization" with "technological progress" that we often hear one or the other of these concepts invoked as an explanation for the decline of sharecropping, as though that were the beginning and end of the story. But mechanization in the South was *induced* by economic incentives, and in the 1930s, these incentives were largely created by government programs. Broadly speaking, the Southern economy was less mechanized before this time because southern labor was relatively cheap. Many writers refer to the 1930s planters "using the government check to pay for machinery," as though the access to cash or credit had been the chief roadblock all along. It is true that capital markets in the South were inadequate, and to many middling cotton growers in the 1930s, finance seemed to be the most pressing constraint. But problems of financing were not the fundamental reasons. The largest planters were wealthy by any standards and could easily have raised funds for investments that promised a high return. To cite one extreme example, Oscar Johnston's giant Delta and Pine Land Company of Mississippi, an efficient, well-financed capitalistic corporate farm if ever there was one, remained essentially unmechanized until World War II.[66]

To be sure, mechanizing the cotton *harvest* was a more difficult challenge than mechanizing the harvest of wheat or other grains, and no individual cotton farmer could crack this technical problem simply by wanting to. But the technology for mechanizing the preharvest operations was available well before the 1930s, yet it was hardly used at all in the South, and least of all in the plantation belt. In the 1930s, however, the plantation areas purchased tractors much faster than the rest

TABLE 7.12

Tractors Per Thousand Acres Harvested, 1930–40

	Nonplantation Counties			Plantation Counties		
	1930	1940	Percentage of Change	1930	1940	Percentage of Change
South	.52	.86	65	.40	.85	113
Southeast[a]	.79	.88	11	.39	.69	77
Delta[b]	.36	.51	42	.51	1.55	204
Alabama	.70	.60	−14	.27	.45	67
Arkansas	.28	.40	43	.46	1.30	183
Georgia	.43	1.02	137	.35	.87	149
Louisiana	.39	.94	141	.43	2.09	386
Mississippi	.54	.46	−15	.55	1.39	153
North Carolina	1.40	.96	−31	1.27	1.11	−13
South Carolina	.74	1.02	38	.58	.86	48
Tennessee	.70	1.34	91	.53	1.90	258
Texas	.88	2.54	189	1.16	1.36	17

SOURCE: Warren Whatley, "Institutional Change and Mechanization in the Cotton South" (Ph.D. diss., Stanford University, 1982), 33. (Based on a 250-county sample.)
[a] Counties in North Carolina, South Carolina, Georgia, and Alabama.
[b] Counties in Mississippi, Louisiana, and Arkansas.

of the South (table 7.12). Through most of American agricultural history, the rapid diffusion of labor-saving machinery has occurred at times of strong commodity markets, expanding acreage, and labor scarcity. Accelerated mechanization in a depressed region, a depressed sector, and a depressed economy is anomalous. But it makes sense in conjunction with the incentives to switch to wage labor that were offered under the federal farm programs of the 1930s.

The recent analysis developed by Warren Whatley has demonstrated that preharvest mechanization in the 1930s may be explained by a variant of the "threshold" model that fits many other cases: investment in a large fixed-cost machine like a tractor only becomes profitable when the scale of cultivation reaches a certain minimum level, or "threshold."[67] The southern plantations seemed to contradict this notion completely, since they were among the largest farming units in the country, yet they were the least mechanized. Most of the *operating* units (the tenants' plots), however, were small. What Whatley has shown is that the relevant concept of "scale" for mechanization is not the entire plantation, but the size of the wage-labor acreage. As argued in chapter 4, this acreage was constrained by the uncertainty of wage labor in relationship to the seasonality of labor requirements in cotton, particularly the as yet unmechanizable harvest. Tenancy was the price planters paid for the certainty of harvest labor. In response to liberal attacks on sharecropping as a "feudal" relationship, Oscar Johnston and other Southerners said with some accuracy that they would be glad to switch to a day-labor system whenever they could.[68] In the late 1930s, the AAA benefits gave them the incentive; thousands of displaced and unemployed farm laborers gave them the short-term labor when needed. As early as 1937, 36 percent of owner-operator cotton acreage in plantations was picked by off-plantation labor, and this percentage continued to increase. Even where the designation "sharecropper" was retained, the plots were often too small to support a family, so that supplementary wage labor came to provide as much as half of the cropper's annual income.[69] So long as the relief administrators cooperated by clearing the rolls at harvest times, southern planters had "labor for the picking" and were able to move toward preharvest mechanization even in the midst of the Great Depression.

The plantation regions like the Delta were certainly not typical of the whole South, and mechanization seemed as remote as it ever had been in the small farm areas in 1940. The experience in the tobacco belt was also markedly different. Farming units were smaller, labor requirements were more uniform across the year, and the technology for mechanization was more distant than in cotton. The inelastic demand for tobacco made it ideally suited for crop-reduction effectiveness, so that those who were fortunate enough to get in on the "allotments" programs beginning in 1934 enjoyed significant economic recovery even before the war.[70] For the longer term, however, the effect of the program was to freeze not only overall tobacco acreage but the number of allotments available. Anyone not on the ground floor would have to seek his economic fortune elsewhere, but not many new opportunities were opening up in any part of the South in the 1930s.

Implications of Changes in the South

At the end of the decade, many observers thought that little had changed. An authoritative 1940 survey on *The Plantation South Today* stated: "Cotton is still king in the South, and the plantation remains an important form of organization in the Cotton Belt. . . . it is chiefly the outward aspects that have changed"; a 1942 prize-winning essay held that "the plantation is as deeply rooted today as at any time in the history of the South."[71] These views were reasonable at the time. Yet with the aid of hindsight, we can see that they were wrong. The "outward aspects" of southern economic life had changed much less than the "inward aspects." The economic underpinnings and social glue that had kept the regional economy isolated were no longer present in 1940.

The first effect was massive out-migration of unskilled labor. The South was planter's heaven by the late 1930s, with generous government subsidies, protection against risk, ready financing for new machinery, and cheap harvest labor to make it all possible. But since agriculture could no longer offer either subsistence security or hope for advancement on the tenure ladder, there was nothing to keep these people in that sector when outside opportunities opened during World War II. The resulting "labor shortage" of the 1940s focused technological energies on breaking the harvest bottleneck, which finally gave way by the end of that decade. Statistical studies show clearly the correlation between out-migration and the incidence of federal cotton programs dating from the 1930s.[72]

The effects of the farm programs have to be seen in conjunction with the effects of federal wage policies. Because unskilled workers, especially blacks, could no longer be absorbed in expanding low-wage southern industry, there was nothing to keep them in the region altogether. Some southern industries, such as seamless hosiery and cottonseed oil, were badly set back by federal wage standards. But most industries did not collapse; instead, by mechanizing and instituting other improvements in efficiency, they found ways to survive and even to grow. What success they had on this basis, however, did not translate into employment; five southern states had fewer industrial jobs in 1939 than they had in 1909, and the South as a whole enjoyed virtually zero net growth in industrial employment between 1929 and 1939.[73] True, it was during the Great Depression; but this performance is a far cry from the growth of southern textiles in the depression of the 1890s, and a further cry still from the performance of low-wage Japanese industry in the depressed world economy of the 1930s. The hypothetical conception of a thriving low-wage industrial South absorbing its own displaced farm workers and developing its own sophisticated labor-intensive technology is not held out here because it was a near historical miss, something that almost happened. All things considered, it was unlikely technologically and impossible politically within the United States. But imagining the possibility is a way of underscoring the point that southern economic progress has been fundamentally shaped by the region's location within a national economy and a national political authority. Southern history is not a "case study in economic development," it is a case of a region being forced off of one growth trajectory and onto another, a case in fact of one large group of people being forced out of the economy altogether, and as we will see in the next chapter, another, more affluent, group coaxed in.

If orthodox market economists want to find examples of well-intentioned liberal interventions leading to hardships for the poor and the vulnerable, they can readily find them in these chapters of southern history. But that is not the full story. With all the suffering, the out-migration of blacks from the South after 1940 was the greatest single economic step forward in black history, and a major advance toward the integration of blacks into the mainstream of American life. At least one economist saw this happening, as early as 1933:

Orthodox economics would have [the Southern labor surplus] drained off through the long process of higher-wage inducements offered by the North. The NRA, on the other hand, proposes to force out the labor reserve by setting such high wage standards in the South that unemployment will result. Through employment exchanges, and other facilities, the surplus labor will then, presumably, be directed into the more profitable channels of Northern or other employment. . . . The agony of it will be more intense at the time, for both workers and owners, [but] the uniform minimum wage would tend to accomplish rapidly what natural forces would accomplish, theoretically, in the long-run.[74]

If the AAA was, as Gunnar Myrdal called it, an "American enclosure movement," then, like its predecessor, it had progressive consequences even while it was inflicting hardships on many people.

But out-migration and better lives in the North were only the first of these consequences. With the decline of the tenant plantation and the effective abolition of the low-wage industrial labor market, southern political and economic leadership no longer had strong interests in regional isolation from outside labor and capital markets. The response to this change in incentives was not immediate or universal, but over the next twenty years, the change in southern political economy was nearly total. Numan Bartley has recently written: "In 1940 the raison d'être of southern state governments was the protection of white supremacy and social stability; thirty years later their central purpose was the promotion of business and industrial development."[75] This change in the fundamentals of southern society ultimately made possible the success of the civil rights revolution of the 1950s and 1960s. As distant as these changes seemed in 1940, the economic bases were already there before World War II.

8

THE NEW ECONOMY OF

THE POSTWAR SOUTH

SINCE 1940, per capita income in the South has persistently grown at rates well above the national average. A glance at figure 8.1 will confirm that there was no sustained trend toward regional convergence before 1930. Since the modest rise during the 1930s primarily reflects the fact that the effects of the Great Depression were even greater in the North than in the South, the southern "takeoff" is most appropriately dated from World War II.[1] A number of interpretations have been advanced for this emphatic departure from previous history. Among the most prominent are these:

1. Southern growth has been stimulated by federal spending, beginning during World War II but with a continuing favorable share of defense dollars ever since.
2. Regional growth (so-called) represents primarily the equilibrating flows of capital and labor to locations of highest return.
3. The South has prospered as a part of the Sunbelt phenomenon that reflects the increasing importance of climate and other amenities in the residential preferences of skilled professional and managerial personnel.
4. The South has experienced the dynamism of the "clean slate," the relative absence of labor unions, entrenched bureaucracies, restrictive legislation, and the overall hardening-of-the-arteries that inevitably comes with economic maturity.

FIGURE 8.1

Per Capita Income as Percentage of U.S. Average, 1880–1980

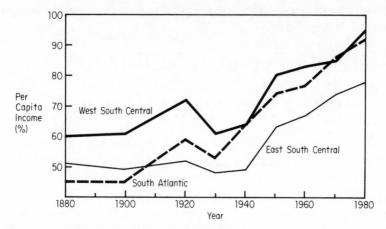

SOURCE: U.S. Bureau of the Census, *Historical Statistics of the United States*, part 1, series nos. 287, 292, 293, 294 (Washington, D.C.: Government Printing Office, 1975). (See note 1.)

Each of these accounts has an important component of truth.[2] What they miss, separately and jointly, is the historical context and the background developments. Why was it that these forces began to operate in the 1940s and not earlier? War plants, shipyards, and military training camps were economically important (and continue to be) in many parts of the South; what was new in the 1940s was the aggressive state-level political pressure for the South's "fair share" of military spending. Massive interregional flows of unskilled labor, skilled labor, and investment capital were critical, but the regional differences in factor prices that prompted these moves were not new in the postwar era. What was new was the drying up of low-wage employment opportunities in the South, and the enthusiastic efforts by public agencies and private interests to welcome outsiders and outside money into the region. The increased attractiveness of southern living to non-Southerners was in some respects new, but these amenities also reflect the conscious effort of the South to remake its image in the interests of a new set of economic strategies and purposes. Of course, voices of boosterism had been there all along; what was new was the balance of economic interests at the state level, the acquiescent silence of the voices of low-wage isolation whose economic future had been undercut in the 1930s.

240

The New Economy of the Postwar South

By the 1980s (and indeed much earlier in many places), a new Southern economy prevailed, located in the same geographic space as the old one, but encompassing a very different package of labor, capital, natural resources, and entrepreneurship: not an advanced version of the old economy, but a new economy. Thus the metaphor of the "clean slate" has basic appropriateness for the postwar South. But the South did not start over with a clean slate all at once as of any precise date. History seldom works that way, and it certainly didn't in this case. There was a distinct transitional phase between the war and the 1960s, and during this period completing the mechanization of the cotton harvest was the dominant regional development (a less devastating replay of a similar scenario has more recently been completed in tobacco). Since then, economic growth and immigration have been rapid in almost all parts of the South, to the point that it is now virtually impossible to find an essentially regional southern identity in economic life.

Southern Labor and the Mechanized Cotton Harvest

During World War II, the labor that had long been bottled up in southern agriculture poured out. The farm population declined by more than 3 million (about 22 percent) as young men responded to induction notices or to wartime job opportunities in the North or South. Most of the departures were not by owners or tenants, but by farm laborers and sharecroppers. Labor shortages in agriculture became acute. As farm wages tripled, women, children, and townspeople were pressed into service, and in some areas, shortages were so severe that war prisoners were ordered to the cotton fields. After a brief postwar "back to the farm" respite, the outflow continued in the late 1940s. The earlier trend toward mechanization was greatly accelerated during the war, but throughout the decade, cotton farmers were unable to complete the mechanization process for one specific reason: the harvest bottleneck. Though the International Harvester Company had begun to manufacture mechanical cotton pickers for commercial sale as early as 1941, numerous problems of operation, adaptation, and cost had kept both production and sales to insignificant levels for the rest of the 1940s. As late as 1950, an authority on southern agriculture could write that there was "little likelihood that mechanization will shortly sweep the entire cotton belt."[3]

Mechanizing the cotton harvest was a formidable task, it is true. The deft picking motion of the hand was much more difficult to replicate mechanically than the sweeping arm motion of the wheat cradle, for example. The successful diffusion of the mechanical harvester in the 1950s was not just a challenge to mechanical ingenuity, but involved the mobilization of a wide range of specialized technical and scientific talents working on complementary developments from weed control to the uniform maturation of the cotton bolls. But even when the full range of technical problems is acknowledged, it is difficult to believe that cotton could not have been mechanized years earlier if the incentives had been strong. As one writer observed in 1937: "A successful cotton picker has been just around the corner for the last eighty-seven years," the first patent having been issued as early as 1850.[4] Promising harvest strategies coming out of Texas around the turn of the century had not been taken up and developed to a state of commercial success.[5] And when John and Mack Rust demonstrated their mechanical picker in a series of tests in the early 1930s, the assistant director of the Delta Experiment Station observed that the Rust model was better as a cotton picker than the Model T Ford had been as an automobile when it was first introduced.[6] But by 1942 the Rust brothers still had only a development shop, the tools from which were sold to pay off their company's obligations. Only with the labor shortage of the 1940s did a giant corporation like International Harvester throw the full weight of its resources behind the effort to develop a commercially successful picker.

In other words, it was the integration of the national market for unskilled labor during the 1940s that created the pressure that led to the concentrated technological effort on the harvest

242

bottleneck. From the viewpoint of the individual grower during the decade, the technical and financial elements were binding; diffusion could not proceed until they were solved. Taking the historian's long view of the matter, however, the technical and financial barriers were broken down because, for the first time, the scarcity of harvest labor was severe enough that they had to be broken down. Or to view it from the standpoint of the machinery manufacturer, enough cotton planters were now potentially in the market for a mechanical harvester that it was worth the investment of time and money to satisfy their demand. Before the end of the decade, Deere and Allis Chalmers had entered the market as well. One may thus view the cotton picker as a delayed effect of the war. One may just as well view it, however, as a delayed effect of the organizational changes in southern agriculture in the 1930s. The planters who relied on wage labor for the harvest before the war now found that these laborers saw no good reason to stay in farming when decent jobs opened up elsewhere.

It is understandable that planters felt that they had no choice but to mechanize, that labor mobility had forced this decision on them willy-nilly. But it is equally understandable that many sharecroppers and farm laborers came to see "mechanization" as the villain, because with the successful breakthrough in mechanical cotton harvesting, the character of the labor market radically changed in the 1950s from "shortage" to "surplus." A dynamic simulation for the Delta region by economist Richard Day vividly portrayed the difference in the labor constraint before and after 1949 (figure 8.2).[7] On the Thomas Hottel Gist plantation in eastern Arkansas, expenses for hired labor fell from $5,215 to $2,428 in this one-year period.[8] The market transition was, of course, not the exclusive result of a single invention, but also reflected the slower pace of the national economy in the 1950s. Once the mechanical picker had been perfected, however, diffusion was far more rapid and thoroughgoing than observers had predicted. The percentage of the American cotton crop that was machine harvested went from 5 in 1950 to 50 in 1960, and was over 90 by the end of the 1960s (table 8.1). The market for unskilled labor has never returned to the level of tightness experienced in the 1940s.

243

FIGURE 8.2

The Derived Demand for Unskilled Labor in Delta Agriculture

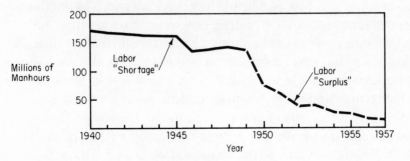

NOTE: Richard Day, "The Economics of Technological Change and the Demise of the Sharecropper," *American Economic Review* 57 (1967): fig. 3.
Figure shows unskilled labor for all crops.

TABLE 8.1

Percentage of Upland Cotton
Mechanically Harvested, 1949–1972

Year	Ark.	La.	Miss.	Tex.	U.S.
1949	1		4	11	6
1950	1	3	3	12	8
1951	2	11	7	19	15
1952	2	13	7	22	18
1953	9	34	13	24	22
1954	16	28	11	21	22
1955	25	28	23	24	23
1956	27	31	25	25	27
1957	15	35	17	37	32
1958	22	43	19	35	34
1959	36	50	38	44	43
1960	42	49	40	58	51
1961	51	56	48	64	59
1962	68	64	58	78	70
1963	73	75	65	81	72
1964	75	78	68	85	78
1965	83	82	76	90	85
1966	87	88	82	95	89
1967	93	93	87	97	94
1968	96	96	93	98	96
1969	96	97	94	98	96
1970	98	99	97	99	98
1971	99	99	99	99	99
1972	100	100	99	99	100

SOURCE: U.S. Department of Agriculture, Economic Research Service, *Statistics on Cotton and Related Data, 1920–1973* (Washington, D.C.: Government Printing Office, 1974), 218.

TABLE 8.2

Farm Operators in the South, 1930–1969
(in Thousands)

	White		Black	
Year	Owners[a]	Tenants[b]	Owners[a]	Tenants[b]
1930	1250	1092	183	699
1940	1384	943	173	507
1945	1526	690	189	476
1950	1553	540	193	366
1954	1454	399	181	283
1959	1151	228	128	138
1964	1017	171	102	82
1969	953	118	72	18

SOURCE: U.S. Bureau of the Census, *Historical Statistics of the United States to 1970*, part 1 (Washington, D.C.: Government Printing Office, 1975), 465.
[a] Includes part owners and managers.
[b] Includes croppers.

The oscillations from a decade of "pull" to a decade of "push" had profound effects on every aspect of human relations in the South. During the 1940s, the labor market was a sellers' market. In late 1944, the general manager of a Mississippi cotton cooperative observed: "Our Negroes have moved away. I don't think they will come back unless forced by necessity." When a labor leader inquired in 1946 about labor displacement in cotton, a Texas agricultural engineer replied that "instead of the machines replacing labor, they were used to replace the labor that had left the farm."[9] Concern for the loss of labor led Southerners to upgrade the level of spending on black schools. Though segregation persisted, a marked decline in racial inequality in education occurred in the South between 1945 and 1950.[10] The outflow of southern tenants and sharecroppers continued, however, long after these labor market conditions had reversed. The number of southern farm operators declined by 350,000 between 1940 and 1950, but by more than one *million* between 1950 and 1959 (table 8.2). Wage-labor employment temporarily expanded between 1945 and 1954 as the first wave of partial mechanization reached completion. With full mechanization, the decline in hired labor was equally precipitous. In this latter phase, it was not just footloose wage laborers

245

TABLE 8.3

*Migrant and Nonmigrant Unemployment Rates
by Race, 1950*

	Nonmigrant		Migrant	
	White	Nonwhite	White	Nonwhite
New York, Area A	5.2	14.6	6.8	33.3
New York, Area G	7.8	11.2	6.8	19.0
Pennsylvania, Area D	5.5	12.2	14.9	44.3
Pennsylvania, Area N	4.8	12.1	7.7	22.0
Ohio, Area A	4.6	16.8	10.1	39.3
Ohio, Area B	3.8	10.6	7.3	17.5
Ohio, Area C	2.3	7.3	5.5	17.2
Ohio, Area E	3.4	10.3	8.3	22.0
Ohio, Area F	7.1	15.2	17.4	38.9
Ohio, Area H	4.5	11.1	10.9	25.5
Ohio, Area K	4.0	12.9	8.4	36.3
Illinois, Area C	3.4	9.9	7.7	21.5
Illinois, Area F	4.9	11.0	4.3	16.4
Michigan, Area F	6.5	10.1	11.7	32.7
California, Area G	9.8	23.2	16.7	40.3
California, Area A	5.3	13.6	9.3	19.4
California, Area F	5.7	14.6	14.5	26.4

SOURCE: Alan L. Sorkin, "Education, Migration and Negro Unemployment,"
Social Forces 47 (1969): 272.

who departed, but established tenant farmers of both races. As
the large tenant plantations transformed themselves into giant,
fully mechanized "neoplantations," neither wage laborers nor
tenants were needed. As Gilbert Fite wrote, "Nothing so mod-
ified the southern rural landscape in the 1960s and 1970s as
the destruction of tens of thousands of sharecropper and tenant
houses."[11]

Displaced tenant farmers poured into the cities in the 1950s,
despite the fact that job prospects were no longer favorable,
particularly for blacks. As early as 1950, black unemployment
rates were between 10 and 15 percent in almost all the major
points of southern in-migration; and the unemployment rates
for new immigrants were staggering (table 8.3). The view of
things that portrays the southern blacks as simply the "next
immigrant group," successor to the European migrants of the
pre–World War I era, is thus seriously inappropriate. After
1950, black migrants, and indeed many southern white mi-

grants, were not moving into areas where jobs were waiting for them, where the industrial employment structure and the educational system was geared to integrating them as quickly as possible into the economy. Instead, they were moving into places where they may have had friends and relatives, but where the economy had relatively little use for them. Now it still may be, taking all relevant factors into account, that the lifetime economic prospects for blacks were better in the North than they would have been in the cotton South even in the absence of mechanization, and thus that the process as a whole was an improvement. It remains the case, however, that they had no choice. As blacks in Tunica, Mississippi, told a reporter in the 1980s:

> At one time, there were houses all over this plantation. . . . We didn't make much money but there was a place to live on the plantation and everybody had a little money. Now there's no work. . . . At first the farmers wanted to keep industry away from their labor, then they wanted to see them gone. They were careful not to do anything that might keep blacks here.[12]

For most white Southerners, it was "out of sight, out of mind." As knowledgable an economist as William Nicholls could write in 1960 that "fears of a parallel Southern enclosure movement, particularly through the effects of mechanization of cotton production, have failed to materialize."[13]

The question naturally arises: Could this history realistically have been very different? Ultimate mechanization may have been inevitable, and yet the speed and heartlessness of the transition did not have to be what it was. The perfection of mechanization involved an all-out research effort by public agencies as well as private firms, with intense concern for the competitive position of American cotton but little for the human consequences. Reflecting on his own early work on agricultural technology, Richard Day observed:

> At a time when the rest of the economy sluggishly ignored the growing influx of displaced agricultural workers, economists and popular commentators ironically suggested policies that would move resources out of agriculture even faster.[14]

247

The example of tobacco offers a glimpse of an alternative scenario. Mechanization of the tobacco harvest was also within technical reach as of the early 1950s, if not before. But mechanization was delayed until the 1970s by limitations on the size of farming operations, limits that were institutionalized in the tobacco allotment system dating from 1938. Because individual allotments could not be transferred and combined, the acreage of a single farm could not expand to the scale needed to cover the large fixed cost of a mechanical harvester. These restrictions reflected the fact that tobacco politics were dominated by small farmers rather than big planters. As pressure for change built up over time, tobacco allotments first became transferable at the county level, and then became detachable from the original acreage. Because of these and additional liberalizations (primarily the elimination of the requirement that leaves be "tied" by hand, which opened the door to bulk curing), large operations have been able to lease allotments and consolidate, passing the forty-acre threshold for economic adoption of the mechanical harvester. As in the case of cotton, when the demand emerged, the technology was forthcoming. No economist would give the tobacco program high marks by the standard of static efficiency (or horizontal equity), but at least the small farmers had a "property right" in the program that prevented gross evictions and hardships. As mechanization has proceeded gradually but steadily since 1970, displaced farmers have been able to find jobs in local industry, with little sign of worsening unemployment or out-migration.[15]

Yet, however different the history of cotton mechanization might have been, it must be acknowledged that for most of the South there was little promise in the future of cotton agriculture by 1950, no matter what arrangements might have been made or policies pursued. The prospects for American cotton were bounded by competition from synthetic fibers on the one hand, and from new centers of cotton production in Asia, Africa, and South America on the other. Quite possibly the high price supports maintained in the United States from 1933 onward served to accelerate both of these trends. But if the price of cotton had been thrown to the market, it could only have

248

accelerated the internal migration of production from the Old South to the new areas of the Southwest and Far West, whose potential was enhanced by developments in artificial irrigation.[16] Sooner or later, therefore, the tenants and farm laborers of the Southeast would have had to leave the farms and seek their fortunes in cities and towns. Hence our attention returns to the labor market, and to the changing relationship between the southern and national labor markets.

Migration and Regional Labor Markets

In recent years, the American economy has moved steadily toward national labor market integration in which wage and salary differentials come to reflect only costs of living and locational amenities. Even in the 1970s, many economists have found that with moderate adjustments for cost-of-living differences, there was little left of the "North-South wage differential."[17] It is tempting, especially for economists, to see this convergence as a long-run market equilibration, the migration of labor and capital to locations of highest return. Direct empirical studies of regional factor movements, however, show that this simple model does not fit the data in any consistent way over the twentieth century as a whole.[18] In light of the analysis of previous chapters, this should not be surprising. The migration of labor had different character at different times, sometimes following labor market channels but sometimes following only in the wake of displacement and desperation. The migration of capital was bound up with the migration of people and all of the social and economic forces that kept the South separate. Nor should it be surprising that studies of long-term trends in regional wage differentials report a bewildering array of conflicting conclusions, ranging from claims of steady, progressive convergence to claims of stubborn persistence over most of the century.[19] We can now see that convergence has occurred, but the process has been anything but steady.

One reason that wage trends have conflicted is that different southern wages have been pushed by different forces. Between the 1930s and the 1960s, wages at the low end of the southern distribution were directly influenced by federal legislation and pressure. In some other sectors, wages were influenced by the policies of national organizations, such as the federal government, national unions, or corporations with branches in the South. Still others may be considered "market-determined," but even this term has a different meaning when referring to people who have Ph.D.'s in chemistry (on the one hand) or to janitors and common laborers on the other. The "North-South differential" has had an unsteady history because the "southern wage" has been a complex average of these different components at different times.

One significant factor in the 1950s and 1960s was the federal minimum wage. Though wages in the South quickly outgrew the prewar floor during the 1940s, a new minimum of $.75 per hour was established in 1950, raised to $1.00 in 1956, $1.25 in 1961, and $1.60 by 1970. Beginning in 1961, coverage of the legislation was significantly broadened to include most retail trade, construction, and service industries, and some agriculture. In every case, the only significant immediate effects of these changes were felt in the South; in the rest of the country, wages were well above these levels. Though early surveys by the Bureau of Labor minimized the adverse effects of these increases on low-wage firms and on employment, closer study shows a lasting impact on the shape of the southern wage distribution, with wages in several industries bunched at the federal floor as much as five years after the initial legislation.[20] The most dramatic effect was on employment in lumber and sawmills, which had been the single most important source of nonagricultural jobs for black teenage males in 1950 (see figure 8.3). Black teenage employment in the industry declined by 74 percent between 1950 and 1960.[21] Thus, it was not just the direct effects of mechanization that forced unskilled blacks out of the South, but the interaction between mechanization, itself the longer-term consequence of federal policies, and the

FIGURE 8.3

Percent of Distribution of Nonsupervisory Workers in Southern
Sawmills by Average Straight-Time Hourly Earnings

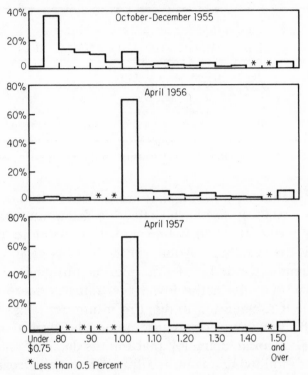

*Less than 0.5 Percent

NOTE: U.S. Department of Labor, Bureau of Labor Statistics, *Studies of the Effects of the $1 Minimum Wage, Southern Sawmills,* Report no. 130 (Washington, D.C.: Government Printing Office, 1957), 15. Graphs exclude premium pay for overtime and for work on weekends, holidays, and late shifts.

decision to impose national wage standards on the South. A recent study by John Cogan demonstrates that the drastic national decline in relative black teenage employment rates between 1950 and 1970 was largely attributable to the disappearance of low-wage jobs in the South (table 8.4). Even in 1950, the northern cities to which these unskilled black teenagers were moving were distinctly uninviting labor markets to them.

More broadly, the minimum wage operated to slow the growth of employment in low-wage industries in all parts of the country, an effect whose greatest impact was felt in the South. The list of industries affected is like a list of prominent southern industries: lumber, furniture, textiles, apparel,

251

TABLE 8.4

Male Youth (16–19 Years of Age) Employment-to-Population Ratios, 1950–70

	1950		1970		Change	
	Black	White	Black	White	Black	White
United States	46.6	40.4	27.0	40.5	−19.6	+0.1
Northeast	23.5	33.2	26.1	39.6	+2.6	+6.4
North Central	28.1	46.7	27.8	45.0	−0.33	−1.7
South	54.8	42.5	27.4	37.7	−27.4	−4.8
West	23.3	33.8	24.6	29.0	+1.3	−4.4

SOURCE: John Cogan, "The Decline in Black Teenage Employment, 1950–70," *American Economic Review* 72 (1982): table 1.

leather.[22] Table 8.5 presents data from a study that compares the period 1939–47 (when no effective minimum prevailed) with the period 1947–58 (when both the 1950 and 1956 increases were in effect). Total southern low-wage industry employment expanded in the first period, but declined in the second; the decline in the low-wage industry share of total employment accelerated under the minimum wage laws in the South, though not elsewhere. In South Carolina through the 1960s, manufacturing job placements declined in each of the periods following a federal minimum wage increase.[23]

The minimum wage laws, however, were only one of several administrative or quasi-political forces that worked to reduce regional wage disparities. In industries in which national unions were in place, strong pressures toward equalization were felt. In the steel industry, for example, the first major postwar wage schedule provided for uniform minimum rates for all U.S. plants except those in Birmingham and Duluth. The plant in Duluth was brought up to scale within three months (April 1947), while under union pressure, the Birmingham differential was cut from seventeen and one-half cents per hour to zero by 1954.[24] Even in the absence of unions, multi-plant companies with operations in more than one region often found that differential wages were hard to justify or maintain. Such firms showed a clear tendency to compress wage differentials or eliminate them entirely.[25]

These various tendencies would not be expected to produce

TABLE 8.5

Employment Changes in Low-Wage Manufacturing,
1939–47 and 1947–58

	Percentage of Change in Number of Workers		Percentage Point Change in Share of Total	
	1939–47	1947–58	1939–47	1947–58
All manufacturing				
Non-South	53	−7		
South	48	15		
Low-Wage Industries				
Non-South	−15	−18	−45	−12
South	31	−4	−11	−16
Lumber				
Non-South	33	2	−13	9
South	48	−30	−.3	−47
Textiles				
Non-South	−56	−51	−71	−47
South	16	−8	−22	−19
Fertilizer				
Non-South	30	75	14	63
South	30	−16	−12	−39
Tobacco				
Non-South	−16	−46	−30	−43
South	46	−16	−1	−27
Sawmilling				
Non-South	33	−22	−26	−16
South	53	−47	3	−53
Furniture				
Non-South	48	−9	−4	−3
South	53	31	3	14
Hosiery				
Non-South	−41	−80	−62	−80
South	−20	−21	−46	−31
Apparel				
Non-South	26	−6	−18	1
South	50	63	1	42

SOURCE: David Evan Kaun, "Economics of the Minimum Wage" (Ph.D. diss., Stanford University, 1963), 126, 131, 135.

a uniform trend toward regional wage convergence. Indeed, after 1950 the short-term effect of agricultural mechanization and higher wages in some sectors was to reduce wages in the uncovered and casual employment sectors of the South. In industries in which political pressures had pushed wages well above prevailing local levels, the effects of "market forces" in the 1950s was toward slower increases in the South and wider

FIGURE 8.4

Average Hourly Earnings^a in Cotton, Silk, and Synthetic Broad-Woven Fabrics, Northern and Southern Regions, January 1950–August 1953

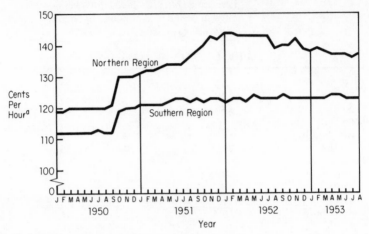

NOTE: U.S. Department of Labor, Bureau of Labor Statistics, *Cotton and Synthetic Textiles: Wage Trends, 1950–53*, Report no. 50 (Washington, D.C.: Government Printing Office, 1953), 8.
^a Excludes premium pay for overtime.

North-South spreads. In textiles, decisions of the War Labor Board in 1943–45 all but eliminated the overall regional gap (while technically reaffirming that the differential should not be altogether eliminated). But the increasing softness of the labor market allowed the industry to defeat a strike for higher wages in 1951, accelerating the decline of the textile unionization that had seemed imminent after the war. The effect was temporarily to widen the North-South wage differential in the early 1950s (figure 8.4). Similarly, in the pulp and paper industry, which paid base mill rates 50 percent higher than the minimum wage, analysts in the 1950s had no doubt that labor market pressures were acting to restrain wage advances in the South.[26]

The more lasting effects of these pressures, however, were to reduce the growth of jobs for unskilled southern workers, to reduce skill premiums within the South, to accelerate mechanization and the upgrading of hiring standards, and to rechannel southern growth away from labor-intensive lines. Migration patterns reflect this reorientation. The South was a region of net out-migration until the 1960s and has been a region of net in-migration since then. But, in fact, immigrants were moving in as well as out through the entire period, and the flows were highly selective along two dimensions: education and race. Here too, numerous studies appear to give conflicting results, in part because of a misguided search for timeless "laws of migration," in part because the nature and directions of migration have changed fundamentally over time. For example, it is often advanced as a general proposition that migration rates increase with the level of education.[27] During the 1940s, however, out-migration from the South was highest at *both* extremes of the distribution, the well-educated and the very poorly educated.[28] Throughout the 1950s, "educational selectivity" looked very different at the point of origin and at the point of destination: those with at least an eighth-grade education were more likely to leave the South, but the *median* educational level of black migrants was only 6.6 years. Southern migrants to the Northeast, Midwest, and West were significantly less educated than the typical resident of the region of destination. By contrast, migrants into the South were highly educated by southern standards (table 8.6). (Both of these contrasts are understated by not adjusting for the lower quality of southern education.) By 1960, more than 35 percent of white males in the South with five or more years of college had been born outside the region.[29]

Selectivity was even more striking by race. Whereas net white migration varied sharply by age and education, blacks left the South at all ages and educational levels. Net out-migration became increasingly black over time, and the reason is evident: most new jobs in the South were reserved for whites. In the Deep South, where blacks were 43 percent of the population in 1950, only 21 percent of new nonagricultural jobs went to blacks. Even these few were mostly in personal services, as blacks actually lost jobs in manufacturing.[30] The arrival of new industries and new non-southern employers was no guarantee of improved job opportunities for blacks. In the rubber tire industry, for example, where a major southward move occurred between 1947 and 1960, the new plants were highly automated and had few openings for blacks. The percentage of black employees went down in the 1950s and 1960s,

TABLE 8.6

Indices of Migration Differentials of White Males
by Educational Level (Areas of Destination)

Level of Education	Middle Atlantic		East North Central		Pacific	
	Pre-1955	1955–60	Pre-1955	1955–60	Pre-1955	1955–60
North						
Elementary (8 years and under)	64.3	37.3	65.2	57.6	61.0	61.2
High School (1–3 years)	41.8	28.8	46.5	35.6	51.0	48.9
High School (4 years)	41.0	41.9	41.7	39.7	47.6	44.5
College (1–3 years)	47.2	59.3	43.6	50.8	47.9	45.5
College (4+ years)	50.7	74.3	48.4	68.4	45.4	54.7

	South Atlantic		East South Central		West South Central	
	Pre-1955	1955–60	Pre-1955	1955–60	Pre-1955	1955–60
South						
Elementary (8 years and under)	32.5	29.8	38.8	27.8	41.7	29.0
High School (1–3 years)	42.5	40.4	44.7	39.5	43.1	40.6
High School (4 years)	53.1	51.7	51.0	50.9	50.5	53.8
College (1–3 years)	59.7	59.9	62.3	65.2	57.5	59.9
College (4+ years)	68.8	72.3	66.8	75.1	63.0	68.3

SOURCE: A. V. Zodgekar and K. S. Seetheram, "Interdivisional Migration Differentials by Education for Groups of Selected SMSAs, United States 1960," *Demography* 9 (1972): 688–89.

and by 1966 was actually lower in southern than in northern plants.[31] It was never as explicitly planned or implemented as in Senator Richard Russell's 1949 proposal for a commission to disperse the black population equally to all parts of the country.[32] But whereas in 1940, almost 80 percent of the American black population lived in the South, by 1970 the figure was barely one half.

Between 1940 and the 1960s, the South thus presents us with an amazing economic spectacle. It was the most rapidly growing region in the country, as measured by either per capita income or industrialization—a region whose political and economic leadership continually complained about the "low-wage" character of its industrial structure. And yet all of this was occurring at the same time that job-hungry workers were leaving the region by the thousands, often to go to cities where they faced hostility, unemployment, and a host of social problems.[33] Was this "southern economic development," or was it the replacement of one economy by another, the two having in common only the coincidence that they both occupied the same geographic space? The "Southern economy" came to look less and less southern over time, but the pressures behind these changes did not come exclusively from outside interests and forces. Southerners who stayed home were actively engaged in selling themselves to the outside world.

The Selling of the South

The imposition of the national minimum wage and the dimming of growth prospects for traditional southern low-wage industries coincided strikingly with the rise of organized political efforts to recruit outside capital into the South. An early survey (1944) noted that "the spread of state-financed industrial programs in the South has been especially rapid since 1937," and the author's interviews with program officials led him to associate this development directly with "recent changes in wage differentials and union status," as well as with the decline in export markets for southern crops. This sort of activity was virtually absent in the South in 1935, yet by the 1940s, every state had some sort of program.[34]

The industrial development promotions of the late 1930s were of modest scope and debatable effect, but a major southern-initiated explosion of such programs came after World War II, and especially after 1950. The devices used to attract industry are described in detail in James C. Cobb's aptly titled

TABLE 8.7

*Print and Broadcast Advertising by State Development
Programs as of 15 August 1964*

	Amount	National Rank
Arkansas	$ 160,000	4
Florida	325,000	2
Georgia	55,000	13
Kentucky	125,000	7
Louisiana	90,000	9
Mississippi	161,265	3
North Carolina	140,000	5
South Carolina	71,181	11
Tennessee	90,000	9
TOTAL	1,217,446	
Average of 31 states reporting	73,202	
Average of 9 Southern states reporting	135,272	

SOURCE: James C. Cobb, *Selling of the South* (Baton Rouge: Louisiana State University Press, 1982), 91.

recent book, *The Selling of the South*.[35] A favorite inducement, pioneered by Mississippi's Balance Agriculture With Industry program, was the issuance of municipal industrial development bonds for plant construction that would then be leased to private firms. Long-term tax exemptions for new manufacturing plants were increasingly utilized, with the South well ahead of the rest of the nation by the mid-1960s. Local industrial development corporations proliferated in the South after 1950, spending substantial sums on advertising and recruitment and offering loans and special services of various kinds (table 8.7). Eventually, the more advanced and successful areas obtained state support for sophisticated technological research centers. The Research Triangle Park in North Carolina is the best known, but by no means the only example; others emerged in Virginia and Georgia in the 1960s, and by the 1970s, even Mississippi had an impressive "R & D Center."

The coincidence of timing is too close to ignore. State-level industrial recruitment efforts began only after federal policies had decisively reduced the regional wage differential, and they became quantitatively significant only after the last technical obstacle to full mechanization of the plantation had been broken through. Southern boosterism had existed before at local levels in programs like the Forward Atlanta movement of the 1920s, or the town-building campaigns of the late nineteenth century. But these advocates were always minorities at the state level. In his classic analysis of pre-1950 southern politics, V. O. Key observed that the "hard core of the political South" was in the black-majority plantation counties that "managed to subordinate the entire South to the service of their peculiar local needs." Referring to the state of Georgia and its county-unit voting system, Key went so far as to say: "In Georgia . . . the only effective vote lies in the country."[36] State regulations sharply restricted cities and towns from offering subsidies and inducements to outside industry. Though Key believed southern political unity revolved fundamentally around the "position of the Negro," the *economic* underpinning was the separate low-wage labor market, and the implicit coalition included not just planters but lumber and sawmill operators, textile millowners, and other employers. Roll-call analysis from the 1930s showed that southern unity was greatest not just on racial issues, but wherever *federal intervention* in the South was involved.[37]

One clue about the posture of state government toward attracting industry is the corporate tax rate. Surprising as it may seem, the South was a high-corporate-tax region prior to the 1950s. Six of the eight states to adopt corporate income taxes in the 1920s were in the South, and all the southern states except Texas and Florida had adopted such taxes by 1934.[38] Between 1950 and 1978, the median corporate tax rate in the South went from 85 percent above, to 13 percent below, that of the rest of the country (table 8.8).

Prior to the 1940s, southern political representatives gave low priority to attracting federal funds to their states and districts, if indeed they were not actively hostile. As W. H. Nicholls wrote in another classic work, "the South has been its own worst enemy in obtaining much-needed and much-deserved federal grants-in-aid for its economic development."[39] The aptness of this indictment for the 1930s is illustrated by the figures on New Deal expenditures by region (table 8.9). Despite the fact that the South was the nation's poorest region, and despite the fact that southern congressmen and senators were

TABLE 8.8

Median Corporate Tax Rates by Region,
1950–78

Year	South	Non-South	South/Non-South (Median)
1950	3.8%	2.0%	1.85
1960	3.8	3.5	1.09
1970	5.5	5.6	.98
1978	5.9	6.75	.87

SOURCE: Robert J. Newman, *Growth in the American South* (New York: New York University Press, 1984), 42.

uniquely well placed to channel funds toward their home districts, the South received the *lowest* level of per capita spending. The responsibility was not just in Congress. Many programs required local sponsorship and at least token local support. But such backing was often not forthcoming in the South. Complaints about the threat to local wages and labor discipline were common.[40]

TABLE 8.9

Per Capita Federal Expenditures,
1933–39

	Expenditures Per Capita	Percentage of U.S. Average
United States	$224	
West	306	137
Midwest	224	100
Northeast	196	88
South	189	84
Alabama	175	78
Arkansas	256	114
Georgia	171	76
Louisiana	221	99
Mississippi	228	102
North Carolina	143	64
South Carolina	198	88
Tennessee	183	82
Texas	205	92
Virginia	175	78

SOURCE: Leonard Arrington, "The New Deal in the West: A Preliminary Statistical Inquiry," *Pacific Historical Review* 38 (1969): 312–14.

TABLE 8.10

*Index Numbers of Relative Per Capita Federal
Expenditures, 1952–76*

	1952	1959–61	1969–71	1974–76
United States	100	100	100	100
New England	103	124	112	109
Mideast	104	104	106	111
Great Lakes	96	79	73	79
Plains	99	88	90	91
Far West	131	136	128	120
South	83	88	96	97
Alabama	83	88	96	97
Arkansas	78	70	76	87
Georgia	77	91	105	94
Louisiana	95	69	83	83
Mississippi	63	72	93	104
North Carolina	56	74	77	82
South Carolina	99	88	84	91
Tennessee	111	66	79	84
Virginia	106	154	148	133

NOTE: U.S. Advisory Commission on Intergovernmental Relatives, *Regional Growth: Historic Prospective* (Washington D.C.: Government Printing Office, 1980), 80–81.

Even by the beginning World War II, this picture had noticeably changed. Southern governors and development agencies pushed hard for their "fair share" of war contracts and industrial facilities, training camps and airfields. In substantial measure they succeeded, obtaining for the region as a whole a proportion of new industrial facilities that was 50 percent higher than the South's prewar share of manufacturing plants.[41] To be sure, the incidence of this spending was highly uneven (the southeastern textile states receiving far less than their share), and much of the activity was temporary. But it was a sign of change. Between 1952 and 1970, the South's share of federal government expenditures per capita increased steadily, from 17 percent below average to virtual parity (table 8.10). Some areas were completely transformed by defense-related activity. Huntsville, Alabama, grew from a small mill town to a major research center under the stimulus of the Redstone Arsenal and the Marshall Space Flight Center. Huntsville drew its electric power cheaply from the Tennessee Valley Authority, itself a major federal investment in one of the poorest parts of the South. Some congressmen, like Mendel Rivers of South Carolina, grew famous for packing their districts with defense facilities. In some states, most clearly Mississippi, defense purchases have been a major contributor to economic growth, but it would be a serious error to suggest that defense spending or federal expenditures generally have been the main force behind postwar regional growth in the South.[42] But the changing position is a good indicator of the complete reversal in the region's attitude toward "outside money."

How influential was the new salesmanship in attracting new industry into the South? For years economists and public policy experts argued that subsidies and tax breaks were wasteful and ineffective, that desirable companies would not require such inducements if a location were fundamentally attractive. In survey responses, business executives rarely acknowledged that subsidies affected their location decisions, and early statistical studies found little evidence that state tax differentials could explain industrial growth patterns.[43] But these conclusions are suspect, not just because businessmen may be unreliable informants about their own motives, but because in a competitive process (resembling a market), differentials that really matter may not be observable for very long because all states quickly follow the tactics of the leaders.

Certainly southern townspeople *believed* that they had no choice but to compete in these ways; for example, the officials of Lafayette, Tennessee, said in 1957:

> The little town that wants industry to stop the flow of young people away from its surrounding rural area does what is called "buying industry" or it does not get any. You listen to the experts tell you "No." Then if you are wise you do whatever it takes to get the plant, and I mean just that, "whatever it takes."[44]

There is undoubtedly inefficiency and waste, from a national point of view, in the whole process of interarea competition for industry. But it is hard to believe that the aggressive entry of southern states and localities into this competition was not an important part of the broad shift of industrial location to the South. The most recent and most systematic study of relative industrial growth does indeed find significant effects, not just for corporate tax rates but for variables representing the vaguer but no less important forms of welcome known as the "business climate."[45]

Some observers in the South have complained that "business climate" is nothing but a euphemism for low wages and anti-unionism, and that boosterism has largely served to tighten the grip of the old cheap-labor economy. It is true that into the 1950s, southern industrial growth continued to be in low-skill, labor-intensive industries, an understandable trend given the low educational standards and narrow scope of industrial experience of most southern workers.[46] It is also true that reports of *opposition* to new high-wage or unionized firms by local employers continued to appear even in the 1970s. As late as 1978 a Fantus Company executive told the *Wall Street Journal*: "There are literally scores of companies that have been turned away from Southern towns because of their wage rates or their union policies."[47] Finally, it is also true that progress toward true national labor market integration for blue-collar workers has been far slower than for professional and white-collar workers, or than the trends in per capita income might indicate. The most detailed studies of interregional wages find that even in the 1970s, though white-collar differentials had disappeared completely (after cost-of-living and city-size effects are corrected), blue-collar differentials by region were still present and still significant.[48]

However, even when all of these qualifications are acknowledged, the decisiveness of the break with the past remains undeniable. Since the end of the era of out-migration in the mid-1960s, the Southern economy has caught up with and moved well past the national minimum wage, and the regional trends of standardized occupational wages have been clearly ahead of the national average.[49] The centers of growth since then have been entirely changed. In a few cases, like tobacco manufacturing, an industry that was initially hard hit by the minimum wage has mechanized so thoroughly that it has moved completely out of the low-wage class. But in this and in almost all of the "traditional" southern industries, employment has shown a steady decline since the 1950s; the five that comprised two-thirds of southern industrial jobs in 1939 (textiles, tobacco, food, paper, and lumber) accounted for less than one-third in 1976, and undoubtedly still less today. In 1980 the chemical industry was the largest in four southern states (Louisiana, Tennessee, Texas, and Virginia), and chemicals, machinery, electronics, and transport equipment were gaining fast in Georgia, the Carolinas, Alabama, Mississippi, and Arkansas. Since modern electrical machinery plants began to move into the Piedmont in the late 1950s, the range of job choices and occupational mobility has notably expanded. To be sure, southern industry is largely nonunion, and one can choose to see this feature as an element of continuity in southern history. But the high-tech corporate antiunionism of the 1980s is quite a different phenomenon from the prewar recipe of tradition, racism, and brute-force isolation. Rather than identification with older southern loyalties, it has been as often the newness of the firms and the jobs and the labor force that explain the absence of unions.

> There is no doubt that by moving South we only escape trade unionism for the moment. . . . But it is supremely important to me that in the years during which I am organizing this new industry and training labor in the plant that I should not have to operate within the straight-jacket of union rules with respect to seniority, featherbedding practices and the like.[50]

Whether the South ever becomes highly unionized, as this man assumed, is an open question. But if it does not, it will be a sign of the late twentieth-century American times, not the persistence of the Old South.[51]

The New South and the Civil Rights Movement

As the South began to move from the political economy of an isolated labor market to the political economics of attracting industry, it was never part of the plan to revolutionize the region's race relations in the process. Indeed, during the transitional period 1930–60 the effect of economic change was to strengthen the supports for racism in two ways: the tendency toward a dualistic wage structure increasingly along racial lines strengthened the association between race and cheap labor in the plantation sector; and the conditions of surplus labor and job scarcity reinforced the interests of white workers in racial separation. With all the increasing talk about the need for more jobs to "stop the outflow of our young people," it was not young blacks that such spokesmen had in mind. One may go further: the increasing integration of national labor markets served to minimize economic pressures to overturn racial segregation, by opening up a wider array of labor force options to new southern employers. Only where blacks had previously built up experience in industrial work were there strong economic incentives to employ or upgrade blacks, or to lobby for better education and social acceptance for black employees. Northern-based firms in such industries as steel, rubber, autos, and textiles typically adopted local segregation lines and did not press for basic changes in racial practices.

And yet the "selling of the South" did contribute fundamentally to the successes of the Civil Rights movement and the overthrow of segregation in the 1960s. One significant factor was that the rise of an urban black voting bloc in the North created a strong force for federal action. Even at the state level, blacks sometimes came to represent a swing vote with enough clout to influence the positions of senatorial candidates. Racial problems in the North were, of course, also plentiful, but this very fact actually increased the temptation to appeal to black voters by attacking the more overt forms of racism in more distant parts of the country. There may have been elements of hypocrisy in the positions of some northern representatives (as Southerners were fond of pointing out), but federal pressure was an increasingly potent force nonetheless. In a state like Mississippi, which received over a billion dollars in federal money in 1964, the direct threat of withdrawal was not to be sniffed at.

But many southern whites did not mind standing in direct defiance of federal authority. The leverage of the Civil Rights forces came from the fact that the southern leadership was no longer trying to protect a fortress; they were trying to bring in outside firms, and this required that they present their towns and cities as safe, civilized communities, and their labor force as well behaved and eager for work. In repeated cases, cities and towns found that turmoil over segregation in schools or other local facilities made the industrial recruitment difficult or impossible. The most famous example was Little Rock, Arkansas, where a promising postwar development program came to a complete standstill when Orval Faubus called out the National Guard to block court-ordered school integration in 1957. Though the city had attracted eight new plants in 1957, not a single new plant came to Little Rock during the next four years, and the figures indicated that the entire state of Arkansas had suffered. One industrial firm that had been considering an Arkansas location wrote:

> You may dismiss ——— from consideration. Our contacts with Arkansas have given us an unfavorable opinion of that state in comparison with Tennessee, Mississippi, or Missouri. We have no desire to be involved in the segregation problems of that state.[52]

The return of prosperity to Little Rock in the 1960s was attributable to improved racial relations, in which local business forces took a leading part. The case was widely discussed in the South, and its lesson widely absorbed, as reflected in the *Wall Street Journal* headline of May 26, 1961: "Business in Dixie: Many Southerners Say Racial Tension Slows Area's Economic Gains."

There were other concrete examples of the cost of racial turmoil and the potential benefits of conciliation. In 1963, Oxford, Mississippi, was reported to have lost two new industries because of its racial crisis. Tourism and convention businesses were badly hurt in New Orleans, Atlanta, Saint Augustine, and other places, during the clashes of the early 1960s. Even in 1970, when the president of Allis-Chalmers Corporation visited Jackson, Mississippi, in the midst of violent confrontations between police and black students on the Jackson State campus, he expressed grave concern about community stability and the school system. Shortly after a seven-year deadlock over school integration was broken with a comprehensive bi-

racial agreement, Allis-Chalmers announced plant construction plans and New York bond-rating firms raised the classi-
fication of the city's municipal bonds.[53]

The coeditor of a systematic review of the role of southern
businessmen in the desegregation crises reached the following
conclusion:

> In the 1950s and 1960s white businessmen across the South found
> themselves pushed—by the federal government and civil rights
> forces as well as by their own economic interests and values—
> into becoming reluctant advocates of a new departure in southern
> race relations.[54]

To be sure, the businessmen were often pushing for mere
tokenism and public-relations "racial harmony." And there
was an element of ex post facto claiming of credit for what had
become inevitable as a result of federal enforcement. As Carl
Abbott has pointed out, "The image of a mobilized business
leadership which could take the city's problems in hand was
a sophisticated form of boosterism as much as it was a description of political realities." Yet with all necessary qualifications,
the new priorities of the southern businessmen and their be-
lated support for concessions were of crucial importance. "The
changes they accepted were the entering wedge for the much
greater changes that have since taken place in southern life
and race relations," proving the ultimate validity of W. H.
Nicholls' view that the South would have to choose between
tradition and regional progress.[55]

The link between economic progress and desegregation was
not, however, the one so often claimed. It had little to do with
labor market pressures, and even less to do with the alleged
openness and rationalism of industrial society. In Alabama,
with one of the longest industrial histories in the South, a survey of firms in all major branches of the economy found not
a single case before the 1960s where management, "drawing
on cost calculations, business norms, or some abstract concept
of justice, chose to desegregate the work place or break down
job discrimination. . . . Even in retrospect, off the record, within
the confines of their own offices, businessmen did not recall
that the racial order created any 'impediments' or 'difficulties'

for their enterprises." In the end, virtually every major manufacturing establishment had to face the federal courts, leading
one officer to conclude: "We know what it is like to be occupied."[56] To be sure, compliance was hastened in cases in which
employers did have potential gains from change, like the textile
and furniture firms in the Carolinas who faced tight labor markets and stiff competition in the early 1960s. But equally tight
labor markets in the early 1900s and 1940s had not generated
lasting change in racial employment barriers in these industries. Carefully specified labor market analysis shows unmis-
takably that the expansion of black jobs in the early 1960s was
a structural break with the past, not simply a labor market
response.[57] In South Carolina, for example, employment of
blacks in textiles has steadily risen since 1961, and is today
higher than the black percentage of the state labor force. Even
in service jobs with high "public visibility," formerly denied
to blacks almost universally, times have changed. Today blacks
are employed not just as clerks and cashiers but as store managers, television cameramen, announcers, and reporters. Like
the rest of the country, the South is a long way from racial
equality in access to jobs and pay; but it is even farther away
from its own past.

The overwhelming testimony from the case studies is that
the business forces that ultimately supported racial change
were motivated by a desire for the absence of turmoil and for
the economic benefits of a good national reputation, and not
by the thought of gains in efficiency or a lowering of production
costs. As important as this understanding is, it is even more
important to recognize the basic contribution of the voices that
were not heard on the other side, the planters and other pro-
tectors of the old isolated low-wage southern labor market. In
Alabama, the Farm Bureau, long the dominant state voice of
reaction and racism, "unobtrusively gave up the race issue"
by the 1960s.[58] As Jack Temple Kirby has recently written:
"Change merely seemed sudden during the 1950s and 1960s,
when foundations, long before undermined, collapsed."[59]

Does it lessen the achievements of the heroes of the Civil
Rights revolution to recognize that their success required a
prerevolution in the countryside and in the labor market? Not

at all. The greatest human accomplishments only occur when they happen to be possible, which was as true of Jefferson's Declaration and Lincoln's Proclamation as it was of the overthrow of segregation. But things don't happen just because they are possible. The evidence shows that Martin Luther King was right when he wrote in his letter from the Birmingham jail that the passage of time alone does not bring change. Vociferous protest was essential to the whole process. If the southern experience has any lesson for South Africa today, it is that the natural forces of economic progress do not break racial barriers unless people speak up through every possible channel.

The breakthroughs of those years were distinctly limited and did not translate magically into rapid economic advancement for the majority of black people. So it is understandable that today's young people have trouble comprehending what all the fuss was about. As a black student at Selma High School told a reporter in 1985: "Try as you can, you can't believe that white people once treated black people that way. It seems like something that happened long, long ago."[60] Her statement is testimony to how thoroughly things have changed.

The South, the Nation, and the World Economy

If this book is accurate, it has chronicled the history of an economy that no longer exists. The South became an economic entity through a series of historical conjunctions dating to colonial times. The tobacco, rice, and indigo regions of the eighteenth century were simply a few more elements among many others in the British colonial empire, with populations and economic structures midway between those of the sugar islands of the Caribbean and the grain-growing colonies of the North. They acquired some political separateness when they joined the American Revolution, and some economic distinctness when the northern states abolished slavery and the southern states did not. This political alignment was in place prior to the great antebellum cotton boom that crystallized the South as an economic entity unified by the market for slave labor. The secession of 1860–61 attempted to insulate this economic entity within an independent political unit, but it failed. Though the abolition of slavery revolutionized the economic structure within the South, with the major exception of the place of the cotton economy in the world, the historical legacy of separateness has carried on until recent times. Though the term has been used polemically and mistakenly more often than not, in a sense *colonial economy* is just the right description of the South's condition: a distinct economy located within the political jurisdiction of a larger country, subject to laws, markets, policies, and technologies that it would not have chosen had it been independent. The ironic conclusion to the story is that the only major act of conscious economic suppression by northern forces, the imposition of national wage and labor standards beginning in the 1930s, was the decisive step in abolishing the separate Southern economy. When southern property owners no longer had an economic stake in maintaining the separateness of the southern labor market, they opened the regional doors to much larger flows of outside labor and capital, with the result that the South as a distinct economic entity has all but disappeared. There are many remnants that still exist, and the whole account may seem fictitious to people working in low-wage, single-industry towns of the Southeast, or to residents of the many rural areas that have not attracted industry and are still losing population. Their problems are real, but they are not southern regional problems any longer. The "colonial economy" no longer exists because "outsiders" have so thoroughly penetrated the South that both the people and the economy have lost their distinct identities, economically speaking.

The southern story has been recounted here in terms of the decade-by-decade interactions between regional, national, and world effects, following what seem to have been the immediate dynamic pressures at each point. There is no question that it could also have been viewed in terms of much larger and longer-term global developments. Cotton would have declined one way or another, and labor has left farming almost everywhere. The automobile and the plane have reduced economic distances while television and other instruments of mass consumption have reduced cultural distances as well. Capital is more mobile and technologies more flexible. Corporations and financial institutions now have the organizational capacity to maintain branches and divisions all over the globe, under more or less unified management. These trends have all occurred for reasons having little to do with the South. But it remains true that every supply has to have a demand. Air conditioning may be essential for today's South, but the technology developed over the whole of the twentieth century, and the particulars of its diffusion in the South after 1950 were shaped by the region's strong new desire to welcome in outside capital and people. Not many of today's Southerners would agree with the Florida woman who said:

> I hate air conditioning; it's a damnfool invention of the Yankees. If they don't like it hot, they can move back up North where they belong.[61]

Similarly, capital and corporations may be more geographically mobile than they used to be, but they still stay away from places with a poor "business climate."

Still, it is difficult to deny that the broad trends in communications, technology, and economics in this century have tended to reduce geographic differences generally, and that in light of these trends, the South could hardly have maintained its labor market and associated cultural isolation into the indefinite future. The object of this book has not been to suggest that the South would have persisted unchanged into the 1990s if it had not been for some bits of legislation passed in the 1930s. The southern states would have moved into the modern era one way or another, but it may well be that the specific shape and character of today's South has been determined by how it got there. Not every colonial economy has the scale and capacity to shape its own technology, its own industrial standards, its own educational system, and its own political culture, but the South might have done it. It might have been a development of and by the southern people rather than an absorption of the southern territory into the U.S. national economy. One can feel sympathy for the southern journalist who deplores the loss of southern regional identity:

> For the last few decades the South has been mightily laboring to mutate itself into a tinfoil-twinkly simulation of southern California, and in the process has unwittingly worked on itself a spiritual impoverishment. Faulkner's Flem Snopes has evolved into a relentlessly bouncy and glitter-eyed neo-Babbit with an almost touching lust for new chemical plants, glassy-maized office parks and instant subdivisions. The mischief is that, in its transfiguration into What-a-Burger drive-ins and apartment wastelands, the South is being etherized, subtly rendered pastless, memoryless and vague of identity.[62]

The larger point of the book, however, is that an economy's performance cannot be evaluated independently of an evaluation of that economy's political legitimacy and culture. We can't overlook the reality that the southern regional polity was not democratic and that large portions of its population were denied access to the political process and other fundamental human rights. Only federal pressure caused these things to change. A genuinely grass-roots development process would not very easily have evolved in the South as it was. In 1928 the doctrine of "self-determination for the Black Belt" was approved in Moscow and passed on to the predominantly black Communist party councils in Alabama, where it raised confusion and interminable issues of interpretation.[63] It is not hard to see why. If the South was a colonial economy, southern blacks were the colonial economy's own colonial economy.

This assessment must be shared all the more strongly by those blacks who are well aware that even today they do not have their proper place in the nation and in the national economy. Overt racial barriers have been abolished, but as the national economy (now including the southern states) has moved toward professional, white-collar, high-tech, high-skill structure, unskilled minority people have become more excluded rather than less.[64] It may be small comfort to them to know that their plight is now more or less the same everywhere.

Some observers still view the South as a colonial economy,

272

pointing out that much of the industry and finances of the region still belong to "outside economic actors." In 1981 a journalist asked "Who Owns Atlanta?" and concluded: "Atlanta has become a city owned by absentee landlords." These facts have led historian Numan Bartley to suggest that the South "may have exchanged one form of colonial dependency for another."[65] At a more basic economic level, Jane Jacobs argues that the TVA and other federal programs to develop the South have "failed" because they have not generated the kind of interactive, indigenous, reinforcing urban technological and economic communities that have been at the heart of past economic success stories, including America's.[66]

These descriptions are accurate enough, but what they miss is the understanding that the economic world has fundamentally changed. If Atlanta is owned by "outside economic actors," these actors are not firmly attached to any other city either. The South is not a colony to any other geographic entity, but to placeless global organizations and markets. What these writers say about the South is true for the country as a whole. The decline of "American manufacturing," for example, has not been a decline in the performance of "American manufacturing firms" so much as a decline in the role of the United States as a geographical location of production. The firms have held their own, but they are not attached to America in the way they used to be.[67] In this one respect, all economies are coming to resemble the economy of the antebellum South, where slave owners were rootless and footloose because their wealth was portable. To a considerable extent, we all have to get used to this idea, because technological and economic communities can now operate over longer and longer distances, and there is no way to turn back the clock to the kind of small-city, closed national economy of the past, however much we might miss it.

Is there any further use or meaning then for national economies? Yes, because countries command the loyalties of people, and they embody the traditions and culture and values of people. Despite, and indeed because of, the global nature of technologies and markets, the character of countries today is more an object of human choice than ever before. With all its faults and hypocrisies, the American national tradition does contain a basis for a decent, humane economic order that does its best to expand opportunities for all its citizens—as the Old South's tradition did not. Accepting this commitment to its people is the proper place of a national economy today, a national economy that includes the South and the Southerners, wherever in the country they happen to be living.

NOTES

Preface

1. William H. Nicholls, *Southern Tradition and Regional Progress* (Chapel Hill: University of North Carolina Press, 1960), 34.
2. Gavin Wright, *Political Economy of the Cotton South* (New York: Norton, 1978).

Chapter 1

1. *Business Week*, 2 September 1972, p. 30; *Fortune*, June 1977, pp. 132–37; *Industrial Distribution*, January 1977, pp. 39–46; *Paper Trade Journal*, July 1984, p. 8.
2. Fred Hobson, "A South Too Busy to Hate?," in Fifteen Southerners, *Why the South Will Survive* (Athens: University of Georgia Press, 1981), 45–46.
3. *Natura non facit saltum* was the great Victorian motto carried on the title page of all eight editions of Alfred Marshall's *Principles of Economics*, 9th ed., vol. 2 (New York: Macmillan, 1961), 35.
4. Stanley Engerman, "Some Economic Factors in Southern Backwardness in the Nineteenth Century," in *Essays in Regional Economics*, ed. John F. Kain and John R. Meyer (Cambridge, Mass.: Harvard University Press, 1971), 292.
5. Sheldon Hackney, "Origins of the New South in Retrospect," *Journal of Southern History* 38 (1972): 195. The author reaffirms the classic "colonial economy" analysis of C. Vann Woodward, *Origins of the New South* (Baton Rouge: Louisiana State University Press, 1951).
6. Jonathan Wiener, *Social Origin of the New South* (Baton Rouge: Louisiana State University Press, 1978), 73.
7. This phrase is from the "oral tradition" of Parker students at Yale. His views on economic history may be sampled in his *Europe, America, and the Wider World* (New York: Cambridge University Press, 1984).
8. Jane Jacobs, *Cities and the Wealth of Nations* (New York: Random House, 1984), 29–36.
9. Walter Prescott Webb, "The South's Future Prospect," in *The Idea of the South*, ed. Frank E. Vandiver (Chicago: University of Chicago Press, 1964), 70–71.

Notes

10. Albert E. Cowdrey, *This Land, This South* (Lexington: University Press of Kentucky, 1983). Cowdrey writes that much southern soil is "mediocre in quality, highly erosive under intensive cultivation" (p. 3), and that the region's "modest and much-abused environmental dower" has been underappreciated as a source of southern economic woes (p. 195).

11. Rupert Vance, *Human Geography of the South* (Chapel Hill: University of North Carolina Press, 1935), 22.

12. Documentation for "southernness" may be found in the work of sociologist John Shelton Reed, *The Enduring South: Subcultural Persistence in a Mass Society* (Lexington, Mass.: Lexington Books, 1971); and *Southerners: The Social Psychology of Sectionalism* (Chapel Hill: University of North Carolina Press, 1983).

13. Calvin B. Hoover and B. U. Ratchford, *Economic Resources and Policies of the South* (New York: Macmillan, 1951), 62.

14. Mancur Olson, "The South Will Fall Again: The South as Leader and Laggard in Economic Growth," *Southern Economic Journal* 49 (1983): 917. The quote from the New Yorker in Atlanta is from the *New York Times*, 11 February 1976, p. 30.

15. Reed, *Southerners*, 4.

16. From T. F. Bayard, "Introductory Letter," in Jacob Schoenhof, *The Economy of High Wages* (New York: Putnam, 1893).

17. Reed, *Southerners*, 35.

18. Holland Thompson, "Effects of Industrialism upon Political and Social Ideas," *Annals of the American Academy* 35 (1910): 142.

19. Ralph C. Hon, quoting Dr. Tait Butler in "The Rust Cotton Picker," *Southern Economic Journal* 3 (1937); Gilbert Fite, "Recent Progress in the Mechanization of Cotton Production," *Agricultural History* 24 (1950): 28.

20. Harriet Herring, *Passing of the Mill Village: Revolution in a Southern Institution* (1949; reprint, Westport, Conn.: Greenwood Press, 1977).

21. Thompson, "Effects of Industrialism Upon Political and Social Ideas," 140–41.

22. C. Vann Woodward, "New South Fraud is Papered by Old South Myth," *Washington Post*, 9 July 1961, p. E3.

23. Arthur Goldschmidt, "The Development of the U.S. South," in *Technology and Economic Development* (New York: Knopf, 1963), 180.

Chapter 2

1. John W. Johnston, "The Emancipation of the Southern Whites," *Manufacturers' Record*, 9 July 1887. Johnston and many others are quoted in Paul M. Gaston, *The New South Creed* (Baton Rouge: Louisiana State University Press, 1970), esp. 35, 54–78.

2. Gaston's book *The New South Creed* is subtitled, "A Study in Southern Myth-making"; C. Vann Woodward concluded: "Among [the southern writers], however, one will search in vain for a realistic portrayal of their own times" (*Origins of the New South* [Baton Rouge: Louisiana State University Press, 1971], 168). From an entirely different perspective, Jonathan Wiener argues that "the New South ideologists embraced the Old South myth because they were not strong enough to attack it" (*Social Origins of the New South* [Baton Rouge: Louisiana State University Press, 1978], 218–19).

3. Robert S. Cotterill, "The Old South to the New," *Journal of Southern History* 15 (1949): 6.

Notes

4. Roger Ransom and Richard Sutch, *One Kind of Freedom* (New York: Cambridge University Press, 1977), 52–53. This paragraph also draws on material from Randolph Campbell, *A Southern Community in Crisis* (Austin: Texas State Historical Association, 1983), 26; Gavin Wright, *Political Economy of the Cotton South* (New York: Norton, 1978), 36.

5. This model is forcefully presented by Roger Ransom and Richard Sutch in "The Long-Run Implications of Capital Absorption in Slave Labor" (Paper presented at the meeting of the Cliometrics Society, Iowa City, May 1983). The authors also review the long history of this idea.

6. Fred Bateman and Thomas Weiss, *A Deplorable Scarcity: The Failure of Industrialization in the Slave Economy* (Chapel Hill: University of North Carolina Press, 1981).

7. See, for example, Roger Ransom, "Public Canal Investment and the Opening of the Old Northwest," in *Essays in Nineteenth Century Economic History*, ed. David C. Klingman and Richard C. Vedder (Athens: Ohio University Press, 1975).

8. David Weiman, "Petty Commodity Production in the Plantation South: Upcountry Farmers in the Georgia Cotton Economy, 1840–1880" (Ph.D. diss., Stanford University, 1983). For the cotton textile industry, see Stephen J. Goldfarb, "A Note on Limits to the Growth of the Cotton-Textile Industry in the Old South," *Journal of Southern History* 48 (1982): 554–58.

9. John F. Stover, *Iron Road to the West* (New York: Columbia University Press, 1978), 89–90. Stover estimates investment per mile at less than $27,000 for the southern lines during the 1850s, compared to $48,000 in the Northeast.

10. Eugene Genovese and Elizabeth Fox-Genovese, *Fruits of Merchant Capital* (New York: Oxford University Press, 1983), 50.

11. David T. Morgan, "Philip Phillips and Internal Improvements in Mid-Nineteenth Century Alabama," *Alabama Review* 34 (1981): 83–93.

12. Charles Ramsdell, "Internal Improvement Projects in Texas in the Fifties," *Proceedings of the Mississippi Valley Historical Association* 9 (1915–18): 100–106.

13. Albert Fishlow, *American Railroads and the Transformation of the Ante-Bellum Economy* (Cambridge, Mass.: Harvard University Press, 1965), chap. 4.

14. These figures are from Stanley Elkins and Eric McKitrick, "A Meaning for Turner's Frontier," *Political Science Quarterly* 69 (1954): 341–42.

15. I discuss the reopening campaigns in detail in *The Political Economy of the Cotton South* (New York: Norton, 1978), 150–54.

16. Ulrich B. Phillips, "Transportation in the Antebellum South," *Quarterly Journal of Economics* 19 (1905), reproduced as the introduction to Phillips, *Transportation in the Eastern Cotton Belt to 1860* (New York: Columbia University Press, 1908), 9.

17. James Oakes, *The Ruling Race* (New York: Knopf, 1982), 77; Wiener, *Social Origins of the New South*, 10; Donald Schaefer, "Migration in the Antebellum Cotton South," *Agricultural History* (in press).

18. The best-known studies are Stephan Thernstrom's, *Poverty and Progress* (Cambridge, Mass.: Harvard University Press, 1964) and *The Other Bostonians* (Cambridge, Mass.: Harvard University Press, 1973). A survey is Thernstrom, "Urbanization, Migration, and Social Mobility in Late Nineteenth Century America," in *Towards a New Past*, ed. Barton Bernstein (New York: Random House, 1967).

19. Drew Gilpin Foust, *James Henry Hammond and the Old South* (Baton Rouge: Louisiana State University Press, 1982), 109–13.

20. See Fred Bateman and Thomas Weiss, *A Deplorable Scarcity: The Failure of Industrialization in the Slave Economy* (Chapel Hill: University of North Carolina Press, 1981), chaps. 1 and 5, though the argument advanced here is somewhat different. For textiles, see Gavin Wright, "Cheap Labor and Southern Textiles Before 1880," *Journal of Economic History* 39 (1979): 655–80.

Notes

21. Alfred Chandler, "Anthracite Coal and the Beginnings of the Industrial Revolution in America," *Business History Review* 46 (1972): 141–81.

22. Edward Phifer, "Slavery in Microcosm: Burke County, North Carolina," *Journal of Southern History* 28 (1962): 144.

23. Michael Wayne, *The Reshaping of Plantation Society* (Baton Rouge: Louisiana State University Press, 1983), 1.

24. Otis E. Young, Jr., "The Southern Gold Rush, 1828–36," *Journal of Southern History* 48 (1982): 377–81; Fletcher Green, "Gold Mining: A Forgotten Industry of Antebellum North Carolina," *North Carolina Historical Review* 14 (1937): 9, 12–13, 135, 151–52.

25. An English correspondent quoted in Lowell Ragatz, *The Fall of the Planter Class* (New York: Century Co., 1928), 63.

26. Carroll D. Wright, *The Phosphate Industry of the United States*, Sixth Special Report of the Commissioner of Labor (1893), 9, 77.

27. Wiener, *Social Origins of the New South*, 141.

28. Kenneth Warren, *The American Steel Industry 1850–1970: A Geographical Interpretation* (Oxford: Clarendon Press, 1973), 68.

29. Ralph V. Anderson and Robert E. Gallman, "Slaves as Fixed Capital: Slave Labor and Southern Economic Development," *Journal of American History* 64 (1977): 24–46.

30. Eugene Genovese, *The Political Economy of Slavery: Studies in the Economy and Society of the Slave South* (1965; reprint, New York: Vintage Books, 1967), 89; Lewis Cecil Gray, *History of Agriculture in the Southern United States to 1860*, vol. 1 (1933; reprint, Clifton, N.J.: A. M. Kelley, 1973), 446.

31. Stanley Trimble, "Perspectives on the History of Soil Erosion Control in the Eastern United States," *Agricultural History* 59 (1985): 175, citing his own *Man-Induced Soil Erosion on the Southern Piedmont 1700–1970* (Ankeny, Ia.: Soil Conservation Society of America, 1974).

32. The Seward quotations are from Eric Foner, *Free Soil, Free Labor, Free Men* (New York: Oxford University Press, 1970), 40–48.

33. Howard Temperly, "Capitalism, Slavery and Ideology," *Past and Present* 75 (1977): 94–118; "Anti-Slavery as a Form of Cultural Imperialism," in *Anti-Slavery, Religion and Reform*, ed. Christine Bolt and Seymour Drescher (Hamden, Conn.: Shoe String Press, 1980). The long history of the belief in a close link between freedom and progress is surveyed in David Brion Davis, *Slavery and Human Progress* (New York: Oxford University Press, 1984).

34. Roger L. Ransom and Richard Sutch, *One Kind of Freedom* (Cambridge: Cambridge University Press, 1977). Random and Sutch estimate the decline in man-hours per capita to be between 28.3 and 37.2 percent (pp. 44–50 and appendix C).

35. Anderson and Gallman, "Slaves as Fixed Capital," 41.

36. Rowland T. Berthoff, "Southern Attitudes Towards Immigration, 1865–1914," *Journal of Southern History* 17 (1951): 328–60; E. Russ Williams, "Louisiana Public and Private Immigration Endeavors: 1866–1893," *Louisiana History* 15 (1974): 153–73; Bert James Loewenberg, "Efforts of the South to Encourage Immigration, 1865–1900," *South Atlantic Quarterly* 10 (1934): 363–85.

37. John F. Stover, *The Railroads of the South, 1865–1900* (Chapel Hill: University of North Carolina Press, 1955), 58.

38. Maury Klein, *The Great Richmond Terminal: A Study in Businessmen and Business Strategy* (Charlottesville: University Press of Virginia, 1970), 7–12.

39. Harold Woodman, *King Cotton and His Retainers: Financing and Marketing the Cotton Crop of the South, 1800–1925* (Lexington: University of Kentucky Press, 1968), chaps. 23–24; Michael Wayne, *The Reshaping of Plantation Society* (Baton Rouge: Louisiana State University Press, 1983), 166.

Notes

40. Carville Earle and Ronald Hoffman, "The Urban South: The First Two Centuries," in *The City in Southern History*, ed. Blaine A. Brownell and David R. Goldfield (Port Washington, N.Y.: Kennikat Press, 1977).

41. Kenneth Weiher, "The Cotton Industry and Southern Urbanization, 1880–1930," *Explorations in Economic History* 14 (1977): 130–39.

42. Wayne K. Durrill, "Producing Poverty: Local Government and Economic Development in a New South County, 1874–84," *Journal of American History* 71 (1985): 767, 770, 774; William J. Cooper, *The Conservative Regime, South Carolina 1870–1890* (Baltimore: Johns Hopkins University Press, 1968).

43. Thorstein Veblen, *Absentee Ownership and Business Enterprise in Recent Times* (New York: B. W. Huebsch, 1923), 135, 142.

44. See particularly David L. Carlton, *Mill and Town in South Carolina 1880–1920* (Baton Rouge: Louisiana State University Press, 1982), 32–34.

45. *Southern Recorder*, 28 November 1865, quoted in Patrick H. Hearden, *Independence and Empire: The New South's Cotton Mill Campaign* (DeKalb: Northern Illinois University Press, 1982), 39.

46. Broadus Mitchell, *The Rise of the Cotton Mills in the South* (Baltimore: Johns Hopkins University Press, 1921); Woodward deals sarcastically with Mitchell in *Origins of the New South*, 112–13, 133–34.

47. This discussion draws on Carlton, *Mill and Town*, chap. 2.

48. Mitchell, *Rise of the Cotton Mills*, viii.

49. This paragraph draws on Tom W. Shick and Don H. Doyle, "The South Carolina Phosphate Boom and the Stillbirth of the New South, 1867–1920," *South Carolina Historical Magazine* 86 (1985): 1–31.

50. Rosser Taylor, "The Sale and Application of Commercial Fertilizers in the South Atlantic States to 1900," *Agricultural History* 21 (1947): 46–52.

51. Ralph M. Tanner, "Some Characteristics of Eight Land Companies in North Alabama, 1863–1900," *Alabama Review* 29 (1976): 124–34; Robert H. McKenzie, "Reconstruction of the Alabama Iron Industry, 1865–1880," *Alabama Review* 25 (1972): 178–91; Justin Fuller, "Boom Towns and Blast Furnaces: Town Promotion in Alabama, 1885–1893," *Alabama Review* 29 (1976): 37–48; Stuart Seely Sprague, "Alabama and the Appalachian Iron and Coal Town Boom, 1889–1893," *Alabama Historical Quarterly* 37 (1975): 85–91.

52. Fuller, "Boom Towns and Blast Furnaces," 38–39.

53. The persistence of the planters is emphasized (in somewhat different ways) by Jonathan Wiener, *Social Origins of the New South*, and by Dwight Billings, Jr., *Planters and the Making of a "New South"* (Chapel Hill: University of North Carolina Press, 1979). On the political programs, see the survey in James Tice Moore, "Redeemers Reconsidered: Change and Continuity in the Democratic South, 1870–1900," *Journal of Southern History* 44 (1978).

54. Carl Degler, "Rethinking Post–Civil War History," *Virginia Quarterly Review* 57 (1981): 264. The prime example, however, is Billings, *Planters and the Making of a "New Class."*

55. Michael Wayne, *Reshaping of Plantation Society*, 204. Other useful references on the need for planters to adjust to new labor market realities are James Roark, *Masters Without Slaves* (New York: Norton, 1977) and Eric Foner, *Nothing But Freedom* (Baton Rouge: Louisiana State University Press, 1983).

56. Quoted in Steven Hahn, *The Roots of Southern Populism* (New York: Oxford University Press, 1983), 248. Detailed accounts of stock law controversies may be found in Hahn, chap. 7; Durrill, "Producing Poverty," 770–77; J. Crawford King, Jr., "Closing of the Southern Range," *Journal of Southern History* 48 (1982): 53–70.

57. King, "Closing of the Southern Range," 69–70.

58. Carl Degler, *Place Over Time: The Continuity of Southern Distinctiveness* (Baton Rouge: Louisiana State University Press, 1977).

Notes

Chapter 3

1. Roger Ransom and Richard Sutch, *One Kind of Freedom: The Economic Consequences of Emancipation* (New York: Cambridge University Press, 1977), appendix F.

2. Richard Easterlin, "Regional Income Trends, 1940–1950," in *The Reinterpretation of American Economic History*, ed. Robert W. Fogel and Stanley L. Engerman (New York: Harper & Row, 1972), 40–43. Easterlin's detailed procedures are presented in "Interregional Differences in Per Capita Income, Population, and Total Income, 1840–1950," in Conference on Research in Income and Wealth, *Trends in the American Economy in the Nineteenth Century*, Studies in Income and Wealth, vol. 24 (Princeton, N.J.: Princeton University Press, 1960).

3. A regression of the log of price on the log of quantity (new production plus stocks) for 1879–1914 shows the following:

$$\ln P_F = 13.6 - 1.10^* \ln Q + 0.034^* t \quad R^2 = .444$$
$$(4.96) \qquad (5.13)$$

where the asterisks indicate statistical significance. In this equation, the elasticity of demand is equal to the reciprocal of the coefficient of $\ln Q$, or 0.91, which is not significantly different from 1.0.

4. This and preceding statements about cotton demand are based on linear regressions of the form displayed in note 3, with shift terms added to capture changes in parameters.

5. This paragraph draws on Julius Rubin, "The Limits of Agricultural Progress in the Nineteenth-Century South," *Agriculture History* 49 (1975): 362–73. See also Robert B. Lamb, *The Mule in Southern Agriculture* (Berkeley: University of California Press, 1963).

6. Quoted in Gilbert Fite, *Cotton Fields No More* (Lexington: University Press of Kentucky, 1984), 117.

7. Ibid., 7.

8. A good example is hybrid corn, the diffusion of which was significantly slower in the South than in the Corn Belt, where the innovation first developed. See Zvi Griliches, "Hybrid Corn and the Economics of Innovation," *Science* 29 July 1960, p. 207–13. Reprinted in Fogel and Engerman, *Reinterpretation of American Economic History*. Griliches shows that good hybrids were not available in the South until the 1940s.

9. The path-breaking article was Theodore W. Schultz's, "Reflections on Poverty within Agriculture," *Journal of Political Economy* 58 (1950): 1–15.

10. Kenneth L. Sokoloff, "Productivity Growth in Manufacturing During Early Industrialization: Evidence from the Northeast, 1820 to 1860," in *Long Term Factors in American Economic Growth* (Chicago: University of Chicago Press, in press).

11. C. Vann Woodward, *Origins of the New South, 1877–1913* (1951; reprint, Baton Rouge: Louisiana State University Press, 1971), 139–41.

12. The quote is from Jay Mandle, *The Roots of Black Poverty* (Durham, N.C.: Duke University Press, 1978), v. See also William Cohen, "Negro Involuntary Servitude in the South, 1865–1940," *Journal of Southern History* 42 (1976): 31–60; Daniel A. Novak, *The Wheel of Servitude* (Lexington: University Press of Kentucky, 1978).

13. Jonathan Wiener, *Social Origins of the New South* (Baton Rouge: Louisiana State University Press, 1978), 69–70.

14. Crandall A. Shifflett, *Patronage and Poverty in the Tobacco South* (Knoxville: University of Tennessee Press, 1982), xii; David Eugene Conrad, *The Forgotten Farmers*

Notes

(Urbana: University of Illinois Press, 1965), 8; Donald H. Grubbs, *Cry from the Cotton* (Chapel Hill: University of North Carolina Press, 1971), 15.

15. For example, Eric Foner, "Reconstruction and the Crisis of Free Labor," in his *Politics and Ideology in the Age of the Civil War* (New York: Oxford University Press, 1980), 118.

16. Michael Wayne, *The Reshaping of Plantation Society* (Baton Rouge, 1983), appendix 2. For the period 1865–80, see the survey by Ralph Shlomowitz, " 'Bound Labor' or Free? Freedmen Labor in Cotton and Sugar Cane Farming, 1865–1880," *Journal of Southern History* 50 (1984): 569–96.

17. Nannie May Tilley, *The Bright-Tobacco Industry 1860–1929* (Chapel Hill: University of North Carolina Press, 1948), 99.

18. Lewis Plantation Records, and George W. Bryan papers, both at the Southern Historical Collection, University of North Carolina, Chapel Hill. A more detailed discussion of these records is presented in Gavin Wright, "Postbellum Southern Labor Markets," in *Quantity and Quiddity: Essays in Honor of Stanley Lebergott*, ed. Peter Kilby (Middletown, Conn.: Wesleyan University Press, in press).

19. Morgan-Malloy Company Records, Perkins Collection, Duke University Library, Durham, N.C.

20. Jacquelyn Hall, Robert Korstad, and Jim Leloudis, " 'Like a Family': Class, Community and Conflict in the Piedmont Textile Industry, 1880–1980," paper presented at the Future of American Labor History Conference, Northern Illinois University, Dekalb, Ill., Oct. 10–12, 1984.

21. Joseph A. Hill, "Interstate Migration," in U.S. Bureau of the Census, *Special Reports: Supplementary Analysis and Derivative Tables* (1906), 305; William O. Scroggs, "Interstate Migration of the Negro Population," *Journal of Political Economy* 25 (1917): 1034–43; Roger W. Shugg, *Origins of Class Struggle in Louisiana* (Baton Rouge: Louisiana State University Press, 1939), 253.

22. Steven DeCanio, "Labor Mobility and Peonage in the Postbellum South" (Paper presented to the First World Congress of Cliometrics, Northwestern University, Evanston, Ill., 1 June 1985).

23. Philip R. P. Coelho and James F. Shepherd, "The Impact of Differences in Prices and Wages on Economic Growth: The U.S. in 1890," *Journal of Economic History* 39 (1979): 73–74; Coelho and Shepherd, "Differences in Regional Prices: The U.S., 1851–1880," *Journal of Economic History* 34 (1974): 569–72. The comparisons are primarily based on urban prices, and do not deny that significant urban-rural cost-of-living differences existed. This was true in the North as well, so it has no bearing on the farm wage comparisons.

24. Coelho and Shepherd, "The U.S. in 1890," 77. Wage ratios quoted are deflated.

25. Wage data may be found in the Seventh Annual Report of the U.S. Commissioner of Labor, *Cost of Production: The Textiles and Glass*, vol. 1, (Washington, D.C.: Government Printing Office, 1891), table XII.

26. Brinley Thomas, *Migration and Economic Growth*, 2d ed. (New York: Cambridge University Press, 1973). Similar statements may be found in Mandle, *Roots of Black Poverty*, chap. 2; Robert Higgs, "The Boll Weevil, the Cotton Economy and Black Migration, 1910–1930," *Agricultural History* 50 (1976): 335–50; W. Arthur Lewis, *The Evolution of the International Economic Order* (Princeton: Princeton University Press, 1978), 17.

27. Report of the Industrial Commission on Agriculture and Agricultural Labor, vol. 10 (Washington, D.C.: Government Printing Office, 1901), 71, 471.

28. Robert Higgs, "Did Southern Farmers Discriminate?" *Agricultural History* 46 (1972): 325–28; *Competition and Coercion* (1977; reprint, Chicago: University of Chicago Press, 1980), 63–66.

29. Robert Higgs, "Racial Wage Differentials in North Carolina: Evidence from North Carolina in 1887," *Agricultural History* 52 (1978): 308–11.

30. Richard Easterlin, "Influences in European Overseas Emigration Before World War I," in *The Reinterpretation of American Economic History*, ed. Fogel and Engerman, 384–95.

31. E. H. Phelps-Brown, *A Century of Pay* (New York: St. Martin's Press, 1968).

32. Peter Shergold, *Working-Class Life: The "American Standard" in Comparative Perspective 1899–1913* (Pittsburgh: University of Pittsburgh Press, 1982).

33. This analysis disagrees with the conclusion reached by Jeffrey G. Williamson in *Late Nineteenth Century American Development* (Cambridge: Cambridge University Press, 1974), chap. 11. Williamson estimates supply functions separately for four countries, none of which were major sources of industrial labor to the United States. He does not apply to the labor market the insight that elsewhere in the book he develops for the wheat market, namely that if there are many countries of emigration and many competing destinations, even a fairly large country is unlikely to affect the "world price" of a standardized commodity.

34. Richard H. Steckel, "The Economic Foundations of East-West Migration during the 19th Century," *Explorations in Economic History* 20 (1983): 14–36.

35. James A. Dunleavy, "Regional Preferences and Migrant Settlement," *Research in Economic History* 8 (1983): 221.

36. Quoted in John Bodnar, Roger Simon, and Michael P. Weber, *Lives of Their Own: Blacks, Italians and Poles in Pittsburgh 1900–1960* (Urbana: University of Illinois Press, 1982), 56. The contrast between blue-collar and white-collar labor market processes is documented in John B. Lansing and Eva Mueller, *The Geographic Mobility of Labor* (Ann Arbor, Mich.: Institute for Social Research, 1967), 215.

37. Michael Piore, *Birds of Passage* (New York: Cambridge University Press, 1979), chaps. 1–4.

38. Charlotte Erickson, *American Industry and the European Immigrant, 1860–1885* (Cambridge, Mass.: Harvard University Press, 1957); Joseph M. Perry, *The Impact of Immigration on Three American Industries, 1865–1914* (New York: Arno Press, 1978).

39. A useful survey of admittedly imperfect and often fragmentary wage data may be found in Robert J. Newman, *Growth in the American South* (New York: New York University Press, 1984), 121–35.

40. Lucy M. Cohen, "Entry of Chinese to the Lower South from 1865 to 1870," *Southern Studies* 17 (1978): 7.

41. Rowland Berthoff, "Southern Attitudes Toward Immigration, 1865–1914," *Journal of Southern History* 17 (1951): 339, 357.

42. From Ed. D. Wicker, 7 April 1906, guide to the records of the Low Moor Iron Company Papers, Manuscript Department of the University of Virginia Library, Charlottesville.

43. Quoted in Stanley Greenberg, *Race and State in Capitalist Development* (New Haven: Yale University Press, 1980), 228.

44. *Report of the Industrial Commission*, vol. 10, 428.

45. Ibid., 497. See similar statements on pp. 119 and 911 of the report.

46. Stanley Lieberson, "Selective Black Migration from the South: A Historical View," in *The Demography of Racial and Ethnic Groups*, ed. Frank D. Bean and W. Packer Frisbie (New York: Academic Press, 1978), table 5.2. See also Lansing and Mueller, *Geographic Mobility of Labor*, 43–50; Michael J. Greenwood, *Migration and Economic Growth in the United States* (New York: Academic Press, 1981), 151.

Notes

Chapter 4

1. There is no single authoritative account of the historical economic geography of the southern crops. For cotton, see Wright, *Political Economy of the Cotton South* (New York: Norton, 1978), 14–15, and the sources cited there. The best source on tobacco cultivation and the sensitivity of quality to soil is still Nannie May Tilley, *The Bright-Tobacco Industry* (Chapel Hill: University of North Carolina Press, 1948), chaps. 1–2. The rigid natural constraints on sugar cane sites are well described by Sam B. Hilliard, "Site Characteristics and Spatial Stability of the Louisiana Sugarcane Industry," *Agricultural History* 53 (1979): 254–69. The rise of rice in the Southwest is covered in Henry Dethloff, "Rice Revolution in the Southwest, 1880–1910," *Arkansas Historical Quarterly* 29 (1970): 66–75.

2. U.S. Bureau of the Census, *Plantation Farming in the United States* (Washington, D.C.: Government Printing Office, 1916).

3. For documentation from different perspectives, see Jay Mandle, "The Plantation States as a Subregion of the Post-Bellum South," *Journal of Economic History* 34 (1974): 732–38; Robert Higgs, "Patterns of Farm Rental in the Georgia Cotton Belt, 1880–1900," *Journal of Economic History* 34 (1974): 468–82.

4. These accounts are from Michael Wayne, *The Reshaping of Plantation Society: The Natchez District, 1860–1880* (Baton Rouge: Louisiana State University Press, 1983), 91–99.

5. Quoted in James T. Currie, *Enclave: Vicksburg and Her Plantation 1863–1870* (Jackson: University Press of Mississippi, 1980), 146.

6. Ronald L. F. Davis, *Good and Faithful Labor: From Slavery to Sharecropping in the Natchez District, 1860–1890* (Westport, Conn.: Greenwood Press, 1982), 95–96.

7. For detailed documentation, see Ralph Shlomowitz, " 'Bound' or 'Free'? Freedman Labor in Cotton and Sugar Cane Farming, 1865–1880," *Journal of Southern History* 50 (1984): 569–96.

8. Quoted in Edward L. Ayers, *Vengeance and Justice: Crime and Parishment in the 19th-Century American South* (New York: Oxford University Press, 1984), 165.

9. Quoted in Ralph Shlomowitz, "The Squad System on Postbellum Cotton Plantations," in *Toward a New South?*, ed. Orville Vernon Burton and Robert C. McMath (Westport, Conn.: Greenwood Press, 1982), 269.

10. Quoted in R. P. Brooks, "The Agrarian Revolution in Georgia 1865–1912," *Bulletin of the University of Wisconsin*, no. 639 (1914): 24.

11. For many maps and diagrams like this one, see Merle Prunty, "The Renaissance of the Southern Plantation," *The Geographical Review* 45 (1955): 459–91.

12. Roger Ransom and Richard Sutch, *One Kind of Freedom* (New York: Cambridge University Press, 1977), 44–47, 232–36.

13. Harold Woodman, *King Cotton and His Retainers* (Lexington: University of Kentucky Press, 1968), chaps. 22–23.

14. Ralph Shlomowitz, "The Origins of Southern Sharecropping," *Agricultural History* 53 (1979): 563. Lacy Ford, "Labor and Ideology in the South Carolina Upcountry," in *The Southern Enigma*, ed. Walter Fraser, Jr., and Winfred B. Moore, Jr. (Westport, Conn.: Greenwood Press, 1983), 30.

15. Charles Stearns, *The Black Man of the South* (1872; reprint, New York: Negro University Press, 1969), 516.

16. This account draws heavily on a forthcoming book by Gerald David Jaynes of Yale University, *Branches Without Roots: Genesis of the Black Working Class, 1862–1882* (New York: Oxford University Press, in press).

17. Lewis C. Gray, *Introduction to Agricultural Economics* (New York: Macmillan, 1924), 384.

18. Journals of John Dent, 15 (3 March 1883), quoted in Charles L. Flynn, Jr. *White Land, Black Labor* (Baton Rouge: Louisiana State University Press, 1983), 78.

19. Pranab K. Bardhan, "Labor-Tying in a Poor Agrarian Economy: A Theoretical and Empirical Analysis," *Quarterly Journal of Economics* 98 (1983): 501–14.

20. Direct evidence may be found in the diaries of the Barrow plantation, reported by J. William Harris, "Plantations and Power: Emancipation on the David Barrow Plantations," in Burton and McMath, *Toward a New South?*, 246–55.

21. Quoted in Brooks, "Agrarian Revolution," p. 46, from an unpublished census plantation survey of 1912. See also Wayne, *Reshaping of Plantation Society*, 122, 133.

22. See the testimony in the *Report of the Industrial Commission on Agriculture and Agricultural Labor*, vol. 10 (Washington, D.C.: Government Printing Office, 1901), xix, 455.

23. Single black women and widows also worked as wage hands, but wives and children did not. See Charles Flynn, *White Land, Black Labor: Caste and Class in Late Nineteenth Century Georgia* (Baton Rouge: Louisiana State University Press, 1983), 61.

24. *Report of the Industrial Commission*, vol. 10, 819.

25. Robert Higgs, "Did Southern Farmers Discriminate?" *Agricultural History* 46 (1972): 325–28. Higgs may have overstated the case slightly, as pointed out by Charles Roberts, "Did Southern Farmers Discriminate? The Evidence Reexamined," *Agricultural History* 49 (1975): 441–47, but the responses to the 1887 North Carolina survey seem decisive. See Higgs, "Racial Wage Differentials in Agriculture: Evidence from North Carolina in 1887," *Agricultural History* 52 (1978): 308–11. The Industrial Commission put the question to John C. Kyle, lawyer and planter from Sardis, Mississippi: "If there is any difference, I do not know it" (*Report of the Industrial Commission*, vol. 10, 471).

26. *Report of the Industrial Commission*, vol. 10, 446.

27. Ibid., 95.

28. Senate Committee on Education and Labor, *Testimony as to the Relations Between Capital and Labor* (1883), vol. 4, 145–46.

29. *Sixth Annual Report of the Commission of Labor* (Washington, D.C.: Government Printing Office, 1890), 680–87.

30. Robert H. Wiebe, *The Opening of American Society* (New York: Knopf, 1984), 151, 299.

31. See W. E. B. Du Bois's 1898 study, "Of the Quest of the Golden Fleece," in *The Southern Common People*, ed. Edward Magdol and Jan Wakelyn (Westport, Conn.: Greenwood Press, 1980), 265.

32. *Report of the Industrial Commission*, vol. 10, xix.

33. Ibid., 77.

34. Davis, *Good and Faithful Labor*, 179.

35. *Report of the Industrial Commission*, vol. 10, 919.

36. T. J. Woofter, Jr., *Negro Migration: Changes in Rural Organization and Population of the Cotton Belt* (New York: W. D. Gray, 1920), 22–23, 90.

37. E. A. Boeger and E. A. Goldenweiser, "A Study of the Tenant Systems of Farming in the Yazoo-Mississippi Delta," USDA Bulletin no. 337 (Washington, D.C.: Government Printing Office, 1916), 6.

38. Woofter, *Negro Migration*, 86.

39. Quoted in Flynn, *White Land, Black Labor*, 75.

40. Theodore Rosengarten, *All God's Dangers: The Life of Nate Shaw* (New York: Knopf, 1975), 117–18.

41. Benjamin Hibbard, "Tenancy in the Southern States," *Quarterly Journal of Economics* 27 (1913): 486.

42. Davis, *Good and Faithful Labor*, 109; Gavin Wright, "Freedom and the Southern Economy," *Explorations in Economic History* 69 (1979): 104. Lee Alston and Robert

Notes

Higgs, "Contractual Mix in Southern Agriculture Since the Civil War," *Journal of Economic History* 42 (1982): 348–49. Alston and Higgs report: "The ownership of work stock by laborers appears to have been decisive in determining whether fixed rental agreements would be used" (p. 351).

43. Steven DeCanio, "Accumulation and Discrimination in the Post-Bellum South," *Explorations in Economic History* 16 (1979): 182–206.

44. R. P. Brooks, "Agrarian Revolution," 60–65.

45. Quoted in Woofter, *Negro Migration*, 53.

46. Robert Higgs, "Accumulation of Property by Southern Blacks Before World War I," *American Economic Review* 72 (1982): 725–37. A more comprehensive summary appears in Robert A. Margo, "Accumulation of Property by Southern Blacks: Comment and Further Evidence," *American Economic Review* 74 (1984): 768–76.

47. Arthur Raper, *Preface to Peacentry* (Chapel Hill: University of North Carolina Press, 1936), 122. Ransom and Sutch show that blacks of a given wealth level held a smaller fraction of their wealth in land than did their white counterparts, in *One Kind of Freedom*, 86–87.

48. Quoted in Brooks, "Agrarian Revolution," 67.

49. Harold Woodman, "Southern Agriculture and the Law," *Agricultural History* 53 (1979): 324.

50. Jonathan Wiener, "Planter-Merchant Conflict in Reconstruction Alabama," *Past and Present* 68 (1975): 73–94.

51. Woodman, "Southern Agriculture and the Law," 333–34; Vernon Burton, "Race and Reconstruction," *Journal of Social History* 12 (1978), reprinted in Magdol and Wakelyn, *The Southern Common People*, 220–26. The era of the laborer's lien is discussed in detail by Gerald Jaynes in *Branches Without Roots*, chap. 10.

52. R. P. Brooks, "Agrarian Revolution," 67.

53. On Georgia, see the forthcoming study of antebellum tenancy by Frederick Bode and Donald Ginter (to be published by the University of Georgia Press). On North Carolina, see Marjorie Mendenhall Applewhite, "Sharecropper and Tenant in the Courts of North Carolina," *North Carolina Historical Review* 3 (1954): 134–49.

54. *Report of the Industrial Commission*, vol. 10, 477. These types of equilibria are analyzed in George Akerlof, "The Market for 'Lemons,' " *Quarterly Journal of Economics* 84 (1970): 488–500; Kenneth Arrow, "Models of Discrimination," in *Racial Discrimination in Economic Life*, ed. A. H. Pascal (Lexington, Mass.: D. C. Heath, 1972); A. Michael Spence, *Market Signalling* (Cambridge, Mass.: Harvard University Press, 1974).

55. The phrase is from Broadus Mitchell's father (1910), quoted in Joel Williamson, *The Crucible of Race* (New York: Oxford University Press, 1984), 440.

56. This distinction has been pressed by Steven Hahn, *The Roots of Southern Populism* (New York: Oxford University Press, 1983), 29–40, and by David Weiman, "Petty Commodity Production in the Cotton South" (Ph.D. diss., Stanford University, 1983).

57. U.S. Senate Report 986, *Report of the Committee on Agriculture and Forestry on Conditions of Cotton Growers in the United States* (Washington, D.C.: Government Printing Office, 1895), 286.

58. Quoted in Hahn, *Roots of Southern Populism*, 142.

59. U.S. Department of Agriculture, *Annual Report* (Washington, D.C.: Government Printing Office, 1876), 151.

60. Charles H. Otken, *The Ills of the South* (New York: Putnam, 1894), 56.

61. These issues are elucidated in exasperating detail in Gavin Wright and Howard Kunreuther, "Cotton, Corn and Risk in the Nineteenth Century," *Journal of Economic History* 35 (1975): 528–36, and "Cotton, Corn and Risk in the Nineteenth Century," *Explanations in Economic History* 14 (1977): 186–89.

62. Ransom and Sutch, *One Kind of Freedom*, 159, table 8.3.

63. See, for example, the 1883 statement by John Peabody of Columbus, Georgia,

U.S. Senate Committee on Relations between Labor and Capital, quoted in Wright, *Political Economy*, 173.

64. David Weiman, "The Emancipation of the 'Non-Slaveowning Classes,' " *Journal of Economic History* 45 (1985): 78–90.

65. Rosser Taylor, "Fertilizers and Farming in the Southeast, 1840–1950," *North Carolina Historical Review* 30 (1953): 314, 327. The decline in fertilizer prices is documented in U.S. Department of Agriculture, Division of Statistics, "The Cost of Cotton Production," Miscellaneous Series, Bulletin no. 16 (1899).

66. Enoch Marvin Banks, *The Economics of Land Tenure in Georgia*, vol. 23 (Columbia University Studies in History, Economics, and Public Law, 1905), 35, 123–26.

67. North Carolina Bureau of Labor Statistics, *First Annual Report* (1887), quoted in Ransom and Sutch, *One Kind of Freedom* (Raleigh, N.C.: Josephus Daniels, 1887), 161.

68. The most careful estimate is by Ransom and Sutch, *One Kind of Freedom*, 128–31, 237–43. See, however, the criticism in Peter Temin, "Freedom and Coercion: Notes on the Analysis of Debt Peonage in *One Kind of Freedom*," *Explorations in Economic History* 16 (1979): 56–63.

69. Wayne, *Reshaping*, 166–77.

70. Ransom and Sutch, *One Kind of Freedom*, 137–46; Hahn, *Roots of Southern Populism*, 184–85.

71. Lewis Haney, "Farm Credit Conditions in a Cotton State," *American Economic Review* 4 (1914): 47–49.

72. The 1887 North Carolina survey estimated that 25 percent of the tenants did not "pay out" in that year (*First Annual Report*, 82–85). George Henry White, the black congressman from North Carolina, described some cases of accumulating debt, but was careful to tell the Industrial Commission: "I do not want to impress you that this is the rule. . . . " (*Report of the Industrial Commission*, vol. 10, 419). Even in 1930, T. J. Woofter found that only 14.0 percent of the cotton sharecroppers actually finished the year in debt (*Landlord and Tenant*, 60, 215).

73. David Montgomery, *Beyond Equality* (New York: Knopf, 1967), 26–31.

74. *Report of the Industrial Commission*, vol. 10, 908.

75. U.S. Department of Agriculture, *Annual Report for 1876*: 149.

76. Hamilton (Ga.) *Weekly Visitor*, 7 February 1873, quoted in Thomas D. Clark, *Three Paths to the Modern South* (Athens: University of Georgia Press, 1965), 37.

77. Quoted in Otken, *Ills of the South*, 75.

78. M. B. Hammond, *The Cotton Industry* (New York: American Economic Association, 1897), 173. The earlier quote and many others are from U.S. Senate Report 986 (1895), an entire set of hearings devoted to "overproduction" as a cause of low cotton prices.

79. This paragraph draws primarily on Robert C. McMath, *Populist Vanguard* (Chapel Hill: University of North Carolina Press, 1975). Other informative recent works on the Alliance and populism in the South are Bruce Palmer, *"Man Over Money"* (Chapel Hill: University of North Carolina Press, 1980); Lawrence Goodwyn, *Democratic Promise* (New York: Oxford University Press, 1976); and Michael Schwartz, *Radical Protest and Social Structure* (New York: Academic Press, 1976).

80. Respectively, the adherents of these views are Schwartz, *Radical Protest and Social Structure*; Palmer, *"Man Over Money"*; Goodwyn, *Democratic Premise*; and C. Vann Woodward, *Tom Watson: Agrarian Rebel* (New York: Macmillan, 1938). The last hypothesis contains considerable truth in the indirect form of disfranchisement, which deprived many poor whites as well as blacks of the vote. See J. Morgan Kousser, *The Shaping of Southern Politics* (New Haven: Yale University Press, 1974).

81. Regression results consistent with this interpretation are presented in Higgs, "Accumulation of Property," 735, and Margo, "Comment and Further Evidence," 771.

82. Douglas Helms, "Technological Methods for Boll Weevil Control," *Agricultural*

Notes

History 53 (1979): 286–99; Douglas Helms, "Revision and Reversion: Changing Cultural Control Practices for the Cotton Boll Weevil," *Agricultural History* 54 (1980): 108–25; Robert Higgs, "The Boll Weevil, The Cotton Economy, and Black Migration," *Agricultural History* 50 (1976): 344–46. The statement on aggregate effects draws on Kent Osband, "The Boll Weevil Versus 'King Cotton,' " *Journal of Economic History* 45 (1985): 627–43.

83. Robert Margo, "Race Differences in Public School Expenditures, Disfranchisement and Public School Finance in Louisiana, 1890–1910," *Social Science History* 6 (1982): 9–33; J. Morgan Kousser, *The Shaping of Southern Politics*; Kousser, "Progressivism for Middle Class Whites Only: North Carolina Education, 1880–1910," *Journal of Southern History* 46 (1980): 17–44.

84. A study that stresses the long-run consequences of southern schooling policy for black progress is James P. Smith, "Race and Human Capital," *American Economic Review* 74 (1984): 685–98.

Chapter 5

1. The best published cost analysis, which uses 1890 data, is David Doane, "Regional Cost Differences and Textile Location," *Explorations in Economic History* 9 (1971): 3–34. An older study that is still informative is Chen-Han Chen, "Regional Differences in Costs and Productivity in the American Cotton Manufacturing Industry, 1880–1910," *Quarterly Journal of Economics* 55 (1941): 533–66.

2. See "Notes on the 170th Anniversary of the Manufacture of Cotton in the United States, 1790–1960," *Cotton History Review* 1 (1960): 83–87.

3. Ernest M. Lander, Jr., *The Textile Industry in Antebellum South Carolina* (Baton Rouge: Louisiana State University Press, 1969), 5.

4. Douglass North, *The Economic Growth of the United States, 1790–1860* (1961; New York: Norton, 1966), 55–58, 162–65; Robert Zevin, "The Growth of Cotton Textile Production after 1815," in *The Reinterpretation of American Economic History*, ed. Robert Fogel and Stanley Engerman (New York: Harper & Row, 1971).

5. This analysis is elaborated in Gavin Wright, "Cheap Labor and Southern Textile Before 1880," *Journal of Economic History* 39 (1979): 661–63. Simkins is quoted in Norris Preyer, "Southern Support of the Tariff of 1816—A Reappraisal," *Journal of Southern History* 25 (1959): 314.

6. Quoted in Steve Dunwell, *The Run of the Mill* (Boston: D. R. Godine, 1978), 158. See also *Hunt's Merchant Magazine* 20 (1849): 672ff.

7. Lander, *The Textile Industry*, 90; Norris Preyer, "The Historian, the Slave and the Ante-Bellum Textile Industry," *Journal of Negro History* 46 (1961): 71–76; Tom Terrill, "Eager Hands: Labor for Southern Textiles, 1850–1860," *Journal of Economic History* 36 (1976): 86. The claim by Robert Starobin, *Industrial Slavery in the Old South* (New York: Oxford University Press, 1970), 13, that five thousand slaves were working in textiles in 1860 is wildly inaccurate.

8. Richard W. Griffin, "Poor White Laborers in Southern Cotton Factories, 1789–1865," *South Carolina Historical Magazine* 41 (1960): 26–40. A recent study argues that inadequate transportation from water-power sites limited the industry: Stephen J. Goldfarb, "A Note on Limits to Growth of the Cotton-Textile Industry in the Old South," *Journal of Southern History* 48 (1982): 545–58. Transportation was certainly a problem, just as humidity and the location of coal deposits were problems. But none of the geographic features explain why growth was so rapid in the 1840s and so slow in the 1850s.

9. Wright, "Cheap Labor and Southern Textiles Before 1880," 673–74.

10. Ulrich B. Phillips, ed., *Plantation and Frontier* (Cleveland: A. H. Clark, 1909), 339.

11. The timing of industry growth is documented in R. W. Griffin, "Reconstruction of the North Carolina Textile Industry, 1865–1885," *North Carolina History Review* 41 (1964): 48–49.

12. These interpretations are advanced, respectively, in Dwight Billings, *Planters and the Making of a "New South"* (Chapel Hill: University of North Carolina Press, 1979); and Patrick J. Hearden, *Independence and Empire: The New South's Cotton Mill Campaign 1865–1901* (DeKalb: Northern Illinois Press, 1982).

13. Carlton, *Mill and Town in South Carolina* (Baton Rouge: Louisiana State University Press), 44–57.

14. Interview quoted by Broadus Mitchell, *The Rise of Cotton Mills in the South* (Baltimore: Johns Hopkins University Press, 1921), 130.

15. A survey of estimates is presented in Alice Galenson, "The Migration of the Cotton Textile Industry" (Ph.D. diss., Cornell University, 1975), 109.

16. Mitchell, *Rise of Cotton Mills*, 108.

17. Thomas Brush and William Lazonick, "The 'Horndal' Effect in Early U.S. Manufacturing," *Exploration in Economic History* 22 (1985): 53–96; Gary Saxonhouse, "Productivity Change and Labor Absorption in Japanese Cotton Spinning 1891–1935," *Quarterly Journal of Economics* 91 (1977): 195–219.

18. Cathy L. McHugh, "Earnings in the Post-bellum Southern Cotton Textile Industry: A Case Study," *Explorations in Economic History* 21 (1984): 33.

19. Nothing could be less appropriate than to characterize the southern textiles industry as engaged in a continuing search for "empire" and foreign markets (see Patrick Hearden, *Independence and Empire*). A reading of the Special Agents Reports issued from various countries by the Bureau of Foreign and Domestic Commerce between 1905 and 1920 should convince anyone that the United States played no more than a marginal and insignificant role in foreign markets. The episodic excursions and comments recited by Hearden serve mainly to illustrate the sporadic and irregular character of foreign connections. Though they were important to some individual firms, exports never reached more than 7 or 8 percent of production, and the growth opportunities were in the domestic market.

20. The count or yarn number is the number of "hanks" of 840 yards each necessary to make one pound of yarn.

21. The interpretation draws on Marvin Fischbaum, "An Economic Analysis of the Southern Capture of the Cotton Textile Industry Progressing to 1910" (Ph.D. diss., Columbia University, 1965).

22. Jack Blicksilver, *Cotton Manufacturing in the Southeast: An Historical Analysis* (Atlanta: Georgia State College of Business Administration, 1959), 19.

23. Thomas M. Young, *The American Cotton Industry* (London: Methuen, 1902), 52.

24. Melvin T. Copeland, *The Cotton Manufacturing Industry of the United States* (Cambridge, Mass.: Harvard University Press, 1912), 51, 53.

25. Ibid., 389.

26. Examples are given in Mitchell, *Rise of Cotton Mills*, 226–28.

27. Ibid., 208.

28. Robert S. Smith, *Mill on the Dan* (Durham, N.C.: Duke University Press, 1960), 102–5.

29. Lois MacDonald, *Southern Mill Hills* (New York: A. L. Hillman, 1928), 45, 86, 121.

30. Lander, *The Textile Industry*, 60–61: "Gregg soon learned that his proposed system of boarding houses did not appeal to the girls, who were unwilling to leave their homes."

31. This comparison is pursued in Gary Saxonhouse and Gavin Wright, "Two Forms

Notes

of Cheap Labor in Textiles History," in *Technique, Spirit and Form in the Making of the Modern Economics: Essays in Honor of William N. Parker*, ed. Saxonhouse and Wright (Greenwich, Conn.: JAI Press, 1984). The contrast between northern and southern labor supplies is emphasized in recent publications by Claudia Goldin and Kenneth Sokoloff, especially "The Relative Productivity Hypothesis of Industrialism: The American Case, 1820 to 1850," *Quarterly Journal of Economics* 94 (1984): 461–87. They conjecture that labor requirements in the major crops must have differed, whereas my analysis stresses the effects of slavery on labor markets.

32. Quoted in Dale Newman, "Work and Community Life in a Southern Town," *Labor History* 19 (1978): 206.

33. Interview in Edgar Ralph Rankin, "A Social Study of One Hundred Families at Cotton Mills in Gastonia, North Carolina" (M.A. thesis, University of North Carolina, 1914), 21.

34. In the 1907 survey, the distributions of "Months Since Beginning Work" were as follows:

	Boys	Girls
12 and below	.080	.090
24 and below	.224	.236
36 and below	.396	.407
48 and below	.574	.568
60 and below	.735	.725

(Compiled from U.S. Senate, *Report on Condition of Women and Child Wage-Earners in the United States* vol. 1, [Washington, D.C.: Government Printing Office, 1910] 826–931, table XXIX.) However, the sample contained 211 girls and only 174 boys.

35. Statement by M. Allred of the Granite Falls Manufacturing Co., in North Carolina Bureau of Labor and Printing, *18th Annual Report* (Raleigh, N.C.: State Printers, 1904), 104. Each annual report contains a sampling of these complaints in the section "Letters from Millmen."

36. Saxonhouse and Wright, "Two Forms of Cheap Labor," 10–11.

37. U.S. Senate, *Condition of Women and Child Wage-Earners*, vol. 1, 453.

38. Irwin Feller, "The Draper Loom in New England Textiles, 1899–1914," *Journal of Economic History* 25 (1966): 320–47; and "The Diffusion and Location of Technological Change in the American Cotton-Textile Industry, 1890–1970," *Technology and Culture* 15 (1974): 569–93. An important new study is William Mass, "Technological Change and Industrial Relations: The Diffusion of Automatic Weaving in the United States and Britain" (Ph.D. diss., Boston University, 1984).

39. Copeland, *Cotton Manufacturing Industry of the U.S.*, 114.

40. Harriet Herring, *The Passing of the Mill Village* (Chapel Hill: University of North Carolina Press, 1949), 5.

41. Herbert Lahne, *The Cotton Mill Worker* (New York: Farrar and Rinehart, 1944), 63.

42. Frank Tannenbaum, *Darker Phases of the South* (New York: G. P. Putnam's Sons, 1924), 43.

43. See the forthcoming book by the University of North Carolina oral-history project, under the direction of Jacquelyn Hall. The disdain of the middle class for the mill people is spelled out in Carlton, *Mill and Town in South Carolina*, 173–212.

44. The report is in Japanese, and is discussed in Saxonhouse and Wright, "Two Forms of Cheap Labor."

45. Frank W. Taussig, *The Tariff History of the United States*, 8th ed. (New York:

Notes

Putnam, 1931), 513; second statement quoted in Dane Yorke, *The Men and Times of Pepperell* (Boston: Pepperell Manufacturing Company, 1945), 91.

46. Smith, *Mill on the Dan,* 262–76, 284–94. Profit figures may be found in Smith, *Mill on the Dan,* 192, and Blicksilver, *Cotton Manufacturing in the Southeast,* 99.

47. My demand curve estimate for 1880–1920 is:

$$\ln(Q_{D/N}) = 2.09 - 0.90^*\ln P_T + 1.05^*\ln(Y/N) + 0.36^*\ln P_w$$
$$(2.59) \qquad (11.03) \qquad (2.72)$$

where $Q_{D/N}$ is per capita consumption, P_T is a cotton textile price index, Y/N is per capita income, and P_w is the price of wool ($R^2 = 0.856$). When the estimating period is extended to 1930, there is no significant change in any coefficient. Details may be found in my "Cheap Labor and Southern Textiles, 1880–1930," *Quarterly Journal of Economics* (1981): 619–21.

48. The following regression for spinners' wages, 1880–1930, illustrates this point:

$$\ln W_S = -3.52 + 0.56^*W_F + 3.25^*EXP$$
$$(2.41) \qquad (3.63)$$

$$+ 0.148^*\ln SP^S + 0.326^*D20S$$
$$(4.25) \qquad (5.10)$$

where W_F is the farm wage, EXP is an age-sex index, SP^S is southern spindles, and D20S is a dummy variable for the 1920s ($R^2 = 0.931$). No coefficient is significantly changed from the 1880–1920 period. The regression indicates that when compositional changes and the growth of spindles are taken into account, we have an "autonomous" rise of 32.6 percent in real terms.

49. U.S. Department of Labor, Women's Bureau, *Lost Time and Labor Turnover in Cotton Mills,* Bulletin no. 52 (Washington, D.C.: Government Printing Office, 1926), 44.

50. Dale Newman, "Work and Community Life in a Southern Town," 211.

51. Daniel T. Rodgers, "Tradition, Modernity, and the American Industrial Worker," *Journal of Interdisciplinary History* 7 (1977), 670–72. The investigators for the Women's Bureau study (see note 49) conceded that the operation of the "spare hand system" made their turnover figures virtually impossible to interpret.

52. Elizabeth Davidson, *Child Labor Legislation in the Southern Textile States* (Chapel Hill: University of North Carolina Press, 1939).

53. See the survey in Jennings J. Rhyne, *Some Southern Cotton Mill Workers and their Villages* (Chapel Hill: University of North Carolina Press, 1930), chap. 14. This observation will be clearly distinguished from the claim that the wage increase itself is merely an artifact of work-force composition, which is refuted in note 48.

54. See the articles "Can You Tell Him?" (*Southern Textile Bulletin,* 26 July 1928) and "The Forty-Year Olds Again" (*Southern Textile Bulletin,* 16 August 1928). I am indebted to Jacquelyn Hall and her associates for these references.

55. Melton A. McLaurin, *Paternalism and Protest: Southern Mill Workers and Organized Labor, 1875–1905* (Westport, Conn.: Greenwood Press, 1971), 69, 93, 131, 144.

56. Herbert Lahne, *The Cotton Mill Worker,* 206.

57. Quoted in F. Ray Marshall, *Labor in the South* (Cambridge, Mass.: Harvard University Press, 1967), 119. For accounts of the major strikes, see Marshall, *Labor in the South,* 101–20; Tom Tippett, *When Southern Labor Stirs* (New York: J. Cape & H. Smith, 1931).

Notes

Chapter 6

1. Sheldon Hackney, "Origins of the New South in Retrospect," *Journal of Southern History* 38 (1972): 195. This thesis has been reiterated even more recently, in more extreme and less defensible form, by David R. Goldfield, who writes that colonialism "fastened a type of regional specialization upon the South that remains to the present day," and that the South has been in "continuous economic servitude to the North." See Goldfield, "The Urban South: A Regional Framework," *American Historical Review* 86 (1981): 1029.

2. From Ray Marshall, "Industrialization and Race Relations in the Southern United States," in *Industrialization and Race Relations*, ed. Guy Hunter (London: Oxford University Press, 1965), quoting Clark Kerr et al., *Industrialism and Industrial Man* (Cambridge, Mass.: Harvard University Press, 1960), 35.

3. Thomas D. Clark, "The Impact of the Timber Industry on the South," *Mississippi Quarterly* 25 (1972): 157.

4. Charlotte Todes, *Labor and Lumber* (1931; reprint, New York: Arno Press, 1975), 75.

5. Abraham Berglund, George T. Starnes, and Frank T. De Vyvver, *Labor in the Industrial South* (University, Virginia: The Institute for Research in the Social Sciences, 1930), 53.

6. Ibid., 54.

7. James Fickle, *The New South and the "New Competition": Trade Association Development in the Southern Pine Industry* (Urbana: University of Illinois Press, 1980), 54, 61.

8. C. F. Korstian, "The Economic Development of the Furniture Industry of the South and its Future Dependence upon Forestry," State of North Carolina Department of Conservation and Development, Division of Forestry, Economic Paper no. 57 (1926); Charles H. V. Ebert, "Furniture Making in High Point," *North Carolina Historical Review* 36 (1959): 330–39.

9. C. Vann Woodward, *Origins of the New South 1877–1913* (Baton Rouge: Louisiana University Press, 1951), 309. The direction of causality from industry attributed to wages is implicit in the many twentieth-century wage studies that "correct for industry mix" before comparing northern and southern wage levels. A comprehensive survey of southern industries from this perspective is Harriet Herring, *Southern Industry and Regional Development* (Chapel Hill: University of North Carolina Press, 1940).

10. Gary Kulick, "Black Workers and Technological change in the Birmingham Iron Industry, 1881–1931," in *Southern Workers and their Unions*, ed. Merl E. Reed, Leslie S. Hough, and Gary M. Fink (Westport, Conn.: Greenwood Press, 1981), 22–42.

11. Fickle, *The New South and the "New Competition,"* 314.

12. R. B. Tennant, *The American Cigarette Industry* (New Haven: Yale University Press, 1950), especially the figures on p. 56. The failure of the Dukes to achieve dominance in cigars is recounted in Robert F. Durden, *The Dukes of Durham* (Durham, N.C.: Duke University Press, 1975), chap. 4.

13. Calculated from data in U.S. Senate, *Report on Conditions of Women and Child Wage-Earners*, vol. 18 (Washington, D.C.: Government Printing Office, 1913), table 8. Remarkably, the weekly earnings of women in the cigarette division (almost exclusively white) were not significantly different between North Carolina and New York.

14. This account is based on Robert H. McKenzie, "Reconstructions of the Alabama Iron Industry, 1865–1880," *Alabama Review* 25 (1972): 178–91; Ralph Tanner, "Some Characteristics of Eight Land Companies in North Alabama, 1863–1900," *Alabama Review* 29 (1976): 124–34; H. H. Chapman et al., *The Iron and Steel Industries of the*

Notes

South (University, Ala.: University of Alabama Press, 1953), 101–5.

15. Quoted in Woodward, *Origins of the New South,* 127. Chattanooga quotation is from Kenneth Warren, *The American Steel Industry,* 69. Details on the early history of Birmingham and TCI may be found in Ethel Armes, *The Story of Coal and Iron in Alabama* (1910; reprint, New York: Arno Press, 1973); Robert Gregg, *Origin and Development of the Tennessee Coal Iron and Railroad Company* (New York: Newcomen Society, 1948). See also William Davis Moore, *Development of the Cast Iron Pressure Pipe Industry in the Southern States, 1800–1938* (Birmingham: Birmingham Publishing Company, 1939).

16. Richard H. Edmonds, *Facts About the South* (Baltimore: Manufacturers Record Publishing Company, 1907), 10.

17. *Birmingham News,* quoted in Kenneth Warren, *The American Steel Industry* (Oxford: Clarendon Press, 1973), 186; *Birmingham Age-Herald* and *Birmingham News,* quoted in Marlene Rikard, "An Experiment in Welfare Capitalism" (Ph.D. diss., University of Alabama, 1983), 29.

18. The strongest statement of this case is presented in George W. Stocking, *Basing Point Pricing and Regional Development: A Case Study of the Iron and Steel Industry* (Chapel Hill: University of North Carolina Press, 1954).

19. For example: "Survival and extension of old firms and the growth of new ones was helped by three aspects of Steel Corporation policy—its co-operative, almost paternalistic stance, the associated price stability, and the development of Pittsburgh Plus pricing. The first two provided a suitable climate for growth, the latter gave extra incentives for new capacity at a distance from Pittsburgh." Warren, *American Steel Industry,* 131.

20. The technical issues are covered in detail by Chapman, *Iron and Steel Industries of the South,* chaps. 5 and 6.

21. Robert Allen, "The Peculiar Productivity History of American Blast Furnaces, 1840–1913," *Journal of Economic History* 37 (September 1977): 605–33.

22. Quoted in Rikard, "Experiment in Welfare Capitalism," 35.

23. A similar verdict on the alleged effects of freight-rate differentials is outlined in Clarence Danhof, "Four Decades of Thought on the South's Economic Problems," in *Essays in Southern Economic Development,* ed. Melvin L. Greenhut and W. Tate Whitman (Chapel Hill: University of North Carolina Press, 1964), 7–68. In their classic *Economic Resources and Policies of the South* (New York: Macmillan, 1951) Hoover and Ratchford concluded that "high freight rates are not now, and never were, a major barrier to the economic development of the South," 65–88.

24. The classic treatment is Nathan Rosenberg, "Technological Change in the Machine Tool Industry, 1840–1910," *Journal of Economic History* 23 (1963): 414–43. A theoretical analysis is presented in Paul David, *Technical Choice, Innovation and Economic Growth* (New York: Cambridge University Press, 1975), chap. 1.

25. For evidence on capital goods, see Louis Ferleger, "Capital Goods and Southern Economic Development," *Journal of Economic History* 45 (1985): 411–17.

26. This account draws on Chapman, *Iron and Steel,* 105–10; Warren, *American Steel Industry,* 182–83; Gary Kulick, "The Sloss Furnace Company, 1881–1931, Technological Change and Labor Supply in the Southern Pig Iron Industry," (unpublished, 1976).

27. Marlene Rikard, "George Gordon Crawford: Man of the New South," *Alabama Review* 31 (1978): 163–81.

28. Stocking, *Basing Point Pricing,* 104–11.

29. George Tindall, *The Emergence of the New South, 1913–1945* (Baton Rouge: Louisiana State University Press, 1967), 84–85; Jack P. Oden, "Origins of the Southern Kraft Paper Industry, 1903–1930," *Mississippi Quarterly* 30 (1977): 565–84.

30. For an analysis of the Japanese adaptation of technology to labor force characteristics and markets, see Gary Saxonhouse, "Technology Choice, Adaptation and

Notes

Quality Dimension in the Japanese Cotton Textile Industry," in *The Comparative Analysis of Japan and Less Developed Countries*, ed. K. Ohkawa and Y. Hayami (Tokyo: The International Development Center of Japan, 1979), 83–120.

31. Accounts of southern marketing by northern producers may be found in G. S. Gibb, *The Saco-Lowell Shops* (Cambridge, Mass.: Harvard University Press, 1950), 241–55, 397–99, 410–19, and T. R. Navin, *The Whitin Machine Works Since 1831: A Textile Machinery Company in an Industrial Village* (1950; reprint, New York: Russell & Russell, 1969), 204–35.

32. Carl V. Harris, "Stability and Change in Discrimination Against Black Public Schools: Birmingham, Alabama, 1871–1931," *Journal of Southern History* 51 (1985): 375–416; Horace Mann Bond, *Negro Education in Alabama: A Study in Cotton and Steel* (1939; reprint, New York: Octagon Books, 1969), chap. 16; Blaine Brownell, "Birmingham, Alabama: New South City in the 1920s," *Journal of Southern History* 38 (1972): 26. A comprehensive study of the U.S. steel program is in Rikard, "Experiment in Welfare Capitalism."

33. Birmingham became one of the chief assembling points for migrants. See Emmett J. Scott, *Negro Migration During the Way* (1920; reprint, New York: Arno Press, 1969), 64 and map on p. 71. The importance of labor experience in foundries is noted in George E. Haynes. *The Negro at Work During the World War and During Reconstruction* (Washington, D.C.: Division of Negro Economics Study, 1921), 42. Experienced coal miners were eagerly sought. U.S. Dept. of Labor, *Negro Migration in 1916–17* (Washington, D.C.: Division of Negro Economics Study, 1919), 63–64.

34. Kulick, "Black Workers and Technological Change," 35.

35. Quoted in Rikard, "Experiment in Welfare Capitalism," 52.

36. Robert Higgs, "Race and Economy in the South, 1890–1950," in *The Age of Segregation*, ed. Robert Haws (Jackson, Miss.: The University Press of Mississippi, 1978), 30. See also William H. Nicholls, *Southern Tradition and Regional Progress* (Chapel Hill: University of North Carolina Press, 1960); Robert Higgs, *Competition and Coercion* (1977; reprint, Chicago: University of Chicago Press, 1980). The classic theoretical statement is Gary Becker, *The Economics of Discrimination* (Chicago: University of Chicago Press, 1957), but see also Thomas Sowell, *Markets and Minorities* (New York: Basic Books, 1981).

37. Paul B. Worthman, "Black Workers and Labor Unions in Birmingham, Alabama, 1897–1904," *Labor History* 10 (1969): 392.

38. Gilbert Thomas Stephenson, *Race Distinctions in American Law* (New York: D. Appleton & Co., 1910) contains no reference to employment or workplace regulation. Charles S. Mangum, in *The Legal Status of the Negro* (Chapel Hill: University of North Carolina Press, 1940), states that "the problem of industrial segregation in the South is usually left in the hands of private business" (p. 174), noting only three exceptions.

39. Pauli Murray, ed., *States Laws on Race and Color* (Cincinnati: Methodist Church, 1950), 341–42, 414–15.

40. Quoted in French Eugene Wolfe, *Admission to American Trade Unions* (Baltimore: The Johns Hopkins University Press, 1912), 124.

41. F. Ray Marshall, *Labor in the South* (Cambridge, Mass.: Harvard University Press, 1967), p. 49; Herbert Northrup, *Organized Labor and the Negro* (New York: Harper and Brothers, 1944), 18–19.

42. See, for example, Worthman, "Black Workers and Labor Unions in Birmingham, Alabama, 1897–1904," 375–407.

43. The best statement is Kenneth Arrow, "The Theory of Discrimination," in *Discrimination in Labor Markets*, ed. Orley Ashenfelter and Albert Rees (Princeton, N.J.: Princeton University Press, 1973). See also Joseph Stiglitz, "Approaches to the Economics of Discrimination," *American Economic Review* 63 (1973): 287–95.

44. U.S. Senate Committee, *Report on Relations between Capital and Labor* (Washington, D.C.: Government Printing Office, 1885), vol. IV, 171, 490.

Notes

45. "Firm-Specific Evidence on Racial Wage Differentials and Workforce Segregation," *American Economic Review* 67 (1977): 236–45.

46. The curves are not actual data points but lognormal curves fitted to the underlying data. Hence they exaggerate the smoothness and regularity of the racial pattern, without doing violence to the available information. The aggregate curves cover building trades, saw and planing mills, cotton and tobacco manufacturers, iron and machinery, and tanneries. The data comes from a larger project on blacks in the labor market, now underway with the support of the National Science Foundation in collaboration with Warren Whatley. Full details on data and procedures will be published in the larger study.

47. Richard J. Hopkins, "Occupational and Geographic Mobility in Atlanta, 1870–1896," *Journal of Southern History* 34 (1968): 200–213; Lois E. Horton and James Oliver Horton, "Race, Occupation and Literacy in Reconstruction Washington, D.C.," in *Toward a New South?*, ed. Orville V. Burton and Robert C. McMath (Westport, Conn.: Greenwood, 1982), 135–51.

48. *Report on Relations between Capital and Labor* 4: 3–9.

49. Ibid., 102, 124, 157, 169, 239, 278, 529, 538, 726, 753.

50. This is the characterization of George Tindall, *South Carolina Negros, 1879–1900* (1952; reprint, Columbia, S.C.: University of South Carolina Press, 1970), 130–32. See particularly the survey of opinion on "The Negro as a Mill Hand" in *Manufacturers' Record* 24 (22 September 1893).

51. Gunnar Myrdal, *An American Dilemma* (New York: Harper and Brothers, 1944), appendix 6, 1110–11.

52. Representative studies are Richard W. Griffin, "The Origins of the Industrial Revolution in Georgia, 1810–65," *Georgia Historical Quarterly* 42 (1958): 355–75; Diffee W. Standard and R. W. Griffin, "The Cotton Textile Industry in Antebellum North Carolina," *North Carolina Historical Review* 34 (January 1957): 15–35, and (April 1957): 131–64; R. W. Griffin, "Cotton Manufacturing in Alabama to 1865," *Alabama Historical Quarterly* 18 (1956): 289–307. More articles appeared in a journal originally titled *Cotton History Review* and later *Textile History Review* that survived from 1960 to 1964. See also Ernest M. Lander, Jr., *The Textile Industry in Antebellum South Carolina* (Baton Rouge: Louisiana State University Press, 1969).

53. Gavin Wright, "Cheap Labor and Southern Textiles before 1880," *Journal of Economic History* 39 (1979): 655–80. The best study of slaves in textiles is Randall M. Miller, "The Fabric of Control-Slavery in Antebellum Southern Textile Mills," *Business History Review* 55 (1981): 471–90.

54. The theoretical basis for this analysis is presented in Kenneth Arrow, "The Theory of Discrimination," and in Brian Arthur, "On Competing Technologies and Historical Small Events" (Stanford University, November 1983). The QWERTY example is taken up in Paul David, "CLIO and the Economics of QWERTY," *American Economic Review* 75 (1985): 332–37.

55. The incident is detailed in McLaurin, *Paternalism and Protest*, 86–87.

56. Allen Heath Stokes, Jr., "Black and White Labor in the Development of the Southern Textile Industry" (Ph.D. diss., University of South Carolina, 1977), 204–8, where other examples are given; McLaurin, *Paternalism and Protest*, 61–65.

57. Leonard Carlson, "Labor Supply, the Acquisition of Skills, and the Location of Southern Textile Mills, 1880–1900," *Journal of Economic History* 41 (1981): 65–71. The account of the Vesta Mill is drawn from Stokes, *Black and White Labor*, chap. 7, but the quotation from the manager is from Broadus Mitchell, *Rise of the Cotton Mills*, 218.

58. This account is based on Durden, *The Dukes of Durham*, 145–48.

59. Joseph Clarke Robert, *The Tobacco Kingdom* (Durham, N.C.: Duke University Press, 1938), esp. chap. 10; Alan Bruce Bromberg, "Slavery in the Virginia Tobacco Factories 1800–1860" (Ph.D. diss., University of Virginia, 1968).

Notes

60. A visitor in 1871 found that many blacks had spent nearly their entire lives in the same establishments. Alrutheus A. Taylor, *The Negro in the Reconstruction of Virginia* (Washington, D.C.: The Association for the Study of Negro Life and History, 1926), 117–18. Continuity is also indicated by the ongoing local debates over whether the freed black tobacco workers were better or worse off than they had been as slaves. See the 1880 Census, vol. 20, p. 40; Bromberg, "Slavery in the Virginia Tobacco Factories," p. 25, citing Trowbridge, *The South*. Citations on the early postwar use of blacks in North Carolina are found in Frenise A. Logan, *The Negro in North Carolina, 1876–1894* (Chapel Hill: University of North Carolina Press, 1964), 91–92.

61. Tilley, *The Bright-Tobacco Industry*, 320–21, quoting the *Kinston Free Press* for 25 September 1900.

62. Billings, *Planters and the Making of a "New South,"* 113–20.

63. Descriptions of the segregation system in tobacco manufacturing appear in Herbert Northrup, "The Negro in the Tobacco Industry," in *Negro Employment in Southern Industry*, ed. Herbert Northrup and Richard L. Rowan (Philadelphia: University of Pennsylvania Press, 1971).

64. See the testimony in *Report on Relations Between Labor and Capital*, vol. 4, 133ff; Lester Lamm, *Black Tennesseans* (Knoxville: University of Tennessee Press, 1977), 142.

65. Greenberg, *Race and State in Capitalist Development*, 231–33.

66. Price Fishback, "Segregation in Job Hierarchies: West Virginia Coal Mining, 1906–1932," *Journal of Economic History* 44 (1984): 755–74.

67. See James P. Smith, "Race and Human Capital," *American Economic Review* 74 (1984): 685–98.

68. Dolores E. Janiewski, "From Field to Factory: Race, Class, Sex and the Woman Worker in Durham, 1880–1940" (Ph.D. diss., Duke University, 1979), 140.

69. Charles S. Johnson, *Patterns of Negro Segregation* (New York: Harper, 1943), 90. Other examples from the late 1920s are noted in Sterling D. Spero and Abram L. Harris, *The Black Worker* (New York: Columbia University Press, 1931), 168–71.

Chapter 7

1. George Tindall, *The Emergence of the New South* (Baton Rouge: Louisiana State University Press, 1967), 53.

2. Quoted in Emmett J. Scott, *Negro Migration during the War* (1920; reprint, New York: Arno Press, 1969), 17.

3. T. J. Woofter, "Migration of Negroes from Georgia, 1916–17," in U.S. Department of Labor, Division of Negro Economics, *Negro Migration in 1916–17* (Washington, D.C.: Government Printing Office, 1917), 86.

4. Robert Higgs, "The Boll Weevil, The Cotton Economy, and Black Migration, 1910–1930," *Agricultural History* 50 (1976): 348–50.

5. Jack Temple Kirby, "Black and White in the Rural South, 1915–1954," *Agricultural History* 58 (1984): 421.

6. U.S. Dept. of Labor, *Negro Migration 1915–17*, 19, 55, 77; Higgs, "Black Migration, 1910–1930," 348–49; C. O. Brannen, "Relation of Land Tenure to Plantation Organization," U.S. Department of Agriculture Bulletin no. 1269 (Washington, D.C.: Government Printing Office, 1924), 44–46.

7. Higgs, "The Boll Weevil," using state data, finds little effect of the boll weevil on migration before 1920. But much more detailed analysis using county data shows a major effect for blacks, 1910–1920. See Neil Fligstein, *Going North: Migration of Blacks and Whites from the South, 1900–1950* (New York: Academic Press, 1981), 124, 126.

8. Tipton Ray Snavely, "Report on Alabama and North Carolina," in U.S. Department of Labor, *Negro Migration in 1916–17*, 63–64.

9. Brannen, "Land Tenure," 45. Fligstein finds an inverse association between tenancy and out-migration for whites (p. 126).

10. Flora Gill, "Economics and the Black Exodus" (Ph.D. diss., Stanford University, 1974), 163–64.

11. The classic description of the 1920s trends in labor policies is in Summer Slichter, "The Current Labor Policies of American Industries," *Quarterly Journal of Economics* 43 (1929): 393–435. An important new book by Sanford Jacoby, *Employing Bureaucracy: Unions, Managers, and the Transformation of Work in American Industry, 1900–1945* (New York: Columbia University Press, 1985) presents a thorough quantitative account and interpretation. Jacoby emphasizes the threat of unionism and questions the expansion of such practices in the 1920s; but the evidence is clear that most of the gains of the war years were not reversed afterward. The uneven access to these well-paid, attractive jobs is described by Frank Stricker, "Affluence for Whom? Another Look at Prosperity and the Working Classes in the 1920s," *Labor History* 24 (1983): 5–33. Studies from the 1920s showing barriers and even retrogression in the status of black industrial workers are surveyed in Louise Venable Kennedy, *The Negro Peasant Turns Cityward* (New York: Columbia University Press, 1930), 80–84, 235.

12. Thomas R. Navin, *The Whitin Machine Works Since 1831: A Textile Machinery Company in an Industrial Village* (1950; reprint, New York: Russell & Russell, 1969), 338–39. The conventional view is presented in Jack Blicksilver, *Cotton Manufacturing in the Southeast: An Historical Analysis* (Atlanta: Georgia State College of Business Administration, 1959), 62.

13. Frank W. Taussig, *The Tariff History of the United States*, 8th ed. (New York: Putnam, 1931), 513.

14. Quoted in Robert Sidney Smith, *Mill on the Dan* (Durham, N.C.: Duke University Press, 1960), 63. Further expressions of industry perspective on the issue may be found in National Industrial Conference Board, *Night Work in Industry* (New York, 1927), and in a symposium in *Textile World*, 4 February 1928.

15. Claudius T. Murchison, *King Cotton Is Sick* (Chapel Hill: University of North Carolina Press, 1938), 20.

16. Ibid., 149.

17. For example: "The Cherry Cotton Mill of Florence, Alabama: An Electric Light Plant Has Been Installed in the Mill, and the Management is Preparing to Put on a Night Force of Operators" (9 November 1894, p. 225).

18. W. A. Graham Clark, *Cotton Goods in Latin America*, U.S. Bureau of Manufacturers, Special Agents Series, Report 31 (Washington, D.C.: Government Printing Office, 1909), 29.

19. U.S. Bureau of Labor Statistics, *Wages and Hours of Labor*, Bulletins 446, 492, 539 (Washington, D.C.: Government Printing Office, 1927, 1929, 1931).

20. Files of U.S. Housing Corporation, National Archives.

21. U.S. Senate, *Report on Conditions of Women and Child Wage-Earners in the United States*, vol. 1 (Washington, D.C.: Government Printing Office, 1910), 284–85. Similar Testimony may be found in Smith, *Mill on the Dan*, 20, 34, 48, 219–20.

22. A more detailed and rigorous theoretical analysis is presented in Martha Shiells and Gavin Wright, "Night Work as a Labor Market Phenomenon: Southern Textiles in the Interwar Period," *Exploration in Economic History* 20 (1983): 331–50.

23. T. M. Young, *The American Cotton Industry* (London: Methuen, 1902), 72.

24. Blicksilver, *Cotton Manufacturing in the Southeast*, 69–70.

25. U.S. Department of Labor, Women's Bureau, *The Employment of Women at Night*, Bulletin 64 (Washington, D.C.: Government Printing Office, 1928), 7.

26. The most thorough account of the CTI efforts is Louis Galambos, *Competition*

Notes

and *Cooperation* (Baltimore: The Johns Hopkins University Press, 1966), 116–18, 141–69.

27. Bureau of Labor Statistics, *Wages in Cotton Goods Manufacturing*, Bulletin no. 663 (Washington, D.C.: Government Printing Office, 1938), 27.

28. Murray F. Foss, "Long-Run Changes in the Work Week of Fixed Capital," *American Economic Review* 71 (1981): 59.

29. Michael M. Weinstein, *Recovery and Redistribution Under the NIRA* (Amsterdam: North-Holland, 1980), 1–15.

30. Ronald L. Heinemann, "Blue Eagle or Black Buzzard? The NRA in Virginia," *Virginia Magazine of History and Biography* 89 (1981): 99.

31. Donald S. Howard, *The WPA and Federal Relief Policy* (1943; reprint, New York: Da Capo Press, 1973), 167.

32. Frank T. de Vyver, "Southern Textile Mills Revisited," *Southern Economic Journal* 4 (1938): 466–73.

33. For example, the successful organization of rubber and steel workers in Gadsden, Alabama. See Charles H. Martin, "Southern Labor Relations in Transition: Gadsden, Alabama, 1930–43," *Journal of Southern History* 47 (1981): 545–68.

34. John F. Maloney, "Some Effects of the FLSA on Southern Industry," *Southern Economic Journal* 9 (1942): 17; National Industrial Conference Board, *Quarterly Review* 7 (1939): 2; H. M. Douty, "Minimum Wage Regulation in the Seamless Hosiery Industry," *Southern Economic Journal* 8 (1941): 176–90, and "Hours and Earnings of Employees of Independent Leaf-Tobacco Dealers," *Monthly Labor Review* (1941): 220–21.

35. James E. Fickle, *The New South and the "New Competition": Trade Association Development in the Southern Pine Industry* (Urbana, Ill.: University of Illinois Press, 1980), 301.

36. Quoted in Tindall, *Emergence of the New South*, 533.

37. Quoted in Howard, *The WPA and Federal Relief Policy*, 166.

38. United States Department of Labor, Bulletin 22, "Proceedings of the Southern Regional Conference on Labor Legislation" (February 1938), p. 33.

39. Elizabeth Davidson, *Child Labor Legislation in the Southern Textile States* (Chapel Hill: University of North Carolina Press, 1939), 25–28, 41–44.

40. Arden J. Lea, "Cotton Textiles and the Federal Child Labor Act of 1916," *Labor History* 16 (1975): 485–94.

41. Charles F. Roos, *NRA Economic Planning* (Bloomington, Ind.: The Principia Press, 1937), 164.

42. Quoted in Roos, *NRA Economic Planning*, 162.

43. Quoted in Fickle, *The New South and the "New Competition,"* 299–300.

44. *New York Herald Tribune*, 21 May 1938, quoted by Stanley Vittoz, "Cotton Textiles and the Fair Labor Standards Act of 1938," paper presented at Conference on "New Deal Economic Policy," Duquesne University, 21 October 1982.

45. National Industrial Conference Board, *Quarterly Review of the Textile Industry* 6 (1939): "Many [southern] mill men who are in the high-wage group, and whose plants are efficient, desire protection against wage-chiseling minorities" (p. 8). Note the internal contradiction: if the higher wages generated higher efficiency, they would have nothing to fear from low-wage chiselers.

46. Tindall, *Emergence of the New South*, 534.

47. Ibid., 373.

48. Raymond Wolters, *Negroes and the Great Depression* (Westport, Conn.: Greenwood Press, 1970), esp. 98–113.

49. Roos, *NRA Economic Planning*, 173.

50. These quotations are taken from an unpublished survey conducted for the NRA by Charles S. Johnson, "The Tobacco Worker: A Study of Tobacco Workers and their Families" (manuscript in National Archives), pp. 278–81, 352. Further complaints

of black displacement are cited in Michael S. Holmes, "The Blue Eagle as 'Jim Crow Bird': The NRA and Georgia's Black Workers," *Journal of Negro History* 57 (1972): 276–79.

51. Unpublished study cited by Gilbert Fite, *Cotton Fields No More: Southern Agriculture 1865–1980* (Lexington: University Press of Kentucky, 1984), 170. Holmes, "The Blue Eagle," minimizes the problem of displacement, but from a short-term perspective and without quantitative evidence.

52. "Proceedings of the Southern Regional Conference" (1938), p. 35.

53. D. Gale Johnson, "Functioning of the Labor Market," *Journal of Farm Economics* 33 (1951): 86.

54. Quoted in Robert E. Snyder, *Cotton Crisis* (Chapel Hill: University of North Carolina Press, 1984), 132. Snyder's book covers the rise and fall of the "Cotton Holiday" movement in detail.

55. A good brief account of the early AAA may be found in Fite, *Cotton Fields No More*, 120–134. See also David Conrad, *The Forgotten Farmers* (Urbana, Ill.: University of Illinois Press, 1965), 37–63.

56. The strongest indictment of the "purge" is in Donald H. Grubbs, *Cry from the Cotton* (Chapel Hill: University of North Carolina Press, 1971), 30–61. The most recent reassessment is Lawrence J. Nelson, "The Art of the Possible: Another Look at the 'Purge' of the AAA Liberals in 1935," *Agricultural History* 57 (1983): 416–35, from which the quotations are taken.

57. This section draws on Warren Whatley, "Labor for the Picking: The New Deal in the South," *Journal of Economic History* 43 (December 1983): 913–26.

58. Arthur F. Raper, *Preface to Peasantry* (Chapel Hill: University of North Carolina Press, 1936), 34.

59. T. J. Woofter, *Landlord and Tenant on the Cotton Plantation*, WPA Division of Social Research, Research Monograph 5 (1936), p. 156.

60. Ibid., 157. A follow-up survey in 1937–38 continued to show relatively moderate changes in the proportions of families in wage labor, cropper, share tenant, and renter categories. See William C. Holley, Ellen Winston, and T. J. Woofter, Jr., *The Plantation South 1934–1937*, WPA Research Monograph 22 (1940), pp. 81–82. Note, however, that these tables refer to "resident families on plantations," and hence neglect nonresident wage laborers.

61. See Grubbs, *Cry From the Cotton*; Paul Mertz, *New Deal Policy and Southern Rural Poverty* (Baton Rouge: Louisiana State University Press, 1978); Sidney Baldwin, *Poverty and Politics: The Rise and Decline of the Farm Security Administration* (Chapel Hill: University of North Carolina Press, 1968).

62. Charles S. Johnson, Edwin R. Embree, and W. W. Alexander, *The Collapse of Cotton Tenancy* (Chapel Hill: University of North Carolina Press, 1935), 51.

63. David Wayne Ganger, "The Impact of Mechanization and the New Deal's Acreage Reduction Programs on Cotton Farmers During the 1930s" (Ph.D. diss., University of California, Los Angeles, 1973), chap. 8.

64. Jack Temple Kirby, "The Transformation of Southern Plantations, 1920–1960," *Agricultural History* 57 (1983): 269.

65. Whatley, "Labor for the Picking," 908.

66. Lawrence J. Nelson, "Welfare Capitalism on a Mississippi Plantation in the Great Depression," *Journal of Southern History* 50 (1984): 244.

67. Warren Whatley, "A History of Mechanization in the Cotton South," *Quarterly Journal of Economics* 100 (1985): 1191–1215. The classic article is Paul David, "The Mechanization of Reaping in the Antebellum Midwest," in David, *Technical Choice, Innovation and Economic Growth* (New York: Cambridge University Press, 1975). David's article has been criticized, most strongly by Alan Olmstead, "The Mechanization of Reaping and Moving in American Agriculture, 1833–70," *Journal of Economic History* 35 (1975): 327–52. But the underlying model has been shown to have great

Notes

scope in American history, especially in the twentieth century. See Nicholas Sargen, *Tractorization in the United States and its Relevance for Developing Countries* (New York: Garland, 1979); and Moses Musoke and Alan Olmstead, "The Rise of the Cotton Industry in California: A Comparative Perspective," *Journal of Economic History* 42 (1982): 389–97.

68. Nelson, "The Art of the Possible," 431.

69. Figures on 1937 harvest labor are in Holley, Winston, and Woofter, *The Plantation South*, 84. The cropper-wage system and other transitional tenure forms are described in James H. Street, *New Revolution in the Cotton Economy* (Chapel Hill: University of North Carolina Press, 1957), 218–22.

70. A good recent monograph is Anthony Badger, *Prosperity Road: The New Deal, Tobacco, and North Carolina* (Chapel Hill: University of North Carolina Press, 1980).

71. T. J. Woofter and A. E. Fisher, *The Plantation South Today* (WPA Social Problems Series no. 5 [1940]), p. 3; Donald Crichton Alexander, *The Arkansas Plantation 1920–1942* (New Haven: Yale University Press, 1943).

72. Roger L. Burford, "The Federal Cotton Programs and Farm Labor Force Adjustment," *Southern Economic Journal* 33 (1966): 223–36; Fligstein, *Going North*, chap. 8.

73. H. M. Douty, "Minimum Wage Regulation in the Seamless Hosiery Industry," 176–90; John F. Maloney, "Some Effects of the FLSA on Southern Industry," *Southern Economic Journal* 9 (1942): 15–23; Vernon Ruttan, "Industrial Progress and Rural Stagnation in the New South," *Social Forces* 34 (1955): 114–18; Calvin B. Hoover and B. U. Ratchford, *Economic Resources and Policies of the South* (New York: Macmillan, 1951), 392.

74. Mercer G. Evans, "Southern Wage Differentials under the NRA," *Southern Economic Journal* 1 (1933): 8.

75. Numan V. Bartley, "In Search of the New South: Southern Politics After Reconstruction," in *The Promise of American History*, ed. Stanley T. Kutler and Stanley N. Katz (Baltimore: The Johns Hopkins University Press, 1982), 160.

Chapter 8

1. The standard regional per capita income figures presented in *Historical Statistics of the United States, Colonial Times to 1970* (p. 242) and widely reproduced, convey the misleading impression that convergence to the national average dates from 1930. The data come from a study by Richard Easterlin that was primarily concerned with estimating regional incomes in the nineteenth century. For the sake of smoothing, "cyclical" effects, Easterlin recorded figures for 1940 that were actually averages for the years 1937–44. The original study by Schwartz and Graham presented annual estimates, which plainly show that the acceleration of growth occurred only after 1940, especially in the South Central regions. See Richard Easterlin, "Interregional Differences in per Capita Income, Population, and Total Income, 1840–1950," in *Trends in the American Economy in the Nineteenth Century* (Princeton, N.J.: Princeton University Press, 1960), 74; Charles F. Schwartz and Robert E. Graham, Jr., "Personal Income by States since 1929," *Survey of Current Business*, (September 1955).

2. Competing theories are surveyed in Bernard R. Weinstein and Robert E. Firestine, *Regional Growth and Decline in the United States* (New York: Praeger, 1978), 48–67, and in Robert J. Newman, *Growth in the American South* (New York: New York University Press, 1984), chap. 4. Federal spending is emphasized in Charles P. Roland, *The Improbable Era* (Lexington: University Press of Kentucky, 1975); Robert Haveman, "The Postwar Corps of Engineers Program," in *Essays in Southern Economic Development*, ed. Melvin Greenhut and W. T. Whiteman (Chapel Hill: University of North Carolina Press, 1964); and in an article entitled "Federal Spending: The Northeast's

Loss is the Sunbelt's Gain," *National Journal*, June 1976, p. 878–91. Equilibrating factor flows are analyzed by Marshall Colberg, *Human Capital in Southern Development 1939–1963* (Chapel Hill: University of North Carolina Press, 1965), and in more sophisticated fashion by Peter Mieszkowski, "Recent Trends in Urban and Regional Development," in *Current Issues in Urban Economics*, ed. Peter Mieszkowski and Mahlon Straszheim (Baltimore: The Johns Hopkins University Press, 1979). The "clean slate" argument is most forcefully presented by Mancur Olson, in *The Rise and Decline of Nations* (New Haven: Yale University Press, 1982), and with specific reference to the South, in "The South Will Fall Again," *Southern Economic Journal* 49 (1983): 917–32. The increased role of amenities is emphasized by Edward L. Ullman, "Amenities as a Factor in Regional Growth," *Geographical Review* 44 (1954): 119–32. Richard J. Cebula and Richard K. Vedder, "A Note on Migration, Economic Opportunity, and the Quality of Life," *Journal of Regional Science* 13 (1973): 205–11.

3. Gilbert Fite, "Recent Progress in the Mechanization of Cotton Production," *Agricultural History* 24 (1950): 28. The best accounts of the development of mechanical cotton harvesting are Gilbert Fite, *Cotton Fields No More: Southern Agriculture 1865–1980* (Lexington: University Press of Kentucky, 1984), chap. 9, and James H. Street, *The New Revolution in the Cotton Economy* (Chapel Hill: University of North Carolina Press, 1957), chap. 6. A brief summary may be found in Jay Mandle, *The Roots of Black Poverty* (Durham, N.C.: Duke University Press, 1978), chap. 7.

4. Ralph C. Hon, "The Rust Cotton Picker," *Southern Economic Journal* 3 (1937): 384.

5. Heywood Fleisig, "Mechanizing the Cotton Harvest in the Nineteenth Century South," *Journal of Economic History* 25 (1965): 704–6.

6. Street, *New Revolution*, 125–26.

7. Richard Day, "The Economics of Technological Change and the Demise of the Sharecropper," *American Economic Review* 57 (1967): 427–49.

8. Jack Temple Kirby, "The Transformation of Southern Plantations," *Agricultural History* 57 (1983): 270.

9. Both quotations are in Gilbert Fite, "Mechanization of Cotton Production Since World War II," *Agricultural History* 54 (1980): 198–99.

10. Stanley Lieberson, *A Piece of the Pie* (Berkeley: University of California Press, 1980), 142–43.

11. Fite, *Cotton Fields No More*, 190. The term *neoplantation* was coined by Merle Prunty, "The Renaissance of the Southern Plantation," *The Geographical Review* 45 (1955): 482–89. On the decline in hired farm labor, see U.S. Department of Labor, *Cotton Harvest Mechanization: Effect on Seasonal Hired Labor*, BES no. 209 (1962), and Kirby, "The Transformation of Southern Plantations," figure 2.

12. Statements of three Tunica residents quoted by Fred Grimm, article in *San Jose Mercury News*, 18 July 1984.

13. *Southern Tradition and Regional Progress* (Chapel Hill: University of North Carolina Press, 1960), 61. By the 1960s, however, many observers did call attention to the "Southern Roots of Urban Crisis." See the article with that title by Robert Beardwood in *Fortune* 78 (1968): 80–87, 151–56, and also John F. Kain and Joseph J. Persky, "The North's State in Southern Rural Poverty," in *Essays in Regional Economics*, ed. John F. Kain and John R. Meyer (Cambridge, Mass.: Harvard University Press, 1971).

14. Day, "Technological Change," 428.

15. Recent developments in tobacco are recounted in William R. Finger, ed., *The Tobacco Industry in Transition* (Lexington, Mass.: Lexington Books, 1981), and Paul R. Johnson, *The Economics of the Tobacco Industry* (New York: Praeger, 1984). A useful comparative survey of mechanization in southern crops is Pete Daniel, "The

Notes

Crossroads of Change: Cotton, Tobacco and Rice Cultures in the Twentieth Century South," *Journal of Southern History* 50 (1984): 429–56.

16. The many advantages of growing cotton in California rather than in the Southeast are discussed in Moses S. Musoke and Alan L. Olmstead, "The Rise of the Cotton Industry in California: A Comparative Perspective," *Journal of Economic History* 42 (1982): 385–412.

17. P. R. Coelho and M. A. Ghali, "The End of the North-South Wage Differential," *American Economic Review* (1971): 932–37; Don Bellante, "The North-South Differential and the Migration of Heterogeneous Labor," *American Economic Review* (1979): 166–72. See, however, the criticisms of these studies in Robert S. Goldfarb and Anthony M. J. Yezer, "Evaluating Alternative Theories of Intensity and Interregional Wage Differentials," *Journal of Regional Science* 16 (1976): 345–63, and Robert J. Newman, *Growth in the American South* (New York: New York University Press, 1984), 116–17.

18. George Borts, "Equalization of Returns and Regional Economic Growth," *American Economic Review* 50 (1960): 319–47; George Borts and Jerome Stein, *Economic Growth in a Free Market* (New York: Columbia University Press, 1964), chap. 3.

19. Long-run convergence is asserted in a report of the United States Advisory Commission on Intergovernmental Relations, *Regional Growth: Historic Perspective* (Washington, D.C.: Government Printing Office, 1980). The absence of any long-term trend to convergence is argued in H. M. Douty, "Regional Wage Differentials: Forces and Counterforces," *Monthly Labor Review*, March 1968, pp. 74–81, and reiterated as recently as 1980 in H. M. Douty, *The Wage Bargain and the Labor Market* (Baltimore: The Johns Hopkins University Press, 1980), 119–20.

20. The most detailed study of the 1950s is David Evan Kaun, "Economics of the Minimum Wage: The Effects of the FLSA, 1945–1960" (Ph.D. diss., Stanford University, 1963).

21. John Cogan, "The Decline in Black Teenage Employment: 1950–70," *American Economic Review* 72 (1982): 629–30.

22. This is the list of industries showing significant wage and employment effects in a study by John M. Peterson, *Minimum Wages: Measures and Industry Effects* (Washington: American Enterprise Institute, 1951), 54–63.

23. James E. Estes, *The Minimum Wage and Its Impact on South Carolina* (Columbia, S.C.: University of South Carolina, 1968), 31–33.

24. Lloyd G. Reynolds and Cynthia H. Taft, *The Evolution of Wage Structure* (New Haven: Yale University Press, 1956), 50–54.

25. Martin Segal, "Regional Wage Differences in Manufacturing in the Post-war Period," *Review of Economics and Statistics* 43 (1961): 148–55.

26. On textiles, see Reynolds and Taft, *Evolution of Wage Structure*, chap. 4. The War Labor Board decisions may be found in *War Labor Reports: Wage and Salary Stabilization, 1942–1945*, vol. 2 (1943), pp. 345–99; vol. 21 (1945), pp. 793–820, 876–87. A general study that stresses downward pressure on southern wages during the 1950s is Victor Fuchs and Richard Perlman, "Recent Trends in Southern Wage Differentials," *Review of Economics and Statistics* 42 (1960): 292–300.

27. Several studies reaching this conclusion are surveyed in Weinstein and Firestine, *Regional Growth and Decline*, 69–70. See also John B. Lansing and Eva Mueller, *The Geographic Mobility of Labor* (Ann Arbor: Institute for Social Research, 1967), 43.

28. C. Horace Hamilton, "Educational Selectivity of Net Migration from the South," *Social Forces* 38 (1959): 33–42.

29. Elizabeth M. Suval and C. Horace Hamilton, "Some New Evidence on Educational Selectivity in Migration to and from the South," *Social Forces* 43 (1965): 540.

30. Joseph J. Persky and John F. Kain, "Migration, Employment and Race in the Deep South," *Southern Economic Journal* 36 (1970): 268–76.

31. Herbert Northrup, "The Negro in the Rubber Tire Industry," in *Negro Em-*

ployment in Southern Industry, ed. Herbert Northrup and Richard Rowan (Philadelphia: University of Pennsylvania Press, 1971).

32. David Potenziani, "Striking Back: Richard B. Russell and Racial Relocation," *Georgia Historical Quarterly* 45 (1981): 263–77.

33. The characterizations are by no means limited to blacks. The problems of "briars," "hillbillies," and "Okies" have been understudied, but some material is contained in a useful survey by Jack Temple Kirby, "The Southern Exodus, 1910–1960: A Primer for Historians," *Journal of Southern History* 49 (1983): 585–600.

34. Paul Barnett, *An Analysis of State Industrial Development Programs in the Thirteen Southern States* (Knoxville, Tenn.: University of Tennessee Press, 1944), 5–11.

35. James C. Cobb, *The Selling of the South: The Southern Crusade for Industrial Development 1936–1980* (Baton Rouge: Louisiana State University Press, 1982).

36. V. O. Key, *Southern Politics* (New York: Knopf, 1950), 5–11, 115–21.

37. Key, *Southern Politics*, 345–68.

38. Newman, *Growth in the American South*, 41.

39. Nicholls, *Southern Tradition and Regional Progress*, 98.

40. In 1974 I published an interpretation of New Deal spending in terms of a national political strategy: the South was a low-priority region for the Democrats because it always voted Democratic in national elections, while the West was uncertain. Gavin Wright, "The Political Economy of New Deal Spending," *Review of Economics and Statistics* 56 (1974): 30–38. This analysis explains much of the national pattern, but I now see that I was missing an important component: much of the southern political leadership didn't want the money.

41. Barnett, *State Industrial Development Programs*, 11–13; Tindall, *Emergence of the New South*, chap. 20.

42. R. E. Bolton, *Defense Purchases and Regional Growth* (Washington, D.C.: Brookings Institution, 1966) found that among the southern states, only Mississippi was in the "growth greatly stimulated" category over 1952–62, while Alabama, Florida, Georgia, North Carolina, Texas, and Virginia were identified as "moderately stimulated" (p. 100).

43. An influential early book was Glenn E. McLaughlin and Stefan Robock, *Why Industry Moves South* (Washington, D.C.: National Planning Association, 1949). Studies from the 1950s are summarized in John T. Due, "Studies of State-Local Tax Influences on Location of Industry," *National Tax Journal* 14 (1961): 163–73.

44. Quoted in Cobb, *Selling of the South*, 58.

45. Newman, *Growth in the American South*, esp. chap. 5; Newman, "Industry Migration and Growth in the South," *Review of Economics and Statistics* 65 (1983): 76–86.

46. See Victor Fuchs, *Changes in the Location of Manufacturing in the United States Since 1929* (New Haven: Yale University Press, 1962), which analyzes changes between 1929 and 1954.

47. Quoted in Cobb, *Selling of the South*, 256.

48. Robert S. Goldfarb and Anthony M. J. Yezer, "Evaluating Alternative Theories of Intercity and Interregional Wage Differentials," 343–63; Charles Hirschman and Kim Blenkenship, "The North-South Earnings Gap: Changes during the 1960s and 1970s," *American Journal of Sociology* 87 (1982): 395; Robert S. Goldfarb and Anthony M. J. Yezer, "Have Regional Wage Differentials Really Disappeared?" *Growth and Change* 14 (1983): 48–51.

49. A wide range of evidence for the 1960s is presented in Newman, *Growth in the American South*, chap. 8.

50. Quoted in Calvin Hoover and B. U. Ratchford, *Economic Resources and Policies of the South* (New York: Macmillan, 1951), 413.

51. Other sources for this paragraph include R. L. Simpson and D. R. Norsworthy,

Notes

"The Changing Occupational Structure," in *The South in Continuity and Change*, ed. John C. McKinney and Edgar T. Thompson (Durham, N.C.: Duke University Press, 1965); Thomas J. Storrs, "The Southern Economy," and Richard A. Beaumont, "Working in the South," in *Southern Business: The Decades Ahead*, ed. David Shannon (Indianapolis: Bobbs-Merrill, 1981); James C. Cobb, *Industrialization and Southern Society 1877–1984* (Lexington: University Press of Kentucky, 1984).

52. Quoted in Cobb, *Selling of the South*, 125–26.

53. A catalogue of examples and incidents from the early 1960s was compiled in a booklet entitled *The Price We Pay*, prepared by Barbara Patternson and other staff members of the Southern Regional Council and the anti-Defamation League, and issued in June 1964. The Jackson case is from Charles Sallis and John Quincy Adams, "Desegregation in Jackson, Mississippi," in *Southern Businessmen and Desegregation*, ed. Elizabeth Jacoway and David R. Colburn (Baton Rouge: Louisiana State University Press, 1982).

54. Elizabeth Jacoway, "Introduction," in Jacoway and Colburn, *Southern Businessmen and Desegregation*, 1.

55. Jacoway, "Introduction," p. 5, and Carl Abbott, "The Norfolk Business Community," p. 101, in Jacoway and Colburn, *Southern Businessmen and Desegregation*; W. H. Nicholls, *Southern Tradition and Regional Progress*.

56. Stanley B. Greenberg, *Race and State in Capitalist Development* (New Haven: Yale University Press, 1980), 231–33.

57. J. Heckman and G. Sedlacek, "The Impact of the Minimum Wage on the Employment and Earnings of Workers in South Carolina," in *Report of the Minimum Wage Commission*, vol. 5 (Washington, D.C.: Government Printing Office, 1981). The authors find a dramatic rise in the black-participation rate in the minimum-wage-covered sector, though their model predicts a decline.

58. Greenberg, *Race and State*, 125. An extensive survey documenting the primacy of the absence of turmoil is described in James C. Cobb, "Yesterday's Liberalism," in Jacoway and Colburn, *Businessmen and Desegregation*, 161.

59. Jack Temple Kirby, "Black and White in the Rural South, 1919–1954," *Agricultural History* 58 (1984): 442.

60. "Selma, 20 Years After the Rights March," *New York Times*, 1 March 1985, A12.

61. Raymound Arsenault, "The End of the Long Hot Summer: The Air Conditioner and Southern Culture," *Journal of Southern History* 50 (1984): 598.

62. Marshall Frady, *Southerners* (New York: New American Library, 1980), 281.

63. Nell Irvin Painter, *The Narrative of Hosea Hudson* (Cambridge, Mass.: Harvard University Press, 1979), 16–17.

64. Among many possible references, see Robert M. Hauser and David L. Featherman, "White-Nonwhite Differentials in Occupational Mobility Among Men in the U.S., 1962–1972," *Demography* 11 (1974): 247–65; Wayne J. Villemez and Candace Hinson Wisivell, "The Impact of Diminishing Discrimination on the Internal Size Distribution of Black Income, 1954–1974," *Social Forces* 56 (1978): 1019–34; Alfonso Pinkney, *The Myth of Black Progress* (New York: Cambridge University Press, 1984); Reynolds Farley, *Blacks and Whites: Narrowing the Gap?* (Cambridge, Mass.: Harvard University Press, 1984).

65. Numan V. Bartley, *The Creation of Modern Georgia* (Athens: University of Georgia Press, 1983), 203 (where the other quotes may also be found).

66. Jane Jacobs, "Why TVA Failed," *New York Review of Books*, 10 May 1984, pp. 41–47, and Jacobs, *Cities and the Wealth of Nations* (New York: Random House, 1984), chaps. 7–10.

67. See Robert E. Lipsey and Irving B. Kravis, "The Competitive Position of U.S. Manufacturing Firms," National Bureau of Economic Research Working Paper no. 1557 (February 1985).

SUGGESTED READINGS

The following is a brief, highly selective list of suggested readings for those who wish to pursue the subject of southern economic history further. The emphasis is on economics and on recent works; only the most durable and influential of the older books are included. It is certainly not my view that the old folks were foolish while the young ones are wise; but recent contributions are more difficult to find listed in one place, and among the older works most readers will be better served by guidance on priority than by a comprehensive listing. The list is organized by chapter; each item is listed only once.

Chapter 1

Degler, Carl. *Place Over Time: The Continuity of Southern Distributions.* Baton Rouge: Louisiana State University Press, 1977.

Nicholls, William H. *Southern Tradition and Regional Progress.* Chapel Hill: University of North Carolina Press, 1960.

Parker, William N. "The South in the National Economy, 1865–1970." *Southern Economic Journal* 46 (1980): 1019–48.

Woodward, C. Vann. *Origins of the New South, 1877–1913.* Baton Rouge: Louisiana State University Press, 1951. Reissued in 1971, with a critical essay on recent works by Charles B. Dew.

Chapter 2

Anderson, Ralph V., and Robert E. Gallman. "Slaves as Fixed Capital." *Journal of American History* 64 (1977): 24–46.

Bateman, Fred, and Thomas Weiss. *A Deplorable Scarcity: The Failure of Industrialization in the Slave Economy.* Chapel Hill: University of North Carolina Press, 1981.

David, Paul A., Herbert G. Gutman, Richard Sutch, Peter Tewin, and Gavin Wright. *Reckoning With Slavery.* New York: Oxford University Press, 1976.

Fleisig, Heywood. "Slavery, the Supply of Agricultural Labor, and the Industrialization of the South." *Journal of Economic History* 36 (1976): 572–95.

Suggested Readings

Fogel, Robert William, and Stanley L. Engerman. *Time on the Cross: The Economics of American Negro Slavery*. Boston: Little, Brown, 1974.

Foner, Eric. *Nothing But Freedom: Emancipation and Its Legacy*. Baton Rouge: Louisiana State University Press, 1983.

Gallman, Robert E. "Slavery and Southern Economic Growth." *Southern Economic Journal* 45 (1979): 1007–22.

Genovese, Eugene D. *The Political Economy of Slavery: Studies in the Economy and Society of the Slave South*. 1965. Reprint. New York: Vintage Books, 1967.

Gray, Lewis C. *History of Agriculture in the Southern United States to 1860*. 1933. Reprint. Clifton, N.J.: A. M. Kelley, 1973.

Harris, J. William. "Plantations and Power: Emancipation on the David Barrow Plantations." In *Toward a New South*, ed. O. V. Burton and R. C. McMath. Westport, Conn.: Greenwood Press, 1982.

Jaynes, Gerald David. *Branches Without Roots: Genesis of the Black Working Class, 1862–1882*. New York: Oxford University Press, 1985.

McDonald, Forrest, and Grady McWhiney. "The South from Self-Sufficiency to Peonage: An Interpretation." *American Historical Review* 85 (1980): 1095–118.

Ransom, Roger, and Richard Sutch. *One Kind of Freedom: The Economic Consequences of Emancipation*. New York: Cambridge University Press, 1977.

Temin, Peter. "The Postbellum Recovery of the South and the Cost of the Civil War." *Journal of Economic History* 36 (1976): 898–907, and subsequent exchange with Claudia Goldin and Frank Lewis, *Journal of Economic History* 38 (1978): 487–493.

Wayne, Michael. *The Reshaping of Plantation Society: The Natchez District, 1860–1880*. Baton Rouge: Louisiana State University Press, 1983.

Weiman, David. "The Economic Emancipation of the Non-Slaveholding Class." *Journal of Economic History* 45 (1985): 78–90.

Wiener, Jonathan M. *Social Origins of the New South*. Baton Rouge: Louisiana State University Press, 1978.

Woodman, Harold D. *King Cotton and His Retainers: Financing and Marketing the Cotton Crop of the South, 1800–1925*. Lexington: University of Kentucky Press, 1968.

———. "How New Was the New South?" *Agricultural History* 58 (1984): 529–45.

Wright, Gavin. *The Political Economy of the Cotton South*. New York: Norton, 1978.

Chapter 3

Cowdrey, Albert E. *This Land, This South: An Environmental History*. Lexington, Ky.: University Press of Kentucky, 1983.

Easterlin, Richard. "Regional Income Trends, 1840–1950." In *The Reinterpretation of American Economic History*, edited by Robert Fogel and Stanley Engerman. New York: Harper & Row, 1972.

Mandle, Jay. *The Roots of Black Poverty*. Durham, N.C.: Duke University Press, 1978.

Rothstein, Morton. "The New South and the International Economy." *Agricultural History* 57 (1983): 38–49.

Rubin, Julius. "The Limits of Agricultural Progress in the Nineteenth Century South." *Agricultural History* 49 (1975): 385–402.

Schultz, Theodore W. "Reflections on Poverty within Agriculture." *Journal of Political Economy* 58 (1950): 362–73.

Chapter 4

Alston, Lee J., and Robert Higgs. "Contractual Mix in Southern Agriculture Since the Civil War." *Journal of Economic History* 42 (1982): 327–53.

Brooks, R. P. "The Agrarian Revolution in Georgia 1865–1912." *Bulletin of the University of Wisconsin*, no. 639, 1914.

Suggested Readings

Davis, Ronald L. F. *Good and Faithful Labor from Slavery to Sharecropping in the Natchez District, 1860–1890*. Westport, Conn.: Greenwood Press, 1982.

Durrill, Wayne K. "Producing Poverty: Local Government and Economic Development in a New South County, 1874–1884." *Journal of American History* 71 (1985): 764–81.

Fite, Gilbert. *Cotton Fields No More: Southern Agriculture 1865–1980*. Lexington, Ky.: University Press of Kentucky, 1984.

Flynn, Charles. *White Land, Black Labor: Caste and Class in Late Nineteenth Century Georgia*. Baton Rouge: Louisiana State University Press, 1983.

Ford, Lacy K. "Rednecks and Merchants: Economic Development and Social Tensions in the South Carolina Upcountry, 1850–1900." *Journal of American History* 71 (1984): 294–318.

Hahn, Steven. *The Roots of Southern Populism: Yeoman Farmers and the Transformation of the Georgia Upcountry, 1850–1890*. New York: Oxford University Press, 1983.

Kousser, J. Morgan. *The Shaping of Southern Politics: Suffrage Restriction and the Establishment of the One-Party South, 1880–1910*. New Haven: Yale University Press, 1974.

McMath, Robert C. *Populist Vanguard: A History of the Southern Farmers' Alliance*. Chapel Hill: University of North Carolina Press, 1975.

Margo, Robert A. "Race Differences in Public School Expenditures: Disfranchisement and School Finance in Louisiana, 1890–1910." *Social Science History* 6 (1982): 1034–43.

Palmer, Bruce. *"Man Over Money": The Southern Populist Critique of American Capitalism*. Chapel Hill: University of North Carolina Press, 1980.

Reid, Joseph D., Jr. "Sharecropping and Tenancy in American History." In *Risk, Uncertainty and Agricultural Development*, edited by J. A. Roumasset, J. Boussard, and I. Singh. New York: Agricultural Development Council, 1979.

Schmitz, Mark. "The Transformation of the Southern Sugar Cane Sector." *Agricultural History* 53 (1979): 270–85.

Shlomowitz, Ralph. " 'Bound' or Free? Freedman Labor in Cotton and Sugar Cane Farming, 1865–1880." *Journal of Southern History* 50 (1984): 569–96.

———. "The Origins of Southern Sharecropping." *Agricultural History* 53 (1979): 557–75.

Thornton, J. Mills. "Fiscal Policy and the Failure of Radical Reconstruction in the Lower South." In *Region, Race and Reconstruction*, edited by James M. McPherson and J. Morgan Kousser. New York: Oxford University Press, 1982.

Woodman, Harold D. "Sequel to Slavery: The New History Views the Postbellum South." *Journal of Southern History* 43 (1977): 523–54.

———. "Southern Agriculture and the Law." *Agricultural History* 53 (1979): 319–37.

Woodward, C. Vann. *Tom Watson: Agrarian Rebel*. 1938. Reprint. New York: Oxford University Press, 1963.

Chapter 5

Blicksilver, Jack. *Cotton Manufacturing in the Southeast: An Historical Analysis*. Atlanta: Georgia State College of Business Administration, 1959.

Carlson, Leonard. "Labor Supply, the Acquisition of Skills, and the Location of Southern Textile Mills, 1880–1900." *Journal of Economic History* 41 (1981): 65–71.

Carlton, David L. *Mill and Town in South Carolina, 1880–1920*. Baton Rouge: Louisiana State University Press, 1982.

Suggested Readings

McHugh, Cathy Louise. "The Family Labor System in the Southern Cotton Textile Industry, 1880–1915." Ph.D. diss., Stanford University, 1981.

Mitchell, Broadus. *The Rise of the Cotton Mills in the South.* Baltimore: The Johns Hopkins University Press, 1921.

Newman, Dale. "Work and Community Life in a Southern Town." *Labor History* 19 (1978): 204–25.

Saxonhouse, Gary, and Gavin Wright. "Two Forms of Cheap Labor in Textile History." In *Technique, Spirit and Form in the Making of the Modern Economies. Essays in Honor of William N. Parker,* edited by Gary Saxonhouse and Gavin Wright. Greenwich, Conn.: JAI Press, 1984.

Smith, Robert Sidney. *Mill on the Dan: A History of Dan River Mills 1882–1950.* Durham, N.C.: Duke University Press, 1960.

Terrill, Tom. "Murder in Graniteville," in *Toward a New South? Studies in Post-Civil War Southern Communities,* edited by Orville V. Burton and Robert C. McMath, Jr. Westport: Greenwood Press, 1982.

Wright, Gavin. "Cheap Labor and Southern Textiles Before 1880." *Journal of Economic History* 39 (1979): 655–80.

———. "Cheap Labor and Southern Textiles, 1880–1930." *Quarterly Journal of Economics* 96 (1981): 605–29.

Chapter 6

Cobb, James C. *Industrialization and Southern Society, 1877–1984.* Lexington: The University Press of Kentucky, 1984.

Daniel, Pete. *The Shadow of Slavery: Peonage in the South 1901–1960.* Lexington: The University Press of Kentucky, 1978.

DeCanio, Stephen J. "Accumulation and Discrimination in the Postbellum South." *Explorations in Economic History* 16 (1979): 182–206.

Durden, Robert F. *The Dukes of Durham, 1865–1929.* Durham, N.C.: Duke University Press, 1975.

Greenberg, Stanley. *Race and State in Capitalist Development.* New Haven: Yale University Press, 1980.

Hackney, Sheldon. "Origins of the New South in Retrospect." *Journal of Southern History* 38 (1972): 191–216.

Higgs, Robert. "Accumulation of Property by Southern Blacks Before World War I." *American Economic Review* 72 (1982): 725–37.

———. *Competition and Coercion: Blacks in the American Economy, 1865–1914.* 1977. Reprint. Chicago: University of Chicago Press, 1980.

Janiewski, Dolores Elizabeth. "From Field to Factory: Race, Class, Sex and the Woman Worker in Durham, 1880–1940." Ph.D. diss., Duke University, 1979.

Kulick, Gary. "Black Workers and Technological Change in the Birmingham Iron Industry, 1881–1931." In *Southern Workers and Their Unions,* edited by Merl E. Reed, Leslie S. Hough, and Gary M. Fink. Westport, Conn.: Greenwood Press, 1981.

Mancini, Matthew J. "Race, Economics and the Abandonment of Convict Leasing." *Journal of Negro History* 63 (1978): 339–52.

Margo, Robert A. "Accumulation of Property by Southern Blacks: Comment and Extensions." *American Economic Review* 74 (1984): 768–76.

Northrup, Herbert R., and Richard L. Rowan. *Negro Employment in Southern Industry.* Philadelphia: University of Pennsylvania Press, 1971.

Reich, Michael. *Racial Inequality: A Political Economic Analysis.* Princeton, N.J.: Princeton University Press, 1981.

Rikard, Marlene Hunt. "An Experiment in Welfare Capitalism: The Health Care Services of the Tennessee Coal, Iron and Railroad Company." Ph.D. diss., University of Alabama, 1983.

Smith, James P. "Race and Human Capital." *American Economic Review* 74 (1984): 685–98.

Spero, Sterling D., and Abram L. Harris. *The Black Worker.* 1931. Reprint. New York: Atheneum, 1969.

Stocking, George W. *Basing Point Pricing and Regional Development: A Case Study of the Iron and Steel Industry.* Chapel Hill: University of North Carolina Press, 1954.

Tilley, Nannie. *The Bright-Tobacco Industry.* Chapel Hill: University of North Carolina Press, 1948.

Worthman, Paul B. "Black Workers and Labor Unions in Birmingham, Alabama, 1897–1904." *Labor History* 10 (1969): 375–407.

———. "Working Class Mobility in Birmingham, Alabama, 1880–1914." In *Anonymous Americans,* edited by Tamara Hareven. Englewood Cliffs, N.J.: Prentice-Hall, 1971.

Chapter 7

Alston, Lee J., and Joseph T. Ferrie. "Labor Cost, Paternalism, and Loyalty in Southern Agriculture." *Journal of Economic History* 45 (1985): 95–117.

Badger, Anthony. *Prosperity Road: The New Deal, Tobacco, and North Carolina.* Chapel Hill: University of North Carolina Press, 1980.

Cobb, James C., and Michael V. Namorato, eds. *The New Deal and the South.* Jackson: University Press of Mississippi, 1984.

Higgs, Robert. "The Boll Weevil, the Cotton Economy, and Black Migration, 1910–1930." *Agricultural History* 50 (1976): 335–50.

Kirby, Jack Temple. "The Southern Exodus: A Primer for Historians." *Journal of Southern History* 49 (1983): 585–600.

———. "The Transformation of Southern Plantations, 1920–1960." *Agricultural History* 57 (1983): 257–76.

Mertz, Paul. *New Deal Policy and Southern Rural Poverty.* Baton Rouge: Louisiana State University Press, 1978.

Miller, Marc S. *Working Lives: The Southern Exposure History of Labor in the South.* New York: Pantheon, 1980.

Nelson, Lawrence J. "The Art of the Possible: Another Look at the Purge of the AAA Liberals in 1935." *Agricultural History* 57 (1983): 416–35.

———. "Welfare Capitalism on a Mississippi Plantation in the Great Depression." *Journal of Southern History* 50 (1984): 225–50.

Shiells, Martha, and Gavin Wright. "Nightwork as a Labor Market Phenomenon: Southern Textiles in the Interwar Years." *Explorations in Economic History* 20 (1983): 331–50.

Snyder, Robert E. *Cotton Crisis.* Chapel Hill: University of North Carolina Press, 1984.

Tindall, George. *The Emergence of the New South, 1913–1945.* Baton Rouge: Louisiana State University Press, 1967.

Whatley, Warren. "A History of Mechanization in the Cotton South: The Institutional Hypothesis," *Quarterly Journal of Economics* (in press).

———. "Labor for the Picking: The New Deal in the South." *Journal of Economic History* 43 (1983): 905–29.

Chapter 8

Bartley, Numan. *The Creation of Modern Georgia.* Athens: University of Georgia Press, 1983.

Suggested Readings

Cobb, James C. The Selling of the South: The Southern Crusade for Industrial Development 1936–1980. Baton Rouge: Louisiana State University Press, 1982.

Cogan, John. "The Decline in Black Teenage Employment: 1950–1970." American Economic Review 72 (1982): 621–38.

Daniel, Pete. "The Crossroads of Change: Cotton, Tobacco and Rice Cultures in the Twentieth-Century South." Journal of Southern History 50 (1984): 429–56.

Day, Richard. "The Economics of Technological Change and the Demise of the Sharecropper." American Economic Review 57 (1967): 427–49.

Jacoway, Elizabeth, and David R. Colburn, eds. Southern Businessmen and Desegregation. Baton Rouge, Louisiana State University Press, 1982.

Musoke, Moses S., and Alan L. Olmstead. "The Rise of the Cotton Industry in California: A Comparative Perspective." Journal of Economic History 42 (1982): 385–412.

Newman, Robert J. Growth in the American South: Changing Regional Employment and Wage Patterns in the 1960s and 1970s. New York: New York University Press, 1984.

Olson, Mancur. "The South Will Fall Again." Southern Economic Journal 49 (1983): 917–32.

Persky, Joseph J., and John F. Kain. "Migration, Employment and Race in the Deep South." Southern Economic Journal 36 (1970): 268–76.

Prunty, Merle. "The Renaissance of the Southern Plantation." Geographical Review 45 (1955): 459–91.

Street, James H. The New Revolution in the Cotton Economy. Chapel Hill: University of North Carolina Press, 1957.

Weinstein, Bernard, and Robert E. Firestine. Regional Growth and Decline in the United States. New York: Praeger, 1978.

INDEX

Abbott, Carl, 267
abolition of slavery, 45; and destroyed basis of southern credit, 87; and effects on economic structure of South, 270
acreage: owned by blacks in Georgia, 106
African slave trade, 33; effort to reopen blocked, 24; proposal to reopen, 129
Agricultural Adjustment Act of 1933, 227–36
Agricultural Adjustment Administration (AAA), 226; abolition of, 232; and farm wages, 230; incentives of, 230
agricultural ladder, 99; blacks' progress on, 104
agriculture: acres in farms, by states, 53t; acres per farm, 54t; and cash crops of the South, 57; and cattle raising, 57; and corn and hog production in South, 35t; and cotton yields, 58t; and export crops, 81; and farm occupancy in 1910, 93t; and farm sizes, 53–54; and farmland in South, 5; and goals of southern landlords, 34; and income in South, 59t; and "King Cotton," 34; and land value per acre of cotton and corn, 36t; and male farm laborers in 1890, 95t; and plantation farming, 12, 81–107; as practiced in South, 29–39; and preeminence of cotton, 59; productivity of South, 55; and regional labor market, 82; and sharecropping, 12; and small farms, 107–15; and southern rainfall, 37; and southern soil, 57
Alabama: and coal, 44; as cotton state, 19; and internal improvements, 23; and iron complex, 47; iron-making in, 163; and iron and steel industry, 165; mineral production of, 48t; mining in, 159, 170; and new industry in 1980, 264; and open ranges, 49; and pig iron production, 169t; as plantation state, 82; and plantation tenants, 65; production of iron and steel products, 169t; and textile industry, 124; and town development, 24
Alamance mill, 142
aliens: arrivals and departures of, 73t
Alliance stores, 115
Allis-Chalmers Corporation, 266–67
American Dilemma, An (Myrdal), 188
American Farm Bureau Federation, 226
American Federation of Labor (AFL), 221
"American system," 14, 173
American Tobacco Company (ATC), 164, 217
Anderson, Ralph V., 36
Arkansas: and labor recruiting, 77; and new industry in 1980, 264; as plantation state, 82
Arkansas River farm area, 231
Arkwright, Richard, 125
artificial irrigation, 249
Ashby, Irene (Mrs. Macfayden), 221
Athens, Georgia, 129
Atlanta, Georgia: and loss of tourism, 266; and occupational mobility, 185
Atlanta Black Shirts, 224
Atlanta Exposition of 1881, 129, 131
Atlantic labor market, 71–72; and southern expectations, 76; wages of, 74
Augusta, Georgia: and strike of 1886, 189
Avondale cotton mill, 178

Index

coal production: in Alabama, 48*t*
Cobb, James C., 257
Coelho, Philip, 67
Cogan, John, 251
coke: first used in iron and steel industry, 165
Coleman, W. C., 191
Coleman Manufacturing Company, 191
"colonial economy," *vii*, 4, 13, 14, 51, 64, 156–64, 173, 270–72
"colonial style": railroad building, 23
Columbus, Georgia, 182
Concord, North Carolina, 191
convergence of wages, 249
Copeland, Melvin T., 135
corn: profitability of, 109
corn production: in South, 1860–80, 35
corporate tax rate: by region, 260*t*; and southern states, 259
Cotterill, Robert S., 19
cotton: acreage, yield, and production, 58*t*; and Bankhead Cotton Control Act, 227; compared to corn, 109; consumption in North and South, 130; and declining prices and wages, 76; as determinant of southern prosperity, 50; eastward shift of production of, 35; and family-size farms, 84; geographic prerequisites for, 81; growth and decline of demand for, 56; and income limitations, 56; and intensification of land use, 35; and international trade, 56; as labor intensive crop, 38; and mechanization, 243–44; and most prosperous growing decade, 128; peak periods of, 91; preeminence in southern agriculture, 59; price per pound, 1879–1915, 118*t*; production and price, 57*t*; production, 1859, 37*t*; production, 1899, 37*t*; production after Civil War, 34; surplus program in 1933, 227; and synthetic fibers, 248; value per acre, 34; world demand for, 12, 117–23; and world depression of 1890s, 115
Cotton Belt, 82, 83*f*; small farmers of, 107
cotton boom: of 1830s, 22; of 1900–1920, 122
"Cotton Ed" Smith, 219, 226
Cotton Fields No More (Fite), x
cotton goods industry: employment in, 127*t*
"Cotton Holiday," 226
cotton manufacturing, 44
"cotton mill drones," 142–43

cotton mill villages, 125
cotton plantation, 92*f*
cotton prices: after 1880, 90
cotton production: and competition from Asia, Africa, and South America, 248
Cotton Textile Institute, 212
Cowles Commission, 224
Crawford, George Gordon, 174
credit: and land collateral, 87; localness of, 97; for small farmers, 110; and southern farmer, 87–90
credit market, 99, 103; *see also* credit
crop lien, 110

Dan River Mills, 147, 217
Danville, Virginia, 147, 178
Day, Richard, 243, 247
debt slavery, 113
DeCanio, Steven, 65, 100
decentralized sharecropping plantation, 91
Degler, Carl, 49
Delta and Pine Land Company of Mississippi, 233
Delta Experiment Station, 242
Dent, John, 91
Department of Agriculture, 108
Department of Labor, 221
disenfranchisement: of blacks, 177; of blacks and whites, 122
disequilibrium wage, 211*f*
doffers, 153
doffing, 132
Draper automatic loom, 144
DuBois, W. E. B., 98
Duke family: investments of, 174; and support of black enterprises, 191
Duluth, Minnesota: and union pressure on steel industry, 252
duplex process, 173
Durham, North Carolina, 178

East St. Louis, Illinois: race riots in, 200
economic mobility: of blacks, 13
Edmonds, Richard, 166

313

Index

Index

Index

National Industrial Recovery Act (NIRA), 15, 213–14, 216; declared unconstitutional, 213; and southern wages, 213
national labor market, 71–77, 201
National Labor Relations ACT (NLRA), 218
national railroad gauge: standardization of, 157
National Recovery Administration, *see* NRA
national unions, 252; and equalization of industry wages, 219
Nebraska: capital ownership in, 62, 63*t*
New Deal programs, 176; expenditures of, by regions, 259; and plantation tenancy, 199; and sharecroppers, 199; and spending in South, 199; wage policy of, 216–24
"Negro Removal Act," 224
neoplantations, 246
New Orleans, Louisiana: and loss of tourism, 266
New South: and civil rights movement, 264–69; new directions for, 16; new economy of, 239–74; ideologists, 19; and migration, 249–57; and the nation, 269–74; origins of, 6; political economy of, 47; and regional labor markets, 249–57; selling of, 257–64; and world economy, 269–74
Nicholls, William H., *vi*, 177, 247, 259, 267
night shifts: percentage of firms using, 209*t*
night-work issue, 207–16, 223
Niles Register, 127
Norgren, Paul, 187
North Carolina: and all-white cotton mills, 178; and all-white furniture factories, 178; and black industrial workers, 180*t*; and bright leaf tobacco, 111; cigarette industry in, 165; courts of, 103; and farm size, 54; and heavily black tobacco factories, 178; labor market conditions in, 162; integrated saw and planing mills in, 178; and new industry in 1980, 264; as plantation state, 82; profile of mill workers, 141; and research centers, 258; and textile industry, 124; as tobacco state, 56
North German Lloyd Line, 76
NRA, 216–24; demise of, in 1935, 217; and wage levels, 216
nuclear household, as farm unit, 90

Oakes, James, 25, 26
occupational mobility: of blacks, 193–95; of blacks today, 268; by race, in Birmingham, Alabama, 185*t*; in textile industry, 185
One Kind of Freedom (Ransom and Sutch), 36
O'Neal, Edward A., 226
open range concept, 49
Origins of the New South (Woodward), 62, 156
Otken, Charles H., 108
out-migration, 14; from the South, 6, 9, 10; after World War II, 15; *see also* interstate migration
Oxford, Mississippi, 266
Ozarks, 5

paper industry, 174
Parker, William N., *vii*, 4
Paterson, New Jersey: and strike of 1886, 189
Pawtucket, Rhode Island, 126
peonage, 113
Pepper, Claude, 223
per capita income, 55, 257; growth of, in South, 239; as percentage of U.S. average, 1880–90, 240*t*
per capita spending: federal, by region, 260, 261
"phantom freight," 168
Phillips, Ulrich, 25
phosphate industry: in South Carolina, 46*t*
Piedmont, the: and cotton production, 35
pig iron industry: in Alabama, 48*t*, 169*t*; and immigration, 71, 73*t*; production by state, 165*t*
Piore, Michael, 75
"Pittsburgh Plus," 168
plantation agriculture, 12
plantation belt, 82
Plantation South Today (Woofter and Fisher), 236
plantation tenants: and migration, 205
plantations, 81–107; acreage of tenant plots, 95; acreage in wage system, 95; area, 83*t*; decline of, after World War II, 238; and mechanization, 246; and New Deal, 199; physical layouts of, 87; and small farms, 54
planter class, 48–50

Index

family-based system, 94; "institutionalized," 101; origins of, 85, 87; in plantation regions, 84–99; under Soil Conservation Act, 232

"sharecropping contract," 97

share tenancies, 99

share tenants: in 1900, 107t; tenure and race of, 121t

share wage, 89

Shaw, Nate, 100

Shepherd, James, 67

Shiells, Martha, ix

Simkins, Eldred, 126

Slater, Samuel, 125

slave markets, 87

slave rental market, 30

slaveholders: block proposal to reopen African slave trade, 129; as capitalists, 20; compared to Europe's landholders, 18; mobility of, 24–25; net worth of, 31; and politics, 31; in postbellum South, 17; and price of cotton, 32–33; and survival of plantations, 84; and value of slave labor, 34; wealth of, in 1860, 19

slavery: impact of, on spatial patterns of economic activity, 35; and migrating tendencies in South, 9; origins and history, 10; and property rights, 11; and retardation of territorial expansion, 33; and southern economic unity, 82; *see also* slaves

slaves: and cotton states in 1860, 19; and industrial growth, 61; in manufacturing and mining, 43; migration of, 26; movability of, 87; as personal property, 17; rental market for, 30; and textile mill work, 126, 128

small farms, 107–15

Soil Conservation Domestic Allotment Act, 232

soil-building payment, 232

soil erosion: in South, 31

soils: of southern states, 57

"sorting equilibrium," 94

South Carolina, vii; as cotton state, 19; and financing of textile mills, 131; and manufacture of fertilizer, 45; mineral deposits in, 29; and minimum wage effects on manufacturing, 252; and new industry in 1980, 264; and phosphate mining, 45–46; as plantation state, 82; rice district of, 90; and textile industry, 124

South Korea: and textile industry, 124

Southern Banner, 129

Southern Council on Women in Industry, 212

Southern Cultivator, The, 87

southern economy: origins of, 4–16; separation of, from mainstream economy, 11, 12; slavery as shaping force in, 33

Southern Farmers' Alliance, 115–16

southern industries, 156–97; barriers to development of, 172–77; black workers in, 179–80t; building trades in, 181; and employment decline since 1950s, 263; iron and steel as, 165–71; and "low wage" characteristic, 257; lumbering in, 159–65; and mechanization, 241–49; and minimum wage, 251–52; mining as, 159; and New Deal wage policy, 216–24; and new industries of 1980, 264; non-union character of, 264; and paper manufacturing, 175; patterns of, 159–164; printing trades in, 181; racial segregation in, 177–95; segregation in, 158; and vertical segregation, 187–95; and wage differentials, 195–97; and World War II economy, 236; *see also* agriculture; cotton; manufacturing; mining; textile industry

southern labor market, 136

Southern Pine Association, 219, 222

Southern Recorder, 43

Southern Regional Conference on Labor Legislation, 221, 225

Southern States Industrial Council, 223

Southern Textile Bulletin, 153

southern wage: and national norms, 52

Spartanburg, South Carolina, 137

spindle hours, 213; calculation of, in southern industry, 214

"spot markets:" for common labor, 13

squad: as farm unit, 90

"squad" system, 86

standard workweek, 150

"standing wage," 89

Stateburg, South Carolina, 126

Stearns, Charles, 89–90

steel industry, 165–71; and recruitment of southern blacks, 207; and union pressure in Birmingham and Duluth, 252

Stevens, O. B., 113

Stocking, G. W., 174

Stover, John, 39

"stretch-out," 154

"subtreasury" scheme, 117

319

Index

Vance, Rupert, 6
Veblen, Thorstein, 43
vertical segregation, 183, 187–95; see also horizontal segregation; segregation
Vesta Mills, 190
Virginia: and chemical industry, 264; and farm size, 54; iron and steel industry in, 165; 1907 wages in, 184, 184t; 1920s wage data for, 195; and research centers, 258; as tobacco state, 56; wage distribution in, 69t, 195
Virginia Bricklayers and Masons, 181
Virginia-Carolina Chemical Corporation, 217

wage convergence, 207–8
wage differentials, 195–97, 249–54; by age and sex, 182; among agricultural workers, 182; under NRA, 216–17, 217t, 224; for strenuous and dangerous jobs, 183
wage distribution: of blacks and whites compared, 70; in Virginia, 69t
wage labor market: coexistence with sharecropping, 91; and races, 96; risks of, 94
wage rates: stability in textile industry, 133; under WPA, 218t
wage stickiness, 150, 152, 153
wages: in Atlantic labor market, 72; below norms in South, 200; of blacks and whites compared, 68–70; of blacks and whites in 1899, 96; convergence of blacks and whites, 183; decline in farm, postbellum, 90; deflation of, by cost of living in South, 201–3; of doffers, 132, 133t; of farmers after Civil War, 76; of farmers 1925–40, 231t; of farmers by states, 202t; "high," and fringe benefits in North, 206; of immigrants, 73; in iron and steel industry, 176; and link to cotton prices, 76; in lumber industry, 203t; minimum, under WPA, 218; of northern and southern mills compared, 130; and North-South gap, 204t; in Old South, 12, 52; per day without board,

66t; in post-Civil War South, 12–13; postharvest, 89; in pulp and paper industry, 254; of Royall Cotton Mill, 149; "share," 89; for skilled occupations, 67; in South under New Deal, 219; of southern farmers, 76t; "standing," 89; in steel industry, 72; "sticky," in cotton and steel industries, 217; of textile and farm workers compared, 69t; of textile workers, 68; of textile workers, and agricultural labor market, 140; of unskilled laborers, 67; in Virginia, 1907, 184, 184t, 195; see also minimum wage
Wall Street Journal, 263, 266
Waltham, Massachusetts: mills of, 132
Waltham system, 138
War Labor Board, 254
Washington, Booker T., 101
Washington, D.C.: and occupational mobility, 185
Watson, Tom, 111
Wayne, Michael, 28
wealth: nonagricultural, 63t; of non-residents of South, 63
weaver, 153
Webb, Walter Prescott, 5, 15
Weiman, David, viii, ix
Weiss, Thomas, 20
Whatley, Warren, ix, 234
whites: and proprietorship, 105t, 111–12; and wage labor, 68–70
white farmers: farm occupancy by, in 1910, 93t; as farm operators in 1900, 107
wholesale price index, 67
Wiener, Jonathan, 25, 64
Wisconsin: capital ownership in, 63
Women's Bureau, 212
Woodward, C. Vann, 44, 62, 156
Work Projects Administration (WPA), 217
World War I, 54, 56
World War II, 56
WPA, 220

yarn number, 134
Young, Thomas M., 135